THE PATH TO PARADISE

Also by Sam Wasson

A Splurch in the Kisser: The Movies of Blake Edwards

*Fifth Avenue, 5 A.M.: Audrey Hepburn, Breakfast at Tiffany's,
and the Dawn of the Modern Woman*

Paul on Mazursky

Fosse

Improv Nation: How We Made a Great American Art

The Big Goodbye: Chinatown and the Last Years of Hollywood

Hollywood: The Oral History (with Jeanine Basinger)

THE PATH TO
PARADISE

A Francis Ford Coppola Story

SAM WASSON

HARPER

An Imprint of HarperCollins*Publishers*

HarperCollins books may be purchased for educational, business, or sales promotional use. For information, please email the Special Markets Department at SPsales@harpercollins.com.

FIRST EDITION

Designed by Leah Carlson-Stanisic
Frontispiece courtesy of Yoshiko Poncher

Library of Congress Cataloging-in-Publication Data has been applied for.

ISBN 978-0-06-303784-7

23 24 25 26 27 LBC 5 4 3 2 1

For Noah Eaker and Jenny Gersten

The path to paradise begins in Hell.

—DANTE

Contents

∞

The Francis Ford Coppolas

The friends that have it I do wrong
Whenever I remake a song,
Should know what issue is at stake:
It is myself that I remake.

—WILLIAM BUTLER YEATS

n this life, he has made and remade movies, won and lost Oscars, won and lost millions, fathered children and grandfathered grandchildren, a great-grandson, lost a son. He has built temples, bombed temples, grown grapes, grown a beard, stomped grapes, shaved his beard. He has written and discarded drafts, completed and then recut movies, fought the studios, battled the current of the times, won battles, lost battles, lost his mind. He has created a filmmaking empire, a hospitality empire, made hell, made paradise, lost paradise, and dreamed again.

"I am *vicino-morte*," he said recently, turning from his current draft of *Megalopolis*. "Do you know what that means?"

"*Morte* . . . I know *morte* . . ."

"*Vicino* . . . it means 'in the vicinity of' . . ."

He keeps changing. They say you only live once. But most of us don't live even once. Francis Ford Coppola has lived over and over again.

In the natural world we all know, he has been, like many of us will be, a child who became old and will die. But in his life as a filmmaker, he lives in new worlds of his own imagining, each a laboratory for his, and others', re-creation. Beginning with his 1966 feature, aptly titled *You're a Big Boy Now*, Francis Ford Coppola initiated a colossal, lifelong project of experimental self-creation few filmmakers can afford—emotionally, financially—and none but he has undertaken. Through the artistic and social ingenuity of his company Zoetrope—in Greek, "life revolution"—his living, dying, living production company and onetime studio, he has marshaled the stubbornly earthbound resources of filmmaking, business, technology, and the natural world to stage—and that's what his Zoetrope laboratory *is*, a stage—literal worlds analogous to those of whatever characters he's creating. As he famously said of *Apocalypse Now*, the paragon of Zoetrope-style filmmaking, he made a war to film war: "My technique for making film is to turn the filmmaking experience, as close as I can, into the experience of [whatever] fiction we're dealing with."

Creating the experience. The experience that re-creates the self. The re-created self that creates the work. These are the life revolutions of Zoetrope. They are what this book is about. How Francis Ford Coppola, leader, driving force of Zoetrope, sacrificed more than the normal man's share to improve the world, the lives of the people in it, one filmmaking community at a time.

As no other filmmaker does, Coppola lives in his stories, changing them as they change him, riding round an unending loop of experience and creation, until either the production clock strikes midnight and the process must stop or, one hopes, he recognizes his new self in the mirror of the movie—for him, a documentary of his new internal landscape—and cries, "That's it! I got it! Now that I know this part of myself, I know what the movie is!"

Sometimes, though, he never gets there. *It* never gets there.

And on a few occasions, he and the movie end up tragically far away.

But artistic perfection has never been integral to Coppola's colossal experiment. Learning and growing have been. Living is. Dying is.

The adventure is.

August in Napa Valley. Lunchtime at Zoetrope, a world apart from the world. But not a dream.

Masa Tsuyuki was vigorously stirring a pan of leftover pasta, talking about the egg, the egg, the added egg, almost singing of its power to transform yesterday's lunch into today's delicious something . . .

Just outside, through the wide-open doors of the kitchen, two apprentices laded twenty feet of picnic table with plums and berries and summer salad and a cobbler someone brought from home. Gazing at the spread in disbelief, a studious-looking fellow paused at the top of the stairway leading down from the library. Wiping his eyeglasses, he volunteered to help, and was laughingly commanded, by Masa, to sit down and eat. He introduced himself to one of the apprentices—Dean Sherriff, artist, brought up to assist Coppola on the visual conceptualization for *Megalopolis*.

Megalopolis is the story—soon to be filmed—Coppola has been thinking about, quarreling with, adding to, altering, and rediscovering for forty years.

Forty years. The story keeps changing.

Coppola keeps changing. His work keeps changing. *The Godfather* he made in a classical style; *Apocalypse Now* opened him to the surreal; *One from the Heart*, he says, he made in a theatrical mode, and *Bram Stoker's Dracula* he built, as an antiquarian, with the live effects of early cinema. But what was *his* style? With *Megalopolis*—sixty years after his first feature—Coppola would at last find out.

In preparation for the shoot, Masa, when he isn't preparing lunch, is rewiring "the Silverfish," Coppola's forty-year-old bespoke mobile cinema unit. Anahid Nazarian, right-hand woman for forty years, is on the phone, ten to five, making sure everything they are going to need will be at the studio in Peachtree City, Georgia, before they need it. Now Anahid sits restfully, eyes closed against the sun. Behind her, a fireworks explosion of orange and gold lantana shoots up the stone wall of the Zoetrope library, once a carriage house. Perched on a garden box at Anahid's feet, a butterfly alights on a zucchini blossom and then flies off.

"Ready!" Masa cries. "Everybody sit!"

Megalopolis is a story of a utopia, a story as visionary and uncompromising as its author; more expensive, more urgently personal than anything he has ever done; and for all these reasons and too many others, nearly impossible to get made. In the eighties, when Coppola, felled with debt after Zoetrope's second apocalypse—the death of Zoetrope Studios in Los Angeles—was directing for money, he read the story of Catiline in *Twelve Against the Gods*, tales of great figures of history who, Coppola said, "went against the current of the times." Catiline, Roman soldier and politician, had failed to remake ancient Rome. There was something there for Coppola. Something of himself. *What if Catiline*, Coppola asked himself, *who history said was the loser, had in fact had a vision of the Republic that was actually better?* Throughout the decades, he'd steal away with *Megalopolis*, a mistress, a dream, gathering research, news items, political cartoons, adding to his notebooks—in hotels and on airplanes and in his bungalow office in Napa—glimpses of an original story, shades of *The Fountainhead* and *The Master Builder* braced with history, philosophy, biography, literature, music, theater, science, architecture, half a lifetime's worth of learning and imagination. But Coppola wasn't just writing a story; he was creating a city, the city of the title, the perfect place. Refined by his own real-life experiments with Zoetrope, his utopia, *Megalopolis* would be characterized by ritual, celebration, and personal improvement, and driven by creativity; it had to be. Corporate and political interests, he had learned too well, were driven mainly by greed. And greed destroyed.

Over the years, *Megalopolis* grew characters, matured into a screenplay, tried to live as a radio drama and a novel, and for decades wandered like the Ancient Mariner, telling its story, looking for financing, or a star: De Niro, Paul Newman, Russell Crowe . . . The story of Coppola's story became a fairy tale for film students, a punch line for agents . . . and in 2001, paid for with revenues from his winery, it almost became a movie. On location in New York City, Coppola shot thirty-six hours of second-unit material. But after September 11, he halted production. The world had changed suddenly, and he needed time to change with it.

He passed the script to Wendy Doniger, University of Chicago professor of comparative mythology (and years before, his first kiss). She introduced Coppola to the work of Mircea Eliade—specifically, his novel *Youth Without Youth*, the story of a scholar who is unable to complete his life's work; then he is struck dead by lightning and rejuvenated to live and work again. Coppola, rejuvenated, made a movie from it. It was his first film in a decade. Thinking like a film student again, he kept making movies—*Tetro* in 2009; *Twixt*, 2011—modest in size and budget, fearing that *Megalopolis*, a metaphysical, DeMille-size epic, was and always would be a dream only, beyond his or anyone's reach. *Utopia*, after all, means a place that doesn't exist.

Then he decided to finance the picture himself, for around $100 million of his own money.

Coppola appeared at the picnic table. He was reading.

Around him, Zoetropers bustled into and out of the kitchen, finished setting places near him, and bustled away again. Coppola kept reading. His eyes on the page, he reached out for a locally grown plum and took a bite. "Mmm," he said to the plum. "This is a wonderful plum." Dean Sherriff cautiously took a seat opposite. "Here is the architect I was talking about," Coppola said, passing his pages to Dean, embellishing a line of inquiry they had been discussing before lunch about what the future should look like. As he spoke, vaulting from architecture to technology, from technology to education, the table around him became populated, quietly, by Zoetropers and their salad, pasta, chicken, and fruit. Though he had come for lunch, Coppola was now the only one without food.

"What do you think?" This question he directed at the table. Everyone looked up.

What do you think? This is how utopia could be attained, how a Zoetrope film would always be made.

There was quiet—a quiet Coppola filled with the wisdom of Goethe and Herman Hesse, two cherished sources. From them, he changed to a painful story of grammar school and his homeroom teacher, the horrible Mrs. Hemashandra.

"Coppola!" she snapped. "What are you doing? What is that *book* you're reading?"

"Biology."

"That's a college subject and you'll never go to college."

No, Coppola says to the table. That wasn't the way to learn, celebrate, improve, create. What if, in the future, teachers were more like hotel concierges? "Good morning. What do you want to learn about today? What interests *you*?" What is your dream?

It could happen. Coppola knows it could. Because it has happened before, great changes to the rules of life. He had seen it happen with each incarnation of Zoetrope. But if it happened again, would it last? If it didn't last, would it teach?

After lunch, the table was cleared. Coppola congratulated Masa on the addition of the egg to the pasta, the Zoetropers resumed their tasks, and he and Dean returned to the library, Dean to a desk, Coppola to an armchair, to decide the future of the world.

I

THE DREAM

The Modern Utopia must be not static but kinetic, must shape not as a permanent state but as a hopeful stage.

—H. G. WELLS, *A MODERN UTOPIA*

Better ideas broke through, crashing against the old, forking with each burst. This was the dreaming Francis Ford Coppola, changed again, this time by the Philippines, rewriting (again) *Apocalypse Now*, spitting bullet sounds through his teeth as he hit the keys, *tchoo tchoo*. He did not know where he was going, where the story was taking him. But what adventurer ever did? *Tchootchootchoo.* Where was he now? Not here, not on his chair at the living room table in Baler, in the jungle, on an island in Luzon, a million miles from home. Was he lost? His story was, but Coppola was a regular in the whirlpool of loss and rediscovery, conviction and uncertainty, ecstasy and despair. Ideas came easy to him; the problem was, the dreaming never stopped. He was writing even when he wasn't writing. He was writing when he was shooting, between setups. He was writing when he was editing! Sleep? If his eyes were closed, he was writing. But until he got to the Philippines, he had never had to write to save his life; to save everyone's life; to save his family, his homes, his friends, the filmmakers (George Lucas, Carroll Ballard, Walter Murch . . .), his assets, his reputation, his dignity—all to save American Zoetrope, their wounded production company, his first, favorite, and biggest dream, the biggest dream anyone in Hollywood, since they first imagined the industry, had ever dreamt. Which, if he, if *they*, dreamed to completion, could grant them the freedom they needed to flee Hollywood or, if it followed their example, transform it entirely. And why stop there? If they could revolutionize the American motion picture industry, what couldn't they change? Zoetrope could be a home for *all* creative people—writers, actors, sculptors, dancers, painters, scientists, even those who didn't know they were creative, or who hadn't found the opportunity to be. It would be an oasis, a paradise of self-discovery and celebration wide open to everyone. With the right financing and the right imaginations, what would stop Zoetrope from reconstituting American or even world consciousness into a single living, loving adventure the size of nations and the span of lifetimes, *La Bohème* for the planet . . .

> *O bella età d'inganni e d'utopie!*
> *Si crede, spera, e tutto*
> *bello appare!*
> Oh, beautiful age of deceptions and utopias!
> You believe, hope, and all
> seems beautiful.

Beauty for all!

And they said it could never be? Why think that way?

Blind to the world, he vanished into his Olivetti. Every late night—even after a sweltering day's shooting and shouting, the physical toil of debating actors, corralling helicopters, praying to explosives, attending budget reports, racing tropical thunderstorms; and even after every morning, when the kids, mosquito bitten and yelling for breakfast, played around his bare feet; and above all, even after the doubts, doubts, doubts: about *Apocalypse*, about his ability to write and direct and produce this movie he still did not understand, about how this coming failure would destroy every plan for his future—Coppola returned home to a house often without electricity, a house illuminated only by candles, tore off his wet shirt, and sat down at the living room table to imagine, on paper, page after terrible, incredible, terrible page, the next day's scene. He did not know what he was doing.

He knew what he was doing. Five Oscars. He had won them, hadn't he? In 1971, Best Original Screenplay, *Patton*; in 1973, Best Adapted Screenplay, *The Godfather*; in 1975, Best Adapted Screenplay, Best Director, Best Picture, *The Godfather Part II*. He was a king, the most powerful, most respected writer-director-producer in Hollywood and—with all the attention and media resources conferred on him—among the most impactful communicators on the planet. That year, one critic wrote that Coppola's "influence over people's minds is much more profound than any American politician's today." Imagine what he could do with that influence!

And yet he still couldn't get Paramount to finance *Apocalypse Now*. Five Oscars and the greatest filmmaking streak in memory—*Godfather, The*

Conversation, Godfather Part II, back-to-back-to-back—weren't enough to get even Paramount, his home studio, patrons of all three (consecutive!) masterpieces, to go for his Vietnam movie. Did Paramount expect Coppola to deliver a *Godfather*—as he had delivered *Godfather II* to be able to make *The Conversation*—every time he wanted to make a movie? That was no kind of freedom.

He had, instead of Paramount, *Godfather* money—and a growing media empire: a commanding eight-story office tower, the Sentinel Building, in North Beach, San Francisco; a twenty-two-room Victorian-style mansion with a bespoke basement screening room not too far away, on Broadway; a breathtaking estate in Napa Valley; a blue Mercedes limousine, compliments of Paramount; shared interest in a private turbojet; property in Mill Valley, where he and his friends could go and write; a San Francisco radio station, KMPX, where he could test material; the Little Fox Theatre, where writers and directors could try out ideas "in a format that's incredibly inexpensive compared to film"; an apartment at the Sherry-Netherland in New York; Cinema Seven, his new distribution company; satellite offices at Goldwyn studios down in L.A.; the rights to *The Black Stallion,* which he had hired Carroll Ballard to write and direct; the rights to John Fante's *The Brotherhood of the Grape,* his next film if it wasn't to be the original musical of the life of Preston Tucker, who had also dreamed bigger than the rest; an unusual TV idea developed at the behest of the Children's Television Workshop entitled *First Contact,* to which Carl Sagan would act as Coppola's scientific advisor; a film he would produce for the eighty-year-old King Vidor to direct; a chronological reimagining of both *Godfather*s into an epic showpiece for NBC; and, until recently, ownership of *City Magazine,* which, had it worked, would have been the veritable writers room of the multimedia network that would publish pieces for Coppola's theater, radio station, and movies. "I don't need more power," he had said. "The most powerful man on earth is a film director. When he makes a picture, he is a god."

What came after that?

"I'm at a Y in the road," he said before he left for the Philippines. "One path is to become a manager and an executive who brings about great changes. On the other, there's a very private notion to put my energy into developing as a writer and an artist. In the next five years I want to break through creatively by my own standards. I don't think any film I have made even comes close to what I have in my heart."

Coppola's heart: in 1968, he had won the initial incarnation of Zoetrope a development deal for seven original scripts by seven of his friends—before Warner Bros. pulled out, stiffing him with $300,000 in debt and decades of old dreams lost. The money he made in the intervening years was enough to get him and Zoetrope out of the red and back in the game, but to change Zoetrope from a little company into its own fully financed, self-sustaining, self-sufficient development, production, and distribution entity, he would need more than just *Godfather* money. He would need Paramount-level money. Imagine it . . .

"Well," Paramount had told Gray Frederickson, producer of *Godfather* and *Godfather II*, months earlier, "we think it's just a little too early for a Vietnam picture."

Paramount, it turned out, was not alone. No one in Hollywood wanted *Apocalypse Now*.

How could that be? *The Godfather*, by one 1974 tally, made $285 million (plus the $10 million NBC paid for onetime-only television rights); then there was the box office from *Godfather II* (13 percent of the gross was his!); and, of course, *American Graffiti*, which he produced for George Lucas, was the highest grosser ever for any film made for under a million dollars— $50 million in the United States alone! And nobody had wanted that picture, either! When would they realize he, not they, was Fort Knox? That he was the future? *Variety* had certainly figured it out: "Coppola's commercial touch thus far verges on the phenomenal."

So, *Apocalypse Now*: he would have to make it himself. He would have to find the money himself. And he would do it without an agent.

In the years after he left Freddie Fields and Creative Management Associates, Coppola didn't take on new representation; Fields had screwed him, he had discovered, on the Zoetrope–Warner Bros. deal. Nor did Coppola need to be charged an agent's percentage for work he, with his track record, could get himself. Nor would it be wise to bring on a traditional lawyer to negotiate his *Apocalypse* deal with financiers. If he or she charged Coppola their hourly rate, Coppola could have bankrupted himself before he raised his first dollar for the movie. But that's where lawyer Barry Hirsch was different. Hirsch, whom Coppola discovered through Pacino, charged, significantly, a percentage. ("That gave us the opportunity to go out and do things that didn't come to fruition without the client having to bear the responsibility of an hourly fee," Hirsch explained.) With Hirsch negotiating on his behalf, Coppola wouldn't have to foot the bill until they had a deal.

They needed about $14 million.

Hirsch flew to the Cannes Film Festival, the international nexus of debuting and selling distribution rights to *finished films*. But Hirsch didn't have a finished film; he had a script about a Vietnam movie to be directed by Francis Ford Coppola. What he sold, territory by territory—and on a scale unprecedented—was foreign presales, the right for international distributors to release the unmade *Apocalypse* in exchange for money up front—winning *Apocalypse* around $7 million. With that first investment secured, Hirsch picked up an additional $7 million for the domestic distribution rights he sold to United Artists, an organization Coppola regarded with special admiration. Since its founding, in 1919, not by executives but by filmmakers Charlie Chaplin, D. W. Griffith, Douglas Fairbanks Sr., and Mary Pickford, United Artists had more than earned its reputation for being the most progressive, filmmaker-friendly financial entity in Hollywood. Fifty-five years later, its current leader, Arthur Krim, was no different. Coppola considered him one of the very great men of the movie business.

The deal Hirsch negotiated wasn't just innovative—probably the biggest prefinancing deal ever won from foreign distributors—it was a beauty. Seven years after the movie's initial release, the rights to *Apocalypse Now* would revert to Coppola. As a studio would, he would own the movie—as he wished he had owned *American Graffiti*—and all the proceeds to the movie, less profit participants, like stars . . .

That was United Artists' condition. He had to sign a star.

Coppola was incensed. Did *Godfather* have stars? Brando had been box-office poison then, remember? And when had movie stars become de facto producers, effectively green-lighting movies? If they could even get Al Pacino—whom Coppola had *made* a star in *Godfather*—how much would his movie star fee cut into Coppola's budget? And what if Pacino *didn't* say yes? If Nicholson didn't say yes? If Redford didn't say yes? "Whose fault is it that there are only six world stars today?" Coppola opined to the trade press.

"We should go back to the old studio system, not in an exploitative, crass way. But every studio should be developing talent. I can't afford to work with people I started with."

Hat in hand, Coppola drove up from Hollywood to Malibu to meet with Steve McQueen. But McQueen said he didn't want to star in *Apocalypse* if it would keep him in the Philippines, away from his family, for three months. Coppola, who was never away from Eleanor and the children (Gio, Roman, Sofia) for more than two weeks, who brought them to every location just as his father, Carmine, had brought his wife, Italia, and his three children (August, Francis, Talia) with him to wherever his flute was needed, urged McQueen to do the same and offered him, instead of the starring role of Willard, the much smaller role of Colonel Kurtz. McQueen said no.

Pacino said no.

Martin Sheen had scheduling conflicts.

Outraged, exasperated, Coppola picked up his Oscars and threw them clean through the dining room window of his big house in Pacific Heights.

It was then back to Hollywood, to Marlon Brando, for what Coppola knew from *The Godfather* would be a fierce negotiation. To play Kurtz, Brando wanted a million dollars a week with a guaranteed minimum of three weeks plus a mouthwatering piece of the first-dollar gross:

"Ten percent," Hirsch offered Brando's agent, Jay Kantor.

"No, no. Marlon hates United Artists. He doesn't trust them. Make it another 1.3%."

"11.3%?!"

This is how a five-time Oscar winner got a movie made? By being squeezed by an actor whose career he rescued in *The Godfather*?

This was Hollywood?

"I began to see," Coppola said, "if this kept up, the industry would someday be paying $3,000,000 for eight hours, plus overtime, and have to shoot at the actor's house."

In the old days, before their production, distribution, and exhibition monopolies were broken up by antitrust regulation, the studios had the resources to keep actors under long-term contracts. Though they had less freedom to choose their own projects, contract players worked more (finishing a picture Thursday, starting a new picture Friday) than they did as freelancers, and in the greenhouse environment of a full-service production enclave, they grew much faster artistically. They weren't prisons, those old studios. They were paradises. "I feel very strongly about term contracts," Coppola said, amid failing to cast *Apocalypse Now*. "If you have a good talent program and the management as it were is interested in acting—and not just [in] business and are not just guys in suits—then it should be a privilege for an actor to be associated with the program." As Coppola saw it, Hollywood studios should invest their own money—$500,000 each, he suggested—to train their actors. "Every studio in this town should have a theater within its walls where it is developing talent," he said. "I liken the movie business to a country that runs on petroleum. They bitch about the price of oil, but aren't out digging for more oil. Movie companies run on talent—performers, directors and writers—but the studios haven't been developing talent." They were scared, shortsighted, living hand to mouth. "They want to know what they are going to get this year," Coppola said. If only they could imagine, with a little time and artistic training, a different and better future of more and better artists, and yes, more money, too, just a little farther down the road . . . But they didn't pay executives to dream . . .

What *did* they pay them for?

As Hirsch settled the deal with Brando's agents on Brando's terms, Coppola and his partner, casting alchemist Fred Roos, forged ahead, signing exciting actors (but not yet stars) Frederic Forrest, Sam Bottoms, Albert Hall, and Laurence Fishburne to *Apocalypse Now*. The proposed seven-year contracts would grant Coppola's actors a full fifty paid weeks a year (as opposed to the forty weeks with an enforced three-month vacation in the old studio days). "It won't be too long before the studios are copying us copying them," Coppola said. "Plus, we'll have a significant reservoir of talent for our films." Furthermore, each actor's agreement would be tailored to the artistic needs of the individual. One clause in particular struck many in the industry as, at best, naïve and, at worst, foolish. Signing term contracts with Coppola, each actor would be offered the dramatic training of his or her choice—anything from conventional workshops to foreign language instruction to music lessons—and Coppola would foot the bill. "Our purpose," Roos said plainly, "is to develop stars." And develop lives:

"I want folks working with me to know there's other things in life than work," Coppola stated. It was a position he would maintain for the rest of his career.

Exclusive in all areas of show business except for television, the contracts allowed for loan-outs to other studios for worthy projects, pending Coppola's approval; attendant salary increases; and down the line, should the money really flow, profit participation. No one was going to get rich quick on this deal, but they had Coppola's assurance—and given his track record, no reason to doubt him—that they would do good work, low on budget, high on art. Perhaps foremost, the contracts introduced into the competitive, highly anxious world of freelance Hollywood a home, a repertory, and, Coppola hoped, a kind of family.

"It's not a baseball team," Robert Altman scoffed.

Harvey Keitel, signed to play Willard, thought Coppola's contract notion similarly absurd. Hand over the reins to his career?

Martin Scorsese, Coppola's pal, got it: "I think it's the right concept in trying to break down the $3,000,000 syndrome."

Then, in February 1976, three months before setting out for the Philippines, Coppola began the ordeal of joining his story to Brando's ideas. They would meet for hours on end in Brando's compound up on Mulholland, expanding and contracting the work in progress, making circular advances in accord with Brando's changing whims and inspirations. Brando could be as brilliant as he could be childlike, one second arguing persuasively for creating Kurtz *against* his counterpart in *Heart of Darkness*, the next second, overcome with an intense fascination with termites, frolicking through a flower field of non sequiturs. Coppola, charged and enervated by turn, welcomed every contradiction: "[Kurtz] is mad, Marlon, I mean his madness is our madness . . . in the larger context, the guy is nuts." It had to be yin *and* yang, Coppola argued: if the lines between good and evil, Willard and Kurtz, were clearly delineated, then the movie would let America off the moral hook for Vietnam. There was no total good, no total evil. This movie had to implicate America. By the end of the movie, you had to understand Kurtz: he was, in a way, a part of Willard. "Willard starts to come apart a little bit," Coppola told Brando, "and the audience feels that 'Ah, that Colonel Kurtz is crazy.' And you begin to get the idea that what makes Kurtz crazy are the same kind of things that begin to have this effect on Willard."

Coppola invited Brando to encroach on his own authority, permitting the actor a creative power aligned with Kurtz's stature. In one sense, this blurring of power boundaries was all part of the seduction: Coppola, acting as his own producer, needed to keep Brando happy to get his movie made. In another sense, Coppola, as writer-director, was a genuine collaborator, always open to the new and better idea, even to the point of confusion.

Whose story was this?

It had started off as John Milius's, a decade earlier. As far back as the mid-sixties, he had talked about doing the Vietnam movie he would eventually call *Apocalypse Now*. By the time Milius, Coppola, Lucas, Walter Murch, Caleb Deschanel, and Carroll Ballard graduated from their respective film schools, USC and UCLA, Milius was still talking *Apocalypse*. They all were. "We sat around in my office on the Warner Bros. lot," Coppola remembered, "talking about our dreams." Maybe Lucas, hitched to Milius since their days at USC, would direct it? Not as the macho, blow-'em-up film Milius had in mind, but as a Strangelovian satire. Lucas would shoot it fast and cheap, somewhere in Northern California, on 16 mm black and white. Coppola would act as producer. Before long, Milius's *Apocalypse Now* would be, along with Lucas and Murch's *THX 1138*, one of the seven scripts—seven was Coppola's lucky number—paid for by Warner Bros. to be developed, under Coppola's aegis, at American Zoetrope, his own production facility up in San Francisco, where they could work with creative independence, not too far from Hollywood and not too close. But after Warner pulled the plug on the whole Zoetrope dream, those scripts, formerly the property of Warner Bros., went back to Coppola.

Five years later, Coppola, owner of Milius's script, offered it to Lucas to direct. But Lucas, agonizing over his space opera, declined, and Coppola decided to direct *Apocalypse Now* himself. He saw in *Apocalypse* the old-fashioned makings of a mainstream hit. It would be huge, Hollywood's first major statement on the Vietnam War. It would be an event, a roadshow blockbuster. It would be that big and he would make that much; and he would invest the returns back into Zoetrope. He said, "I was really thinking of [*Apocalypse Now*], as I'm always thinking of it, as a way to finance ultimately what I have in mind for Zoetrope." Think *The Longest Day* for Vietnam. "I figured this is a chance," he said, "which was always the holy grail, [to] make some huge picture that makes a ton of money and then make little Roger Corman type budget art films."

But Milius's script, upon closer inspection, wanted changing. "It wasn't that the script wasn't working," Coppola explained. "It's that whenever you direct a script, even a good script, you suddenly understand its architecture and what its problems are." And Coppola was not John Milius. He was not interested in combat per se. In Milius's ending, Kurtz dies in a climactic attack on his compound; U.S. Army helicopters come to Willard's rescue, and he whips up his M16 and starts firing at them, laughing crazily. But Coppola had changed since that draft. By the time he got to the Philippines in March 1976, having already tangoed for days on end with Brando in Los Angeles, it would be hard to reason out one alternate ending from the next, separated as they were by thousands of discarded pages, so much time and space. One draft had ended with Willard meeting Kurtz's widow in California; one, echoing Conrad's opening to *Heart of Darkness*, began with Willard aboard a yacht in the Potomac. One draft opened with a shot of Willard's head emerging ominously from dark water; one ended with Willard, Chef, and Lance floating downstream with Kurtz's body . . .

Where was *Coppola* in this material? So many of Milius's ideas—his soldier surfers, the napalm dreams of Colonel Kilgore, the kooky madness of what Coppola termed "an L.A. war," with its drugs, sex, and Jim Morrison—appealed to Coppola's taste for spectacle. "I wanted to remember it like a dream," Milius had said of Conrad's novel. "I wanted to use the novel as a sort of allegory." But an allegory for what? Coppola wasn't political. He had never been to war. Did he understand this?

"Best wishes for a great picture," Lucas had telexed. "Zap the VC . . ."

Who did Coppola think he was? He didn't know how it felt, body and mind, to live and sleep in the jungle, to be separated from his family for years, to wake up afraid and to sleep afraid, to be *only* afraid. And he was going to tell them where to put the camera? What a heart of darkness was? He grew up on Long Island! He hadn't *lived* that story. Not the way he had lived the *Godfather*; he knew dynasty, Italy, guilt, and tradition. He knew what it was to be a second brother and a big man's son. He knew the mind of *The Conversation*. He knew surveillance—that was his life, growing up alone, watching, listening from the outside. He knew *The Rain People* because he had lived it as he had made it, being on the road, imagining what it was to run from family. This was different; Vietnam had never been *his*. Nor had he experienced the moral paradox of war on a metaphorical level. He didn't know what it was to lose himself in the spiritual spiral of doing bad to do "good," as Willard would learn, as Kurtz had learned before he lost himself.

Had he ever lost himself?

No.

Had he ever lost *his* story?

No.

What if *that* was the story he was telling?

A story of how *losing* was actually becoming . . .

If so, what were its plot points? Its act breaks?

He didn't know.

And yet, there they were. In the jungle in the Philippines.

There was the Olivetti. There were the keys, there was the page.

There were Eleanor and the kids. There were Dean Tavoularis, Fred Roos, Gray Frederickson, the magnificent Vittorio Storaro. All of them, his families. They had come all this way—from San Francisco, L.A., New York, Rome—because of him. Wagering their time, careers, comfort, reputations, goodwill—in some cases, their own families—because of him. Who did he think he was?

He couldn't know the ending until he was certain he knew the beginning, but he couldn't be sure about the beginning until he knew why and how it ended, and not knowing how it began or how it ended, he couldn't be sure he knew what, in the most fundamental terms, the story was *about*, who Willard was, who Kurtz was, or why he, or they, were there at all.

He wasn't like Brando, who sometimes would just open his mouth, and out would come genius, expertise on anything, a perfect soliloquy . . . Or there was his big brother, Augie, a real intellectual, who was naturally brilliant and effortlessly talented, who didn't have to die and come back to life every time he sat down to write something . . . Or his father, Carmine, who could just lift the flute to his mouth and then . . . *music* . . .

O bella età d'inganni e d'utopie!

But him? Alone, he sat at the typewriter making bullet sounds, *tchoo* . . . *tchoo* . . .

A half-hour chopper ride from Coppola's living room typewriter, on location in Baler, little rickety Cessna planes small enough to land on jungle airstrips had flown in production equipment that was trundled over narrow dirt roads and onto the beach not far from where a Philippine coconut plantation had been transformed into a Vietnamese village of seventy or so bamboo and thatch huts with a view of a 250-foot pier destined for destruction by gunship and rocket blasts from low-flying helicopters and A-5 jets. One could forget—it was hard to remember—that none of it was real. "With my helicopters," said pilot and Vietnam veteran Dick White, "the boats and the high morale of the well-trained extras we had, there were three or four countries in the world we could have taken easily."

The sequence required nearly five hundred technicians, actors and extras, a small armada of naval craft, more than a hundred assorted vehicles, surfboards and surfers, and a chopper squadron on loan from Philippine president Ferdinand Marcos—until the choppers were temporarily recalled, sometimes without notice, to contain an outbreak of Communist rebel forces in Mindanao, 150 miles to the south, only to be returned to Baler, their painted colors having been changed from U.S. back to Philippine colors, needing to be repainted U.S. again, and rerigged. "You never knew when you were going to lose a helicopter or four or five," assistant director Doug Claybourne said. "So it was hard to plan a day's shooting for the assistant director team, when you're unsure of how many helicopters you're going to have." Giant floating fishnets, bomb-blasted out of the sea during a take, flew skyward. "My god," thought Gray Frederickson, "if a helicopter rotor caught one of those fishnets, that would be the end of everybody inside . . ." One copter flew so close to a tree that it chopped the crown off, and the crew below ran from the hailstorm of coconuts. Dick White's chopper caught fire in the air. "[It] burned the socks off the guy in the back seat, flames came between my legs, blinded me . . . I jumped out and ran up on the side and put the water in my eyes to try to be able to see, so that was pretty scary." ("I was responsible for that," Coppola said. "It was supposed to burst into flame in the scene and I made the charge a little too strong.") Down on the ground, Joe Lombardi's special effects cortege carefully arranged explosives in and out of the water, maintaining raging fires of different sizes timed to sync with the choreographed aircraft attacks overhead. If one wrong wire—of two hundred thousand feet of wire—were accidentally cut, the thing wouldn't detonate or, worse, only part of it would: half the village would blow, and they'd have to do another take, which would cost more time, more money, more nervous emotion of cast and crew. They had to wrap at six each evening. And were up again before dawn.

From out of the trees, actual Vietnam vets—"lost souls," Tavoularis observed, "who drift around the Orient"—peeked through the jungle. They talked about the real war, how it changed, forever, the insides of soldiers and civilians, the smoke bombs . . .

"Black smoke or white smoke?" Tavoularis asked.

"No, no. There were a range of colors."

"Get them. Let's look at them."

Great gales of smoke, purple, red, green, yellow, marijuana, licked up by whomping chopper blades, the smell of burned rubber from the fire clusters along the shore . . . The landscape was unrecognizable, real but unnatural, like a believed dream.

There was the rumor that the rebel forces to the south were in the hills as close as ten miles away.

All that remained of this once-quiet quarter of Baler was the jagged maw of broken bamboo and palms X-ing in the rubble, a picture of annihilation drawn by an angry child.

Coppola was white-knuckling himself. The helicopter sequence was taking far longer than expected, and with so many variables impossible to control, it was physically and artistically without precedent, and dangerous beyond reckoning. "What gets me so berserk," he was saying, talking to anyone who would approach him, speaking nonstop, in one unbroken monologue of present and anticipated fears and practical and wishful solutions, "I think I can handle big problems pretty well. If they tell me a typhoon came and wiped out the set, or the guerillas attacked and killed all of us, I can deal with those kinds of problems, you know. But when they tell me that we blew a whole shot because some guy didn't know something and wasn't there, then I go crazy."

George Lucas had warned him: "Francis," he had said, "it's one thing to go over there for three weeks with, like, five people and sort of scrounge a lot of footage using the Philippine army"—this was the 16-millimeter *Apocalypse* Lucas would have made years before—"but if you go over there as a big Hollywood production, they're gonna kill you. The longer you stay, the more in danger you are of getting sucked into the swamp." But if he allowed himself to see the parallel between what he was doing to and in the jungle and what America had done to and in Vietnam, he would fold in self-recrimination. And then there would be no part of him left to consider the numbing details of making a movie on location. Or the ending.

Behind him, they whispered. They always whispered, Coppola thought. They had whispered on the first *Godfather*: *This guy is full of shit. Fire this guy. He doesn't know what he's doing.*

In a way, they would be right. He *didn't* know what he was doing. But he *knew* that he didn't know. "What I do," he said, "is create chaos and then try to control it." But there were two kinds of chaos: chaos in the pursuit of spontaneity, the golden moments in which Coppola seized his cameras on "the life energy," and then there was, not too far from the act of creation, a bedlam that preceded destruction.

Brando, meanwhile, was threatening to take the million Coppola had paid him up front and run—before he'd even arrived at the location. "I mean," Coppola sputtered to Barry Hirsch by phone, "that means the man is going to seriously not, I mean, take his money and not *deliv*—" He listened as Hirsch counseled. "Yeah, but that's fine, that's a lot of guys in offices. But here I am in this fucking country with about fifty things that are just quasi-in-my-control, like the Philippine government and the fucking helicopters, which they take away from me whenever they feel like, and they've done it three times already, and I'm shooting around *that*." What would that do to the story? The ending he didn't have? "Why should I make a picture less well than it's possible to do because of some peculiar vise that I'm in. It seems to me the so-called deal which we're trying to preserve is not more important than just my career as a director, and I feel that now as a producer, I'm being compromised as a director, and I don't feel I should be in that position. You know, all I'm asking for is for Marlon to allow me to start him a little later, and what this all comes down to is that he wants to be there when his kids get out of school, well, Jesus. . . . Let's go, let's blow the deal and go to Redford." Coppola insisted he would assume responsibility. Let them say it was his fault, *fine*. "I assumed there would be some malleability about Marlon. And I also didn't realize the immensity of the constructions and stuff. I mean, the picture's bigger than I thought, it's just gigantic. . . . I mean it'd be very easy for me now just to say, 'fuck it, it's just too big, what should I do?' But I'm not, we're hanging on, and all I'm saying is that. We're hanging on."

In desperation, he wrote to Arthur Krim, head of United Artists:

In the nutshell, Marlon put a very restrictive condition into the deal . . . that gave me two immense problems. it meant I had to do the last 30 minutes of the film. the most ambitious and most critical, i e, the ending . . . early on, totally out of continuity. Normally I don't mind shooting out of continuity, but since this film is the story of a journey, with the main characters changing as they go along, it means I have to guess at what they will look like, be like, what experiences they will have seen etc . . . and jump right into the last portion. as you can imagine, this will eliminate any wonderful surprises, accident, improvisations that might be happening during the journey . . .

a second problem is that the cambodian temple set at the end of the river journey is a massive and spectacular set, and although we are working on it 24 hours a day, literally, we are all terrified that it will not be done soon enough to get marlon out by june 10th, as he requests. . . .

the last reason is simple, me, myself. I am presently in the big helicopter battle sequence of baler. this is an enormous action, special effects, helicopter sequence on a beautiful but very difficult distant location. we are having a hell of a time shooting scenes, coordinating effects, helicopters, action stunts and doing it with the Philippine armed forces. . . . it is very trying and frustrating, and each night I go to sleep just praying that I'll be able to get the helicopter battle at all.

The exposed negative had to be flown to Rome for processing, so rushes took as long as a week and a half to get back to Coppola's makeshift projection room in the Philippines. Until then, he and his team couldn't be certain what shots they really had or which they only imagined they had. When the first weeks' rushes had arrived in the Philippines nearly three weeks after they were shot (along with the De Cecco pasta the Italian crew couldn't get through customs), Coppola faced the highly distressing fact that his Willard, Harvey Keitel, was miscast. "His style of acting did not work for Willard," Coppola conceded. He needed a calm presence, a face to mirror the audience's, a watcher. A former marine, Keitel was himself uncomfortable with Coppola. He could not accept the so-called truths of Coppola's Vietnam fantasy, to say nothing of his dangerously irresponsible, run-amok production, or the incarcerating, Keitel thought, seven-year contract only Frederic Forrest had signed—and he and Coppola parted ways in mid-April.

Which left Coppola with another crisis. Attempting to assume the guise of Filmmaker in Control, he shaved off his black beard, "as a sort of outward symbol, that even when he is really in trouble, he is capable of change," and hurriedly flew to Los Angeles with Fred Roos to greet the replacement candidate—mercifully, one of Coppola's original choices for Willard—recently of *Badlands*, Martin Sheen. Their meeting at LAX was brief but sufficient; whoever Willard was or what his soul had seen, Coppola still saw in Sheen, in his watchful eyes, red worlds within. He was a man of precipices, although of what and where they waited, neither could be certain. He had the part.

Back in the jungle, Robert Duvall was pulling all he could from Coppola—the tantrums, the fearlessness, the charisma—and feeding it to his surf-mad, napalm-loving (the smell, that is, in the morning) naval officer, Lieutenant Colonel Bill Kilgore. A Zoetrope mainstay since *The Rain People*—*Apocalypse* marked their sixth collaboration—Duvall found Coppola, once again, the most satisfying director he'd ever worked with. It was the mutual freedom his worlds facilitated, the leash the director gave the actor—Duvall, not asking permission, did it differently every take (and will "only do two or three takes," Coppola said)—and likewise the freedom Coppola gave himself, his vulnerability and inhibition, how he lost himself, so to speak, in the part of director. Pointedly *not* a director in control, Coppola was even moodier than the actors, Duvall thought, directing like a colonel to his soldiers—Duvall also applied this to Kilgore—shouting, exasperatedly hurling his megaphone into the air.

Early in May, with Coppola and Duvall and their armies storming the beach, special effects began to prepare the long-awaited napalm strike. Nearly a mile and a half from the camera, Lombardi, physically ill and pushing through a dirt trench fifty feet from the shore, had readied twelve hundred gasoline gallons to race through a mile of pipe and detonate the six-hundred-foot stretch of waterfront palms at the precise moment airborne F-5 jets, synchronized and on cue, were to drop their canisters.

There was no margin for error—not from the jets, not from Lombardi, nor from Coppola's crew. The slightest hesitation or oversight would destroy all that had been prepared for. And even if they thought they had the shot, in full or in part from one or all five cameras stationed to capture the inferno, they couldn't be certain until they had the rushes weeks later.

It was near impossible to rehearse. The Philippine government kept sending new pilots, each different from the day before. They didn't know the drills. They flew improperly, wasting thousands of dollars and numberless hours. Some could barely fly at all. "So our pilots," producer Gray Frederickson said, "would fly next to them as copilots and tell them to do certain maneuvers and so forth. But it was a little hairy because . . . we were [asking them] to do certain things that sometimes were dangerous. So a lot of times we had our fingers crossed when they would go flying into a cloud of smoke and—three helicopters from different directions. You just hoped that they didn't collide in the middle. And after a take, they would just circle around and head back over the hill, and you'd be waiting for them to come around for take two. And they'd disappear. They just . . . would go home. And that made Francis crazy." His mind looping now on worst-case scenarios, Coppola imagined some kid wandering into the jungle at the exact wrong moment and saw his little body tossing in the flames, his face burning. They would have to find his mother. He saw her, too: She would be wailing, beating her chest, tearing her hair. Would she kill herself?

Kneeling in the mud, looking skyward, at helicopters that might not make it into the shot in time for the blast, Coppola thought, "There's got to be a better way to do this." A studio . . .

Noxious helicopter exhaust spread headaches through the crew. Then the napalm—or what felt like it. The heat from the explosion was so hot, the boom so convulsive, it hit them a mile and a half away. Over there, orange sky turned a sickened gray, and palms rocked in turrets of flame.

"It's really, really Vietnam," Dick White said.

Coppola wasn't making a movie; he was shooting a documentary.

He was not making the movie, Eleanor knew; it was remaking him.

As she had so many times before, since the very moment she first saw him, the writing director of *Dementia 13*—pajama pants on, shirt off, hairy chest out, sitting in a circle of script pages on the floor—Eleanor Coppola had, then as now, the sure knowledge that this man Coppola was "a risk-taker, and commanded a vision of what he wanted." She said, "You had a sense, too, of his focus and dedication and commitment to go forward—ready or not—into this production." He had not changed, she could see that these fifteen years later; he still lived *there*, in the movie.

Watching him turn out new scenes at the dining room table in their house in the Philippines, typing his original script into mimeo masters that went to the mimeo printer with no way to make corrections or changes, Eleanor was ever mindful not to hover, but not to stray too far. Francis needed people around. She knew that. He talked through story issues and ideas to whoever was on hand, talked as he wrote, flying up on a rocket of story so fast that it often left the earthbound scrambling for sense. Not her, though. The dreamer's wife was a dreamer herself, an artist, a friend of artists; she knew how to stand on earth and hold out, if he fell, strong arms to catch him. Some nights, though, he never got off the ground. Others, he flew up into his own typhoon and never came back. On the nights he did return, she woke up beside a new him, recolored somehow and deepened. But either way, earth or sky, every night, when his dining room production meetings ended, after the plates were cleared and Dean, Vittorio, and the team ambled home, it would be down to her arms to hold him.

It was never a question of honesty. Eleanor knew she had to be honest. She would remind him, as she had before, that panic was his custom. He would insist that this time it's different; she would say he always said that. He would insist, no, this time it really is.

Some would say he needed hell to get to heaven. Coppola rejected that.

He looked different. Silly, their daughter, Sofia, thought, without the beard. He had lost, Eleanor guessed, thirty-five pounds since coming to the jungle, and normally, in real life, he wore glasses; in the Philippines, he had switched to contacts. Easier to look through the camera that way.

Their home in Manila was a stage set, as if created by Tavoularis, with plastic plants and the proplike bric-a-brac of fifties jungle kitsch, "mental milk of magnesia," one observer described it, emblems of another time and place, not theirs. "My reality feels like a foreign movie," Eleanor would write. "Part of me is waiting for the reels to change and get back to a familiar scene in San Francisco or Napa." They wouldn't be home again for five months.

In the meantime, United Artists had told Coppola they were sending a small crew to shoot a five-minute promotional piece about the film, something they could run on TV. But Coppola, beset with enough difficulties he didn't need UA knowing about, informed them they'd do it in-house.

"Ellie," he said, "you do it."

She was, he knew, a wonderful handheld cameraperson, one of the very best in the world, he thought. But Eleanor resisted. She'd made a short art film, but documentary filmmaker didn't sound like her. Was he just trying to keep her busy, or did he really think she could make something of value? She didn't know. What would *her* movie be about? She didn't know that, either. "If I knew what the basic idea was, I could be more specific about what to shoot," she wrote to herself. "I guess I am counting on the concept eventually appearing obvious to me and being better than anything I could figure out in advance." She was starting to sound like *him*.

Not knowing where she was headed, she began. She taught herself to use the 16 mm newsreel camera he bought for her, and with no crew, save for the young man who projected dailies by night to record sound and carry the tripod, Eleanor started gathering material.

"At home," she said, in the Philippines, "Francis would start talking about his problems, and I would just stick the tape recorder on the table and turn it on. He didn't care. He was too overwhelmed with what he was saying. By the end, I had sixty hours of film and forty hours of sound tape."

Eleanor Neil Coppola was not a writer—at least, not in her mind. "That was never my strength," she decided. "I'm a little dyslexic." But in the jungle she found herself writing. The notes she was taking on the film would be practical, a log for the documentary, a way to order her footage in advance. Scribbled furtively in spiral notebooks and on cocktail napkins, they were like little Instamatic snaps of Francis at work, she thought.

Her fortieth birthday came and went. *My kids are terrific*, she assured herself. *I love my husband, I am fine.*

She had always dreamed of marrying a man of overpowering talent and perhaps finding, or losing, her story in his. Which she had done, both. Mr. and Mrs. Coppola had created a bountiful world for themselves and their children, folding them into his films in the communal Zoetrope fashion, giving them adventures beyond imagining, at home and abroad. They had always done it, fame or no fame, with incredible wealth or with almost nothing at all. As long as the Coppolas were together, creating alone in their rooms but dreaming as a family, they would endure.

But she worried about Francis. The helicopter battle at last behind him, he faced an urgent threshold in the schedule: he must transform from a director of an airborne spectacular into a director of intimate human exchanges. This scared him. For not much longer could he continue to hide from the essential questions of character and story he did not completely understand. Actors needed answers. He could already feel their eyes on him, waiting for direction; Eleanor, a seasoned empath, felt him feeling them. Their minds pressed into hers. "There is the exhilaration of power in the face of losing everything," she noted, "like the excitement of war when one kills and takes the chance of being killed. Francis has taken the biggest risk possible in the way he is making this film. He is feeling the power of being the creator/director and the fear of completely failing," a remote, hazy wisp of Kurtz. It scared her, too.

Scarier still, it would seem he could not stop it. After *Godfather II*, which began for him as any other film and ended by consuming him and isolating her—she suffered silently, becoming Kay again—he stated to her and to Walter Murch and others that his next film, *Apocalypse Now*, would not tax his reality. It would be a fun action movie, a job, like the ones he used to do for Roger Corman—like *Dementia 13*, where he and Eleanor met and fell in love. He would do it fast, not for his soul, but for his wallet: for Zoetrope.

But that was before he breathed the clouds of colored smoke, back when Milius's John Wayne ending kept Coppola at a safe, commercial distance from himself.

The rains came with the wind, and the palms outside bent as if trying to run. Typhoon water ran into and through the house, out of closed bedroom doors, downstairs, and floated rugs and carpets off the floor like great waterbeds the kids splashed up and down. The front door flew open with more watery wind, and in swept a dozen crew people and Francis's friend, concert promoter Bill Graham. None of them could get home; they all would feast together in the big house of rain. Francis, who relished any chance to shoot in inclement weather, as he had to excellent results in *You're a Big Boy Now* and *The Godfather*, merrily threw pasta into a bubbling pot and rocket-blasted *La Bohème* over the windowpane rattles and crashing tree limbs and thunderclaps. There was singing, too, from the back lawn, now a lake of chorusing frogs. After dinner, the power went out and the music stopped and the table was set for dessert. They ate their bananas flambé smiling in quiet candlelight. "It was really beautiful," Eleanor recalled. "Francis was marveling at how the people at the table were so perfectly staged."

And then, all of a sudden, the power came back on, the needle fell back on the record, and *La Bohème* played again for all.

Three months before the beginning of typhoon season, the worst typhoon the Philippines had seen in forty years pummeled the Coppolas' home; it pummeled the cast and crew in their hotel in Iba, on the South China Sea; it pummeled the stunt guys jumping off the hotel roof into the pool; and it pummeled an estimated 80 percent of the sets, including the empty stadium built for the Playboy Bunny sequence. The typhoon threw Willard's little PBR, a patrol boat, up onto a helicopter pad; it spun the river into a whirling lake; buried costumes for eight hundred extras; buried Jeeps and a generator truck; and washed away tents readied for what should have been their next location, the medevac set. It buried dolly tracks in mountains of mud, destroyed roads, destroyed communication between production camps and the rest of the world, and stranded Sam Bottoms and Frederic Forrest on a pier in Manila with two Playboy Bunnies/actresses and their lobster dinners. It stranded further Bunnies in rivers in their cowboy boots ("You have twenty minutes to take cover," they heard. "The typhoon is coming!") and sent them running toward their flooded limousine, which became a hot tub on wheels. "You couldn't see an inch in front of your face," Gray Frederickson said; rain, Laurence Fishburne said, "hitting you so hard it hurt"; "115-mile-an-hour winds for almost three days" (Scott Glenn); like a 747 flying overhead (Albert Hall); "this yellowy light" (Dean Tavoularis) whipping invisible heavy objects—by the sound of it, sheets of aluminum roofing—through the air, shutting down electricity, air conditioning, running water, spreading dysentery and mold odor through the old hotel and starting fights. The typhoon dumped forty inches of continuous rain in six days, flattening bridges and huts, breaking apart whole boats in the sea, and, Coppola saw—he could not have dreamed it—entire ocean liners washed up onto shore. By May 21, the rain was like stones. A tree crashed into the hotel; in the rubble, the mayor of Iba, illumined by candles, saluted the sky with a sip of Chivas. "It's bad," he said to the carnage. "It's bad. As bad as I've ever seen." By May 23, the wind was double the force of a hurricane. "It seemed like days and nights we lost track of time," said "Playmate" actress Cindy Wood, "and we all feared that possibly we may not make it out alive, we really did." She saw it in their faces: "These men that normally were very collected and very cool and very masculine became very vulnerable, and I could see the fear. And it was really scary being a woman seeing the men that I would normally feel inclined to be protected by, reduced to a level where it made me really realize, gee, I mean, this is really a serious situation." Wood pushed a chair against her door at nights, afraid, somehow, that someone might do something crazy to her. "We were all losing it," she said. A dam burst, and Scott Glenn and Doug Claybourne raced out to see if and where they could help. They found a desperate woman in labor. Had they ever delivered a baby? "Yeah," Glenn answered her, "I delivered my second daughter in our home in Topanga Canyon." Burly Dick White, Vietnam vet, braved the air in a helicopter, flying sideways in the storm, replenishing food and water to a hundred members of the crew who had been stranded somewhere for three days.

A day or two later, cast and crew emerged from what was left of the medevac set. What they beheld was muddy water in all directions and, here and there, Filipino families clinging to floating rooftops. One by one, radios buzzed on to announce that hundreds had been killed. Arriving by helicopter, Coppola and Storaro found a dolly three feet under mud some two hundred yards from where they had set it. Coppola told Storaro he was shutting down the movie right away. "It's not possible," he explained as they surveyed the devastation. "We can't control everything." But then he turned back to Storaro and said through the rain, "Vittorio, what do you need to shoot something here?"

Beginning May 27, covered in plastic rain gear and up to their hips in mud, Coppola, Storaro, and a small crew returned to the medevac set to shoot, documentary-like, on the fly. Doubling as grips, extras pitched in to push the PBR into the surging Agno River and quickly tether it in place. Coppola yelled "Action" into the rain, and Sheen and the other actors leapt off the boat, but Sam Bottoms slipped and disappeared under the hull, and Coppola dove in after him. They tried again. "Every time we went out there, it was impossible," said Bill Graham. "And yet, if it was at all possible, Coppola wanted to try to capture it because of the madness of it." He was always telling Graham it wasn't that bad, that they were going to get through it. Graham wasn't sure. "I was concerned more than anything about Francis' mental stability," he said. *Apocalypse* was a demon, Graham thought; there was something inside Francis, something ugly he did not understand. *Apocalypse Now* was the record of its exorcism.

"The typhoon was our passage into a black hole," Sam Bottoms said, "and it changed everything." "I guess it was our hallucination, some of us," Cindy Wood said, "that the film was jinxed. That *Apocalypse Now* had some sort of magical, maybe negative spell attached to it. I remember even at one point there was a woman present who proclaimed herself to be a witch. And I don't believe in all this stuff, but so many strange things happened, we were beginning to believe it is possible that somebody could actually put a spell on this production."

They decided to close down for six weeks to rebuild.

In Manila, Francis and Eleanor were checked into a hospital for dehydration and malnutrition. Their test results, the doctor told her, looked like they'd been taken from concentration camp survivors.

"When Marty [Sheen] came home after the typhoon, he was real scared," Sheen's friend Gary Morgan recalled. "He said, 'I don't know if I am going to live through this. Those fuckers are crazy, all those helicopters and really blowing things up.' It was freaky; at the airport he kept saying goodbye to everyone."

The Coppolas went home to Napa.

Waking up in their own bed and opening the door to the sunlit vista of blooming dogwoods, oaks, and Japanese maples was like the moment Dorothy opens the door and faces her imagination, Oz, "the point," Eleanor wrote, "where the dream world and the real world meet."

It was late spring, and there were blossoms on the big magnolia tree. Vineyards rolled up over and down the far hills, all theirs. The Coppolas drank sacred, old cellar wines and picnicked on cheeses and read and slept outside on the lawn under the new moon, where Francis had nightmares about his ending.

Coppola knelt on the sidewalk outside the Transamerica Pyramid, United Artists' San Francisco headquarters, head lowered and hands clasped in prayer. "Please don't let me be a failure," he unjokingly joked. "I want to make money for you on this movie."

Way behind schedule and over budget, Coppola had returned to United Artists, for an additional $3 million. This time it was a loan.

Which meant if *Apocalypse Now* didn't turn a profit sufficient to reimburse United Artists, Coppola would be personally on the hook for overages. "The guarantee of the loan was all of my estate."

With *Apocalypse Now*, Coppola would do, he felt, the only thing worth doing in this life, something he should have done all along: invest more, invest in himself, put all his chips on lucky number seven and win. And he *would* win. Because, up to now, he had *always* won. But this time, with his own money in the film, he would win bigger than he or anyone else ever had; owning *Apocalypse*, if it hit—and it would—he would be one giant step closer to financial independence, perhaps even rich enough to transform Zoetrope into a studio . . . or something bigger than a studio . . .

What was bigger than a studio?

"I will do good with this picture," Coppola, kneeling, pledged on the sidewalk. "Someday I won't just own *this*," the Sentinel Building, visible from the Transamerica building, standing behind him, "but I'll own you too. You guys won't own a piece of my picture. I'll own you instead."

The Sentinel Building—eight cluttered floors of Coppola Company offices, alternately bustling and vacated with the ebb and flow of production, reorganized at a moment's notice in accordance with Coppola's fortunes, new ideas, and unexpected special projects—was no one in Hollywood's dream of a production headquarters, but Coppola was, despite his incredible success, no one in Hollywood's dream of a businessman. On his desk in his penthouse, he kept a stereo, a tape recorder to speak *Apocalypse* scenes into, piles of books of Vietnam research, his typewriter, a phone, and an original Edison phonograph, a reminder of his boyhood North Star: innovation.

"Read," he directed, from behind his typewriter, at Fred Roos. "You're supposed to be reading."

Roos held new *Apocalypse* pages. "Francis, I'm having a hard time following it."

"These last five pages are crucial," Coppola explained. "The jungle will look psychedelic, fluorescent blues, yellows, and greens. I mean the war is essentially a Los Angeles export, like acid rock. Like in *Heart of Darkness*, Kurtz has gone savage, but there's this greatness in him." Coppola was racing, lit with story. "We are all as much products of this primitive earth as a tree or a native whooping around. The horror that Kurtz talks about is never resolved. As Willard goes deeper into the jungle, he realizes that the civilization that has sent him is more savage in ways than the jungle. I mean, we created that war."

A floor below the penthouse sat and scurried a handful of employees either overworked or underworked, rarely in between. The stylish Mona Skager, once a set gofer and now a manager of the Coppola Company's growing list of properties, had been with him the longest, since *The Rain*

People, and like most others in his company, she had a history of filling in where needed, doing everything. "Mona acted as a screen for Francis," Colin Michael Kitchens said. "She was like the mouth of a baleen whale: she just sucked out the protein Francis needed to know about." Across the hall from Mona was the resolute Jean Autrey, the one-woman accounting department, who once had the happy task of calling Paramount to say Francis wanted another million dollars of his *Godfather* money. ("They sent it," she said.) As for his expenses, she had to bite her lip. "People would complain about what Francis was doing," Autrey said. "My standard pitch was, 'It's his money. He can do whatever he wants with it.'" Perusing the charges, whether from Francis or his employees, she often seemed, to herself and others, the only adult in the building. "People would come in wanting to be reimbursed for expenses, and I'd say, 'What's *that* for?'" It was not a question heard often in the Sentinel Building.

From his seat in the penthouse, Coppola zestily resumed the course of empire. Riding eureka surges of inspiration, he did not hesitate to buy from his heart, spending money he didn't have, or didn't know he didn't have, or felt he would have very soon. His recklessness—or hopefulness—amused Autrey, when it didn't annoy her. ("It's stunning what you can do with no money down," she whispered to Barry Hirsch.) But there was only one way to abundance, as he explained to his future sound designer Richard Beggs, and it was not caution. Stopping by Beggs's recording studio in the basement of the Sentinel Building, Coppola described "with gusto and enthusiasm" his plans for his own Zoetrope studio, Beggs said, "this very utopian idea about what would be a creative playground of sorts. He very much saw himself as an artist *and* as a leadership force to further those things." He would talk about his idea, "right out of *Metropolis*," Beggs said, "like a donut with everybody sitting around in a circle, and in the center was this core, which would be the explorative analogy of a mainframe computer. Each department head would plug into this, and everything else would melt away, and we'd be working in this filmic nirvana or something."

The beginnings of such a transformation were already taking shape at the Sentinel Building and Coppola's around-the-corner-and-underground postproduction bunker known as the Facility. One such innovation, the "film chain"—the process by which *Apocalypse* dailies were transferred to videotape and sent to the Philippines—was one of many Coppola-inspired production phenomena found nowhere else in the world. It was overseen by Mitch Dubin in the Facility. "First, the negative would get shipped to ENR, Ernesto Novello Roma [in Rome], and undergo a chemical process to retain more of the silver in the negative," Dubin explained. "They would make a print and ship the print to San Francisco, and then, literally, we would project it onto a little screen in the screening room and would sit there with a video camera and videotape them in Betamax and send the Betamax tape to the Philippines. That's how they would watch dailies."

"We were always, always running the film chain," said Karen Frerichs, stationed at the Facility switchboard. "Either it was breaking down or being put back together," and always, it seemed, in the middle of the night. As many were, Frerichs had been hired in a pinch, in her case to play the part of receptionist for both the Sentinel Building and the Facility, because, as Tom Sternberg told her, "The person who is supposed to be here isn't doing it." "That's how things happened there," Holland Sutton said. "Someone would realize they needed something, and someone would be asked," or hired, to get it, or, as was more often the case, invent it. Dubin said, "We were just making it up as we went along."

Late in July 1976, the Coppolas returned to the Philippines. Sofia was enrolled in first grade at a Chinese school where no one spoke English ("Francis said it would be a terrific experience for her," Eleanor recalled), and, the day before production was to resume, Eleanor dreamt heavily. At breakfast the next morning, she told Francis she was afraid to proceed with the documentary she was making about *Apocalypse Now*. She wasn't a professional, she insisted. It just wasn't her. Then it started to rain.

Coppola dreamt he was in the Saigon hotel room with Martin Sheen and a nameless Green Beret who was telling Coppola he wasn't getting Willard right; he needed to convey something unprocessed in Willard's "very textured soul," and film, somehow, a private event that "would bring out the devils in him." But Sheen's Willard, Coppola saw in dailies, wasn't reading deep enough to contain devils. He was reading bland. "It's the Stanley and Livingston of morality," Coppola had implored Sheen, as if imploring himself, too. "The journey to find out. That's why I say it's a mythical journey into oneself. That is the question that I would love this movie not to answer, cause I don't know that it can be answered, other than to say basically that the answer is you, you now, you are it." Coppola persisted, scouring the "hidden levels" for dark synchronies "in the actor's personality and in the personality of the character he plays." Again, it didn't work. It looked like Sheen was acting. But the job of the actor was *not* to act. "Marty, it's *you*," Coppola insisted. "Whoever you are at the moment, that's all we got. If the sun is shining, you don't hold the umbrella up because the script says it's a rainy scene. Or if it's raining you don't pretend that the sun is shining because the camera is going to photograph you at that moment in time doing whatever it is or not doing whatever it is. And the camera's going to tell the truth." Coppola confided in Storaro he had done everything he could think of "to fuck him up," including opium, but Sheen's reaction always seemed somehow put on. "There isn't an honest layer for maybe five layers down," he told Storaro.

These guys are vain, the Green Beret in Coppola's dream told him. *Get Willard and Marty looking into their faces in the hotel room mirror, get them admiring their beauty, their hair, their lips . . .*

They shot the scene on August 3, 1976, Martin Sheen's thirty-sixth birthday.

It was a small hotel room, cramped with crew, equipment, and wet summer heat. Steve Burum set up two bright lights outside the window and, inside, arranged small lights in clusters to create patches of darkness around Willard's bed. He placed the harsh glow of a naked light bulb at his mirror.

On the far side of the room, near the bathroom door, Coppola sat up on a dresser to have a clearer eyeline to Sheen.

By then, Sheen had been caged in the room days on end, just as Willard was meant to have been. "I was a raving lunatic," he said.

It was the night of the day Willard's divorce is finalized. He's been trying and failing to get in touch with his ex-wife, in Ohio, Sheen's birthplace. All present on the set, having fought long-distance loneliness in their own hotel rooms, related.

By the time the cameras rolled, Sheen had been drinking all day. Per his dream, Coppola had encouraged Sheen to get himself a bottle and peel away the dishonest layers between his vanity and himself. No one knew what would happen next.

Gradually, under the influence of Coppola's off-camera prodding, the actor's masks fell away. Sheen the righteous, the Catholic; Sheen the artist ... he began to dance, to take off his clothes ...

"Marty, go look at yourself in the mirror," Coppola called from across the room. "I want you to look at how beautiful you are. I want you to look at your mouth, your mouth and your hair ..."

He did as he was told. He did look beautiful, standing naked in front of a mirror. He had been practicing judo, and it showed. He looked strong.

"You look like a movie star."

Coppola was tense. He was afraid of what he was about to see and of what it might say about him, as a director and as a man. "Now frighten yourself, Marty ..."

Nothing is faster than your own reflection, the actor reminded himself. Judo had taught him that.

Sheen shrank and lunged forward, ashamed of pretending. He knew he had been hiding his brokenness and that in keeping it from Francis, he was failing them both. Failing the truth, he was failing two of his own brothers, both Vietnam veterans. Disgusted, he drunkenly punched Willard's movie star face in the mirror, shattering it, cutting open his thumb, and stumbled back, half-conscious of what was changing in him.

Coppola didn't jump down from the dresser. He didn't call "Cut." He waited, Sheen unraveling, watching him.

How long would he wait?

Before a hushed crew and rolling cameras, both were finding out.

Coppola waited.

Sheen was drifting, glaring at the blood in his hand. He was so drunk he could hardly stand.

"Okay, cut," Coppola said. "Do we have a doctor?"

"No, let it go," Sheen insisted. "I want to have this out right here and now."

He was in chaos. Slumped on the floor, against the bed, he was wailing, an animal. There was blood on the bed, on his bare chest.

He had been acting his entire life until that moment. It was, in a sense, why he was an actor: to protect himself from having to feel like Martin Sheen, handsome and virile and, as Coppola dreamed, vain, but angry, alcoholic, married and alone. He was fragmented, "almost nonexistent," he realized, "not in touch with my spirit at all." "He's angry with the Church," said his brother Joe Estevez. "It did so much good and it caused so much pain." He turned on himself.

"You fucker . . ." He was crying on the floor. "You *fuckkkkerrrrr* . . ."

He had failed as a father and a husband, emotionally abandoning his wife, Janet, to become Willard.

Coppola badgered him for being evil. *I want the hatred in you to come out.* "You tell that to a guilt-ridden Irish Catholic," a crew member later said, "and he hasn't a chance."

"Think about it," Francis demanded, taunting Sheen. He didn't know the man was an alcoholic. "Your wife! Your home. Your car . . ."

"My heart is broken . . . *God damn it!*"

It was not natural to watch the deliberate breaking of a human being and do nothing. "Francis," one crew member said, "did a dangerous and terrible thing. He assumed the role of a psychiatrist and did a kind of brainwashing on a man who was much too sensitive." There was in the room the unreal feeling that if Coppola let the transformation continue, Sheen or Willard might attack him or someone else, or worse. Coppola himself shared the feeling, but he was plagued by another: if he didn't continue, if he called cut now, he could lose whatever came next.

Then, quite unexpectedly, a calm overtook the actor. "It was a landmark in my life," Sheen reflected. "And that scene in particular revealed something to me about myself."

Coppola would say, "As you go up the river, there are things on your right that you can choose and there are things on your left that you can choose—and usually possibilities are contradictions. I began to realize that I was not making a film about Vietnam or about war, I was making a film about the precarious position that we are all in where we must choose between right and wrong, good and evil—and everyone is in that position."

A nurse standing by in the hotel room was called forward, and the man on the floor, Martin Sheen, was bandaged.

Eleanor would watch Storaro and his crew walking out of the hotel room, solemnly, unlike themselves. Inside, she found her husband alone with Sheen. He was dangerously drunk on the bed, raving about God and love, singing "Amazing Grace," begging Eleanor and Francis to sing with him, squeezing their hands so hard he bled more through the bandage, and the nurse was called in again to redress the wound. Taking the nurse's hand, Sheen had her join them in song and prayer, and she did, emphatically assuring him throughout, "Jesus loves you, Marty. Jesus loves you." Then Janet and their son appeared out of the rain, and Sheen joined their hands together and asked them to get on their knees to pray and confess with him.

He had met Coppola on a Good Friday. On Holy Saturday, he had learned he got the part, and on Easter Sunday, he had read the script. "Martin paid a lot of penance for that film," said his brother Joe. "Willard is symbolic of his life. Martin is such a lonely man."

Reaching the majestic squalor of Dean Tavoularis's bombed-out Do Lung Bridge, constructed from the remains of an actual bridge bombed by the Japanese in World War II, Coppola immersed his company, hundreds deep, in the symbolic atmosphere of the bridge: a soldier's crossing between realities real and dreamed and, as lit by Vittorio Storaro against the night rain, mad contrasts of nature and artifice. "I try to have a parallel story to the actual story," Storaro explained, "so that through light and color you can feel and understand, consciously and unconsciously, much more clearly what the story is about." An impression of his unconscious, the parallel story he was light-writing into *Apocalypse Now* was the story of its own creation, very much like *Heart of Darkness* and the American infiltration of Vietnam, "the conflict between natural energy and artificial energy," he would explain, the conflict between the harsh white light of American electricity and the blue glow Storaro had seen, he said, in a Philippine jungle tree.

The sky was a psychedelic smile of carnival lights against bamboo scaffolds and the crossing beams of massive arc lights. Fires burned and rockets and phosphorescent loops rose and fell like disco balls into the black river and tungsten flares leapt crackling and died slowly into the far distance.

With one eye open, the vista was beautiful; with two, it was insane. Tavoularis explained: "It's dark and, like soldiers in the film, you can't see anyone." But you could hear. Though what you could hear—shouts, explosions—you couldn't understand.

Eleanor was there with Roman, sleeping and waking under a coconut tree. Gio, in black makeup and full uniform, carried an M16. He was almost thirteen.

Leaving his mind, Willard and his crew pushed deeper into the jungle, and Coppola, shooting almost entirely in sequence, moving himself and Willard closer to Kurtz, still had no ending. "[Willard] is falling apart into two separate guys," Coppola reminded himself. "One is very sweet, very considerate, very loving, very reminiscent or nostalgic about things that happened to him in his life, or things, or things that he observed. Becomes very concerned for the younger guys. And the other aspect of him is really violent and pushing and relentless." But here, at the bridge, it was a question not of writing, but of directing. He needed to make imagery. "The metaphor is you're going into hell," he told Tavoularis, "you're going into your own soul and you're going into a very dark place. What can we do to enhance this pictorially? Is it just the same river as the day before? As they progress, what's different? What happens?"

He didn't know.

He *had* to know.

"For Willard," he stammered to Sheen, "the conclusion he comes to, is that there is no going back. It's falling apart. It's the end of the world."

What was the cinematic language of a breaking mind? As a writer, he could hide, he could hold off crucial choices of execution, but at the Do Lung Bridge, he was made to decide, as a director must, the exact frame of his camera's awareness. The surreal was upon him and, in desperation, Coppola was grabbing on to anyone. His mind was his mouth now; he had to look to others' faces to see it. What was Willard even doing in the trenches? Storaro didn't know:

"We haven't, right now, a reason why he's come in here."

"Well," Coppola said, "I think the reason is—is that he realizes or he comes to realize that there is no one in command. . . . There is no one in command."

Storaro, however, was not scared. In his perfectly pressed linen shirts and gold chains, he still was a poet-prince, calmly sitting out the war to discourse on color theory and the processes of his own conscious and unconscious minds. Other directors had no patience for such discussions. Other directors, Storaro knew, were not adventurers; they drew clear the lines between worlds. "This doesn't happen with Francis," he said. "You can live your personal life while you're filming." The confluence allowed Storaro uninterrupted access to his complete creative person, and the extreme conditions of *Apocalypse Now* "give that kind of idea even more," he said, "because [it] was so far away, was so long, was so expensive, was so difficult, was so dangerous." He thrived under Coppola. "Francis is, without a doubt, the director who gave me the most freedom to express myself," he said.

"Remember *Paths of Glory*?" he asked Storaro. "They were in the trench?"

"Yeah."

"It bothered me all night. I kept dreaming about it . . ."

For the bridge, they decided on a dolly shot, a long one. Rather than breaking a moment into pieces, long takes gave Coppola and his actors more of a real-time sense of the imagined experience and, if Coppola did it right, maybe even the experience itself, with all the surprise of life. The dolly he and Storaro designed was incredibly treacherous, almost five continuous minutes of careful choreography in the half light, time-consuming and—after the hours spent designing and arranging with only their 3 a.m. instinct to tell them if they got it—perhaps too much. Had he crossed into pretension?

"What I'm worried about is that I'm getting into a self-indulgent pattern," Coppola would say to Eleanor.

"Yeah, but don't you, on the one hand, feel like that's where your gifts as an artist are working? They're on that brink of not knowing what to do. What if you just scream out to the heavens, 'I don't know what the fuck I'm doing'?"

"I've done that. That's another form of self-indulgence."

He decided he was sabotaging himself with his dolly, showing off. Once he got into the cutting room, he'd chop the shots up anyway.

"What I'm coming to is that what I think I did wrong is I tried to hold it all. Maybe you can't hold it all. And that's what's giving me trouble. Maybe this is a sequence that really should be shot very point of view . . . Is this gonna be Willard's point of view, which the picture has to be, or is this Lance's point of view? Or do I have two points of views? Can you have two points of view?"

At the end of the day, he would try to discover himself by listening to himself talk to her:

". . . and the thing I don't do well, is I tend not to jump into the heart of the matter. . . . I tend to start the scene for the things that lead up to the scene, and end up spending all my energy in that prime time working on this. And then suddenly, there I am facing the heart of the matter, which I then either do very quickly or don't do and have to do the next day."

This is what he was doing on the bridge: searching, and not merely for his movie.

"It's a crime the time I'm taking. It's not making the picture any better, it's not making anything any better. It's just getting me depressed and costing a lot of money. It's a total waste of money, the time I'm taking. So I'm gonna see if tonight I can enjoy the essence of the scene, and what the scene means, and nothing else. Not get bogged down in all this bullshit."

Was she really listening to him, or was she just shining him on? He needed her to say he was going to be okay. But then, whenever she said it, he dismissed it.

"What I have to admit is that I don't know what I'm doing," he told her.

This was how he worked. She knew he shot long. She knew he came through strongly when, behind the gun, his instinct was forced to emerge. "Well," she began, "how do you account for the discrepancy between what you feel about it and what everybody else who sees it feels?"

"Because they see the magic of what has happened before. I'm saying, 'Hey, it's not gonna happen! I don't have any performances. The script doesn't make sense. I have no ending.' I'm like a voice crying out, saying, 'Please, it's not working! Somebody get me off this.' And nobody listens to me! Everyone says, 'Yes, well, Francis works best in a crisis.' I'm saying, 'This is one crisis I'm not gonna pull myself out of!'"

Could it be that she was using his crisis? He'd come home and tell her he was dying, "but instead of her telling me, 'It's not so bad, you're doing a good job,' all she said was, 'Could you say that a little louder?'" She was making a film, too. But what had begun as a film about a movie was fast becoming a film about an artist, his process—a subject far more interesting to Eleanor than the helicopters and explosives of Vietnam.

Likewise, he knew now his wasn't a war film; it was a breakdown. It was the horror, the center of Conrad's novel, to which he needed to return. The letter of the script he had abandoned, and in its place, Coppola would reference the green paperback copy of *Heart of Darkness* he carried with him everywhere, its dog-eared pages creased and single- and double-underlined.

"From the bridge on," he would say, "it's pretty much *Heart of Darkness* and me."

They marked the boats they were going to blow up with red flags, so the helicopters would know not to fly too close, but after ten takes, a rope holding a boat in place caught fire, setting the vessel loose. It drifted downriver, burning, as a trio of low-flying helicopters grazed the flames and men fell out of the sky.

One minute, Coppola was wasting his money; the next, he was wasting his time *not* to spend more money. If you're gonna be in debt for $3 million, what's the difference if you're in debt for $4 million?

He started smoking: Balkan Sobranie cigarettes. "When you're in the midst of this kind of carnage and devastation and horror," he explained, "it is amazing what the human being will seek out to be interested in."

He started smoking grass. He said, "It was like Vietnam—it was there, and everybody was doing it." It dulled the self-critical voices, focusing him.

There was cocaine for those who wanted it, and booze to work off the steam. Tavoularis said, "There were people who went over the edge, started drinking, basically had to be shipped back, couldn't function." Some days, it was so hot the cocaine melted.

At Do Lung Bridge, Sam Bottoms was so whacked out on speed he thought he accidentally shot Martin Sheen in the arm. "Every time I look at you," Coppola had told him, "it looks like you're on vacation." Coppola was right; that's about how Bottoms had felt, originally, coming to the Philippines, hanging out in the sun with Fred Forrest, Larry Fishburne, and Sheen on the PBR. Who knew how long this would last? Just trying to enjoy himself, Bottoms spent a lot of the shoot drinking or stoned. Once or twice, he dropped acid while on camera. "I just wanted to feel like . . . it was a dream," Bottoms said. "Like I was just experiencing a dream." Coppola folded it into the character to the degree that Bottoms wasn't certain they were acting anymore. "A lot of marriages broke up," Bottoms recalled. "A lot of guys over there would spend time with the local girls. Prostitution is something that's legal in the Philippines . . . I think Vietnam was the same thing . . . And, if the rains would come, everybody would run off to the massage parlors. It was pretty insane. And there was a lot of gonorrhea going around too, as I remember." At Do Lung Bridge, he felt what he thought was a python slither up his arm.

Fred Forrest flipped. "I don't know, Francis," he would say, over and over, "I'm just not here. I'm somewhere else. I'm walking down the street in Beverly Hills with my friend. I'm gonna go in and get a Coke and a hamburger."

"Freddy, that's your character," Coppola said one day. "Just keep thinking that. I'm in the middle of all this, just keep thinking I'm not here."

It caught on. Where are you today, Freddy? They would ask. I don't know. I'm in Waco, I'm in Des Moines. I'm in Montana making a movie with Jack Nicholson. But I'm not here.

Forrest wasn't acting, but he wasn't not pretending, either. He said, "It was like you were in a dream or something, you know."

It was that way for the others. "The character basically evolved out of my thoughts and concepts," said Albert Hall. True to his character, Chief Phillips, Hall kept his distance from the other guys on the PBR. "He was the mother of the ship," Bottoms said. "He kept very much to himself. He's a very private person." Hall spent his days alone, in self-reflection. Chief Phillips "dove deeper and deeper into my mind," Hall said, "started waking up another feeling in me—a desperate need to survive."

Coppola had the actors fire live ammunition, break down and clean their guns, and when the boat gave up, as it often did, he had them fix its broken engine. In place of script pages calling for "Scene Unknown," he had them improvise. In that weather, it was easy. Heat melted personality. "That is how we got to be a family," Hall said. Coppola was in control of all of it, Bottoms surmised, but it—whatever it was—was obviously also in control of him. That was obvious to all of them. This could kill Francis, Bottoms worried; he could actually die here. That is, if he didn't kill himself accidentally or, somehow, be reborn. The possession, expanding the awareness of the afflicted, sometimes did just that, manifesting as revelation. "Everybody was opening themselves up," Bottoms said. "We were liberating ourselves in many interesting ways."

". . . When you start fooling around with metaphor," Coppola said, "the metaphor fools around with you."

In mid-August, after about two weeks at the bridge, Coppola wrapped the extras at sunrise. Along with the real veterans who had started trailing the production, extras climbed into buses and headed back to the hotel. The vets aboard drank from rum flasks, murmuring among themselves. "The fucking Charlies," said one, shaking, "they threw all of their miscellaneous shit at us. They really wanted the bridge out. They *really* wanted the bridge out."

Brando was coming. Brando, King of the Actors, the actor's dream.

The photojournalist's dream. *A great man*, Dennis Hopper's character would call Kurtz.

Hopper—cast, almost spontaneously, on location, to play a character inspired by the Russian of *Heart of Darkness*—prepared for immersion in the coming world, which would be Marlon Brando's. Anticipating Kurtz's arrival, Hopper cleaned himself up, stepped into a brand-new captain's uniform, and gathered his troops, the Montagnards, headhunters. He would be ready for Colonel Kurtz's appearance: he, their captain, drilling the troops in all-night war games. As they got word of an insurgency in the mountains—real, it seemed—Hopper ordered his soldiers, who seemed just as real, to take possession of bridges, scout the enemy, and arm and ceremoniously fire their guns.

When Brando finally arrived, Hopper led him to greet his troops. In his honor, they "got weirder and weirder," Hopper said. In a frenzy, their uniforms tore. Their face camouflage melted. Some appeared with parrots and snakes. In grand ceremony, they marched for Kurtz in parade formation, and displayed for his pleasure their perfected jujitsu technique, their beautiful canoes. At last, Hopper thought, they were a spectacular fighting machine ready for their king. And he had delivered them.

"It was the most amazing thing that I've ever experienced in my life," Hopper said.

Outside his mind, it never happened.

Hopper and Eleanor watched as young Ifugao, in loincloths, grabbed pigs, tied their legs, and delivered them to the foot of an old priest—about eighty, Eleanor had been told—stationed in a nearby glade. There was chanting from the tribe as the holy man danced beside the pigs, drinking from a cup of rice wine before sprinkling it on the largest one. Then caged chickens were carried out, and other Ifugao tribesmen joined the dance. The priest then selected a chicken and danced with it before setting it down atop the chosen pig.

The ceremony lasted an hour. Finally, one of the Ifugao dancers appeared with a great knife and drove it into the first pig and systematically slaughtered the others, biggest to smallest. "So many non reasonable [*sic*] things have happened to me since I have been in the Philippines," Eleanor wrote. "I no longer try to make them fit a reasonable linear context. I see things, notice them, the way you do in dreams."

Francis joined her that afternoon, on the set, for the next sequence of the ritual—the killing of the carabao, a water buffalo. They watched two chanting priests whack away at the animal with bolo knives. How startlingly high, Eleanor thought, its blood spurted in the air. How basic it all was to them, Coppola thought. The proximity of death. How matter-of-fact the Ifugao were about killing—as if sacrifice wasn't really killing, as if the animal, perishing, hadn't actually died. He watched with fascination as carabao entrails were distributed among the tribesmen; he watched them pour the animal's blood into yellow buckets and put aside its meat for the feast. The carabao's enormous dripping heart, traditionally reserved for the priest, they presented to him, their director.

"The violent, angry part in me, Eleanor, is the most pure part of me that there is. It is probably the most beautiful part of me because I am not lying,

I am not feeling malice, I am not doing it to be mean. In other words if I get angry at you I am not doing it to be mean to you. It is the crystal clear expression of how I feel. It's neither good nor bad, it's just my emotion."

He was talking to her about Kurtz. Brando had arrived, and Coppola still didn't have an ending. Because he still didn't know who, or what, Kurtz was.

"We say that anger is bad. But if you viewed my anger as a very sincere, honest expression of myself in the moment, and trust that I will not hurt anyone really, the fact that it is preventing me from getting ulcers and probably is good for me, and for that"—he was stammering—"it allows me to put an end to what I obviously consider an unbearable situation because I can't—"

He was paying millions for Brando, and Brando hadn't lost the weight he had promised he would—if anything, he was fatter, "gigantic," Coppola said, "bigger than a water buffalo," far too big to credibly play, as written, a former Green Beret. What if they put him in a sarong and really leaned into the fat? No, Brando said. He didn't want to be seen as fat. But he *was* fat, so . . .

Coppola and Brando would spend days discussing the character, the story, the war, in Brando's houseboat, rehashing the narrative elements as if they were still in preproduction, while the crew shot nothing—*Knock knock*, "Francis, should I send the crew to lunch?" "Send the crew to lunch"—running up the budget (eighty thousand dollars a day, give or take) and Coppola's personal liability, bigger since interest rates had since skyrocketed to an astonishing 20 percent.

They had to move quicker. But if Coppola the producer said that to Coppola the director, the latter would tell him to take it up with Coppola the writer. The movie couldn't just end, happy, sad, or ambiguous, the writer would argue back; it had to end answering some very hard moral-metaphysical questions on about forty-seven different levels at once, and it had to do it fast, in a few scenes, because at this point in the movie, nearly the end, it had to be over. But there was no way to write that well, or at all. To put mystical language in characters' mouths, *self-purgation, epiphany, soul*—not even Marlon Brando could rescue these words from pretension. "But those *are* the words for the process," Coppola would insist to Eleanor, "this *transmutation*, the *renaissance*, this *rebirth*, which is the basis of all life." What else would you call it?

Or was it better to not use language at all?

"How do you judge him?" he asked her. "Would you kill him? Should Willard kill him?" Maybe that's how he would release the movie—with a question for the audience. Let *them* direct the picture. "All those who want Willard to, push button A and you see the movie that way. God! Wouldn't that be great if I did that—a double ending?"

It was so *simple*, just a single choice, really: he had to pick a motivation for Brando, just *one*. "One drive [for Kurtz] is to in fact make Willard his disciple and carry the word. And the other is to torment and kill Willard. You know what I mean?" If he could just choose. But Kurtz was still less character than idea, and a conflicted idea at that, embodiment of the lurking Vietnam in America, the evil in the good. Unless, of course, he was the good in the evil? Or were these rather big questions, not motivations, questions that shouldn't absorb the actor's mind? Or was Coppola being too binary? Brando, not just any actor, contained multitudes. Why not use them? "It's to be relaxed enough to use your own instinctual stuff," Coppola explained to Storaro. "It's the same struggle as the theme. You've gotta reconcile your own mystical part and just [imbue] your inclinations and your instincts with some kind of logic so that you have structure." He would be artistically irresponsible *not* to go mad and, therefore, equally irresponsible not to let Brando, one of the world's great artists, an actual living genius, Coppola thought, not go as mad as he ever had been before. "Everything in this production is telling me to be practical," he was saying to Storaro. "I mean, just by sheer force of presence. I mean, I got too many people, it cost too much money, the issues are too volatile and it's ironic that as it's telling me to be more and more practical, I find myself less and less able to be practical, which is exactly the right decision. You know what I mean?"

"If you say I'm stressing with stuff that would crack a lot of people," he was saying to Eleanor, trying to speak to this thing that was happening to him, "then letting off steam is good for me and it's not petulant. I mean, I'm not complaining about the fact that the grocery bill didn't get paid or something, you know. I mean, I'm trying to stay sane wrestling with problems that are bigger than I am.

"But I don't know what my limits are. I have no limits. I could hack a body. No, I'm not going to my limits. I'm going—there's a line in Conrad where he said he went beyond the bounds of permitted aspirations. That implies there are bounds? But saying 'permitted' implies that there's some moral system. So I'm not saying that there *isn't* a moral system. I'm saying that it's a *bigger* one. . . . What I'm saying is that although I know all about me, it is very possible that I am generating an impression of another aspect of me which I'm not even aware of. So what I'm trying to say—now that's hard to tell an actor. That there are two—that there are two yous. Although that's what the movie is saying. Isn't the movie always talking about that?"

Should she be recording this?

"It's like trying to blow up a gorge in a cliff with pitchforks. You gotta use dynamite. We have to use moral dynamite. We have to, we have to try to use a system of—you can't get to the moon with 18th century physics. You have to get there with 20th—and you can't get to Mars with 19th century physics. We're capable, I think, of expanding ourselves. Equally so, you cannot view these moral outer galactic things, such as the Nazis or Vietnam, you can't view them through 19th or 14th or morality that was created 2,000 years ago. We have to be prepared to enter a new age of morality, and we are afraid to do it because we think it will be immoral. It will not be immoral. It will be a new morality, and we hope with all our hearts that it will not include all these blood-lust things. But we must let go. We're afraid to let go of that old morality, because we're frightened. But in holding on to it, perhaps we're perpetuating the very thing we're frightened of. This film does not want to advocate killing, it does not want to advocate blood-lust, it really doesn't. But it's saying we must step into the future unafraid. And that means the future in physics, the future in morality, and the future in logic, and the future in concepts of existence. We must be unafraid, we're afraid of the unknown, we're afraid of our true nature. We can't be afraid of our true nature, because our true nature is all we've got. We must merely expand our moral view of it, and an event like Vietnam only illustrates once again how our moral system has more than allowed these horrors, it has encouraged them. So once and for all we must be clear, it doesn't work. It can't work. We must, we must not be afraid of our true nature. We must struggle with it, if we're to break into a new level. And that's what I want the movie to say. Now, God help me, please help me, how do I say it? I've been trying to say it in words. It's all right to say it in words, only after I've put the event and let people say it in their own words as best they can. Let them grapple with it. I can't teach them because I'm grappling with it. And I'm not that kind of talent, I don't have the kind of genius mind of a Shaw or one of those guys. I'm not that kind of mind. All I can do maybe is put something that smells of it. I'm not a Conrad. God, I wish I were, but I'm not a Conrad. I can admire Conrad is all I can do. And I can sort of, like a fucking centipede, with some intuition, throw a bunch of elements and have courage, which is about all I have, to just fuckin' throw them together on this 17 million dollar canvas. And I realize that I can't. But even Conrad, he's a twenty-times greater man than I am, 120 times greater artist than I am, he couldn't do it. But he didn't even try to do it. He did it with less. He gave you an image. He used language, he used poetry to evoke the meaning, so that it would stick in our craw and we would talk about it and I would follow after it like a little dog trying to do it. And maybe if I make this movie, even if it doesn't open it up in the way I want to, some kid or old man will see it and say, 'Oh, I get it,' and he'll make a film, or he'll write a book, and he'll get it. You know what I mean? He'll reach the freezing point of water and it will gel. Or maybe it won't, maybe it'll happen twenty years from now. Maybe the movie will be misunderstood. Doesn't matter. But in a practical sense what I've learned is that I have been going crazy between the literal and the realistic. You know, it's not important what Green Berets would do there. I've already gone beyond the ken of logic with this, it didn't happen this way. I don't pretend that it did. It's a poem. You can't tell Vietnam, Vietnam has a trillion faces. No one face of Vietnam will resound to the true Vietnam, it's not possible to do. I have to realize it is not possible, what I'm doing. I can only make a poem, I can only give an impression. Bob Scheer, so and so, they're all experts on one aspect, General So-and-So is an expert, Ho Chi Minh, someone who knew him is an expert on one thing. Each one has the little window that they think tells the whole Vietnam war, but none of them do. Only something mad and something illogical and something poetic can tell it, in the form of an odyssey. And it has to be about morality. And that is what I am trying to throw fuckin' together. And I really am trying, I mean it's—I have no cynicism, I don't think I can pull over anything on anyone. In fact my self-criticism has now reached a point where it's hurting the project. In other words, I have no audacity of, you know, 'I'll do this and fuck it.' I mean, presumptuous, pretension. I wish I had some of the brashness that I had when I was twenty-three. That kind of Stevie Spielberg wonder and love of it, that you just do it, fuck it. You know, I'm too old, I'm too wise, I know how good I am and how good I'm not."

He climbed up the scaffolding to a lighting platform thirty feet in the air, where no one could find him, and lay down in the rain alone.

Marlon hated everything Coppola had written. Everything he owned was on the line, and everyone he respected, the greatest crew in the world, was out there waiting for him to know what neither he nor anyone else had the ability to understand.

I t was a very magical childhood," Coppola would say. Loyal to the end, even if it meant his own, he was given to remembering his family happily. His father, Carmine, was a magician.

That was how Francie, as he was called, heard the word *musician*.

A flutist and composer, Carmine would bring home pressings of his newest demo recording, and the family—mother Italia, older brother August, Francie, younger sister Talia—would gather to listen to their father's music, which they knew well from hearing him practice, with an actual orchestral arrangement. Talia would dance, Francie would sing, and Augie would play along on his imaginary flute, as silver as the real thing.

Their house—on 212th Street in Queens Village, New York—teemed with music and stories about music, tales Carmine told his children of the great operas and their composers. There was *Carmen*, about a Spanish soldier who meets his downfall after he deserts his true love; and there was Georges Bizet, the opera's composer, the man who wrote it. The children knew that Bizet, who was a genius, a maker of beautiful melodies, had died thinking his work was worthless and that he himself was worthless because, in his time, the late nineteenth century, *Carmen* was a failure, even though today, Carmine reminded his children, it is one of the most beloved operas in the world. In fact, some of the best operas were once flops, and some of the most gifted composers were misunderstood in their time. Genius often is.

Carmine Coppola was born in New York City in 1910. In 1928 he won a four-year scholarship to Juilliard, where he studied flute, composition, and conducting; in 1930 he made his debut at Carnegie Hall; and in 1933 he married Italia Pennino, whose father, Francesco, the story went, came to America in 1905 as Caruso's pianist; Francesco's Paramount Music Roll Company, he claimed, was later to inspire the name "Paramount Pictures." Leaving New York, Carmine and Italia moved their growing family wherever he could find work: Detroit in 1937—where Francis, his middle name a tribute to Carmine's playing for *The Ford Sunday Evening Hour* radio program, was born in 1939—then back to New York at the beginning of World War II, where Carmine, in 1941, took the esteemed position of first-chair flute for the great Arturo Toscanini and the NBC Symphony Orchestra.

Agostino, Carmine's own father, born in the southern Italian town of Bernalda, had been a music lover. He played guitar and mandolin and pumped the church organ for his blind cousin and mentor, Donato Carella, who knew how to play only one composition, the march from *Aida*, which he would perform for funerals and weddings. Agostino's favorite opera, *Lucia di Lammermoor*, which features the flute, he first saw in the town square of Forlì when he was eighteen or nineteen; he went back so many times, it was said, he memorized the entire score. Professionally, Agostino was a man of science, apprenticing to a machinist of great repute, the one, they said, who brought electric light to the south of Italy. In 1904, he followed his brothers to America, where he would eventually engineer and build a prototype of the Vitaphone, an improved turntable used to record sound for motion pictures. Among its most innovative features were a revolving table as wide as twenty inches, permitting the production of longer recordings; a lever to vary the turntable's revolutions per minute (rpm), "for experimental recordings, if so desired"; and a noiseless, vibrationless mechanical motor. Quite memorably, the Vitaphone was used to record sound for, among other features, *The Jazz Singer* in 1927. "Modern methods for the production of disc records demand ideal conditions," concluded *Motion Picture Projectionist* magazine two years later, "and the present design by Coppola would seem to successfully meet all conditions."

A machinist by trade, Agostino Coppola was a storyteller by passion. With his grandchildren at his feet, he would describe the long-ago and far-away village he called "Bernalda*bella*" with the force and fancy of a new lover. "It sounded like an almost mystical place," his grandson Francie would say. A little tipsy, Agostino would embellish "stories of bandits," Coppola said, "and murder for the honor of the sister," of first hearing the sweet mad flute music of *Lucia di Lammermoor*, and of leaving Bernaldabella for Upper Harlem. That's where, in a tenement on Lexington Avenue and 110th Street, every Sunday at 2 p.m., Francie's grandfather gathered his family to sit silently around the radio and behold the sound of Toscanini leading the New York Philharmonic. Opening wide his arms and raising them high above the table, he would beseech all present to join the maestro in conducting from their own chair. "Everything had to be remembered and told in stories," Francie's older brother, August, remembered, "so that they became imbued with passion." Storytelling, he continued, was "an emotional act rather than veracity." And so, Agostino would tell of making his very own wine from concrete fermenters he kept in his basement; and of how his sons would tie their brother, Francie's uncle Mikey, to a rope and lower him down to steal the precious grapes their father had imported from California; and of the time the rope snapped and Uncle Mikey fell splashing into the wine.

Agostino Coppola and his wife had sons, seven. They were Archimedes (violin), Carmine (flute), Michael, Pancrazio (cello), Antonio (piano, oboe), and the twins, Edward and Clarence. His chosen path for them was clear: they were to be musicians, and they were to be rich and famous. But Agostino was reckless with money. Come the Depression, he was strained further, but with seven talented, dutiful boys to his name, he could be assured that one would come to the family's rescue. His best bet was his first son, Archimedes, the violinist. But the boy fell ill with pneumonia. It was then that Carmine, the second son, came to his brother's bedside and, at Archimedes's request, serenaded him on his flute. "Carmine," his brother implored him, "never forget the music. Never forget your gift." Archimedes's death promoted Carmine from understudy to star, and in his father's dreams, the sound of the violin was replaced by the music of the flute.

"He was sort of like the Italian-American Gatsby," Carmine's son August wrote, "appearing in concert with his rented tuxedo, a brilliant gleam to his hair and silver flute, the cut figure of Latin deco, who could be anything, a prince, a god, a magician, a star . . ." But Carmine wanted to be a composer, not a flutist, and though his instrument brought him renown and acclaim from his peers, it kept him, he feared, from writing songs and operas and symphonies like his idol Gershwin.

When his firstborn son, August, threatened to drop out of medical school to pursue a life of literature, Carmine, seeing a parallel between his son's writing and his own composing, and therefore a parallel fate, wrote August an anguished letter demanding his capitulation. "No one knows better than I that a writing career is a precarious one. Many doctors have become writers, but they were doctors first; if I had depended upon my writing, believe me I would have starved to death. The choices are slim for success; however, if one has some sort of job teaching etc, then, one can always write. I work on a job, but then, no one can stop me from writing, I write when I can, and I have written—there is always time but *security first* [underlined twice]. This now brings me to what I'm aiming at you; and it's with *double-barrelled guns* [underlined twice]. *YOU MUST* [underlined twice] *FINISH* [underlined six times] *YOUR SCHOOLING* [underlined twice] *NOW* [underlined five times]. . . . You might counter now," he wrote, "that after all, it is *your life*, why should I interfere? Remember, I gave you your life and I do not aim that you should throw it away. It is my duty as your father to guide you in it. Please do not mention again, 'It is my life to do as I choose.'"

Carmine grew hard. The farther he fell, the harder Italia struggled to defend him from insults actual and perceived, compiling for their vindication scrapbooks of his modest successes, ensuring that their house, even when the children were home, was dead silent when he needed to practice. Carmine's triumph would be not just her pride but also her revenge—against his mother, a tyrannical woman Italia despised—just as it would be his revenge against a world that had for too long undervalued him.

When at last Carmine left Toscanini and his chair in the NBC Symphony Orchestra and moved in 1951 to Radio City Music Hall to arrange music for the Rockettes, his children began to observe the change in him, in the house: Its mood was no longer dreams; it was compromise. Then it was rage, and that rage followed Carmine from Radio City to the road, wherever work—not the work he wanted, but the work he took—took him. This was the life of a great composer? Carmine, not one to conceal his passions, grieved openly. He wailed.

Francie watched, blaming himself. Maybe if he were *better*, did more . . .

The kids at school must have been right: something *was* wrong with him. Why did his father never ask him "How are you, Francie?" Or "How do you feel about things, Francie?" Why did he no longer tell his children opera tales of *Carmen* and *La Bohème*? Why did he sneer when Francie's friends opened the family fridge and helped themselves to a Coke?

"Dad, at their house, I'm welcome to take orange juice—"

"I don't care. It's my house."

Francie watched others degrade his father the way his mother would degrade his father's brothers—dwelling still in "the little-town mentality," as Coppola would come to understand it, of Italian families divided by pride and shame, with the resources to pick only one child, one son, the best, onto whose future they would latch the full weight of their dreams.

"Francis," his father had asked, "what do you want to be when you grow up?"

"A nuclear physicist."

"You can't flunk algebra twice in a row and be a nuclear physicist."

"Why not? Einstein wasn't a great mathematician. I have a good imagination. I could do it."

"You can't be it."

Walking by the kitchen, he overheard Uncle Mikey and his father deciding his future.

"Well, he's never going to go to college . . ."

"What about a trade?"

"Printing . . . ?"

And yet, the son had always supported *him*, the father. They all had. "We were very involved in my father's talent," Coppola would say. "That was the focus of our family."

Waking, Francie discovered that the pain in his spine had spread to his neck. He knew he shouldn't be going back to school. But his sixth-grade year was beginning, and his father had insisted.

It was his teacher who sent Francie to the school nurse, who told him he was fine. Boys his age were stiff from running around too much. But Francie wasn't a runner.

The next time he awoke, it was to a doctor, a serious look on his face, glaring down at him. He had been admitted to Queens General Hospital.

"Breathe deeply, release . . ." he was instructed. "Breathe deeply . . . release . . ."

Francie had never seen this man before, and neither his parents nor his brother was at hand. He was floating, Francie thought; he was rolling down all-white hospital corridors. He could have been moving a hundred miles an hour; he could have been lying completely still. In the sameness, he could have been living a month in a second. Then the sign, "Polio Ward," a spinal tap, and the diagnosis confirmed.

They kept him in the hospital for two weeks.

He was wooden, sore. It was hard to move, as if the strings to his arms and head had been clipped.

He lay there.

For four days he was restricted to bed.

He lay there, looking.

But there was nothing too look at, just white.

He would look elsewhere, within. He would say, "The reality in which we live is beyond our immediate perceptions. Even as a kid, I knew the stars were not little balls of fire in the sky." Maybe they were little pinholes and behind them was a great white light.

Thinking was better than looking, and dreaming was better than thinking. Dreaming he wasn't in that white room or any room, or his bed, he was running and kissing girls and getting 100 percent on his exams. He was at his desk at school, his books laid neatly before him, smiling at his new teacher, this time a male teacher, a sure sign of growing up. Dreaming, he wasn't contagious, but outside the hospital window. He wasn't him, but "they," the people who got to make decisions, who did stuff, not to whom stuff was done. He knew that dreaming was a lot like praying, and fairy tales like the story of Jesus and Mary. They were his comforts. Mary was his benefactress, and "Hail Mary" his "Abracadabra."

Outside his door, the gurneys were stacked three abreast. He couldn't always see, but he heard them crying in their beds, ten thousand crying kids.

When no one was around, he lifted himself up out of bed and landed on the floor. His entire left side was paralyzed, arm and leg.

The doctor said he'd never walk again.

They moved him home, to Seventy-Seventh Avenue and Bell Boulevard, and pinned him to the bedsheet.

No one came to visit him: not adults, no children. He was diseased, contagious.

From his bed, he watched life on television. People dropped off presents—there was a movie projector, a tape recorder given to him by his grandfather Francesco, his mother's father. Alone, he listened to the radio, *Captain Midnight* and *Tom Mix* and *Let's Pretend*, and learned that stories, like sounds and music, create worlds that live in your head. He owned an autographed picture of ventriloquist Paul Winchell, who just like him had contracted polio as a boy, and he had his own Jerry Mahoney puppet, which his grandmother had outfitted in a tiny tuxedo. Francie's puppets he could make do and say whatever he wanted—in his Mickey Mouse voice. Wouldn't it be great if he could change the channel on the television without having to get up and turn the knob on the set? If he could just press a button from some imagined handheld device from his bed and watch another story? It would be like time travel: Press a button and you're in a new world. Press it again and again, a new world, a newer world, a better world . . .

He was a wooden boy like Pinocchio, but he was also an inventor like Pinocchio's father, Geppetto. Like David Sarnoff, who started radio at RCA. Or Thomas Edison and Alexander Graham Bell. If he ever walked again, the first thing he would do was race downstairs to the basement and build his own pretend television studio with sound booms and cameras and a control room of his own. Imagine: a whole room of buttons. Color TV . . .

He missed all of sixth grade. The normal kids were out having a good time, and the popular ones were hoisting themselves up ropes of blond hair, kissing girls in towers. "But the kid who is ugly, sick, miserable or schlumpy sits around heartbroken and thinks. He's like an oyster growing this pearl of feelings out of which comes the basis of art."

The pearl, the magic potion of fairy tales, a treasure of transformation.

He was thick-lipped, friendless Francie Coppola—like his father, a disappointment, oyster-ugly, no better than himself.

But the pearl. "MY BEST FRIEND IS ME," an original lyric from his Hofstra University musical adaptation of H. G. Wells's *The Man Who Could Work Miracles*, would not surface unit 1957.

MY BEST FRIEND IS ME (he would write)

I know, to have lots of friends,
Is a very good way to be . . .
but mine are very few,
not even one or two,
My best friend, is me . . .
Some say, I should take a wife,
Although I can't see why,
I'm the very best of cooks.
And I go to bed with books,
My companion . . . is I.
I still have hair,
well in my head,
And no one to share,
my happy bed . . .
My best and my only friend, is me!

He spent over a year in bed. Despite the doctor's advice, in came the white-haired Miss Wilson from the March of Dimes, and with great care and patience, she exercised Francie's limbs to mobility. Before long, he would be back in school with only a little limp, but branded, in his own mind, damaged goods.

His father was the artist, Talia the beauty. "Augie's the bright one," his mother would say of his brother, August. Thus was it proven true. Francie? He was the stupid one, he thought, stupid and ugly, a disappointment to his parents.

Augie was five years older and more affectionate than either parent. He would be forever ahead of Francis in learning, wisdom, cool, and girls, worlds Augie generously opened to his little brother's wonder every night. In their bunk beds, eyes on the ceiling, Augie whispered grown-up tales of academic and social mastery, of hangouts with the big boys and brassieres magically unfastened . . . and the more he heard, the more Francie agreed with his mother's choice. Augie was the one. He had been born the older son for a reason.

Even to the other boys in the neighborhood, Augie was a figure with the force of myth, a leader, movie-star beautiful, the one they told stories about. Francie, who starred only in the stories he told to himself, indebted himself to his charity. He understood that Augie didn't have to include him, literally or vicariously, in his adventures, and never dreamed of eclipsing him. Only of being by his side forever. "He was so nice to me," Coppola said. "He took me everywhere. He protected me." It was Augie who cut school to take Francie into Manhattan, to FAO Schwarz, to buy the chemistry sets he had saved up for; it was Augie who signed his short stories "August Floyd Coppola," so Francie started calling himself "Francis Ford Coppola." It was Augie who gave him *The Catcher in the Rye* when he needed it most, who gave him the birthday gift of folios embossed with the initials *FFC*, a place of his own to write in, to be in. It was Augie who took him to the Center Cinema in Queens to behold the unworldly wonders of *Things to Come* and *The Man Who Could Work Miracles* and *The Thief of Bagdad*, all movies connected to the exotic name Alexander Korda, a name Francie would never forget. Above the other Korda pictures, *The Thief of Bagdad* was the miracle to Francie, "a fairy tale," he said, "beyond imagining." The flying carpets, the wily Abu, the king's magical mechanical inventions, the candy-colored adventure lands, the hot eyes of harem girls behind bewitching blue veils. "I didn't think it was a manufactured thing," he would explain. "I thought it was, in fact, a living story." It had happened, hadn't it? Even if it wasn't true, it had happened before the cameras, it *was* real.

Whatever Augie dreamed, he dreamed in sharp-focused close-ups; Francie dreamed in telephoto. When Augie decided he would be a doctor, the very first in the family, Francie chose ophthalmology. (He did like light.) When Augie decided he would be a great novelist, Francie decided he would be a playwright. He submitted a highly precocious, one-hundred-page paper on Hemingway, one of Augie's favorites, to his English teacher. "I always wanted to be the junior version of my brother," Coppola explained. "I wanted to be like the Huxley brothers or Henry James and William James."

It was only many years later that Francie's English teacher discovered that the Hemingway paper's real author was August Floyd Coppola.

Proudly accepting his role as *secondo*, Francie further indemnified the family order behind and beneath Carmine, king, high and central on the throne—"There can only be one genius in the family," Carmine had drilled into Augie, "and since I'm already it, what chance do you have?" To upset the balance would be to disrupt tradition and home, the fairy tale told to maintain continuity and safety for all.

If Francis was Abu, then Augie was lean and handsome and older, the caliph, Ahmad, and together they would have adventures, and Francis would sing "I want to be a sailor, sailing off to sea!" and they would fly to the highest peak of the highest mountain in the world. His nightmare was that the bad people were trying to push Augie down a manhole, and Francie, who wasn't big or strong enough to save him, was running frantically from house to house, trying to find a phone so he could call for help.

"If it wasn't for Augie," his mother said after Coppola's second Oscar, "Francis would be nothing." And Francis agreed.

Every night, at the end of his prayers, Francie would say, ". . . and give Daddy his break." He didn't even know what his daddy's "break" was. The brake of his car? But saving the most important for last, he prayed for the break anyway. "All I had to do was say a Hail Mary, and it would come true," he knew. He had once gone fishing and said twenty-two Hail Marys, and so caught twenty-two fish. But this was different, because when it came to his father's break, they all prayed: Talia, Augie, their mother, and Francie.

The tragedy of his father's career was like the tragedy of Preston Tucker, automobile inventor and visionary, in whom Carmine had invested the significant sum of ten thousand dollars, five thousand in the Tucker Company itself and an additional five thousand in the down payment on a Tucker car.

"When's the Tucker coming? When's the Tucker coming?" Francie, sharing his father's enthusiasm, would ask.

"It's not going to come," answered his father one day. "They won't let him buy steel."

"Why?"

"The car is too good." That is, too good *not* to be put out of business by his more powerful competitors.

It was an injustice, the boy thought; something good for the world, a man's innovation destroyed. Because of business? For money?

So, Francie prayed for his father—not for money, but for artistic renown. "It was just agonizing," Coppola said, "and we lived through it with him."

Until one day.

A telegram arrived. Western Union. It was from the head of Paramount Pictures' music department, a famous name in the Coppola household: Mr. Louis Lipstone. Francie—who had been working at Western Union—hand-delivered the telegram to his father: "Dear Mr. Coppola," it read. "We have selected you to write a score. Please return to L.A. immediately to begin the assignment. Sincerely, Louis Lipstone."

"It's my break! It's my break!"

The Coppolas were going to California. To Hollywood.

And then Francie told the truth. He wanted it to be true, he didn't know why he did it, but *he* had cut and pasted together the little yellow strips of telegram paper himself.

Carmine reached for his belt. Francie would keep praying, but not for himself. Augie was deserving, and his father, Coppola would say, "hated anybody who was successful."

He would go to the basement as often as he could, building and wiring; then he would bug the house. They didn't know that all he had to do was push a button and an explosion would go off in the backyard. They didn't know that he would hide little microphones in every radiator in every room and, that way, he would hear what everyone was saying, and he would find out what his parents didn't want him to know and what he was going to get for Christmas, and the best part was, they wouldn't know that he knew. They would be having dinner, and he would be grinning to himself because he had outsmarted them.

Surveillance and communication—that's how he would have his revenge on the bullies at school, the guys with the pretty girlfriends, the guys who would steal his lunch money, leaving him with nothing though he begged them to let him keep just one nickel to buy a pretzel. His plan was to round up all the smart kids who were, like him, picked on and good at science, and together they would develop a secret paramilitary organization and defeat the mean kids in a rumble that would win them their freedom and the hearts of their tormentors' girlfriends. Francie's army had prepared cobalt bombs to temporarily blind their enemies. With their blue-filtered glasses, they could protect their own eyes from the blast, and if they found they were in danger, one of Francie's gang would sound a siren hidden in a secret suitcase and the cops would come running to their rescue.

No bully would know just how prepared they were. They wouldn't know that Francie kept all his make-believe military papers in the file cabinet in his basement workshop, or that Francie knew how to make actual explosives. They didn't know he was going to be a nuclear physicist. They didn't know he had his own atomic energy lab he had gotten with his own money from A. C. Gilbert Company, nor that it had a Geiger counter and a cloud chamber and a little radioactive needle, which his sister, Talia, had broken off but he could fix. They didn't know he had invented a color television system of his own; they didn't know he was the brigadier general of his secret army, nor that when the army met somewhere secret, they devised ingenious weapons with a button for everything: a button for outrunning the mean kids, a button for holding on to their lunch money, a button for getting the girls, and a button for winning real wars, like the war in Korea. They would come back to school conquerors, because they had outsmarted them like Abu did. And there would be confetti in the air and street-long ticker tape parades in their honor, and the girls would kiss him, and his parents would be so proud they would cry out, "That's Francie! That's him there!"

It was his mother who first grew suspicious. She had a hunch what was in the file cabinet—pornography. But it was Carmine who carried the cabinet upstairs, broke the lock, and found Francie's files, the secret military memos he didn't know were fiction.

"If you're so interested in this," he told the boy, "maybe you should go to military school."

He did—New York Military Academy—and went AWOL. Shamed by a dishonorable discharge and fearing the wrath of his father, who had taken out a loan to send him, Francie sold his uniform for two hundred dollars and hid in New York City, taking cover in flophouses and dance halls, waiting out two weeks of nights before he knew the coast was clear at home. "I was scared to go home," he said, "because I was afraid dad would beat me, or worse, send me back."

The sense of innate shame had been with Francie as long as he could remember, well before he was sent to military school. Moving for his father's work—and because "my mother really didn't want me in the house"—Francie had attended, by his count, fourteen different schools—nine alone before high school—each with its own dream girl, its own set of bad boys. Moving with his father to Los Angeles, where Carmine was qualifying for the musicians' union, Francie had been entered into Le Conte Middle School, where the girls were prettier than in Queens. He'd watch them at lunch, sticking together, walking around one another in chatty circles. "I used to wonder what they were like," he said, "and why they kept walking around and around and around and why they were so fantastically beautiful." He was ashamed of his name ("'Francis' is a girls' name!"; "Francis the Talking Mule!") and of course he didn't like his face. At school, they called him "Pregnant lips" or "Ubangi lips," for the fat mouth his mother said he should have fixed.

Every night in Los Angeles, Francie and his father would eat a dinner of tamales and RC Cola, saying nothing to each other. "Basically regularly I was hit with the strap whenever I did something bad or got bad grades or I did something that was considered salacious or too interested in sexy things," he wrote, looking back. "I would get hit for that, and rejected by my mother, and ridiculed. I have to say that the most terrifying thing in my life, even now, is to be embarrassed in public, the idea of them singling you out and everyone laughed and you were caught and ridiculed for doing something bad so that nobody would like you or want to know you and you would never get a girlfriend." He didn't qualify for the football teams, but was actually useful in the theater department, where he was too afraid to approach even those girls he thought might actually find him interesting. "I'd get *tremendous* crushes on girls that I didn't ever get to talk to," he said. "You would see her, but you wouldn't have the wherewithal to meet her. So I lived a tremendous fantasy life . . ."

No one told him—he didn't have guy friends and his brother was living with his grandmother—but he figured out, as a boy scientist would, how babies were made. What happened was, first a man and a woman *slept* together. He had overheard that part. Then, after embracing for six or seven hours, the man's testicles radiated a signal which, like a projector, cast a picture of a baby inside the woman's womb. Once the picture was developed, it would become an actual baby.

As for the erotic feelings he had, Francie came close to going to a priest and telling him about his "problem." It wasn't until he was riding the trolley on the way to school and overheard a cluster of boys talking about girls that he understood there were others like him.

He was so lonely living in Los Angeles. "When a student appears, two months after the semester has begun, they don't take him seriously . . . I would always say, 'Oh I'm working on a special project in the shop, or I'm doing this, or I'm doing that . . . and I would go to the theater department, because that's where the girls were." But they never saw him.

For consolation, he would escape his father's tiny walk-up apartment, ride the trolley, and wander the neighborhood alone. At Santa Monica Boulevard and Las Palmas, he would stick his nose through the closed gate of one of Los Angeles's oldest studios, Hollywood General. It was just soundstages and bungalow offices and parking lots, but Francis had some idea of what went on inside, and what he didn't know, he could imagine: people, none of them lonely, working together, having fun making movies. There were surely musicians and film composers in there whom his father admired, even envied, giants like Dimitri Tiomkin, Bronislau Kaper, Bernard Herrmann . . . His father would never work there. But what if *he* could?

What if everyone could?

"I've tried to believe that someday I could make a dream world for myself," he would one day write to his parents, "now I realize that this is what it will be, merely a *dream* world. I've wanted so many things, some I've gotten, others . . . At first this will be a joke. Something for Daddy and Uncle Mike to laugh about over their glasses of $3.00 a gallon wine. Maybe it is funny, but as their [sic] laughing at me, let them know that someone is laughing at them, the only difference is that I know that I'm the clown, and they don't realize that to someone bigger, they're clowns also."

He was friendly with a kid at school who was in the play. Francie, of course, went to see it alone. He sat in an audience of proudly adoring parents, and afterward, he was told he wasn't invited to the cast party. "All I ever wanted to be was part of a group, and theater was a group," he said. He walked away from the school play weeping, telling himself that one day he was going to be the one to have the party, he was going to be the one to decide who could come and who couldn't, but he would invite everyone, and the pretty girls would come, he thought, as he passed, once more, the closed gates of Hollywood General.

One day, he would write the lyrics to a musical he would also direct.

TINKERBELL

I've fabricated princesses
I know can never be . . .
I've whistled and I've whispered
In the hollow of a tree
And every time
An echo came
It never came to me . . .
I've fabricated princesses,
I think . . .
Or have they
Imagined me?

Taking refuge in the hollow of a tree, Francis Ford Coppola invited Dennis Jakob to the Philippines. In addition to being somewhat insane, Jakob was a vast and cluttered library of advanced and esoteric learning and loved to talk. Leaping from Nietzsche to Freud to Conrad, he could review with Coppola the philosophical bases of *Apocalypse*'s possible endings and, it was hoped, persuade him, finally, to make a choice that would free him from crisis. But Jakob—on the company payroll for doing no one, save Coppola, knew exactly what—was terminally competitive with Coppola, forever threatening to write a scandalous novel about Coppola and Carroll Ballard, their comrade from UCLA. But Coppola, a brother to the end, continued to feed the mouth that bit him, waving Jakob in to comment on scripts and rough cuts and parse his spews of sporadic brilliance.

Arriving in September, Jakob could not believe just how hot it was in the Philippines, how anyone could sleep with the air conditioners, when they *did* work, rattling away like old Fords. He regarded the whole living theater as a torture trap of Coppola's creation. "It took genius," Jakob would say, "to create the inferno here on earth." Wherever he looked, someone was asking himself what it all meant, why they were there and when it would end. All around him, people were stoned and suicidal, but his old friend Coppola, Jakob saw, was the most endangered of all. This world of anguish had sprung from his own unconscious—he, they, everyone was living in Coppola's mind, but it was not, Jakob surmised, Coppola's to control. Then again, on the subject of reality, Jakob was hardly an authority.

He met Coppola at his place in Hidden Valley, an oasis of hot springs and cabanas set in a dead volcano not far from the Kurtz compound. They dined on a kingly breakfast of grapes, mangoes, and imported espresso and quickly got down to the big question: Who lives and who dies? Kurtz or Willard, or both, and why?

As they colloquied to Beethoven and bird calls, drifting from Goethe's *Elective Affinities*, its revolutionary ideas of marriage ("the greatest fucking frontier is between people and people!"—Jakob), to Conrad, Jakob's mind turned from *Apocalypse Now* to the man opposite him. Coppola had lost weight, he was chain-smoking, and the marijuana was turning what remained of his mind to jelly. "Why, Francis," Jakob demanded, "why, why have you put yourself into this position?"

They took a break, and when they returned, they discussed Willard's story within the mythical framework of a Grail quest. Willard begins on a journey to terminate Kurtz, but, Jakob said to Coppola, "the journey is not really about him terminating anything. It's about a door that's opening to him about the possibilities on the meaning of life and death that he could have never imagined, just being a simple assassin, because he gets caught up in an ancient, ancient tribal ritual that demands that he kill Kurtz in order for the crops to grow. That's the meaning of the rejuvenation process—that is, the meaning of death and why death exists in the world is so that renewal is possible.... That is the meaning of the change of life, the change of seasons."

It was a perfect reading for Coppola. The idea of ritual, with its foundations in community, theater, and storytelling, and its eternal cycles of life, death, and rebirth, had produced some of his most memorable scenes in *The Godfather* and *Godfather II*. Even *The Conversation*, the Corleones' nightmare inverse, about a man without a community, ends with Harry Caul tearing up his apartment and returning to his saxophone, signaling his death and, through music, restoration.

Jakob had turned Coppola on to Jessie Weston's *From Ritual to Romance* and James George Frazer's *The Golden Bough*, which takes as its subject the primal myth, the ancient and pervasive ritual killing of the king or, in metaphorical terms, the father. The ordeal of succession: Coppola, approaching middle age, understood. There was something there.

Coppola told Eleanor he needed to be on his own for a few days, and he left the location in Pagsanjan. She didn't know where he went.

*   *   *

While away, he reflected. He tried to remember. What was it he once thought he might have been good at?

It was never writing. Rarely, if ever, did he glide into his chair behind the Olivetti and think, *This is it. Now I've got it.* Even *Godfather II* and *The Conversation*, movies he was most proud of, he had rewritten throughout production—Tavoularis called his new pages, reissued daily, "the newspaper"—and even then, after all the film was shot, there was still that final rewrite, editing. Then the *final* final rewrite: sound. The film's release, which always seemed to come too soon, was really the first moment his story was actually set in stone, but even then . . . he still wondered. Yes, but. *What if?* As long as the concept of "better" existed, things could always change.

What if?

He'd always loved directing plays. What if he wasn't really a filmmaker?

What if he was really less of a director and more of a conductor? A bringer-together of people and their talents?

What if Warner Bros. hadn't reneged on Zoetrope? Who would he be then?

What if *THX 1138* had been properly distributed and did the kind of astonishing business *American Graffiti* later did? What if Lucas were right this minute making his next movie, *Star Wars*, for Zoetrope instead of Fox? Would the world be different? Better?

Would the world be different if Zoetrope had made, when no one else would, that Orson Welles movie? Would Orson still be working today, making more movies? Instead of what he was doing, begging for money . . .

Or King Vidor?

Nicholas Ray, down and out when he came to Zoetrope . . . sleeping with Chinese takeout under the flatbeds, his eye patch slung over the door handle . . .

Imagine what Michael Powell, one of the directors of *Thief of Bagdad*, who hadn't directed a major movie in years, could do, with no one to tell him no, at Zoetrope . . .

Think of the numberless unknowns whom Coppola might have discovered, or been first to hire, just as he was the first one to say to Lucas, "You want to make a movie? I'll get you the money . . ."

How many careers would have been started, jump-started, that the Hollywood studios never would have given a chance?

How many film productions, each an experiment in communal creativity, would give rise to how many new worlds?

How many new worlds would change how many lives?

Hollywood—like any business, like any bank, sensibly risk-averse wherever possible—could permit only so many variables before its investment became a gamble. But what if—*what if*—partway up the river of production, someone had a better idea? What if fate arrived with a typhoon no special effect could match? What if the filmmakers, in the course of filming, changed or learned or grew?

Coppola knew an alternative system was possible. Following August to Hofstra University, he had experienced it for himself. There, surrounded by like-minded young adults, making theater, he enjoyed, for the first time, creative freedom, community, the world as it could be. "I went from being this lonely kid who had no friends to being like the king of Hofstra," he said. "I had all the keys, I ran everything." His enterprise was astonishing. "I played a very political game," he explained. Through force of will, he wrested from faculty control Hofstra's two drama organizations, the Kaleidoscopians, the musical comedy society, and the Green Wig, the drama club. In 1958, the eighteen-year-old Coppola, president of both organizations, combined and transformed them into a wholly new theatrical community, the Spectrum Players. His first decree: only students would direct shows. "It was," he said, "the first time I learned how you could [get] kind of true independence from the people of authority . . ." Professors referred to Coppola's coup as his "regime." The faculty responded with an order that no theater student could direct more than two plays a year, so Coppola promptly switched into the English Department. "The drama department was always trying to rein me in," he said. To afford professional violin players for one musical's orchestra ("the weakness of musicals is always in the string section"), Coppola increased the size of the show's playbill, netting more ad space, which he sold easily to pay for the violinists. But when the faculty discovered Coppola's workaround (he was also an editor of *The Word*, one of Hofstra's literary magazines), they insisted that all proceeds from the program's ad sales go directly into the student fund. So, Coppola published the program instead as a stand-alone issue—and the violinists were paid. "In the end," he said, "our musical sounded like a Broadway musical."

Led by Coppola, the Hofstra ritual chant—"Poowabah! Poowabah! Poowabah!"—would henceforth mark the beginning of his every production, stage and screen, for the rest of Coppola's life.

Those years of making theater he called a golden age.

At Hofstra, Coppola published his first short story, five pages of "broken ideals and dreams," "about a kid who used to sneak into a garden of this girl—a princess—and she was so beautiful and so perfect and at the end he was disillusioned with her." He appeared in *Once in a Lifetime* and *As You Like It* and directed O'Neill's *The Rope* ("he must have had eighty-seven light cues," said classmate Joel Oliansky), with a flute score by Carmine Coppola; played the French ambassador, duetting with classmate Lainie Kazan, in *Of Thee I Sing*; wrote book and lyrics to a musical, *Inertia*, based on H. G. Wells, Hofstra's first production written and produced entirely by students; and authored book and lyrics and created a rope and sandbag system for all the avista changes for a musical called *A Delicate Touch* (with, Oliansky said, "eight hundred scenes, ninety-two songs, a cast of millions . . .").

Those days and nights, Coppola would remember, began his second life. Dreams had always been there just off-stage, but Hofstra gave him a precedent and, with it, power and purpose—and all of it against his mother and father's will. Art was Carmine's calling, the family's limited resources Carmine's to use. And Francis, a senior at Hofstra, wanted to go on to Yale? To study theater?

He was sitting there, outside the Hofstra Little Theater, waiting for rehearsal to begin, the day he saw the sign. "Today: 4:00. Sergei Eisenstein's *Ten Days That Shook the World*."

He went in. The movie began. "I was astonished," he said. "It was a silent movie, but you could hear everything just through the editing." When he emerged from the theater he decided: he wasn't going to Yale. He was going to make movies.

But how? Struggling in Hollywood after college, he wrote his parents, "I would hope that I might receive a little personal communication from my family. You don't know how I waited, hoping for a letter from you telling that you cared and were interested in what was happening. Instead all I get is a card saying that I'm lazing around. Well, I'm trying so hard to get a job so I DON'T HAVE TO GO TO SCHOOL. I know Daddy is apprehensive about the money I'll cost to live, and I want more than anything to find something. Even something small, just as long as I don't feel I'm throwing away two years working as a messenger or a page at NBC when I could have been in school getting that all important, priceless Master's Degree. Well now, if I did what you said, and worked in NY for the summer, then . . . I would never know how or where or what the score was to try to get a job in this business. I had to try and I am still trying. I don't like not making money, believe me, I don't have a cent . . . and I don't like it one bit . . . and this is what I have to do." The hypocrisy was not lost on him: "Why do you say I'm lazing around when you yourself Daddy knows what it's like to try to get a break and have everyone string you on. I never said *you* were lazing around when I lived with you in those hotels and changed school after school when you were trying to get a break."

"Dear Mr. Selden," he wrote on April 27, 1960, to the UCLA chairman of the department of theater arts, "I would like to study Motion Picture writing, direction and production. I see these three aspects as one, and so I would like to study to become a Motion Picture Artist."

He was accepted. But rather than the golden age of Hofstra theater, he found the film school at UCLA to be an unfriendly institution hobbled by limited resources and red tape. The spirit of collaboration he had felt and loved was nowhere near. "The theatrical spirit is like a family," he would say, "but the cinema tradition is you're much more alone." Those film students who could get their hands on production equipment hoarded it for themselves.

He didn't have any money, barely enough for food, a quarter for breakfast, fifty cents for a Kraft macaroni and cheese dinner, his car was always breaking down, and his future in film—any film student's future in film— looked bleak. There was one moderately comforting precedent, brothers Denis and Terry Sanders, UCLA film graduates, Oscar winners for their 1954 documentary short, A *Time Out of War*. But who else?

He thought of quitting and going home, back to New York. It would be easy, he thought, sitting outside an art department bungalow, to go back to the theater and get a job somewhere as a stage manager or assistant stage manager, make enough money, have a little life.

"What are you doing?"

It was Miss Arzner—Dorothy Arzner, director, editor, writer, UCLA film professor. Beloved by her students, she would tell them a great kiss had to be held for three arm lengths of film and bring them cookies. She knew some, like Coppola, were that hungry.

"Oh, Miss Arzner, I don't know . . . I don't feel I'm doing well."

"You'll make it," she said. "I've been around and I know."

That made all the difference. He stayed.

At UCLA, Coppola met fellow film students Carroll Ballard, whom Coppola thought the most talented filmmaker of the bunch, Dennis Jakob, and Jim Morrison. ("He came to my house once—this was before he'd had a record out—with some acetates, demos, asking if I could help.") They toiled in dingy wooden bungalows in a far corner of the campus. To Ballard, Coppola was about the only thing going. Coppola had him working as a grip on *Ayamonn the Terrible*, a short about a sculptor who dreams his self-portrait is screaming at him. . . . Not only did Coppola manage to convince Forest Lawn Cemetery, which refused even established Hollywood filmmakers, to let him use the location—it'll just be a little crew, Coppola assured them— but he got a Chapman crane, the best there was, and showed up at the cemetery with the biggest crew any student filmmaker had ever had.

As if sprung from a lifetime of confinement, Coppola was writing, directing, selling, hustling, and when the other students shrugged and said "What's the point, Francis? Maybe if we're lucky, we'll end up making industrial films, but we'll never get jobs in Hollywood, and even if we do, they won't let us make the kind of films we want to make, personal films like Bergman and Fellini and Antonioni," Coppola looked at them like they were out of their minds. And then he went on to prove it: At twenty-two, while still enrolled at UCLA, he went out and shot *The Peeper*, a nudie short, and then partnered with a softcore outfit and combined his footage with their footage into *Tonight for Sure*, a nudie *feature*. Meanwhile, money was so scarce he couldn't pay his phone bill. Following up on an ad, posted on a school bulletin board, for a job with Roger Corman, he waited by his phone for a call back, praying both that he would get an interview and also that they hadn't yet discontinued his service. Then the phone rang. He got the interview. And the phone shut off.

"Do you know anything about Russia?" asked Kinta Zertuche from behind her desk at Corman's office.

"Oh, *yes*," he fibbed.

"Roger's got this Russian film. He wants someone to sort of rewrite the script. It's about these two idealistic Soviets. Roger wants them converted into two monsters, one that looks like a female organ and one that looks like a male organ. You'd have to do the looping—"

"I can do that!"

What was he now? He'd work like crazy on *Battle Beyond the Sun*, getting to the office before anyone else and staying later, deliberately staging his appearance to make it look like he had spent the night. From there, Coppola was everywhere Corman needed him. "Roger was such a cheapskate," Coppola explained, "he would have me work as dialogue director [on *Tower of London*] in the morning, then I would leave and be his personal assistant for free," washing Corman's car, mowing his lawn, moving heavy sod, rewriting his scripts, cutting and dubbing, whatever—Coppola wasn't saying no, not to Corman and not to money, not to getting to Corman's sets before Corman did, prestaging scenes for his boss to then restage, maximizing time and money, both in short supply for employer and apprentice. They were suited in productivity and speed, and like his new, young associate, Corman was always looking for an angle, a way to make two and two into ten. *We only have x to spend. Can we shoot two features—never mind what they are—instead of one? If we don't get location y, could we make it a bike picture instead of a Western?* (Yes, always yes.) At Corman's side, Coppola learned that producing—what he had been doing naturally since Hofstra, or even before, as a boy, arranging secret battalions to decimate his enemies, inventing phony jobs for his father to save his dignity and his family—was, when practiced expertly, as imaginative as writing.

Was that what he was? Foremost a producer? Like Corman?

Writing was the dream that producing brought to life, and unlike producing, it could be done by night and at the speed of thought. In a single night Coppola wrote *Pilma, Pilma*, a script about a boy who murders his older brother. For his work, he won UCLA's Samuel Goldwyn Award—a shock, given the prize was customarily awarded to writers of prose fiction.

(That year, Carroll Ballard won second place.) With his prize money, two thousand dollars, Coppola bought a new Alfa Romeo. But with the recognition that came with being the first-ever screenwriter to win the award, he got Ben Benjamin, his first agent.

"Francis," Corman said one day, "you went to UCLA. Do you know of any young guy who can be a sound mixer?"

"I can!"

So, it was off to Europe to hold the boom (and shoot second unit) for Corman's *The Young Racers*. ("Francis had *guts*," said actor Bill Campbell. "He picks up the goddamn handheld camera, he gets out on the racetrack, and he's shooting pictures of these damn racing drivers driving past him within six feet!") "I knew that Roger would always make a second film wherever he went," Coppola explained, "because he would have the company pay for the first one, which was AIP, and since everyone was there and the equipment was there, he'd always do one on his own to average out the costs." Here was Coppola's chance. What if *he* directed that second film? With customary speed, he wrote "a *Psycho*-like scene I thought Roger would buy." Corman matched Coppola's scene to a title, *Dementia*, and Coppola raced to Ardmore Studios in Ireland to direct the movie—his first feature—which still had no story. But he came up with something, reverse-engineered to suit the budget (twenty thousand dollars), location (a castle), schedule (ten days), and the macabre set pieces Corman had requested. Still without a script, Coppola offered his father a job ("I have a small budget on this *Dementia* film," he wrote, ". . . but it's one that you could do a great big score for . . . so I'll try to get as much money for music as possible . . .") and turned around and sold the British rights to the unmade picture for an additional twenty thousand dollars up front. When Corman heard about the new investment, he went to withdraw his original seed money, only to find that Coppola, already outstepping the master, had deposited it into another account under his name.

On location in Dublin, Coppola met Eleanor Neil, a freelance designer. She'd come to visit her boyfriend, the cinematographer, and to work for the production wherever needed. When she met Coppola, he'd been up all night writing the movie, and he hadn't shaved, she estimated, for days.

Coppola completed postproduction on *Dementia 13* (the title *Dementia* was already taken, so Corman added the 13, thinking it might be a fun hook to show it on the thirteenth of every month), and drove across Europe with Eleanor to check in on another Corman production in Dubrovnik. She would return to L.A. for a teacher's assistant job at UCLA; he to Big Sur to direct for Corman some of *The Terror* (starring Jack Nicholson). He flew back to L.A. "a wreck." Eleanor picked him up at the airport.

"I have to talk to you," she said.

"What?"

"I'm pregnant."

They married in February 1963.

Or was he, if not a novelist and not a playwright, a screenwriter? It was Coppola's agent, Ben Benjamin, who got him into Hollywood via a writing contract with Seven Arts Productions. Starting at $475 and then $630 and finally close to $1,000 a week, Coppola wrote at all hours, pounding down coffee to stay awake, playing music to keep him charged. There was his adaptation of Carson McCullers's *Reflections in a Golden Eye*; his adaptation of Tennessee Williams's *This Property Is Condemned*; an original, *My Last Duchess*, "a crazy comedy," Coppola called it, written in a week ("I always wanted to write original material, but I knew I wasn't good at it"); his adaptation of *Shame, Shame on the Johnson Boys* (from a novel by Hofstra classmate Joel Oliansky); his adaptation of Budd Schulberg's novel *The Disenchanted*; and finally, the flailing *Is Paris Burning?*, which he was sent to Paris, with Gore Vidal, to save—they didn't. Freelance again, he bought a house in Mandeville Canyon and gambled twenty thousand dollars on the stock market—thinking he'd finance a movie with his profits—and lost it all. With a wife, two babies, no job, he took a meeting at Fox. They were looking for a writer to do a script on General Patton. "Mr. Coppola," began producer Frank McCarthy, "we hear you have military experience." "Yes, sir." (He *did* run away from military school, after all.) For fifty thousand dollars, he wrote *Patton*, but its star, Burt Lancaster, hated Coppola's script and his option was not renewed.

He had (while toiling on *Is Paris Burning?*) started writing yet another script, a coming-of-age comedy about a nerdy New York boy, the bad girl he falls for, and the corrosive family he must escape. This one Coppola intended to direct himself. But how—when he had written it while under contract to Seven Arts? He dreamt up a chess master's scheme: he optioned the rights (a grand) to *You're a Big Boy Now*, an English novel with a story somewhat like his own script, so that when Seven Arts—as he had hoped it would—made a play for participation in Coppola's "adaptation," Coppola could maintain, option in hand, a producer's control of the project. The thousand-dollar gamble paid off. ("You should have seen it," an amazed studio press agent recalled. "Typical conference-table session, with all these stuffy executives sitting around offering the moon to this funny-looking guy with a beard in blue jeans.") The old men of Seven Arts judged the "adaptation" hip enough to accept Coppola's terms: he would direct. Putting aside an offer of $75,000 to write a script for an entirely different project, Coppola accepted a mere $8,000 to write and direct *You're a Big Boy Now*. "So, again," he said, "I took the risk."

He still hadn't graduated from UCLA.

Acting as his own producer, Coppola would make *You're a Big Boy Now* as far from studio control as possible. "I would like to shoot 75 percent of the film on natural locations, using the freedom and spontaneity of films like *Hard Day's Night* or *The Knack*," he wrote to a Seven Arts representative. "Hopefully, the film will be done under the camouflage of a small, unheard-of independent company, so that I can be free to get the production values I want for the minimum money. If it is labeled as a Paramount, or even Seven Arts picture, all the figures involved shoot up, some of them even doubling." He added: "Most important is that it be a small, enthusiastic unit"—like his Hofstra theater ensembles—able to move fast around locations and slip past unions.

Without so much as an introduction, Coppola called stars Geraldine Page, Rip Torn, and Julie Harris and signed them to the project, raising the status and budget of his intended little film from $250,000 to $1.5 million; under the gun, he talked Mayor John Lindsay's office into expediting permits and convinced the New York Public Library to break its ban on filming and let them shoot inside, as he did with Macy's, and he persuaded the guardians of the Accutron signs over Times Square to stop flashing the news and to flash instead, for his cameras, "Barbara Darling," per his script. Moreover, he started innovating instantly: In sandals and a red T-shirt with the word "Underplay" written across the front, Coppola greeted his company in radio producer Himan Brown's production facility at 221 West Twenty-Sixth Street for their first day of rehearsal. What he did next was unheard-of for the director of a feature film: he presented his cast with two distinct scripts, one prepared to shoot and the other, with extra dialogue, for them to rehearse like a play. "There are two kinds of acting," he said, "stage acting by which you evolve the character through rehearsals and discussion, and film acting, in which you better have the character right now and which is a terrible limitation on the actor." Initiating a process that he would develop for years to come, he filmed his *Big Boy* rehearsals and took the footage home to study. "It taught me a lot," Coppola said, "how to make shortcuts, how to turn fat characters into thin ones, how to shoot three and four scenes at a time, how to handle the actors. That's why writers often make bad directors—they have to film it the way they saw it on paper. Not me." But once rehearsal ended, his challenges began. "I forget things like yelling 'cut' at the end of scenes," he confessed during the production. "This whole thing is over my head. Everyone wants every shot to be perfect. Every time I turn my head, the actors are putting on more makeup. Well, maybe some scenes are not supposed to be perfect. With all these big stars and all these producers with dollar signs in their eyes, I don't know what I'm doing any more."

You're a Big Boy Now earned Coppola both his MFA from UCLA and an invitation to the 1967 Cannes Film Festival—the only American entry in the competition that year. "*You're a Big Boy Now* is the most thoroughly contemporary film in years of memory" (*The Hollywood Reporter*) and "Francis Ford Coppola . . . is someone to keep an eye on" (*The New Yorker*). It won Coppola his first major round of national press. Who *was* this kid?

A fool or a nut, apparently: "I want to make films in Denver, Hartford, Seattle," he announced, "places [where] nobody ever makes films. Give me $400,000 and six guys who love to make films and I'll do it"—a statement his Hollywood elders would have derided. Follow a big splash with a B movie? "We also have an army of vigorous youngsters in films," Coppola informed the press. "I think we're at the beginning of the golden age of filmmaking—if we can eliminate the promoters who aren't qualified to control." He became—with good reason—spokesman for his generation of filmmakers. Will there be more film schools, Mr. Coppola? "No, there shouldn't be another film school," he said. "There should be something that enables young filmmakers to get a subsidy, like a ministry of culture gives in Europe, an organization that would take a little bit of money from the grosses of all movies, like 2 percent, and it would go into this fund to finance student films."

No matter how challenging Coppola's ideas, Hollywood's greatest generation would have to agree that the introduction of a youngster into the fore was quickly becoming commonplace. But the particular case of Francis Ford Coppola was another phenomenon entirely. The young men of *The Graduate* and *Bonnie and Clyde*—Mike Nichols, Arthur Penn, Warren Beatty—were established show business big boys; they had achieved their influence in Hollywood only after years of recognition and success. Where had this Coppola come from? UCLA Film School? A school for . . . movies? As they understood it, one became a director in Hollywood only after a period of *apprenticeship*, either in the second unit (in the old days) or in television, or after a hoard of one's screenplays had been produced, and in any of these cases—unless one was Orson Welles or Mike Nichols, an indisputable wunderkind proven in the theater—it required work from inside the studio gates, knowing someone, being liked by the right people, or having a father or uncle already in the business. "The real scandal of the closed doors," Coppola said that year, "or the people really responsible, are the young directors who've made it. The Stanley Kubricks [age thirty-seven] and the John Frankenheimers [thirty-five] are the ones who should and could do something. They carry the weight. If they agreed somehow to be present during the shooting, a young filmmaker could probably make his first movie."

Back when he was at Seven Arts, Coppola had conceived an entirely new future for Hollywood: on television. In the tradition of the great live dramas of the 1950s, programs like *Playhouse 90*, he wrote, "I would like to see Seven Arts begin a 'Project 120' of its own or a 'Project 90' or a 'Project 100'—essentially, feature films designed to be a feature film and not a television film." The networks showed high-level studio movies on TV; why not *make* them, at a high level, *for* TV? They could be like plays. He knew about that. Wouldn't there be considerable savings, in production and postproduction, if these dramas were shot and aired—as they once were—live, *like* a play? Like John Frankenheimer's live masterpiece, *The Comedian*? Sprung from a lifelong inspiration, a TV adaptation of H. G. Wells's future history, *The Shape of Things to Come*, would be the cornerstone of Coppola's program. "Essentially, it's a utopian look at the future, not in a science-fictiony way, but in a carefully and intelligently thought out manner. It examines society or an area of what things will be like in the year 2000. . . . 'Things to Come 1984–2000+,'" as he called it, was "the idea [that] interests me more than the others."

In one form or another, it always would be.

Is that what he was? Not a born film director, but a futurist?

Scorsese, he would think . . . Spielberg . . . they were *born* to do it . . .

He remembered first meeting Scorsese at a film festival outside Naples. Martin Scorsese, still struggling through his debut feature, years in the making, *Who's That Knocking at My Door?*, recalled meeting Francis Ford Coppola in a loft on Great Jones Street. Coppola was in town to promote the New York opening of *Big Boy* and had packed the loft with forty or fifty young people, in denim, fringe, and beads—Scorsese had never seen this species at a Hollywood party, which, incredibly, this was. Scorsese was equally amazed by this guy Coppola. He had never come face-to-face with a director his age, a New York–Italian American like him who had made his own little movie *and* had written for the big Hollywood studios. Which one was this guy? Scorsese did not recognize in this new breed the complacency of what he thought of as a studio working man. He saw in him the kind of filmmaker he himself dreamed of being: both of the system and an iconoclast. "You have to want to make a film so badly," Coppola told the crowd that night on Great Jones, "that you would kill for it." *That's me*, Scorsese thought. *I want to make Hollywood films—my own kind*. "He's like the older brother," Scorsese said.

Steven Spielberg was just a film student at Long Beach State, almost twenty-one years old, when he heard Francis Ford Coppola was at Warner Bros., directing as his next movie *Finian's Rainbow*—and "his door was open to any young film student anywhere in the world. You can just walk in and meet Francis." To sit and talk about movies with a young filmmaker in his own office at Warner Bros.? Spielberg was nervous. He had first met Coppola through actor Tony Bill, who had appeared in *Big Boy*, but suspected he and Coppola didn't dream in the same vernacular. Spielberg's tastes were by his own estimation slightly old-fashioned; he didn't love the European "art" filmmakers with the same passion as his friends did; he loved classical Hollywood, David Lean, Michael Curtiz, "and I didn't think there would be room for me." But Coppola, in his Warner Bros. office, took the time to listen. "That was a blessing in those days," Spielberg said.

And there was another young filmmaker.

A solemn little kid in glasses, "standing there in his black chino pants, white T-shirt, and white sneakers day in and day out," an observer of George Lucas recalled. "He had a little goatee and looked like a back-room engineer. He was just very quietly always there, watching, looking, and listening." He had been hanging around the *Finian's Rainbow* set "bored out of my mind," thinking, *This is just another big, dumb Hollywood musical*, when Coppola at last looked up from his work and saw him, the only other guy at Warner Bros. with facial hair. In a way, almost a skinny version of him. He went over.

"Hi," Coppola said. "Whatcha lookin' at?"

"Nothin' much."

"How come you're here?"

George Lucas was there on a scholarship, he said. He'd hoped to put in some time in the animation department, he told Coppola, but the place, like most of Warner Bros., was empty, drafting boards and chairs. Even Jack Warner, Lucas heard, had sold his interest and left.

"I heard a UCLA student was shooting," he added, "so I thought I'd take a look."

"Well, if you want to come and be part of this, you're welcome. On one condition."

"What's that?"

"You have to come up with one brilliant idea a day."

For instance, those dancing leprechauns. Coppola had to shoot them galivanting around a pot of gold. To finesse the obvious challenge, Lucas suggested Coppola cast normal-size actors, use an oversize pot, and shoot the scene with an anamorphic lens turned vertically to create a "squishing" effect. *Wow*, Coppola thought, *this kid has talent*.

As agreed, Lucas came up with brilliant ideas, one a day, but three days of singing and dancing leprechauns later, Lucas couldn't wait to leave Hollywood. In six long months, when his Warner Bros. scholarship finally ended, he intended to go back to USC, finish his master's degree, and then move back up to San Francisco, where (if he was lucky) he'd get work shooting commercials and educational films to finance what he really wanted to do: make avant-garde films.

Coppola had to agree: he didn't want to be there, either.

As he had with *Big Boy*, Coppola had rehearsed *Finian's Rainbow* like a play: six weeks (paid) with a full cast and a one-night-only performance, in the round, outdoor at Warner Bros., for friends and family. (Carmine brought his flute to join his son's orchestra.) Coppola said, "By doing this, the camera schedule, which could have taken double or triple the time, has been trimmed to 13 weeks for a tremendous saving, possibly $3,000,000 to $5,000,000." Even still he faced serious opposition. Harried by studio restrictions and sets (he wanted to be shooting on location), the stodgy taste of senior crew people, and the implacably outdated material, Coppola couldn't bring *Finian's Rainbow* to life. He wanted to be doing his own thing, working on other ideas, like *The Conversation* or *The Rain People*, which he had begun writing. Why wasn't he? It was the offer to direct a movie with such a musical pedigree; it would make his father proud, his "Achilles' heel," Coppola said. Those incredible songs . . . "I thought, 'What would my father think?' My father would finally think that I was a success. My father would finally accept me as someone who had sort of made it, which is something that he had wanted all his life."

George Lucas Sr. was a man of modest ambition, a store owner: office desks and copying machines mostly. "He was very strict with George," Coppola said. "George's father, Mr. Lucas, had advice about how to run a business," recalled Lucas's friend from USC, Matthew Robbins. "Never hire a man who smokes a pipe. Because he's going to take time standing around, emptying the pipe, scraping out the old ashes, cleaning out the stem . . ." Coppola's family, a traveling circus, lived impulsively; George Senior punched in and punched out. "Mr. Lucas was a skinny Babbitt," Robbins said, referring to the protagonist of the 1922 Sinclair Lewis novel. Coppola compared him to Polonius, never loan, never borrow. George Senior expected his son to work at the very same store in Modesto, California. But George Junior vowed, "I will never go to work every day doing the same thing day in and day out." He just wanted to race cars (he had a glove compartment full of unpaid speeding tickets) and pick up girls.

Lucas imagined he was manning a race car as he gunned his Fiat Bianchina over sixty, turned left onto the dirt road toward home, and was knocked over by a Chevy, the Fiat flipping six or seven times and bashing into a tree. "When I was pulled out," he said, "they thought I was dead. I wasn't breathing and I had no heartbeat. I had two broken bones and crushed lungs." When he woke up in the hospital, he resolved to stop, as he said, "living my life so close to the edge." He would go to junior college and study—something.

But what? Having survived the wreck, Lucas urgently recognized the dangerous, thrilling companionship of humans and machines. Who controlled whom? He became "interested in how the culture relates to machinery," and at Modesto Junior College, he was driven to the social sciences and photography—cameras being yet another fulcrum of humans and technology—and made experimental short films. "We did trick animation," he said, "ran our movies backwards." Moving images, he recognized, had the power to form our unconscious thoughts—that was also man and machine. "As families begin to break up," he said, "kids are left more to the television and they don't hear bedtime stories. As a result, people are learning their mythology from TV . . ." Where once they turned to religion, or children to the fairy tales their parents told them, humans were turning to popular culture. "That's when George really started exploring," his best friend, John Plummer, recalled. "We went to a theater on Union Street that showed art movies, we drove up to San Francisco State for a film festival, and there was an old beatnik coffeehouse in Cow Hollow with shorts that were really out there." Stan Brakhage, Bruce Conner, Jordan Belson, Bruce Baillie and his Canyon Cinema screenings, their shared interest in the machinery of film . . .

To satisfy his father, he would study anthropology at San Francisco State.

"Come to USC with me," Plummer said toward the end of sophomore year, "we'll have fun down there."

"What can I do?"

"They've got a great thing called the cinema department, films, and it's very easy, anybody could get through it."

Lucas got in, one of about fifty. Studying art, he knew, "would have upset my father, but cinema, that's obscure enough, he didn't know what it was and he didn't care as long as I wasn't in the art department."

In 1964, Lucas said, "Nobody wanted to be a film student. There was no point in it, because you couldn't get a job in the industry and the most you could hope for would be becoming a ticket taker at Disneyland or working for Lockheed making industrial films."

Sitting on his desk, an unlit cigarette in his teeth, cameraman-professor Gene Peterson would scan the eager, nervous rookies. It was the same every year—hopeless. Anyone interested in a degree that wouldn't open a door to its own trade was, by definition, weird, somewhere between hippie, nerd, and dropout. "Well, my advice to you boys is to get out now. You're never going to get in. You're never going to make it."

This was lesson one.

"There's not enough work for even a fraction of you," he persisted. "And in the years to come, it's going to get much worse. You can get your money back if you drop out now."

Many did.

Nineteen sixty-five: in his first class, Animation, with Professor Herb Kossover, Lucas thrilled to the experimental arrangements of tiny parts and pieces, technological and narrative. "I was fascinated with the mechanics of it," he said, "coming out of cars and what have you." They gave him about a minute's worth of film, just to test the camera with. Instead, Lucas used it to make an actual film, one inspired by Arthur Lipsett's avant-garde short 21-87, which he had seen twenty or thirty times. It was his creativity and industry: Lucas shot stills he had cut out of *Life* magazine, added music and a voice-over, and—lo and behold! Where others had merely tested the camera, he had made *Look at Life*. And it was good. "Suddenly," Lucas said, "I was a rising star at the school." From then on, he was in his paradise, living on chocolate, Coca-Cola, and coffee and thinking of nothing but movies.

In the studious quiet of the university darkroom, Lucas met the tall, courtly, intellectually promiscuous, handlebar-mustachioed audiophile Walter Murch. "Neither of us talk very much," Lucas would explain, "so we got along very well."

Unlike George Senior, Walter Murch's father, Walter Senior, was an artist, a painter. He worked out of their apartment on Riverside Drive in Manhattan. Its long hallway was carpeted in giant unpainted canvases and watercolor Arches, the swaths of paper he taped to the floor. Walter Junior insisted his friends step right across them. "Walk on it!" he told Matthew Robbins as he entered the apartment. "My father wants you to! Everyone must walk on them!" When the sheets of paper were scuffed at last to his satisfaction, Mr. Murch would take them up, like small sails, and carry them into his painter's studio, what was once the Murches' dining room, and paint all night. He was a night painter. "I remember him falling asleep on the sofa," Walter Junior would say, "and having nightmares, calling out against his agent, who was making him do something he didn't want to do." While Mr. Murch dreamt, Mrs. Murch, who had sung "My Darling Clementine" to her son in her womb, tucked little Walter into bed with a reading from *The Wonderful Wizard of Oz.*

Nothing ever dies in Oz, little Walter learned; it only changes.

"'My Darling Clementine,'" he said, "has a peculiar quality to me when I hear it, because I heard it before I knew who I was." He would later learn a four-and-a-half-month-old fetus experiences sound almost exclusively. Sound, keeper of memories, the door backward into our lost self.

As a child, his ears stuck out.

When Walter, a boy, didn't know the word for a thing, he would make its sound.

He spliced together sounds on his Revere tape recorder, breaking down a phrase and remaking it, like looking at a diamond through its different facets.

From Johns Hopkins, he went to USC to study film on a full fellowship that paid his tuition and $200-a-month living expenses. "There were very few people at school who were interested in sound," Murch said, "since it was seen as unglamorous, and people assumed that you had to have a high technical engineering interest in amperes and ohms and all of these obscure terms. I didn't have an engineering background, and I approached the work . . . with what you might call an aggressive aesthetic approach . . ."

"Okay, Murch, we know about you," his sound professor said when introducing himself. "We know you did this tape recording stuff, but you have to forget all that because that's not the way film sound works."

"Oh, how *does* it work?"

"Well, we turn the camera on, we take the lens cap off and we hold a microphone, and we record the picture and the image, and that's what it is. We can't change it. We just record the world."

But there were sounds the world hadn't heard yet. How could a microphone record *them*?

Walter and his wife, Aggie, lived near the USC campus, in an apartment where a dozen film students would cram in to watch a movie as she, home late from hospital swing shifts, would try to sleep in their Murphy bed, not easy with a movie playing three feet above her head. But this was, Aggie knew, Life with Walter.

"I never should have married you!" she would protest. "It was ridiculous to marry you! You have a mistress!"

"Yes, I do. Yes. And her name is Moviola."

With Murch and Lucas at USC was surfer-storyteller-rifleman and amiably right-wing provocateur John Milius, who squeezed all his classes into three days so he could go surfing the rest of the week. There were also Murch's friend from Johns Hopkins, the warm and literate Matthew Robbins, and their pal, also from Hopkins, French New Wave–loving Caleb Deschanel and his Bolex . . . Rather than compete for jobs they knew didn't exist after graduation, they stuck together. "George was the master of machines and mechanism," Milius said. "And he could handle the concepts of editing, you know, so he edited everybody's films. He also knew how to run a Moviola"—which Lucas learned he could drive like a car—"which nobody else did. He could make a splice properly." And Murch "really was, even in those days, quite superior with sound," Lucas said. "We all wanted to get him to help us with our mixes." The general lack of equipment nurtured their communal ethic (though Milius hid the Eclair film camera in his Land Rover), and their ramshackle close quarters—a couple of editing rooms, a small screening room that doubled as a mix stage, which "backed into the patio where everybody hung out," Lucas said, "so if you had a good soundtrack on your movie, it would sort of draw all the students into the screening room to see what was going on"—kept them engaged in one another's minds and work. It was by the patio where, Milius said, "we all sat on the grass and spun our wildest dreams," watched girls (through zoom lenses), told one another their big movie ideas—like Lucas's plan to make a "student film about a soldier doing hand-to-hand combat with a P51 Mustang," which could be combined with the idea Milius had, to make a funny movie, like *Dr. Strangelove*, about the war in Vietnam. Those buttons the hippies are wearing, "Nirvana Now!"? His script would be titled *Apocalypse Now!*

"We were all looking at each other's movies," Matthew Robbins said, "and were very free with our opinions. Everyone was up late because everyone shot around the same time and everyone recorded their sound at the same time, and you gotta have your movie ready by Friday, right? So you're all there. 'Hey, can you look at this cut? Is this smooth? Is this jumpy?'" They cross-fertilized. Natural editors learned to think like writers; directors like cameramen—and under the ear-opening influence of Professors Ken Miura and Dan Wiegand, they all discovered the hidden value of film sound, a most inexpensive, practical, and playful way to augment or even rewrite stories late in the filmmaking process. Among students, it became "a real obsession," Lucas said, "to focus on the relationship between sound and picture and really give the soundtrack as much attention as we do the picture track."

They would never forget the day Lucas, Milius, Robbins, Murch, and a few of the others were summoned by certain concerned members of the faculty to their picnic table on the patio and told they were troublemakers. True, Milius could get rowdy and spar with his professors—there were rumors of an actual fistfight—and Deschanel had broken into the editing rooms after hours (trash can to drain pipe to roof), and many of them falsified records to keep equipment for themselves, but none was a pothead or terribly active politically (or sexually).

"We're gonna go around the table," the faculty decreed, "and everyone's going to tell us what you're going to do. Why are you in film school?"

That stopped them.

"*National Geographic* documentaries," Murch fumbled, vamping. "Trips down the Mississippi . . ."

"John, what about you?"

Milius pounded his fist on the table. "I want to be a mogul!"

They all laughed—not a chance. Like wanting to be king.

Nineteen sixty-six: Lucas got his bachelor's degree, met and fell in love with editor Marcia Griffin, and picked up film work here and there, including a gig assisting USC professor Gene Peterson in teaching production to navy cameramen—a shrewd move: Lucas knew USC gave its navy students color film stock, access to choice locations, a comparatively generous budget, and their pick of equipment. If he skimmed a little off the top, he could make a short film on a scale that neither he nor any of them had ever attempted . . .

At a party at Professor Kossover's, Lucas sneaked up to Robbins and Murch in the kitchen. "Are you guys gonna do that film about the guy trapped underground?" Robbins and Murch didn't have much, just a short outline with a twist ending—the hero climbs through a hatch, and it's revealed that he's been underground all along—and anyway, they'd already moved on to another idea. So, their underground man went to George.

Completed in just three months, Lucas's *Electronic Labyrinth: THX 1138 4EB* was tightly structured, highly visual, and cleverly enhanced with optical effects (and made for far less money than it appeared). An action short disguised as an experimental film (or vice versa), *THX* didn't have much in the way of performance and almost no intelligible dialogue, but it was the best of George Lucas slathered in eerie moods he had inherited from the avant-garde—and it raced like a Hollywood rocket.

The film was an instant and ubiquitous sensation, celebrated everywhere, from USC to Universal—"Jesus, who the hell did *this*?" asked executive Ned Tanen—to the rival quads of UCLA, where it was screened at Royce Hall as part of a festival of student work. "It absolutely stopped the festival," said Long Beach State's Steven Spielberg. He was floored—by the technique, by the size of the vision, by Lucas's complete immersion in science-fictional world-building. For the young Spielberg, the screening was a deliriously complicated experience of abject jealousy, awe, and, finally, inspiration: Lucas, a guy his *own* age, had created unforgettable imagery—and with so little and within such a short period. "It was certainly, to me, one of the greatest science fiction movies I had ever seen," Spielberg would say. After the screening, bashfully making his way backstage, he would have a chance to greet the filmmaker in person. Given the scope of the film, he had imagined a giant, someone physically powerful enough to dream up entirely new worlds and haul them into real life. But the figure Spielberg encountered "reminded me a little bit of Walt Disney's version of a mad scientist," small.

Spielberg's was the approximately typical reaction to encountering Lucas, the local legend. "Partly because it was a disconnect," Murch said, "between his persona and what you saw in the films he made," a little like "discovering your anonymous next door neighbor has this fantastic career as a world-famous orchestra conductor." When Spielberg's moment to approach finally arrived, he gushed, and Lucas, just as bashfully, murmured his nervous thanks. ("That's George, you know," Spielberg would say.) Having been rejected by both USC and UCLA film schools, Spielberg decided that night that age was no barrier.

Electronic Labyrinth: THX 1138 4EB won first place at the National Student Film Festival, and Lucas shot ahead, picking up more awards (in addition to scholarships left and right) and, from Columbia Pictures, the chance to shoot a behind-the-scenes documentary of *Mackenna's Gold*, a Hollywood feature, and to observe up close "such opulence, zillions of dollars being spent every five minutes on this huge, unwieldy thing. It was mind-boggling to us because we had been making films for three hundred dollars, and seeing this incredible waste—that was the worst of Hollywood." And then came Warner Bros. with its contest for an apprenticeship opportunity, a photo finish, as it turned out, between USC's finest, Lucas and Murch. Lucas won. Not that he had any particular interest in what was going on at Warner Bros. "The only reason I took the scholarship was to give it a chance," he said. "Oh, I'll go and see what it's all about, just so I can say I really don't like it."

Which is how he met Francis Ford Coppola filming *Finian's Rainbow*.

"That started our friendship basically," Lucas would say. "I'd go around with a Polaroid and take camera angles and show 'em to him and basically help him in any way I could." In time, the two found they had complementary gifts: Francis for story and character, writing and directing actors; George for cutting and camera work. Constitutionally, they were just as complementary: Francis was impulsive, charismatic, improvisational; George looked before he leapt . . . if he ever leapt. "George comes from a conservative Northern California family where money is kind of serious business," Coppola said. Of

Coppola, Lucas would say, "He calls me 'the kid with the seventy-year-old mind.' His head is up in the clouds—he dreams. I always used to say that he was crazy in a good way—the kind of guy, like in the old movies, who goes out there and pulls off things while everybody else says, 'No, no, Francis! You can't do that!'" Coppola sang, actually sang, as he worked.

"I can sing anything! Give me a song! Any song! Any song! From any show!"

They didn't make 'em like that in Modesto.

Coppola's office on the lot—which other film school graduate had one?—became the unofficial clubhouse for their generation of Hollywood up-and-comers: Lucas, Milius, Deschanel . . . Ron Colby, a friend of Coppola's from Hofstra . . . Carroll Ballard, whom Coppola hired to shoot the terrific opening sequence for *Finian's Rainbow* . . . They had plans. Coppola's success made them seem possible. Milius was talking about *Apocalypse Now*, which maybe Lucas would direct . . . Ballard was talking to producer Joe Landon about directing a film version of *Heart of Darkness* . . . And always, always asking could they do it cheaper, faster? How could they get a camera, get a Moviola, and really go to work? What if they owned their own equipment? The cameras were smaller, more portable than ever. They could even be like a studio but not *at* a studio. They would have power: Francis, the gang asked him, which director do you admire most?

"Would you believe Howard Hughes?"

"I consider myself a very romantic human being," Coppola would say, "and I really feel I was well suited to do this project," *Finian's Rainbow*. "But it's not my personal kind of filmmaking, which I may never depart from again, by the way." Lucas would sit there, saying nothing, hands in his pockets. "I'm disgruntled," Coppola confessed. "I could make a lot of money by just grabbing up three pictures and having writers write them and having cutters cut them, and just—zoom—go right through them. I could pile up about a million dollars, which I would surely like."

But which came first, the pictures or the money? They would chicken-and-egg that one for hours (with Coppola doing most of the talking). You do not wait for permission, Coppola taught them. You just *go*. And when the studio execs find out you're making a movie, they'll fall all over themselves to buy in. But if they lay out the money first, Coppola advised, they'll *own* you. That was the whole problem with, say, Warner Bros. They don't hire you because they want you; they hire you because they want you to work *for them*. New ideas, the very essence of creation, innovation, civilization, and happiness, they all sound crazy to studio executives. Most are paid *not* to take chances. But they didn't know the history of the world. They didn't know all visionaries begin as misunderstood; they haven't yet changed the world to match their vision. "What I'm thinking of doing, quite honestly, is splitting," Coppola would tell the press. "I'm thinking of pulling out and making other kinds of films. Cheaper films. Films I can make in 16 mm. No one knows whether there's a valuable market for that kind of film yet." All Coppola and his fellow filmmaking aspirants had was talent, but maybe that was enough. Maybe they really could make money *and* change the world . . . "The establishment wants no part of the young filmmakers," Coppola would say, "and the young filmmakers want no part of the establishment."

Spielberg, nearly eight years younger than Coppola, was intimidated by the big ideas coming from Francis and his cohort, their talk of revolution. He was, he said, "a young anachronism. And I didn't think there would be room for me because I did see that the times they were a-changing, and maybe I was too old-fashioned, even at 20 years old, to be a part of those times."

But Coppola and Lucas were different. They were at odds with the world without. The system depicted in Lucas's *Electronic Labyrinth: THX 1138 4EB* was twinned to their Hollywood nightmare, the imagined consequence of social and emotional oppression; so, too, was isolation in Coppola's script *The Rain People*, about a woman alone, and his gestating tale of privacy and paranoia—titled, maybe, "The Secret Harry," "The Personal Harry," "The Unspoken" (. . . and, finally, *The Conversation*) . . .

But, first, *Finian's Rainbow*, a mistake, as Coppola told the gang in his Warner Bros. office, he vowed never to make again. "A lot of us were involved with those discussions about how to get through *Finian's Rainbow*," Ballard recalled. For his part, Coppola would not see *Finian's* postproduction to completion. Instead, he would finish writing and then go out and direct *The Rain People*, the script, paid for by Seven Arts, that he had put aside to direct *Finian's Rainbow*—just as the pregnant heroine of *The Rain People* leaves her life and husband behind to . . . go where? It didn't matter; not to the fictional Natalie, not to Coppola, as long as they did it together, an adventure in filmmaking on their own terms—with George Lucas as his assistant. "By then," Coppola said, "he was like a kid brother, so I wanted him—and he wanted to go on this adventure. We were going to get a van and make a camera van and go across the country."

"Francis's attitude was, 'We'll just start making it and they'll have to catch up with us,'" Lucas said. "So he put up some of his own money"—about $20,000 or $30,000 Coppola estimated—"and got us going. We started casting and scouting locations and hiring an art director and doing all kinds of things before Warner knew what was going on. Finally, [Coppola] just said, 'Look, you're either going to make this movie or not.'"

"Well, you know," Francis mused to George, "we could get money in the budget for you to do a documentary on the making of the film, but really you could be writing your script"—the script being a full-length version of *THX 1138*. So it was that the Coppola Company, on January 30, 1968, offered George Lucas his first screenwriting deal: $2,500 for a treatment and first draft.

Lucas insisted he couldn't write. He hated writing.

"You're never going to be a good director unless you become a good writer," Coppola advised him.

"Francis, I can't write a screenplay."

"Sure you can."

"But this is not my thing."

"You have to learn how to do this."

"He always said we were the Trojan horse," Milius recalled, "but that wasn't quite true, because he was inside opening the gate. None of those other guys—Lucas, Spielberg, all of them—could have existed without Francis's help. And his was a much more interesting influence than theirs. Francis was going to become the emperor of the new order, but it wasn't going to be like the old order. It was going to be the rule of the artist."

"Look," Coppola said to Warner Bros., in what was certainly not a bluff, "I'm starting to shoot on Monday and I need some money and if you don't give it to me, I'll get it from someone else." Afraid to lose him, Warner bought *The Rain People* for fifty thousand dollars ("And I never showed them the script"), and off they went: Francis, George (filming his documentary all day, writing all night; "I worked on *THX* from four in the morning until six in the morning, and then I'd work on the picture," as "the third assistant director, the third assistant art director, the third camera assistant—the third assistant everything"), Mona Skager ("I was the do-all," she said, "the guard at the gate. You couldn't talk to Francis until you came by me"), Ron Colby (producer), Barry Malkin (a friend from Francis's Great Neck days, as editor), and the Coppola kids big brother Gio and little Roman ("my first memories are during *Rain People*," Roman said), along with Eleanor and her brother Bill, Francis's pal the poet Tony Dingman, actor James Caan (a friend from Hofstra), and star Shirley Knight. Coppola said, "I supported that cast and crew of almost twenty for nearly five months."

Cleverly, Coppola elided union constraints. "Because we had representation of every union in the crew, by my definition, we could shoot anywhere in the country," he said. "But there were some questions from some teamsters." Beginning in New York, Dingman was on Teamster watch—"They were just kind of monitoring what we were doing"—but Coppola's crew was at least small enough, and their equipment portable enough, to, in a pinch, hide behind the cover of "documentary." "They didn't even classify us as a movie," Skager said, "because then we would have had to hire Teamsters. And we were not about to do that. We had no money"—and therefore, no definite plan. "We started out in Garden City, Long Island, and we borrowed everything. We borrowed from Ford Motor, we borrowed the cars. We made a deal with hotels, you know, so we could get reasonable, relatively free lodging. And we just took off. We just started driving." The only set they had arranged for in advance was sixteen hundred miles away, in North Platte, Nebraska. "And that was a snake farm," Skager said. But to get there, they had to get out of Garden City, where the Teamsters had traced them, in the middle of the night. "Literally under the cover of darkness," Colby recalled, "we all got into the vehicles and we drove on out of town."

Forced to improvise, Skager said, "Francis was rewriting to the situations. When something happened, we raced to that site," or when the weather changed, when the sun went up or down, when a location fell through, or when a new (or old) idea hit him, and the captain turned his seven-vehicle caravan around again and raced them all back, dispatching in haste art director/location scout Leon Ericksen to okay the environs a hundred miles ahead of them so producers Ron Colby and Bart Patton could get a jump on negotiations should the production, in constant communication by walkie-talkie—"Was that the turnoff? Did he just *miss* the turnoff?"—arrive at its destination ready to roll camera before an agreement had been made. The star of the caravan was the mobile unit Coppola and Lucas had devised, a remodeled Dodge Travco packed to the windows with all that gear Coppola had bought with his own money: cameras on one side, sound on the other; in the kitchenette in the back, a flatbed editing table for Barry Malkin; rewinds mounted on the sink; on the roof, an old dolly and track, a few twenty-inch quartz lights without any lenses. And the whole thing doubled as a dressing room—"more or less," Coppola said, "a whole studio on wheels," which George called HAL 9000 in honor of Kubrick's 2001 and which Malkin christened "the Magical Mystery Tour." For a little extra cash, Coppola rented the whole package back to Warner Bros., charging it against the budget of the picture. Now, *that* was producing.

Lucas took note. Though he was never a spender, somewhere in the middle of America in the middle of 1968, he had to concede that the best way to independence was owning your own gear. "Everything I learnt as a producer," he said, "I learned from Francis." It meant, also, owning the underlying rights, the movie material, as the Coppola Company owned Lucas's (still-developing) THX. The big money, a way to sustainable independence, was in owning everything. Therefore, writing. Whoever owned the script called the shots. Here again, Francis had a head start; he wrote. Lucas could barely type. ("He didn't spell very well," Skager said. "He didn't know where the keys were." At night, she would type for him. "Everybody just helped everybody else," she said. "That was just the attitude.")

Down the Appalachians to Chattanooga, Tennessee, back up through Amish Country, Pennsylvania (Blue Ball, PA!), learning how to alchemize resources every step of the way: "We would send our film to New York for processing, and it would be sent back to us," Malkin said, via Greyhound. "We occasionally would get to a city and rent a movie theater late at night, where we would try to run our dailies . . . We had a lot of fun doing it, and you can't often say that about moviemaking."

"[Lucas and I] were sitting in the motel lobby," Skager remembered, "waiting for Francis and Ellie to arrive, and George was watching *Flash Gordon* on the television. All of a sudden, he started talking about how he should make a movie like that, with holograms and everything. I didn't even know what a hologram was."

America was a new world. Adventuring through the country's most rugged subcultures, the *Rain* guys were wise to shave their beards in advance and keep their liberal politics to the van. Coppola even went so far as to change his wardrobe. In jumpsuits bought in bulk from the surplus store, he could have passed for a mechanic, Eleanor thought. "He was sort of dressed like Everyman, and I think the idea was really to sort of blend in and not be anything threatening to any place that they tried to stop and shoot." He woke up in Tennessee and threw James Caan, in character, into an actual parade—and rolled camera. And when he needed to shoot a burning home, he bought a house and burned it down. "We didn't need a special effects man or anything," Coppola said. "We just needed a match, and it looked more real than other fires I've seen."

He had made other movies before, with others' money, others' budgets, people, and scripts; but never before had he made a movie entirely on his terms, in his way, allowing the mad muses of chance to transform his story. Coppola was directing *life*. Fate was his uncredited cowriter, and the story, true to any first telling, was a lived improvisation with an ending always unknown. "What I always learn about Francis," Eleanor said, "is that in every movie, he is asking himself a question." "The ideal way to work on a project," he concurred, "is to ask a question you don't know the answer to." Question: What would become of Natalie, the heroine of *The Rain People*? Question: What is a woman's responsibility to her family? He could not answer this until he had achieved, through the lived metaphor of his independent production, the independence the character was seeking. "The film is the force," he would say of his impending methodology, "and we're all trying to tame it, trying to make it do the things that we want it to do, but in the end we can't. It's pushing us around as much as we're pushing it. And it is a struggle. And it's a struggle, I think, always on the brink of failure."

An unfavorite child, his parents' second son, a polio survivor and social outcast—Coppola lacked much, but what he had was a gift for overcoming failure. Extremity propelled him. It raised the stakes, lit the flame. The scent of calamity gave him the emotion to live the story, to shoot the movie—

like a Method actor *behind* the camera—autobiographically. "All you have is yourself to invent the character, so as you work on it, little by little, the character and you get closer and closer." Until now, Coppola hadn't had the means to get that close. How could he "live" *Finian's Rainbow* when they were always telling him no? "With *The Rain People*," he said, "I planned deliberately to complicate matters, to follow the housewife wherever she went—to literally take the trip." Shooting entirely in sequence allowed him and his actors and his crew to breathe the same air as his characters, to change with them. Wherever possible, he would write (and at night and off camera, rewrite and rewrite) to those transformations. "My films are unusual partly because I look at art as an adventure," he said. Why else live? To wake up, in your bed in Brentwood, the same person you were yesterday?

By June 1968, having shot over a hundred days in over fifteen states (and mainly outrun the unions), the production came to their last stop, Ogallala, Nebraska. Colby watched, elated, from James Caan's motel room, as Bobby Kennedy took California.

"That's it," he said, standing to turn off the TV. "It looks like we're gonna win, 'cause this guy's gonna win."

Colby left for his own room and slipped into bed beside his wife. He gave her the great news and fell asleep.

Ten minutes later, there was a pounding on his door.

It was Caan. "They shot him! They shot Bobby!"

The assassination galvanized talk of change. Now that the last scene of *The Rain People* was upon them, so, too, was the inevitable return to Los Angeles and the Hollywood way, a depressing thought, given that Coppola had proven, to his crew and to himself, that *his* way of making movies really did work. More than work: they were thriving. Nebraska was idyllic; beautiful, even; the plains, the total immersion in art and family, the creation of a life apart. "We had the big preview of *Finian's Rainbow* today," Jack Warner cabled Coppola care of the Paradise Motel, "and the picture went over fantastically. I could see the wonderful touch and the warmth you personally put into the film. This is just the beginning of a very important future that will rank among the tops." But what kind of future, Warner had no clue. By the end of June, after five full weeks of living and working in Ogallala, Malkin worked out a rough cut in the back of the Dodge. It was apparent, foremost to Coppola, that "he could make a film studio anywhere," Eleanor said. "In fact, they wanted him to stay and make a studio right there."

Coppola, too busy wrapping the movie to accept an invitation to speak at the California Council on the Arts Conference in San Francisco, sent an associate in his stead. "Hi," Coppola's emissary—"this rather thin, young guy in blue jeans and tennis shoes"—greeted fellow panelist, filmmaker John Korty, moments before the conference began, "I'm George Lucas." Lucas took a seat at the table behind the name card "Francis Coppola" and proceeded to speak, "mainly about what Francis had been doing," Korty said, "trying to break out of the system in various ways," driving across the country, shooting, learning, cutting as they went. "We obviously had a lot in common right there," he observed.

An independent filmmaker in the little Northern California town of Stinson Beach, Korty was already a giant step ahead of them: "I mean the idea of going to Hollywood or being part of the film industry never really occurred to me," he said. "I was interested in filmmaking the way someone gets interested in carpentry. I was like, oh, there's a camera. It was the tools and it was the craft, and I didn't mind being responsible for my own financial future in it, whether it was making commercials or whatever." Five years prior, he'd finally made a move. "I was in this tiny apartment in Brooklyn Heights," he said, "and was actually going through a divorce with my first wife, and I wanted to go to Northern California. I was very clear that I didn't want to go to Southern California. Everything I heard about San Francisco sounded like my kind of place. So I came out. I packed up and I drove a VW bus across-country in the winter of '63, got a place in Stinson Beach, California. A wonderful old house right on the beach . . ."

Korty soon found out he could make five-minute animated films, on his own—the design, animation, music, photography, everything—in about five minutes, which led to *Breaking the Habit*, which he submitted, on a lark, for Oscar consideration, in 1965; it got the nomination. His first low-budget feature, *The Crazy-Quilt*, followed in 1966, and another, *Funnyman*, came a year later—all "little soulful independent movies," as Lucas would describe them—and, remarkably, they were actually making money, not a lot, but enough to keep Korty working in the studio he made out of the big old garage by the ocean he rented for $150 a month.

As soon as the panel in San Francisco ended, Lucas grabbed Korty's arm. "Come on. We're gonna call Francis." They found a phone booth downstairs. Lucas dialed, and Korty observed the Lucas version of enthusiasm.

"Francis," he told the phone, "I just met John Korty and he's doing exactly what you said you wanted to do and we've got to get together . . ."

"That's it," Coppola said from Nebraska. "That's what we should do."

Lucas hung up and faced Korty. "As soon as Francis is done, since he is on the road anyway, he'll come and see you in Stinson Beach."

Days later, *Rain People* in the can, Coppola, Lucas, and Ron Colby, along with Eleanor, Roman, and Gio, caravanned their (now beat-up) station wagons 1,370 miles west from Nebraska to the Pacific Coast Highway and down to Stinson Beach. They arrived at Korty's barn on the Fourth of July. "It looked terrible on the outside," Korty said—there were literally holes in the wall—"but inside we had an editing room with the first 355 Steenbeck on the West Coast, a screening room with two 35 mm projectors, and Nagra tape recorders for taking sound. Francis and George walked in and their mouths dropped open."

"This is what I want," Coppola announced.

Lucas and Colby were in complete and instantaneous agreement. "And it just seemed like such a perfect environment," Colby said, "because it was like you're being a writer in the country, but yet you have the tools . . ."

Never one to miss a ritual celebration—the joyous convergence of community, tradition, and living theater—Coppola had come prepared with fireworks, which they shot up, throughout dinner, and colors rained down onto the barn.

"We're gonna be back Monday," Coppola assured his new friend Korty. "We'll be back Monday and we'll go look for a place and we'll get this place and we'll all be together in this big filmmaking community."

The search for their headquarters began, taking them to West Marin, and someone mentioned how beautiful Bodega Bay was, "and they had fishing boats and things," Korty added, so off they went to the seaside village where Hitchcock had shot *The Birds* five years earlier.

"That's it," Coppola announced. "We'll set up a studio in Bodega Bay."

Korty laughed. "Francis, it's over two hours from the city . . ."

The difference between Francis and George, Korty thought, is the difference between an Italian opera and a comic book. Coppola had, in his imagination, already moved into their headquarters on the sea, his children at his feet as he expounded philosophically on Herman Hesse and Orson Welles with writers and musicians, photographers and singers, gamblers and architects . . .

In another reality, Coppola's editor, Barry Malkin, was moving back to New York with *The Rain People* still in cans.

"Do you know anybody that knows anything about sound?" Coppola asked Lucas.

"I know just the guy. He's a genius."

Walter Murch. Now graduated from USC Film, and expecting his first child with Aggie, he lived on Cheremoya Avenue in Hollywood, not far from where he was cutting commercials at Dove Films, Haskell Wexler's company—which is where Lucas introduced him to Coppola in the summer of 1968.

"Come with us up the street," Coppola said to Murch, "and have a look at this new computerized editing system."

Computerized editing? *Computers?*

Coppola was shopping. That day, he and Murch had a good look at the CNX Memorex system, with its crappy black-and-white picture, its intolerance for more than five minutes of footage at a time. A very good idea, they agreed, but not yet up to snuff. In a flash, Coppola was in Cologne, Germany, at Photokina, a film equipment fair, where he discovered "a candy store of technology," bought an Eclair PR, "a very beautiful camera," he said (lightweight, quiet, 16 mm), and beheld the new array of Steenbecks and KEMs, far better suited to the mixing of sound elements than anything else in Hollywood.

"God, we can have our own mix studio," Coppola recalled thinking. "And so I kind of went all crazy," he said. "And I figured, well, I'm going to sell my house. I'll have enough money. So I don't know how much money I went in the hole." Following a trip to Denmark, to Klampenborg, Coppola pressed his nose to the lustrous windows of Laternafilm, a villa on a hill by the sea.

Coppola was awestruck by the people, their process, the life. Its cohabitants had transformed their mansion into a filmmaking collective, "a Korty-like existence," as Ron Colby put it, of administrative offices, a garage turned into a mix studio, bedrooms changed into editing rooms, each with its own Steenbeck, beautiful Zoetropes, and other antique film artifacts—and outside, in the garden, in the perfect picnic spot, they were treated to salmon and herring and aquavit and beer. *This is heaven*, Coppola thought, *this is paradise. To make movies surrounded by lovely colleagues in a beautiful place with all this equipment by the sea.*

Returning to Los Angeles, Coppola was "in a daze." He sold off his summer house and home in Mandeville Canyon, started buying film equipment, and poured the vision into Lucas: "We'll have a place out in the country and we'll make the bedrooms editing rooms and we'll discuss the script in the garden and we'll have lunch together and there'll be all these young people working there."

Lucas could see it, too: a Victorian estate, maybe, whirring with splicers and sprocket clicks, in the woods just outside San Francisco . . .

"Then," Coppola added, "we'll be independent . . ."

So, it was back up to Marin to find the perfect setting for their paradise—and fast, before the equipment Coppola had ordered arrived so Murch could mix *The Rain People*, so they could release it, so they could declare themselves and set an example for the world. "If *The Rain People* dies a dreary death," Coppola explained, "it's not just me who will be hurt. I can make a big hunk of money doing a lot of different commercial pictures. But my chances of doing a film like this again—or anyone's chances—will be in jeopardy if this risk [that] Warner-Seven took doesn't pay off. The people who will be hurt most will be all those others who feel that a meaningful picture can be brought in on a reasonable budget, and who are willing to try something new." In the town of Ross, Coppola found Fernhill, a late-nineteenth-century mansion in the Hudson River style. Coppola put in an offer and lost. Next time, he vowed to Lucas, he'd bid higher.

They kept looking and losing, finding, falling in love, and then losing again. And the equipment was on its way.

Lucas, meanwhile, was editing his documentary about *The Rain People* in his rented hillside cottage on Portola Drive in Benedict Canyon. It was the laughable opposite of Fernhill, off a dirt road and dollhouse tiny. Even so, Lucas, who was always building, managed to install a screen and a make-shift projection booth (lined in cork to muffle the noise) in the upstairs living room, where Matthew and Janet Robbins came to hear the *THX 1138* pitch he was fashioning to outsmart the executives. "He made a presenta-tion for how he was going to use special effects using 'rotary cam photog-raphy,' which was total bullshit," Matthew Robbins recalled. "It was really scurrilous high school kind of shit" and made them all laugh. "George had a goofy sense of humor," he added. "With his friends, he was perfectly chatty, but if there were other people around, he was far more silent than he is now. Never withdrawn, just kind of cautious."

Ten miles east, on Cheremoya Avenue, Walter Murch had converted his second bedroom, intended for the baby's nursery, into a sound studio—and started to hunt, but carefully. As a nonunion ex–film student working on a studio feature, his first, he wouldn't show himself at film libraries on the trail for prerecorded sound. What if they asked who he was? The whole picture—and potentially their fledgling film collective with it—could be shut down. So, he would collect his sounds himself. "Come on, darling," he said to Aggie, NAGRA in hand, "we're going to go out . . ." and they climbed into their 1937 Bentley to capture some "squeaky leather sounds" for the long interior car ride that was *The Rain People*.

George moved in with his fiancée, editor Marcia Griffin, and Matthew and Janet Robbins took over the busy little house Lucas had vacated on Portola Drive—"It was like a club," Robbins said—where Murch continued to glean and polish audio morsels out of the searchlight of the unions. "It probably was good in the long run," Murch said, "because it forced me into thinking up techniques and ways of doing things that I had to pull out of myself, rather than asking somebody who'd done it fifty times, 'What is the way to do this?'" Murch converted the living room Lucas had made into a screening room into a mixing studio, with Moviola and transfer machine. Here and there, he asked Janet Robbins to lend a hand. "I would help make sounds and weird stuff like that and do some rewinding of reels. I had to drink a bottle of 7UP and make a *glug glug glug* and put my finger in my mouth and make a popping sound."

On the eve of *Finian's* New York premiere, in October 1968, writer Joseph Gelmis found Coppola, in his suite at the Plaza Hotel, "nervous and under great emotional stress." He had his ups, now he was down. Was he really a director? Or was he really more of a supervisor, a catalyst for other people's talents? Was he wasting the time and effort he had on those other people and their dreams? "It's come to the point where I just want to get out altogether," he confessed to Gelmis. "I just want to go do my own thing. And I may do that. I'm fed up. It takes too much out of you. You don't get enough for it, in whatever commodity you're dealing in." He had read his press. He felt critics' contempt for his spending and early recognition and the implication that success had gone to his head, as if wanting the system to be different and having the means, maybe, to change it was megalomaniacal. But they were wrong. His largesse was not ego. "They just think I'm living this golden life and they don't realize that I am really straining and endeavoring to find some honest balance with myself in terms of the work of the future." He had spent all his money, everything he had made on *Finian's*. "So, after today," he said, "I may not get the offers that I was hoping I would."

Finian's Rainbow flopped with critics and audiences, and Coppola's uphill battle inclined further. How would he, branded a folly, interest a distributor in *The Rain People*? In Lucas's documentary?

In Carroll Ballard . . . John Milius . . . Walter Murch . . . ?

In the future?

At home, Eleanor would reflect on *The Rain People*, its story of Natalie Ravenna, the pregnant wife fleeing home and husband. Francis would say her flight had been inspired by a story from his mother's life. "My mother never loved me," he would confess to Eleanor, and indeed, Coppola's steely portrayal of Natalie bears the scars. But Eleanor could see that *she* was implicated, too. "I was interested," Coppola said, "in the idea that she loves her husband, but she didn't want to be a wife." As played by Shirley Knight, born in 1936, Natalie was Eleanor's age exactly, and a WASP married to Vinny, an Italian American. "I just realized that I am sharing his life," she tells her mother in an early draft. "I go where he goes, I live where he lives,

I'm interested in his work. But what about me?" As with Gio, Natalie's first baby came fast—"I . . . we . . . hadn't planned on it," Natalie tells her doctor in a scene written but never filmed—before Eleanor discovered (and later than Natalie, perhaps even too late) that Francis had already cast her, as his father, Carmine, had cast *his* wife, to play out her life in accord with their growing family.

Gio was then five. Roman was three. Eleanor was thirty-two. *The Rain People*, she would think—how could Francis claim to know and understand Natalie's struggle for independence but not hers?

In December 1968, Motion Picture Academy president Gregory Peck introduced Coppola to a theater full of its members, discerning middle-aged representatives of the Hollywood establishment. They had gathered for a "Director's Choice" screening of—Coppola's only personal feature to date and therefore his only real "choice"—*You're a Big Boy Now*. "We're very pleased and proud," Peck told the audience, "to present to you this afternoon one of the youngest of the American major film directors, one with whom I'm sure you'll have a great deal in common. You'll have a great deal to talk about with him and he has a beard."

But Coppola didn't go by the plan that day. He didn't show *Big Boy*, nor did he present himself as director of the hour. That afternoon, he made a different choice. "What I would like to show you, if I may," he said, "is a film that was made by George Lucas." Lucas, somewhere in the theater, was hiding in embarrassment. "Some of you know him. He's a young filmmaker. Very talented. He came on this four month safari across the country trying desperately to make a movie at sometimes very adverse conditions, and George made a movie about us trying to make this movie. It's not a promotional film. . . . I haven't seen the film. I have to say that also this film is George's without censorship. . . . It tells perhaps a way of making films that is going to be a reality and something you can share in and hopefully flourish in yourselves."

Only the night before had the Academy finally been outfitted to project 16 mm—preference of the new low-budget youth. Now there was trouble with the sound, "a tragedy," Coppola told the crowd, "because poor George has been up day and night for the last four weeks getting this ready to show you." So, Coppola invited the audience to get up from their seats around the theater and gather close enough to the screen to hear *Filmmaker*, a title

Coppola confessed didn't reflect his own view. The enterprise of filmmaking was, he believed, the work of many, not one.

After the film ("George died," Coppola said), the Q&A:

"Can you tell us something about your film school?"

"That's a misconception," Coppola responded. "I'm not going to start a film school"—at least, not yet. "I myself am personally moving to San Francisco and I am attempting with some luck and the people associated with me—a lot of the people you saw in the film—to start a film company really designed to do so-called 'personal' films, for lack of a better term." He told them his organization would not—unlike they of the Academy—be unionized. This would set his gang still farther apart from Hollywood, perhaps prohibitively so. Or, perhaps not: the strictures of union filmmaking, "this pigeonholing of people," Coppola explained to the pigeonholers of the Academy audience, not only prohibited up-and-coming talent from breaking into Hollywood, but prevented already unionized talent, *them*, from expanding their range of creativity. Confined by regulation, how did they expect themselves to truly expand as artists? "Unions were designed for a 1935 kind of thing, and what we need is a new approach to unionism and film production based on smaller crews . . ."—which he would attempt as soon as he finished sound recording and then mixing *The Rain People* . . . on the equipment he had gone broke buying in Germany . . . in their nonexistent outpost in San Francisco.

All they had was a name. Lucas had pushed for "TransAmerica Sprocket Works," but Coppola chose "American Zoetrope."

"Zoetrope," for the nineteenth-century optical toy Coppola was gifted at Laternafilm. "I thought it would be a good symbol," he said. A primitive miracle of physics and cinema, the zoetrope—relative of the magic lantern that was the symbol of Laternafilm—condensed many facets of the Francis Ford Coppola dream: technology and art, egalitarianism (anyone could work a zoetrope; you just had to spin it), and transformation: *zoe* was Greek for "life," and *trope* meant "movement, turn, revolution." The revolutions Coppola had in mind were not political per se. "It's the wheel of life," he said of the zoetrope. "The whole idea of our company was that everybody— all the filmmakers—could do whatever they wanted." That couldn't happen in a union town.

With *The Rain People* still in postproduction in Los Angeles, Coppola's frustration with the Hollywood way only mounted. Lucas's *THX* was turned down first by Warner Bros. and then, late in December—after the Academy screening of *Filmmaker*—by United Artists. "Despite many clever things in the screenplay," concluded UA's Herb Jaffe, "I think it becomes very redundant and boring, and while I think Lucas is a man to be reckoned with, I don't think *THX 1138* is for us."

Warner Bros. was, at the moment of its turning down *THX*, transforming. Effective January 1969, the Kinney National Service (its specialty: parking lots and funeral homes) had put the final touches on its studio takeover. Out went eighteen of twenty-one older executives and in came, as head of production, a spick-and-span cool customer, thirty-nine-year-old John Calley. He was the new breed, inmate *not* asylum, or at least, wanted it to seem that way. "He was so hip," Peter Biskind wrote, "he didn't even have a desk in his office, just a big coffee table covered with snacks, carrot sticks, hardboiled eggs, and candy." (Jack Warner had cigars.) Calley wore—like the directors, writers, actors—jeans, as if he were one of them. He read books! Flaunting his friendships with talent—he and Mike Nichols were truly close—Calley understood that in post-studio Hollywood, where long-term contracts were a thing of the past, mutual loyalty was the coin of the realm. It was who you know. He said, "What [Warner chairman] Ted [Ashley and I] were trying to do when we got there was create a universe in which directors felt that they could come to us with projects and say I want to make it and they would either find support, or we would help them find support in the purely business and technical aspects of producing a film, but that, in the main, we favored the creative input of filmmakers rather than producers." They would be openly hands-off where Robert Evans, their young competitor at Paramount, was covertly hands-on. "I thought that the studio system was ridiculous," Calley confessed (though he had to admit it was efficient where independent film was slow, erratic, chaotic).

Well before the first day of the new regime, Lucas was itching to bring them *THX*. "Come on," he implored Coppola. "We'll get this thing made."

"We gotta wait a while until these people show up for work."

In his own office at Warner Bros.—spying distance from Calley—Coppola ran cuts of *The Rain People* for Carroll Ballard and John Milius, who had himself been making slow but steady progress—no script yet, just notes—on *Apocalypse Now*.

"How much do you need to live for a year?" Coppola asked Milius.

"Fifteen grand."

"I think I can get it for you."

As he had on *The Rain People*, Coppola convinced Lucas to begin pre-production—at least in his own mind—of *THX 1138*, though he had no deal. "We'll just pretend like we've already started it," Coppola advised, but before Lucas could look, Coppola leapt, and charged Ron Colby, Hofstra pal, with casting the picture . . . and called Robert Dalva, a friend of Lucas's from USC, to edit . . .

Across town from Warner Bros., lazing with Ballard on a sailboat off Marina del Rey, Coppola asked, "What do you think about going to San Francisco?"

"Well, just think of Caesar," Ballard answered. "The first move that Caesar made was to leave Rome and to get out of the hot bed and go out there and gather your army and then come back when you're strong."

A few weeks later, Coppola finally reached out to Calley. A jokey telegram: "Shape up or ship out." Coppola had timed his approach perfectly. Presenting his idea for American Zoetrope and the hoped-for future of film, he found Calley receptive.

What Coppola offered Calley/Warner Bros. in American Zoetrope was a package of assembled filmmakers and scripts and, further, relationships with the future of film in the form of Milius (whose idea for *Apocalypse* intrigued Calley), Lucas ("who everybody thought was extraordinary"), and others from USC and UCLA—and of course Coppola ("as the parental figure," Calley said), who would supervise all in San Francisco. In a way, Calley figured, Coppola's proposal was not outlandish. While in Mexico, making *Catch-22* with Mike Nichols, he had been early to see *Easy Rider*—a giant hit, economically produced, in a similar fashion, by BBC for Columbia—which struck Calley as a successful proof-of-concept for Zoetrope, "a way of doing films," he said, "that was not traditional."

Warner Bros. was in. Seven scripts. Coppola's lucky number.

Coppola burst into the little theater on Beach Street, where Lucas was casting *THX*, with the incredibly good news: "George, I gotta tell you, we succeeded."

Actors, waiting to be seen, looked to Coppola, baffled.

"Not only did I get *THX* off the ground, but I got six other movies off the ground. I even got that film that you and John are working on, the *Apocalypse Now*, I got that off the ground too. I got seven movies! And I got a go-ahead to do *THX*! We're on our way, and they're gonna fund American Zoetrope!"

None of them could believe it—until it came true: "The idea," said Milius, "that [Coppola] had sort of conned them somehow into bringing this motley entourage . . ."

And just in time, too. The eighty thousand dollars' worth of German equipment Coppola had ordered was fast arriving, and Korty, in lieu of their dreamed-of Victorian mansion in Marin County, had found, in March 1969, a storage space in San Francisco: the top floor of an empty warehouse, formerly a recording studio, with ample garage space to park their equipment truck, in a sketchy neighborhood, South of Market, at 827 Folsom Street. "We used to call it Wine Country," Mona Skager said, "because that's where all the winos were."

"And that's where American Zoetrope essentially started," Coppola said, on a fierce budget, a lot of freedom, and, racing to finish *The Rain People* in time to submit it to the San Sebastián Film Festival, a serious deadline.

Walter and Aggie Murch—with "a weekend, a baby and five thousand dollars with which to find a home in two days"—loaded up a rental truck with equipment and reels and reels of sounds and took off north from Los Angeles to Folsom Street. Exhausted from overwork, Walter fell asleep on the way to San Francisco, his head on Aggie's lap as she drove, their baby, Walter Junior, bedded down on the floor by her feet. "We were going to change the world," Murch said.

The Murches put a down payment on a houseboat in Sausalito, but Walter spent day and night in the warehouse on Folsom: "Literally a KEM sitting in a warehouse and a lot o' dreams," Lucas described it. Hastily converting into an office space and postproduction facility, the warehouse buzzed and clanged with the sounds of teardown and installation and the echoes of the cavernous, dusty storage room where Murch had to mix *The Rain People* on a state-of-the-art KEM that kept breaking down and whose instruction manual was written only in German. What else could they do? "I spent the budget we had for mixing on that machine," Coppola said, "so we had no choice but to use it." (Fortunately, the telex machine worked, so they could troubleshoot with an expert in Germany, one telexed question at a time.) But even when they had a semi-functional KEM ("I don't think we ever got it to completely work," Coppola said), barely two weeks before their San Sebastián premiere, they didn't have projectors. So, they put the film on a dubber, and Coppola filmed it with an amateur Sony camera, but the image, when they played it back on the monitor, appeared upside down.

"I'll work with this German equipment," Murch declared, "but I'm not going to mix the picture upside down."

Coppola seized the monitor. "Look!" He flipped the television upside down. That's it!

For the next three days, they toiled: Murch; composer Ronnie Stein; Eleanor's brother, Bill Neil; sound recordist David Macmillan; and Mona Skager, with Coppola on hand and in and out of consciousness, sleeping and emerging from cardboard boxes the equipment had arrived in. "I think more than anything else," Macmillan said, "it was just that youthful spirit with Francis that you were willing to try anything." There was, in fact, no other choice but to try. "[American Zoetrope was] always in over our head, technologically speaking," Murch said. "I kind of enjoy that. . . . You're trying to both make the film and learn this new technology. It keeps you from getting too settled in your ways." If necessity was the mother of invention, then American Zoetrope would be the mother of necessity.

At two o'clock in the morning on the day they had to get *The Rain People* on a plane to Hollywood so a clean optical track could be made for San Sebastián, they all began coughing uncontrollably, "what looked like simultaneous seizures," Murch said.

"It was me," Coppola confessed.

"What do you mean?"

"I bought a ballpoint pen filled with Mace," he said: research for *The Conversation*.

Five hours later, they were on the plane, with the film, headed to L.A.

The clock ticking on their San Sebastián premiere, Coppola tended the garden of American Zoetrope, toiling on his ideas for *The Conversation*, encouraging Milius to just "keep going, keep writing" *Apocalypse Now*—Milius had heard that Ariel Sharon went scuba diving after the Six-Day War; so, why not surfing in Vietnam?—and catching up on Lucas's latest draft of *THX*. "Boy, you're right," Coppola told him, "you really *can't* write," and he hired him a cowriter, a playwright-novelist who didn't get what Lucas was trying to do, so Coppola then added the *THX* script to his own workload. He brought Lucas up to his cabin in Big Bear, and for a week they thrashed it out together before Coppola himself cried mercy. "Do you know anybody else that could help you with this?" he asked Lucas.

"Maybe Walter. He's strange like me."

Murch, whom with Matthew Robbins at USC had written the two-page treatment for Lucas's student film version of *THX*, hit the ground running. For about a month, he and Lucas traded pages back and forth, scribbling scenes in longhand. Their collaboration was seamless: anticipating possibilities for sound supplied Murch with story ideas that, in turn, gave Lucas directorial ideas that Murch reconstituted into new ideas for sound. "That sort of mutual influence is something we experienced in film school," Murch observed. Was there ever before a sound designer–screenwriter? "That was part of the American Zoetrope dream . . ." Murch said, "to hire fewer people and have them on longer, rather than hire a bunch of people at the very last minute to do something . . ." Not likely in the unionized world of Hollywood. As Murch was learning, "if you did have enough time, a single person could actually do a very good job doing everything on a film."

Meanwhile, Eleanor Coppola was responsible for much of the Folsom Street décor. There was, of course, no money in the budget for a professional decorator and almost nothing for furnishing, so, true to Zoetrope, she took a leap: "I somehow passed myself off as a designer," she wrote. She ordered 110 yards of black Duvetyne (to mask the screen in the screening room, still under construction) and scraped off the plaster to expose the wood beams and brick, but the rest of the new Zoetrope building, color-blasted in mustard (to cover the dull gray soundboards on the walls), silver (wallpaper in the lounge), and Marimekko (wall hangings), was cheerily psychedelic, though it wasn't Eleanor but the construction workers who were actually dropping the acid, creating a certain amount of concern—but then again, without the money, whom else could they get? Colored inflatable chairs and sofas popped against orange and red and purple striped walls hung with portraits of the gods: Griffith, Eisenstein, Kubrick, and Kurosawa looking down over Zoetrope's loftlike lounge. The lounge, open to all, was right off the Folsom Street entrance and centered on an antique oak and blue baize pool table and an industrial-size espresso machine that stretched gleamingly high, like an artwork from the future. Nearby, in a place of prominence, was a display of actual zoetropes reverently maintained in Lucite.

In June 1969, *The Rain People* won Coppola San Sebastián's Golden Shell for Best Film, but a month later the film was released modestly to mixed reviews.

Following the desperate flight, never fully understood, of pregnant Natalie Ravenna from her husband, Vinny, *The Rain People* is saturated in isolation—Natalie's from herself and, disconcertingly, ours from her. "The way women come out in my movies," Coppola would admit, "is very strange." The problems he had directing Shirley Knight are apparent throughout; in her tension and discomfort, her remorseless self-absorption, Knight's Natalie is an alienated character out of Antonioni. Her presence edges *The Rain People* into a story about emotional withdrawal, failure to connect—a condition Coppola, boyhood loner, understood. But the outlines of a different story are evident in the progressive brightening, rain to shine, the shift from cage imagery—obstructive branches, fences, telephone booths, animal farms—to the wide-open vistas of the American West. This is the story—a story of connection—it seems Coppola had hoped to tell.

He had, he said, always wanted to make a love story. One day he would.

On Lucas's first day of shooting the feature-length *THX 1138*, Coppola gathered together the crew—"strictly bench players," cinematographer Stephen Lighthill called them—inside the Zoetrope garage on Folsom Street, where the old *Rain People* utility van was waiting, ready with gear, and told them a story, *theirs*: It was "about how they were going to challenge Holly-wood," composer Jim Mansen said, "that Hollywood was dead and that the quality of the people that we could bring into the San Francisco scene to make things happen was going to carry the idea and the success of Zoetrope going forward." They needed reminding: San Francisco was a 16 mm town, and the THX crew, mainly documentary filmmakers, was, like their direc-tor, George Lucas, new to dramatic film. "I'm not sure a Hollywood crew would have given George the same level of dedication," Mansen said.

Lucas's riskiest decision was also his smartest: to shoot *THX 1138* like a documentary that didn't *look* like a documentary; to use real locations; to rely on natural lighting and three cameras for maximum coverage, includ-ing an Eclair borrowed from his friend and mentor Haskell Wexler; and, finally, to save the lion's share of innovation for postproduction, when he and Murch would have maximal freedom at minimal expense. Wisely, they would be stealthy and covert. "The financing was iffy," Mona Skager said, "and we never knew if [Warner Bros.] would like the rushes or if they were going to pull the plug." Shooting shallow focus for a two-dimensional look, Lucas knew, would both visualize the feeling of claustrophobia and free them from having to light and decorate the entire shot. Faster was cheaper. "A lot of the time, I didn't rehearse at all," Lucas wrote. "It felt like work-ing on a very large student film," Murch said. Permits? With only a fifteen-person crew, they could slip in and out just in time without them. "We were sort of getting in there, getting our shots before the police came and then running as fast as we could," Lucas said. He was having fun, though you wouldn't know it to watch him; while working, he ran the emotional gamut from opaque to distant, more like an accountant than an artist, but his long suits—clarity and efficiency—won him admiration from the crew.

Coppola rarely appeared on set. As it was, he had enough on his hands, early in December 1969, preparing for American Zoetrope's opening night party; supervising construction on Folsom Street; recruiting scripts from Robbins, Ballard, Milius, et al.; keeping Calley at a friendly distance with happy progress reports; and personally greeting the drunks, vagabonds, thrill seekers, young hippies, old Beats, punk kids, filmmakers, and artists of every stripe who had heard Francis Ford Coppola was keeping his door open to good ideas. Unlike a Hollywood executive who traffics in professional talent,

Coppola devoted one day a week to hearing stories from civilians, no matter how inexperienced. If they came recommended, he heard them. (And always: "How about an espresso?") He welcomed even those with only a casual interest in filmmaking. If they wanted to direct at American Zoetrope, his only stipulation was their story had to be *theirs*, an original screenplay—no adaptations. His policy of embrace was murder on the Zoetrope secretary—on a given day, Coppola estimated that as many as twenty newcomers would pour through—who gamely greeted walk-ins from behind her hyperfuturistic glass front desk. But no one took a job at American Zoetrope because the work was easy and paid well; they came for the adventure, and on that score, Coppola never failed.

"Film students walk in and get weak at the knees," he told one of about a dozen journalists who toured his ten thousand square feet and a half-million dollars' worth of freedom: the offices that doubled as recording studios; the seven editing rooms that doubled as offices, with two KEMs and two Steenbecks *each*; the screening room, which could transform into a mixing stage around the three-screen Keller dubbing machine Coppola had bought in Germany, the only one of its kind in the United States, fit for anything, Super 8 to 70 mm, whirring forward *and* back at twenty-four, forty-eight, or one hundred frames per second . . .

"The company itself is financed by me, essentially," Coppola told the journalists. "The films are financed by the major studios, primarily Warner Bros., although we're beginning to talk now with others. We're trying to have a few high-profit projects to ensure our survival." Hopefully, Lucas's next effort, "about an army colonel who's an insane surfer and takes a post in Vietnam because the waves aren't breaking right," would bring in the blockbuster grosses to finance the rest of their slate, each done for under a million and a half.

In addition, American Zoetrope was moonlighting in documentary and television, the latter an ideal venue, Coppola thought, to give those first-time filmmakers their break. He would hold weekly screenings of their work at the Thursday Night Film Festival, and would serve up North Beach Chinese on the house. John Korty, who had taught film at Columbia, was even talking about holding weekend seminars so anyone "could see and hear as much as possible in two days," one of many nonprofit programs geared toward sharing film and the filmmaking experience with the Bay Area community.

Community—Zoetrope would do whatever it could. Perhaps even more than it could. In November, Korty got a panicked call from "these hippie filmmakers" covering the Native American Occupation of Alcatraz, asking to borrow Zoetrope's cameras (Coppola said yes) and then, days later, its film stock (yes again), and eventually, lab fees ("In the end, I'll always say yes") that they never paid back. "I was a patsy," Coppola said. "I never had anything as a kid, so whenever anyone needed stuff I would be prone to give it." Then there was the time, in December 1969, when the Maysles brothers, documentarians, came to shoot the Rolling Stones' concert at Altamont— Lucas and Murch showed up with a 16 mm Arri-S with a 1,000 mm lens— there had been a murder, which they had caught on film, and they requested access to Zoetrope's KEM. Coppola wanted them to have it gratis, "but we've just painted all of the floors at Zoetrope, and it's locked, and you can't go up the stairs or walk because it'll be totally ruined."

"Oh, we'll pay. We'll pay to repaint it."

Coppola okayed this, too, and on the designated weekend, the Maysles met him at the Folsom Street entrance, ruined the paint job as expected, watched as Coppola loaded the film onto the KEM—"No one knew how to work it"—and found it for them: the moment of the murder. A shooting. "And you saw the hand come out," Coppola remembered. "And you saw the gun. . . . Of course they never paid us for the rental. They never paid us for the floor." Henceforth, Coppola vowed he would be careful about who would be allowed access, but when Warner Bros. called to ask for Zoetrope's KEMs—three new KEMs Coppola had been expecting for three months—to cut their documentary *Woodstock*, Coppola consented to have the machines shipped to New York, "mainly," he explained, "because of Marty [Scorsese]," one of the picture editors. The KEMs—as Mona Skager would have predicted—were returned beat-up and unpaid for. One of them Coppola then rented to Fox. When it broke—"They were threading it wrong," he said—the studio called for help, and Coppola himself appeared to fix the problem. That's how he discovered that *Patton*—starring George C. Scott instead of Burt Lancaster—was finally getting made, and to Coppola's astonishment, his script had been reinstated. Only a few battle scenes had been beefed up by writer Edmund North, who would share screen credit with Coppola. "I was so happy," Coppola said. It meant a highly visible credit on what looked like a popular and critical success and the promise of much-needed income.

A few times a week, Lucas would pop into Zoetrope, "and there would be all these crazy things going on down there. Not only people just sort of walking off with equipment, but people yelling and screaming and all kinds of arguments and threats and people stealing other people's movies. Just craziness." Lucas would just shake his head, muttering, "I don't know how you guys can stand it down here," and retreat to the safety of his own attic in Mill Valley, his own bucolic Zoetrope apart from Coppola's urban Zoetrope, and edit *THX* with Marcia, assistant and wife. They had asked Murch, himself editing sound on the Moviola downstairs, to help them heave the giant Steenbeck up into the attic. (Murch got under it; the Lucases pushed.) "Walter and I were working simultaneously, so I could react to his sounds and recut the film according to what he was doing," Lucas said. "We were inspiring each other as we went, rather than just doing the picture and attaching sounds to it."

As former film students, Murch and Lucas approached postproduction sound with a historical awareness most of their forefathers had lacked. In the four decades since *The Jazz Singer*, the shift from optical sound (recorded and printed next to the film images for accurate synchronization) to magnetic sound (recorded separately for maximal flexibility) had not done much to shift audio aesthetics in Hollywood, where the prevailing "hear what you see" approach largely confined movie sound to the literal: see the gun being shot, hear the bullet. This was the stock "library" approach. But, with the exception of a single punch and a flash of lightning, all *THX* sounds were handmade, recorded by Murch, and not intended to convey the literal. Their new sounds were the "instruments" of Lucas's *THX* orchestra: the tinkling of an old music box slowed way down; "a vague clinking" Murch pulled from the air of San Francisco's Exploratorium; women screaming as loud as they could in a Zoetrope bathroom; a haunting tincture of Murch shouting in tongues over rushing water . . . "There are a few electronic sounds," Murch said, "but mostly it's organic sounds that are taken out of context and distorted and turned upside down and put in another context."

Adding to the picture, they implied more world than was seen, "the sonic equivalent of depth of field photography," as Murch explained it. "That's the greatest thing, I think, that film can do," he said, "that is, to provoke an image or a sensation that is not on the screen but is elicited from the mind of the audience."

As Lucas's cut evolved, Murch's sonic world changed. Having all the equipment at hand and only him, Lucas, and Marcia at work on the film enhanced the unity of expression, blurring the distinction among dialogue, music, and effects. Working the Zoetrope way, they moved faster, and their creative engagement heightened. This would have been impossible in Hollywood, where the sound editor turned his sounds over to the sound mixer—as inefficient and artistically counterintuitive as having the director of photography light a scene for the operator to shoot as he liked, Murch thought. In Lucas's attic, sound editor Murch was free to be his own mixer, on a movie he himself had helped conceive and write. It was, Murch said, "a paradise for us as film students."

"*THX* was the best experience I had," Lucas agreed. "I was the editor, the director of photography, the lighting cameraman." In fact, it was the best filmmaking experience he would *ever* have. "I owe it all to Francis," he said. "Instead of having to pay the bills or do a rewrite on some movie, I got to do something I really wanted to do."

"There's no question that *THX* would have taken 14 weeks for a major Hollywood studio to shoot," Coppola said. "We shot it in seven. There's no question that it would have cost them at least $1.5 million; it cost us somewhere near $800,000. As for post-production time, they could probably get it done quicker. Why? Because my filmmakers don't want to turn their post-production over to an army of other people. They want to do it with their own hands."

Through intimacy, innovation, interdisciplinarity, and independence, they had grown as artists, technicians, friends. "The friendships of the guys are deep," Aggie Murch observed, "and of pure love. Their respect for each other grew quickly as they recognized the courage they needed, and found, to put their work out into the world." The same applied to her and Eleanor: "If one of us got sick, really sick, suddenly, there were four more women in your kitchen, bringing a picnic or whatever," Aggie explained. "Ellie and

I would take turns feeding the big boys and the crew and/or watching out for the little ones. But often they—Gio, Roman, and Walter Junior (Francis called him Walter Minor)—could be found playing and sleeping in piles of cables, with the film coming together around them." Little Roman would hide under the mixing console, explore his dad's rolltop action desk (compartments!) and dress up in bulky battery belts left lying around (Batman!). His older brother, Gio, illustrated newsletters with cartoon portraits of Lucas, of his mother, and of his bushy-bearded father. "So it was really more of a lifestyle, almost, than it was like a film company," Coppola said.

American Zoetrope formally debuted in Hollywood's consciousness on December 11, 1969—"I've been waiting all my life for this," Coppola told a local reporter—with a full-page ad in *Variety* of a black zoetrope against a white background and only a single line of explanation: "ZOETROPE MEANS LIFE REVOLUTION."

It was party time—opening night. "Who's the most beautiful woman in San Francisco?" Coppola excitedly asked a visiting *Chronicle* reporter.

"Joanne Kobrin."

"Invite her. Invite them all. My wife is giving me four hours off during the party."

The next day, the Folsom Street headquarters was "packed, just packed with people," Mona Skager said, for a wild launch that lasted, by Coppola's clock, all day. True to form, Coppola had invited everyone for food, grass, and dance: Bill Graham, Jerry Garcia, Zoetropers and their families of course, the acid-brained carpenters (who still hadn't finished the job) . . . "You had dyed in the wool hippies," Milius said, "you had communists, you had Maoists, you had anarchists . . ." Milius called himself a Zen anarchist. "We were gonna change society," he said. There was self-appointed designated drinker Tony Dingman, who was rumored to have a law degree but had given it up to write poetry and hang with fellow poets Lew Welch, Gene Ruggles, and Lawrence Ferlinghetti . . . That night, Coppola was "impresario and public dreamer," Robbins said. John Milius brought Murch up to speed on *Apocalypse*; Carroll Ballard, paranoid about earthquakes, stared down the crack that ran through the building; John Calley and Freddie Weintraub clung executive-like to the colored walls. At one point, Ron Colby spotted a guy nobody recognized disappearing with an Eclair camera under his raincoat, and, it seemed, Calley and Weintraub vanished with him. "It was like a little bit of bedlam," Colby recalled, nothing like a Hollywood party. "The little office on Folsom was exciting," Dean Tavoularis said, "because it wasn't a big studio but a little studio, a studio run by artists. So, you felt empowered somehow. You didn't feel like when you work at, let's say, Columbia [and] all these big moguls were there. There was Francis. Francis was a guy you hang around with."

The opening night party had set the tempo. People simply wanted to be at American Zoetrope. Lucas brought a friend from USC, Willard Huyck, to show Coppola *The Naked Gypsies*, his script about a theater troupe that travels the country scandalizing citizens with their radical, sometimes nude performances. It was a road movie.

"I read the script," Coppola told Huyck at their first meeting on Folsom Street, "and I think it's really great. It's the kind of thing American Zoetrope wants to make." Drawing a stack of papers from his desk drawer, he said, "I've got a contract for you to join us." He handed Huyck the papers.

"What does that mean?"

"It's a contract to write and direct six movies."

"Great. Well, I've just got an agent—"

"That's a problem. Now you're going to want your agent to get into this."

"Yeah, but I'm paying him ten percent. I should at least call him."

"Go ahead and call him."

Huyck dialed Mike Medavoy. "Mike, I'm up with Francis Coppola and we just had this meeting and he wants me to sign a contract—"

"What contract?"

"It's a six picture deal. I get to write and direct."

"Well, you can't sign. What does it say?"

Huyck signed anyway, and *The Naked Gypsies* was brought into the fold, joining American Zoetrope's *Santa Rita* (about the tragedy and consequences of "Bloody Thursday," the uprising at Berkeley's People's Park), to be written and directed by Zoetrope's "token radical," Lucas's friend Steve Wax; *Have We Seen the Elephant?* (a madcap tale of a garbage man and his fascination with the California gold rush), written and directed by John Korty; Milius's

Apocalypse Now; Lucas's follow-up to *THX*; and *Who's Garibaldi?*, a love story written and directed by Coppola and starring Broadway actor Al Pacino. And there was more, always more: *The Air Conditioned Dream*, a script from Huyck and wife Gloria Katz; *Night Ride Down*, a black comedy about the porn industry also by the Huycks; *The Privateer*, a motorcycle picture from Matthew Robbins and USC film grad Hal Barwood, to be directed by Robbins; Carroll Ballard's feature debut, *Vesuvia* (a soldier returns from the war and descends into madness and fantasy); *Atlantis Rising*, an original musical from experimental filmmaker Scott Bartlett; and of course Coppola's *The Conversation*, which he'd written, he hoped, for Marlon Brando. Further projects included Robert Dalva's program of industrial and educational documentaries, including a series for the President's Cabinet Committee for Voluntary Action and the Office of Economic Opportunity; Korty's documentary short about American photographer Imogen Cunningham; and August Coppola's curriculum for a university-level course in film study. There was conference room talk of a film about Eldridge Cleaver . . . a potential investment from Mike Nichols . . . maybe a project with John Schlesinger . . . something with Haskell Wexler . . . Kubrick wanted to have a look around . . . Even Stanley Kramer, Hollywood's leading middlebrow extraordinaire, called for a visit . . . and, yes, Orson Welles.

Coppola was doing the dishes in the conference room when word came that the man himself was on the phone, wanting to speak with him. Coppola ran. "And I'm talking to Orson Welles," he recalled in disbelief. "I'm trying to be, you know, appropriately grown up." Coppola listened as that "resonant voice" told a tale he refused to accept: Orson Welles, perhaps America's greatest filmmaker, could not find work in Hollywood? It was a sad sign of the times, a horrifyingly inspiring validation of sorts. This is what American Zoetrope was for! Zoetrope meant life revolution! As Walter Murch explained it, "[Zoetrope] was, in a sense, a revolution of the hopeless," and what could be more hopeless than a god in need of saving, or more hopeful than having the means to rescue him?

Unless, of course, that god was stubbornly, self-destructively refusing to pitch his idea—what would be *The Other Side of the Wind*—to Warner Bros., despite Coppola's urging. When the call ended, Coppola returned to the conference room, where he had left the water running . . . all over the floor, the carpet, everything—"and we never had the money to fix it." ("That was like a typical day at American Zoetrope," Wax said.) Money? If money was the problem, they had no problem. Money, like the future, would come. Coppola talked of one day buying a country estate with an airport and a fleet of helicopters to fly equipment out to locations, of building inflatable soundstages that could be blown up and set down anywhere, of movies shot on videotape (!) so a director didn't have to wait for dailies to see what he'd shot and could even cut his movie immediately, as he shot it, making cinema virtually at the speed of one's imagination . . .

Coppola burst into Folsom Street one day with a little Beaulieu Super 8 camera under his arm. "This is it. This is the future of filmmaking. I'm gonna make all my films with this."

Korty thought, *What kind of quality is he going to get with that?*

"To hell with Arriflexes, to hell with Mitchells. We're gonna make all of our films with little Super 8 cameras."

Lucas saw in Coppola the zeal of a bright-eyed father on Christmas morning hurriedly assembling the bike before the kids woke up—without the instructions. But what revolution came with an instruction manual?

"What I'm creating here is a shiny little convertible," Coppola explained to Steve Wax. Coppola was P. T. Barnum waving people in for the grand tour. The parties, the girls, the machines, he said, were all part of the publicity plan. More begat more. Abundance drew filmmakers, and investors made headlines. But it was the 1970 release and widespread acclaim of *Patton* that conferred the greatest glory yet on the Folsom Street gang. In the years since Coppola wrote his draft of the screenplay, his fame had remained relatively local, his story—wunderkind on the make—of interest mainly inside Hollywood. With *Patton*, however, he won his first highly visible national raves. Formerly the leader of his generation, Coppola was now a player on the mainstage. And only thirty-one. They'd come from miles around just to experience his energies for themselves. "Francis," Steve Wax observed, "was the greatest magnet to celebrities and creative people the world has ever known."

"You know you're like the Shadow in that radio show?" Wax told Coppola.

"Yeah? What's *The Shadow* about?"

"It's about this guy who clouds men's minds, and that makes him invisible. The only difference is you make yourself visible."

A decade before the idea of synergy—cross-marketing film and other media—became the driving force in Hollywood, Coppola wrote to Warner Bros., urging them to make good on the commercial assets of *Woodstock* and its ilk. But rather than cynically engineer carbon copies, he advised, "we have to go the next step, into a new unknown generation of musical films," and create "an electronic-musical film" using—to the astonishment of Warner executives, surely—video technology. It was only 1970, but: "The idea is to select and build a varying and stimulating soundtrack of musical excerpts from some of the important Warner's Rock and Contemporary music names: The Grateful Dead, Jimi Hendrix, etc. And then utilizing very advanced electronic techniques in Video-taping, and Video-feedback in color, come up with an almost religious, LSD, 1970 *Fantasia*." The project evaporated along with others as Coppola "scurried around arranging emergency loans to pay off the exorbitant remodeling costs of the Zoetrope facility," writer Jesse Ritter observed, all while trying to fix the busted Kellers and Steenbecks he needed to rent in order to keep American Zoetrope going. When Ritter approached him about *Santa Rita*, the still-unwritten script based on his source material, Coppola "would evade charmingly, sending me off in a glow of generalized enthusiasm. There seemed to be something lacking at his center, a hollow place where problems should be faced." Instead, Coppola, shell-gaming, cheerfully posted twenty-thousand-dollar dunning notices to Los Angeles banks and talked of the new writers' retreat he had purchased in Marin, where Zoetropers could get away from the activity and constant distractions of Folsom Street.

"That's a good story," Coppola replied.

Lucas and Milius had caught him up to their new draft of *Apocalypse Now*, its outlandish, high-personality action-satire of the first rock'n'roll war, its melding of American imperialism and California youth culture à la the unforgettable Lt. Col. Bill Kilgore, who orders his boys to surf in the middle of an attack. Buried in there, amid the fantastic set pieces, the madness and chicanery, Coppola saw literature and metaphor. "It sounds like *Heart of Darkness*," he said, "you know, going up the river . . ."

"It was too crazy at Zoetrope," Wax said. "There was just too much going on there. We'd be working and, suddenly, it would be 'Oh, look! Come see the new machines Francis bought!'" Like the two projectors in the screening room/mixing stage, which, improperly installed, threw a skewed image onto the screen and overheated. (Ice packs were applied to the motors and changed every half hour.) Nor were the necessary repairmen, so far from Hollywood, easily available. As with the KEM in the same room, which would start to fail at around four thirty in the afternoon—"You could almost time it," Robert Dalva said—no one could figure out why. Its belts were either too tight or not tight enough and sync was always slightly off. When Murch heard that teeth-snapping sound, he felt it in the pit of his stomach: again, the exasperation of having to stop, fix, rewind picture and sound to the head, and start over. And the feeling that it would probably happen again.

Business managers came and went.

Coppola needed more money. Three hundred grand, in fact.

In April 1970, Warner Bros. agreed to invest further. Meanwhile, when would they be seeing *THX 1138*? How long, the studio wondered anxiously, did it take to edit a little low-budget movie? And when would they get those scripts Coppola was supposedly developing? What was going on up there, so far from Burbank? To the studio, Coppola said, I'm handling George; to George, he said, I'm handling Warner.

In May, after months of successfully holding off Warner Bros., Coppola finally flew down to Los Angeles with a rough cut of *THX* and a beautiful black box proudly inscribed with "American Zoetrope." Lifting the lid for Willard Huyck, who had picked him up at the airport, Coppola revealed their offering, seven original Zoetrope screenplays, including *Apocalypse Now* and *The Conversation*. "Look at this," Coppola crowed to Huyck. "This is what I am going to present to the brass at Warner Brothers."

Before the big screening of *THX 1138*, Coppola alone faced Calley, Warner chairman Ted Ashley, and the other executives waiting in their seats. He then did what he had come to do and what he did so well: raised the room with a full orchestral account of how the film they were about to see was perfectly and prophetically representative of the way they did and would continue to do things at American Zoetrope. Then, at the moment of climactic enthusiasm, he cued the film to roll.

Calley didn't know what to make of *THX*. Certainly, he knew he couldn't sell it. It was too odd, he thought. But something else about this Zoetrope business was far more troubling to him. Originally, Coppola had assured Warner Bros. that he would be a hands-on executive, allowing Lucas freedom to create with the caveat that he would protect Warner's interests, keeping the film close to the screenplay—a story similar to *Brave New World*, Calley recalled—they had approved.

Calley turned to Coppola, sitting beside him, after the film ended. "It's not the screenplay."

"I know."

The other executives hated *THX 1138*.

"What happened?" Huyck questioned Coppola on his way out of the screening.

"They thought the scripts looked really neat—and the box . . ."

"What *about* the scripts?"

"I don't know."

Coppola's most daunting task still lay ahead of him: telling Lucas that Warner Bros. didn't "get" *THX 1138*. Delivering the bad news, he would have to play a new role, closer, in its own way, to Warner Bros. studio executive than leader of the revolution, or even, it could be construed, ally. But it was in everyone's best interest to bring Lucas to a compromise, to encourage him to recut the movie to suit Warner Bros. and get *THX* the release it deserved—or else, very likely, it would be dropped into theaters and forgotten. Coppola was responsibly playing the long game, but compromise was precisely what American Zoetrope had been founded to avoid.

What Zoetrope hadn't foreseen was their reliance on Warner for distribution. Lucas said, "As long as they have that stranglehold, we're just going to keep trying to get things done and never get them done."

It would be a problem for all young filmmakers. Production financing was one thing, but how independent could Zoetrope, or any fringe filmmaking enterprise, really be when the studios basically controlled what movies got into theaters?

Their dream was in Warner's hands now.

American Zoetrope divided. There would be speculation that Coppola froze, buckled, reneged, that he chose to keep an amicable relationship with Warner Bros. over *THX*, that he was sacrificing Lucas, even using his friends' future films, if need be, to clear the way for his own. Such speculation presented him as more salesman, showman, and producer than director. After all, how good *were* his movies? *Finian's Rainbow*? *The Rain People*?

Isolation. It was the cold tower of leadership. Ironic, given that Coppola had founded Zoetrope only to immerse himself in a troupe, a community, the way he had at Hofstra. Where were his thanks? Who else had sold his house to keep them afloat, weathered the accusations of megalomania and wasteful indulgence he read about in the press? Why was it so hard for even those on his team to accept that his intentions were pure? Like Harry Caul, protagonist of *The Conversation*, it was he who was suddenly being watched, traced, threatened. Or, at least, it often felt that way. And then despair: "What am I doing? Am I doing what I want to be doing? Everything is so hard. Nobody likes me." And the rages would set in . . . the shouting, the throwing . . . The failure . . . the failure to save his family . . .

"I think that Francis was caught between a rock and a hard place," Milius said. Korty, too, was among the compassionate. "There was a change in the whole industry," he reflected. "It was a gamble Francis made when he opened Zoetrope at a time everyone expected good things from *Rain People* and [when] *Easy Rider* was the freshest thing on everyone's mind." In the ensuing year, *Airport*, a giant, star-studded studio disaster movie, had won the box office, rocking Hollywood from its counterculture dream, "and the ground beneath Zoetrope," Korty said, "started shaking." Had the days of *Easy Rider* passed so quickly? Or was all Calley's talk about the filmmaker just a come-on? "I felt Calley was a very attractive and a very smart guy who was a movie intellectual," concluded Coppola, "but underneath it all he was the same kind of movie executive dog-eat-dog guy." Warner's Ted Ashley argued in *The Hollywood Reporter*, "We have not changed our concept of making pictures. Some of the material Coppola submitted to us did not interest us, didn't make sense for us. But there has been no change in policy. We are looking for interesting films and we are continuing our agreement with Coppola and his company"—with the understanding, that is, that Lucas butchered *THX* to fit their satisfaction. It's as if they took your four-year-old daughter, he told Robbins, and said, "We know how to make her better. We'll just cut off one little finger. She'll still have nine left."

Coppola was instructed to return to Warner Bros. and screen the film for their editorial department. Terrified that someone at the studio would abscond with the print, Lucas instructed Robbins, Murch, and Caleb Deschanel to personally escort him and his canisters of *THX* past studio security and through the gates of Warner Bros. and wait for him while he screened the film. Then, after the screening, when the moment was right, they were to steal into the projection booth and shuttle the film to a secure location off the lot. All agreed, and on the day of the heist, Robbins drove Lucas in his Volkswagen van, which was big enough to hide Murch and Deschanel, past the unsuspecting guard, and unloaded Lucas and the film at the designated screening room. Then they waited, playing cards under the Warner Bros. water tower for the exact running time of *THX 1138*, and appeared, not a minute too late, at the projectionist's door. "We're here to pick up the film." They were handed the film, and off they went.

Now what?

Seeking peace, Coppola called his troops together for a meeting at Zoetrope. "They don't like this film," he explained. "We have to do something. What are we gonna do about this? Are we gonna re-cut it, or are we gonna go make another film? What are we gonna do?"

What choice did they have?

"Dear John," Coppola telexed Calley.

My call earlier this week was to confirm that your meeting
with George Lucas went to your satisfaction. I have talked
with George at length about the measures he is taking
to move the film on to its next stage. He is clarifying
the narrative of the first third of the film, making
the story points fully evident, and although it differs
to a degree from the exact narrative as scripted (it is
simpler), I believe it will work to all our satisfaction
and expectations.

I am a realist about things and fully understand that you
were disappointed by this rough cut. It is a very unusual

film but we all feel sure that it will be well accepted
in this difficult to predict market both critically and
financially.

Pushing for genre, Warner wanted Lucas to get to the action quicker. But Lucas still wouldn't budge, not enough. Tired of being the go-between, Coppola lost his patience and insisted that Lucas and Warner Bros. speak directly. As expected, the Warner/Lucas meeting degenerated into a shouting match. Fred Weintraub kept pushing Lucas to introduce the supernatural creatures earlier in the film, in the first act ("put the freaks up front" became the grim Zoetrope slogan of the hour), but that change wouldn't address the studio's issue with the film's pacing, Lucas argued. You can't add *and* subtract. It was one or the other. Both, Weintraub argued back: They'll forgive you anything if you grab 'em right away, and also take out all that weird sound. And make it more of a love story. But it's not a love story, Lucas countered. It's about freedom. It's about fighting the system.

"Just cut five minutes from it," Weintraub insisted. "Otherwise we're not gonna release it."

"Okay, we'll cut it."

And that was the end of it.

All that over five minutes of film. That's it. "So there was no point for them to do it," Lucas concluded, "other than to exercise some power and say, 'We can screw around with your movie so we're going to.'" By the same token, Warner would complain, all this hassle for only five minutes? Who needs these kids?

On June 1, Warner Bros. formally rejected Willard Huyck's *The Naked Gypsies*.

In September, they rejected Steve Wax's *Santa Rita*.

In October, they rejected Matthew Robbins and Hal Barwood's *The Privateer*.

Then they turned down *The Conversation*.

"You don't like this?" Coppola pleaded with executive Jeff Sandford.

"I must tell you, I don't think this is going to be an interesting movie."

On Thursday, November 19, 1970—"Black Thursday," as it would always be known at American Zoetrope—Warner Bros. summarily extricated itself from all dealings with Coppola's organization. It had been only one year and five days since the signing of Zoetrope's incorporation papers. What did they have to show for it?

Lucas—three years of his life spent, penniless; with a maligned movie that wouldn't be released for half a year (and would probably be dropped)—took it out on Coppola. "You didn't fight hard enough."

But Coppola had other wars. He had come to Steve Wax with the idea of starting an entirely new union. "Pretty soon," Wax said, "we had about a hundred people coming to meetings," writers, editors, directors. They called themselves the Film Workers Union. "The idea," Wax explained, "was that all the unions were full of shit and we were going to create our own organization," in which workers from each union would join together, thereby increasing their bargaining power.

But Hollywood found out.

"We got to stop it," Coppola told Wax one day over the phone. "The studios don't want to have an alternative union."

"You can't stop a union."

How many dreams could a single dream hold? Coppola's was not foremost a political revolution, but how successful could American Zoetrope hope to be artistically if it was still and forever shackled to Warner's purse strings—as the ongoing calamity of *THX* demonstrated—"independent" in spirit only? "My enthusiasm and my imagination had simply gone beyond any financial logic," Coppola would concede. "The only principle was that of freedom and of young directors; that was vague, very vague."

The dispute over the union idea ended Wax's relationship with Zoetrope. Moving on, he founded Cinema Manifesto, a "completely communist" (Lucas said) filmmaking collective. Their productions would be characterized by complete uniformity of power, a political dream, Coppola maintained, that clashed with the artistic one. "What happened was that you had everybody on the crew telling everybody what to do," he said. "It was hopelessly naive and ridiculous." It was a position that would earn Coppola further criticism, even charges of hypocrisy; Francis the "idealist" was, in truth, Francis the manipulator, they sneered. He had claimed a film was a collaboration between "orchestra" and "conductor." But surely his critics had to understand that even the most utopian arrangement needed leadership, or else it would succumb to anarchy.

Had he led?

Life on Folsom Street absorbed the feel of failure. Some grumbled that Coppola, always on the financial brink, was exploiting his people, all non-union, both below and above the line. Film editor Richard Chew was among those "working minimum wage, long hours, hundred dollars a week, seven days a week, and it was always like, 'Hey, we're artists, we're creating something here!' You know, 'Don't worry about that. You can eat tomorrow! You know, this is gonna last forever!'" Carroll Ballard surmised, "[Francis] was a den mother, but he was also co-opting everybody. That was my sort of cynical view of what was really behind a lot of what he wanted to do with Zoetrope."

"That's what destroyed the whole idea of Zoetrope, in my opinion," Ballard said. "It required a certain amount of loyalty for everybody to each other, and it didn't happen. Ended up being every man for himself." Believing that Coppola had introduced to Lucas and Milius the notion of using *Heart of Darkness*—which Ballard had been talking about adapting since film school—for *Apocalypse Now*, he exploded, betrayed. Steven Spielberg had foreseen dissolution. "I just feel about groups and getting together that it's great to have friends who are directors, because you trade scripts and points and conversation and gossip and everything else," he would say. "But when it comes time to getting a business together, it gets so nasty. And the attorneys move in, and suddenly the person you used to call four nights a week just to rap you can't talk to anymore because the attorneys have sort of put a restraining order on your conversation."

The attorneys did move in. That $300,000 Warner Bros. had invested in Coppola?

Dear Francis:

As requested I am setting forth below a breakdown of the amounts
paid to you or in your behalf in regards to the $300,000 loan to you
and American Zoetrope . . .

It was a loan.

"No one told me," Coppola said. "I didn't know it was a loan. I thought
it was like any other deal."

It was a loan that Coppola, having spent the money for its intended purpose, couldn't pay back. And with those Zoetrope scripts—*The Conversation*, *Apocalypse Now*, etc.—in the possession of Warner Bros., languishing
in turnaround, he had nothing on hand to sell.

Suddenly, the situation was dire—and unmistakably punitive. Calley
would say that his hands were tied, but $300,000 of Warner Bros. money
was not much of a rope. They could have offered Coppola a writing or
directing deal and called it even. That they demanded reimbursement
knowing full well that Coppola couldn't afford it seemed a pointed effort
to publicly brand American Zoetrope as Coppola's folly, to guillotine the
insurgents in the town square and fly high the banner "Don't Fuck with Big
Hollywood, Dream as You're Told."

It was a bad Christmas 1970. American Zoetrope faced imminent bankruptcy.

Still, Coppola gave a holiday party on Folsom Street, albeit a small one.
That night, he gifted David Macmillan, who had tried his best, since *The
Rain People*, to keep the KEMs running, a Swiss Army Knife.

"Francis," Macmillan responded in thanks, "I have about four thousand
dollars. That's about all I have . . ." He made $2.50 an hour.

That Christmas saw the release of Paramount's *Love Story*. Based on Er-
ich Segal's blockbuster novel, it would gross $100 million in four months
and send studios scrambling—as they had once scrambled for the "next"
Easy Rider—for America's next weepie. "[The] American film business once
again is in a state of total confusion," Coppola wrote to *New York Times* col-
umnist Guy Flatley, "looking for trends that are of course not there . . . and

furious at the youthful filmmakers whom they tried to exploit and whom they now feel exploited them."

It was Mona Skager who noticed that Lucas, attempting to get a project off the ground, had amassed a long-distance phone bill of $1,500. Diplomatically, she approached him. "George," she said, "why should Francis and Zoetrope pay for this?" Lucas, baffled at the expense, went to his father for help and borrowed the uncomfortable sum he needed to reimburse Skager, straining relations between father and son. "I knew nothing about this," Coppola explained later. "I would have told Mona, 'Well, George has a right to.' I never would have charged him." It marked the beginning, Coppola felt, of "a break of faith" between them. "That was when George began to say, 'Well, I'm going to have [my own company]. Zoetrope is Francis's.' It was heartbreaking and unnecessary."

Helpless, Coppola raised the rent, lost the better part of his team, shouldered the blame, and mortgaged what he could, thousands of pieces of equipment, furniture, art: Arriflex cameras; Eclair viewfinders; Caméblimps, the soundproof carrying cases for Caméflex cameras; 12 V DC batteries and chargers ($200 each); Beaulieu Super 8s; zoom lenses (Nikkor, Vivitar, Angénieux . . .); gels; filters; light meters; NAGRAs; windsocks; transformers; microphones; headsets; twenty-four 9 V transistors ($1.50 each); an oscilloscope; speakers; TV monitors; his Keller dubbing machine and twenty-channel stereo mixer with individual fader control; white-and-gold reflector umbrellas; hundreds of bulbs; a Mole-Richardson reflector stand ($30); six Mole-Richardson baby-soft lights; tripods; a Mitchell hi-hat; a Colortran crab dolly; a western dolly; three 8-inch C-clamps ($7.50 each); a rainmaking machine; a Bölzer two-way radio; Halliburton cases; 35 mm splicers; Moviola editing bins; a Wellack film rack; synchronizers; a 35 mm portable projector; a projection screen; multicolored inflatable chairs and sofas; multicolored cube tables; photos of Kurosawa, of Fellini, of Eisenstein, of D. W. Griffith, of Orson Welles; an espresso machine ($1,400); an Olivetti typewriter ($500); a Dodge van camera truck ($4,000); and a three-hole punch ($4) . . . "Zoetrope," Coppola would say, "was picked clean." But Coppola's debt to Warner was still outstanding.

"Did Francis and George's dream come true?" Robert Dalva mused in retrospect. "Almost."

Warner Bros. dumped *THX* in a couple of theaters and yanked it after a few weeks.

"It's basically the death of a dream," Ron Colby conceded.

"The dream," said Lucas in anger and despair, "never existed."

Far, far away, in the Kurtz compound, in the high huts watched over by coconut palms, Kurtz's tribe of 250 Montagnards, played by the local Ifugao, slept, ate, celebrated. They were living there, on the location, in their complete and actual jungle village realized by Dean Tavoularis, that did not look like a set at all. To behold the awesome totality of the vista was to be not where one stood, surrounded by cameras and crew, in the Philippines in 1976, but somewhere on the lost river leading back into the heart of old Cambodia.

It is like an exhibition, actor Christian Marquand observed to Eleanor, but somehow better.

Eleanor understood something of what he meant. Before coming to the Philippines, she herself had experimented in the creation of living artworks. "In the museums, occasionally there'd be some very famous woman, Georgia O'Keeffe or someone. But it was ninety-seven percent male artists. We"—she and artist Lynn Hershman—"realized we didn't have a chance in the establishment . . . so we thought, well, we would rent a storefront and just make our own space. Then we had a better idea": They each took a room at the Dante Hotel in North Beach, just up the street from Francis's offices in the Sentinel Building; in her room, Eleanor staged poet and friend Tony Dingman. He simply lived there. "I would come every few days," she said, "and take photos of how the room changed, how his dirty clothes piled up, and how his towel was crumpled in a different way on the rack." At any hour of the day or night, people were welcome to pick up the room key at the front desk and watch Dingman live. "I would take these Polaroids," Eleanor said, "and put them on the wall, so people could see the evolution of time."

Something about the artistic event or shared experience naturally appealed to her, more so than even the art object itself. Perhaps that's really what she was seeking in the Philippines, standing at the center of a great event, the creation of a new world. "Francis is actually the conceptual artist, the ultimate conceptual artist I have been wanting to know," she concluded. His great concept—tempting hell in the jungle—was, paradoxically, a heaven on earth. "He has always wanted to be in this wonderful community of artists at the moment that people would talk about later as some golden era," she wrote in the notebook she had begun just before leaving for the Philippines. His films, it sometimes seemed, were just a pretext for re-creating those communities. *The Rain People*, *The Godfather*, *The Godfather Part II*. Each was a happening, a living theater. But never before had this kind of living come so close to reality. Here in the Philippines, on *Apocalypse*, he had, at last, the money and means to stretch their lives to his imagination's breaking point—and he had been stretching it for so long, and so far from home.

The rebirth: she had seen that. The dying was new.

Coppola and Brando, in Coppola's houseboat, had been talking and talking for hours, interrogating the mystery of Kurtz from every angle—psychological, literary, historical—and as massive Brando, improvising aloud, stood, moved, sat his bulk down again, the boat rocked, and the light on his bald head changed shadow to light to shadow. Seeing the great man in the half-light was facing the presence of something gargantuan but not entirely real, Coppola thought, like an entity of the mind.

It would be a difficult feeling to explain to anyone, let alone cinematographer Vittorio Storaro, who was only just learning English. "You feel him," Storaro clarified. "I don't know, just the presence. He came . . . like a king . . ." It would be dark, but Storaro would push the film a stop . . .

"But you can't see him," Coppola tried, "you must—"

"No, it just—"

"The idea."

"*Sì*, the idea."

From the semidarkness, Storaro and Coppola would summon only a notional Kurtz. The audience would be made to complete the picture for themselves . . .

"This is difficult to understand," Storaro said.

Perhaps they would only show him in pieces, through synecdoche—a part for the whole—his empty lair, his empty bed . . .

"Maybe in an image that we can come up with," Coppola suggested to Storaro, "we can give the presence of Kurtz, the *feeling* of Kurtz, but so your mind can imagine him."

And so, Kurtz would be lit in extreme contrasts—bright light and dark shadow—consciousness and the unconscious, as Storaro formulated it; good *and* evil, order *and* chaos, creation and death. On Kurtz's table, Coppola would place a copy of *The Golden Bough*, an almanac of ancient ritual and a symbolic indication that this king, far from fearing his inevitable assassination, welcomes death as any enlightened figure would the natural cycle of rebirth.

Coppola had cue cards prepared for Brando, but Brando used them only intermittently. Out of laziness, mischief, or inspiration—accounts vary—he would almost exclusively improvise. With Coppola's encouragement, he spun arias as long as forty-five minutes, stunning all present, even himself; for all his expertise in film acting, he had never been allowed so much freedom to live in character. "It was probably the closest I've ever come to getting lost in a part," he would say, "and one of the best scenes I've ever played." Brando was so attuned to the present, so serenely relaxed in Kurtz, that amid one improvised soliloquy, he could reach into the dark and grab a buzzing fly without breaking his thought. This astonished Martin Sheen. When Coppola called cut, Sheen watched with even more astonishment as Brando opened his grip, allowing the fly to escape.

His intuition was remarkable, Sheen thought. On and off camera, he demonstrated an awareness of everything, including the minds of those around him. "Are you free of others' opinions of you?" Brando improvised as Willard prepared to assassinate him. "Are you free of your own opinion of yourself?"

The question stunned Sheen. Since that drunken night at the hotel, he had been asking it himself.

"Hey, Dick White," Coppola radioed, "can I fly this helicopter?"

"I, you know, yeah, it's your helicopter."

On the same channel, Doug Claybourne heard the engines starting up. "Dick White, can he really fly that thing?"

"Sure, he can fly it." Meaning he knew how, not that he was permitted to. (He had no pilot's license.)

White and Claybourne looked up to witness Francis Ford Coppola lifting the chopper six feet into the sky and Dean Tavoularis jumping the hell out.

"My God," Claybourne yelled. "Dick, is—is he gonna be all right? Is he gonna—"

"Sure he'll be all right, but he'll never come back."

"What do you mean he'll never come back?"

"He can't navigate, and he'll never find this little hole. He's got about an hour and a half of fuel."

"My greatest fear," Coppola railed to Eleanor while in Pagsanjan, "is to make a really shitty, embarrassing, pompous film on an important subject, and I am *doing* it! I *confront* it! I *acknowledge*! I will tell you right straight from the most sincere depths of my heart, the film will not be good!"

"It's like going to school," she offered. "You finish your term paper and maybe you get a B instead of an A-plus that you wanted, so you get a B."

He shouted, "I'm gonna get *an F*!"

She would listen coolly, objectively. In keeping notes on *Apocalypse Now*, she was, like a spy, keeping notes on her husband, on his disintegration, his split—splitting herself, wife and author, down the middle, too. Her big NAGRA was sitting right there, recording.

"Why can't I just have the courage to say it's no good?!" he rebuked himself.

Panic, she knew, was a natural outgrowth of his process. "I remember the anxiety he felt and the struggle he had with the script of *Godfather II*," she wrote in her notebook, "and it seems, in retrospect, at that time he was himself dealing with the same themes in his own life—money, power and family. Now he is struggling with the themes of Willard's journey into self and Kurtz's truths that are in a way themes he has not resolved within himself, so he is really going through the most intense struggle to write his way to the end of the script and understand himself on the way." Perhaps this was why he worked: *to* resolve. But he was no painter resolving with paints. Every time out, he "put us all in a circumstance [that] would most likely bring out a piece of work that reflected what the movie was about . . ." He was resolving with *them*, his family.

She was glad to be creating, filming a documentary, albeit a documentary about *his* movie, but *filming* nonetheless. She had often felt like a dilettante, spread thin by the diversity of her commitments, the ties of motherhood, the unknowns of artisthood, and the bouts of self-consciousness working as a woman among men: "Look lady, you've still got the cap on your lens!" But watching Francis through her viewfinder, Eleanor sustained a sense of purpose that, now, when she needed it most, was organizing, saving her inner life. She did not—as she once thought—have to work at home in a studio. She could see the world everywhere. This was a stasis of the "balancing act" she had written her mother about: to make art and to live *simultaneously*. Her camera, as portable as life, would be the way in to herself, filming her husband, giving her her best subject, him.

"This film is a twenty-million-dollar disaster!" he yelled to her. "Why won't anyone believe me? I'm thinking of shooting myself!"

She saw he was also Willard staring down his dossier on Kurtz, his mission, flogging his mind to answer the question "How does a man go bad?" She could see he was beginning to despise the half of himself that couldn't see to the end of the other. "I always had the idea of Willard and Kurtz being the same man . . . And I feel that Willard arriving at the compound to meet Kurtz is like coming to the place that you don't want to go—because it's all your ghosts and all your demons."

All this plus three children, more than a decade of marriage, and her gathering revelation that she was no longer his only sounding board, his first and best audience. It wasn't just the rumors of infidelity; he was promiscuous with his genius now, too, in desperation, sharing it with anyone at hand, collaring housekeepers in the kitchen to listen and respond to his ideas as once only she had.

This is the way the world ends, not with a bang but a whimper.

"It refers to the reality that you die, man, with a whimper and not with a bang," Hopper was telling Coppola. "'Cause you never hear the bang because the—because like you know, the bullet travels faster than the sound. 'Cause light travels faster than the sound, and now we're dealing with light and sound together, but—"

"What I'd like you to try to do, whenever possible, Dennis, is to relate the symmetry and these ideas to America and Vietnam."

"Okay, but like I'm—like I'm ready, like you know, we can do twenty-eight takes, man—we print one."

But it didn't work that way. Directing Dennis Hopper, Coppola thought, was like starting a storm and then trying to control it.

"Cut!" Coppola yelled. "Cut, cut, cut!"

By take ten, Hopper was screaming at him. By take twenty, he had lost it completely, his jugular vein bulging. "Fuck it! What do you want from me?" He was coked up and smelled like filth. They said he was so into the part he had stopped showering. "I've *directed* a fucking million-dollar-movie, man!"

Playing a photojournalist, Hopper had wanted to put actual film in his prop camera, but Coppola refused him; he didn't want images to get back to the States before his movie came out. Hopper called him paranoid, but Coppola knew the press was saying the film was never going to be finished, that he was losing his mind, which made it harder, with each horror story, for him to protect his credit and credibility. They were already saying he had gone AWOL, like Kurtz. But, in fact, he was still fighting. "I wanted to be thought of as American and that America would be proud that if I had $30 million of my own money that I would fearlessly invest it in a movie that had serious themes," he complained. "I was crushed that they ridiculed *Apocalypse* because it seemed to be such an out-of-control financial boondoggle, and yet for *Superman*, which cost so much and was about nothing, there was respect."

Hopper and Tony Dingman went crazy at night. Outside the Rapids Hotel, screaming up at the moon, they disobeyed curfew along with everyone else. Insurgents in the mountains? Have another beer. Have two. "Will notify" was often the only instruction on the call sheet. Cackling, cast and crew pounded caseloads of San Miguel in the Pit, the sunken hotel restaurant, "turning over tables and chairs," Laurence Fishburne said, "and breaking bottles and screaming real loud"; they got hand jobs and more at the Dampa (which promised "Friendly Serving Wenches"); Hopper got low and watched lizards crawl on the ceiling and crash into little pieces on the floor, he got high and heard the guy who claimed he was from Bank of America had a hit on him and sent his girlfriend screaming naked into the halls. Someone lit a mattress on fire and threw it out the window into the pool. "You know, you go to Disneyland, you're gonna act like a little kid," Fishburne said. "Francis had it all worked out."

"Now, conceptual art we were gonna talk about, right?" Hopper asked Eleanor. She was behind the camera.

"Right."

"Okay. Is this conceptual art? I think it's way beyond conceptual art. Conceptual art is something that is a tribal unit enjoying an experience together, which this is . . ." No. Francis, Hopper corrected himself, is building a church.

Coppola would tell his dreams to Dean Tavoularis. In the Philippines, far from his known life, he would tell his old friend how he planned to "make a better telephone, develop a more efficient toaster, improve the style of baseball uniforms, build a beautiful little restaurant, run a revolutionary design school such as Germany's prewar Bauhaus." Tavoularis would remember how he began, dreaming of imaginary spaces, wandering, as a boy, through unbuilt worlds of Rudolph Schindler, Dion Neutra, and Frank Lloyd Wright, the shapers of his architectural fantasies. He saw a garret: *I'd like to go to Paris*, he thought, *and live in a garret and paint*, the La Bohème dream he called a sickness.

Early in 1971, depleted by the gutting of American Zoetrope, Coppola was at zero, alienated from his community, alone.

The Folsom Street headquarters had all but emptied.

Save for Robert Dalva, dutifully cutting commercials (Rice-A-Roni) for money, and John Korty, in postproduction on a TV movie, *The People*, what remained of the dream was a flimsy corporate advertising division, and behind them all, accountant Jean Autrey, dispatched to clean up the mess. Opening a forgotten closet door one day, she discovered boxes upon boxes of unpaid bills. ("I gasped.") The next six months she spent on the phone with collection agencies: "We can give you ten dollars. If you don't want the ten dollars, I can send it to somebody else . . ."

After Warner's betrayal, Coppola had no next move. Without the means to self-finance a personal film, he was likewise averse to returning to any studio, hat in hand, for what would surely be another *Finian's Rainbow* situation. He stayed at home, writing.

Then came Paramount, via Peter Bart, with a glorified soap opera about the Mafia. Coppola read about fifty pages of the novel by Mario Puzo and turned it down.

But Peter Bart, like Coppola, was also out of ideas. Every director of stature had passed on *The Godfather*; alone among them, at least Coppola was Italian. Giving it another shot, Bart traced Coppola to his place in Mill Valley, where he was toiling, under the cover of giant redwoods, on *The Conversation*. Lucas was in a nearby room writing the script Coppola convinced him should be his next movie, *American Graffiti*. Not that the dying of THX gave him much of a chance of making it. That's when Bart's call came.

"Francis, you're just a kid," Bart pleaded. "You can't live your life this way. This could be a commercial movie." He knew all about Coppola's $300,000 debt to Warner Bros. It still had to be paid off. "It'd be irresponsible of you not to do it."

His hand over the receiver, Coppola turned to Lucas. "George, what should I do? Should I make this gangster picture or shouldn't I?"

If Warner's decimation of Zoetrope was Coppola's public defeat, taking *The Godfather* would be his humiliating surrender.

"Francis," Lucas said, "we need the money."

We.

"Okay," Coppola answered Bart. "I'm in."

Caleb Deschanel would say, "Everybody who knew Francis thought he was selling out." What choice did he have? The city had threatened to chain the doors on Folsom Street.

Pregnant with Sofia, their third child, Eleanor followed her husband back to New York for *The Godfather*. While he worked, she took Gio and Roman, seven and six, to MoMA and the Met. "There is infinite art around us if we choose to see it," she had said. Why, then, couldn't this life, this Being a Mother, this Waiting for Francis life, be a work of art? "With Francis, everything is mixed," Storaro had observed. "There is no difference between living with the family, and directing, and shooting." Eleanor envied that.

In adapting the novel, with Puzo, Coppola was proceeding less like a screenwriter than the creator of a bildungsroman, supplying detailed sense memories of his own childhood growing up Italian American, in thrall to a powerful father and star brother, to expand, rather than contract, Puzo's potboiler. Coppola may have lived—in his own mind, *still* lived—as a Fredo, but while re-creating *The Godfather* as a screenplay, there came—on February 23, 1971—an empowering signal of success and a foreshadowing of the inchoate Michael to come: he was nominated for Best Original Screenplay for *Patton*, one of the film's ten nominations, which included Best Picture. Coppola was not yet thirty-two.

On the page (and, later, on the *Godfather* set), the exact emotions were immediately at hand. Michael's sister, Connie, would be played by Coppola's sister, Talia; Carmine, his father, would write the score; baby Sofia, his daughter, would later appear as Michael's baby; and Pacino would end up seeing more of Michael in Coppola than in himself. "So, yes of course it reeks of family," Coppola said. "Because it is a family. It's a real family." Kay, Michael's wife, was a portrait of Eleanor rendered by Diane Keaton—"It's the WASP wife who is not Italian," Eleanor said, "not really a member of the family, always a little on the outside, excluded"—in collaboration with Coppola himself. "Think of how many husbands have kept their wives and held their families together by promising that things would change just as soon as they became vice-presidents or had a hundred-thousand dollars in the bank or closed the big deal," he said. "I've strung my own wife along for thirteen years by telling her that as soon as I was done with this or that project, I'd stop working so hard, and we'd live a more normal life. I mean, that's the classic way husbands lie. Often the lies aren't even intentional. And it's easy to string a woman along for years by doing exactly that." The stage was set, the illusion total. He was making, he said, the most expensive home movie in Hollywood history.

Then the thing that always seemed to happen, the thing that Coppola had always said would never happen again, happened again. Losing himself in the process, immersing himself in the world of the film, Coppola began to change.

His *Godfather* transformation was not, at first, characterized by anything more than an influx of emotion: agitation. The studio was crowding him.

Throughout preproduction, Paramount fought him on Pacino, Keaton, and Brando; they wanted the film to be contemporary and shot in Kansas City. Now, in production, they were still fighting his every move. He wasn't being a leader, they said. "Running a set means you gotta be the guy that makes it go forward," one detractor remarked. "And it just wasn't happening. Nothing got done"—that is, except endless (by Hollywood standards) rehearsals and rewrites. And the schedule kept changing. With its basis in theater, Coppola's discursive method certainly appeared sloppy. Or could it be that, still discovering his story, he wasn't as lost as he seemed?

Paramount freaked. It was the rushes: too shadowy. They couldn't see, they complained. They couldn't hear: Brando was incomprehensible. Coppola obediently offered to reshoot the scene in question; it would take only a day, he assured them, but Paramount refused. Why? They hated the scene, didn't they? No, he realized: It was Warner Bros. vs. Zoetrope all over again. It was *him* they hated. Studio head Robert Evans hated him. The crew hated him. He was being edged out, excluded like a polio boy from the sixth grade. Like Francie, Mr. and Mrs. Coppola's no-good son. "What do you think of this director?" he overheard in the bathroom one day. "He doesn't know anything! What an asshole he is!" He wasn't imagining this.

Jack Ballard, Paramount's head of physical production—"a henchman," production designer Dean Tavoularis described him—would appear on set to scrutinize his work down to the crown moldings. Nor did Coppola have an ally in director of photography Gordon Willis, surly and intransigent throughout. To Coppola, Willis didn't understand actors. To Willis, Coppola didn't understand camera. "I was so frightened and depressed," Coppola said, "that I just wanted to get through the night and day."

But the nights: he wasn't sleeping. It was the recurring nightmares of Elia Kazan, a great director, a giant, a god—at one time, the studio's choice to direct—arriving on set to take over. That had been their plan all along, Coppola decided. Paramount had hired him, a director with no hits, to control him. Line producer Gray Frederickson confirmed that there would be a coup. Coppola said, "My editor, who wanted to direct the movie himself, was meeting with them, telling them that the footage couldn't be cut. He and the assistant director were actively conspiring to get me fired. My producer Al Ruddy was also working behind my back to dump me." It was clear now. He was totally alone—and powerless.

And if he was fired, he would be finished.

On April 15, 1971, he was with his friend Scorsese in New York, watching the Oscar telecast. It was bittersweet: to be nominated, with Edmund H. North, for *Patton*, while *Godfather* was crumbling. Except, he won.

"I don't think they're going to fire you now," Scorsese told him.

It was a surge of self. Scorsese was right and Gray Frederickson agreed: the Oscar was Coppola's restoration. Seizing the power that was his, he summarily fired a traitorous assistant director and a number of disloyal others—"a peremptory strike," he said, one that threw Paramount into "a total dither"—and promptly reshot the "problematic" Brando scene to perfection.

It was his movie now.

His sister, Talia, witnessed the transformation. "When you play a role of force, a king or queen," she said, "and you have not been by casting or nature that size yet, it suffuses you. You saw Francis emerge . . . not just from people applauding, but from something of the epic size of the project and of the central character—a dark character, a Machiavellian character, but a man also appealing." Making *The Godfather* was Coppola's education in power. The ordeal instilled in him a young don's command of diplomacy, cunning, and—against Paramount's Robert Evans—necessary force. Insisting, against Evans's wishes, on housing postproduction at Zoetrope in San Francisco, Coppola expeditiously funneled funds, garnered from facility rentals and his *Godfather* salary, back into Folsom Street. "Thank god," he said, "I had my studio and my people."

As Coppola edited (with William Reynolds and Peter Zinner), Zoetrope general manager Christopher Pearce touted a revived open-door policy with the "Associates of American Zoetrope" program, "a group of people who can come in whenever they want and play pool or drink coffee and talk and see what is going on," as Pearce put it. From freelance cameramen to established directors, filmmakers of all ranks were once again invited to make Folsom their base of operations, "especially if you're young and just starting out," Pearce explained. To that end, the company published the

Zoetrope Film Book, a monthly comic book primer on filmmaking for high school students—a project initiated by August Coppola—in addition to founding an adjunct company, Trimedia Educational Systems, "basically a think tank," said Pearce, "for educational films that grew to encompass all forms of communication."

Throughout, Robert Evans continued to threaten Coppola's hold, insisting that he would yank back *The Godfather* if Coppola's cut exceeded two and a half hours—and Coppola played him beautifully. He lifted, he said, the twenty-five minutes he needed to keep him working, out of Evans's reach, at Zoetrope. "I figured, 'I'll show it to them, and little by little I'll get it back in.' But Bob Evans said, 'Well, you pulled out the best parts of the film. We'll bring it to L.A.' They brought it to L.A., Evans ordered me to put it all back, which I happily did, and then he said 'See!'" Wisely, Coppola had allowed for Evans's vanity, a pawn's sacrifice to checkmate. Coppola "was able, by force of his personality and his energy, to turn [*The Godfather*] into one of our films," Murch said, "meaning a film made the way we made it."

Still convinced that *The Godfather* would end in disaster, Coppola took a quick-money job for Paramount, adapting *The Great Gatsby* for director Jack Clayton. Throughout, he grappled with how to represent Gatsby's love obsession for Daisy, "a dream girl," as Clayton described her to Coppola, forever out of reach, Coppola agreed, to Gatsby, "the poor boy hopelessly in love with the rich girl." Coppola well understood the nature of such a lonely passion, and in his adaptation, he struggled to find a way to convey, in the form of a scene, what was so rooted in his own and Gatsby's imagination. How did people in love behave? he asked Clayton. How did they show it? Beyond the clichés, did they speak about it? Coppola could imagine Clayton layering the imagery—as Walter Murch might layer sound—contrasting two realities, superimposing Daisy's face over Gatsby's at key moments . . . as if Gatsby was imagining her, or remembering, or dreaming . . . Was that how to film a love story? Was that what love, if it could be seen, would look like?

Released in March 1972, and distributed with uncommon ubiquity and speed, *The Godfather* was an instant and staggering success, soon to trounce *Gone with the Wind* for the title of biggest movie of all time. "That changed my life," Coppola said, putting it mildly. The titanic glory and power he achieved upon the film's release was matched only by that of his on-screen counterpart, Michael Corleone. "I can fail for ten years now," Coppola confided in filmmaker Paul Schrader. (*Coppola's wrong*, Schrader thought. *He can fail for fifty years now*.)

Eleanor wrote to her mother from New York, telling her the movie had received

the most good reviews a film has gotten in 10 years or so . . . and there are lines around the block at the five theaters where it is playing in N.Y. City. They are now expecting it to be one of the big 10 money makers of all time. Brando didn't show up at the premiere at the last minute, which sort of made Francis the next most important star, and we were seated by H[enry] Kissinger, several senators, the heads of Paramount [and the] Gulf & Western Pres. Etc. There was a party afterwards on the roof of the St. Regis Hotel with Italian food and waiters dressed as 40's [*sic*] gangsters. Francis' father conducted Italian music at intermissions of the dance band. Tally [Talia Shire] came, and everybody was in high spirits.

I am very happy over F. success in that it was really his ideas that made the picture good. I am happy to see him gain success over his good ideas instead of a chance real estate investment or fluke stock deal. It is also some sort of satisfaction to see the people at Paramount who opposed F. having to back up and admit they were wrong. Anyway it looks like F. may get rich & famous—or at least out of debt & famous—and I am trying to keep my feet on the floor because changes—any kind—good or bad—are always an adjustment in marriage.

My own path seems to be getting more & more into focus. The drawing I sent to the national show was accepted and the gallery in S.F. gave me a definite date—September—for my first little one woman show . . .

Anyway, I am especially excited about the prospect for my life— present & future—at the moment. I just have to get it all in balance.

The whole world turned to face Francis Ford Coppola, the world's newest great filmmaker. In the wake of the *Godfather* phenomenon, none other than Jean-Luc Godard appeared at the production offices of Zoetrope to inform him—the new don, as it were—"that it was [his] obligation," as the maker of films as successful, respected, and widely visible as *The Godfather*, to sponsor the filmmakers of the world.

But first, he would have to clean house. Returning his attention to Zoetrope after a year and a half of fighting for *The Godfather*, he found his Folsom Street headquarters in disarray. There was, for starters, a $40,000 charge to Coppola's account at the corner gas station; someone, he was shocked to learn, had used his name to get personal projects off the ground. "Every incarnation of Zoetrope afterwards was always the same problem," he said. "I'd always have to set things straight after being away."

Indemnified by sudden triumph, Coppola would now think—as perhaps a Michael Corleone was intended to—in terms of empire. "I had money," he said, "for the first time in my life." He bought a magnificent twenty-two-room, sky-blue Queen Anne Victorian mansion at 2307 Broadway in Pacific Heights, which Eleanor reimagined in the big, bright colors of American Zoetrope's first home on Folsom Street. Her renovation, overseen by contractor Peter Dornbach, proved to be, like any Francis Ford Coppola production, a growing improvisation that revealed itself in its own time. "I was supposed to be there for like three weeks or a month," said Dornbach. "I was there for two years."

Inside, the old-growth redwood wainscoting was painted dark mahogany and needed restoration. Eleanor had it painted a rich oak to lighten the entry and hallway. Done to Francis's specifications, the downstairs ballroom—"You couldn't believe the size of it," Dornbach said—was transformed into not just a screening room, but an actual cinema, done up in Coppola's favorite Art Deco. Thus was the Broadway house a living portrait of the Coppola marriage, classical and modern. The living room was crisp in white walls, minimal Italian furniture, and neon tubing running along the ceiling. Next to it was Francis's study, its two Art Deco sofas designed by Dean Tavoularis, its walls of orange felt, and "the soft, cushy, touchy-feely of everything in it," Jean Autrey said. "And it was astounding, the difference in the two styles."

Two miles away, Coppola purchased for $500,000 what was then called the Columbus Tower, a triangular flatiron masterpiece looming over the corner of Kearny and Columbus Streets, only blocks from the City Lights bookstore and the legendary Beat bar Vesuvio. Here in North Beach, amid the strip joints and the vagabonds on the outskirts of Chinatown, would be the new home of American Zoetrope. From its street-level café, Zim's (formerly "Caesar's," thought to be home of the famous salad); to its first floor, for postproduction; up farther to more floors, for offices; and finally, to Coppola's eighth-floor penthouse office, it was giant step up from Folsom Street.

Down beneath Zim's, in the basement that was once the hungry i nightclub, worked Richard Beggs, in his recording studio. He'd been there, making music with the latest multitrack technology, when Coppola, without explanation, appeared in his studio with an entourage of architects.

"What's going on here?" Beggs asked.

The intruders were talking among themselves, pointing at the ceiling.

Beggs called upstairs to Coppola's assistant. "Mona, who are these guys?"

"Didn't anyone tell you?"

"What are they doing?"

"My understanding is you're being incorporated into the organization."

Seeing the future, Coppola invested in Richard Beggs's studio, and their lifelong collaboration began. "Francis always saw that the multitrack technology in [the music industry] was very advanced in some ways, compared to film," Beggs said, "and he saw that as the way to approach the soundtrack of a picture."

Coppola would conscientiously restore the white-painted Columbus Tower—at eight floors, one of turn-of-the-century San Francisco's first skyscrapers—to its original incarnation, the copper-green Sentinel Building. Principally, the whole of the tower's painted exterior was to be stripped down, with much trial and error, in pursuit of the stripping solution that would reveal the restored copper's authentic shade—until Coppola, former boy scientist, and Peter Dornbach finally settled on hydrochloric acid, which Dean Tavoularis approved.

Coppola would hardly have made a design move, at home or at work, without consulting Tavoularis, his right hand since *Godfather*. But among all Tavoularis's creations, none was more beautiful—or more demonstrative of Coppola's charge to better life with art—than the penthouse office he designed for Coppola atop the Sentinel Building. It was a setting so beautiful, in fact, Coppola would tell Tavoularis he wouldn't let anyone photograph it. Encased in paneled white oak with Art Deco inlay, and boasting a panoramic city view, the eighth floor of the refurbished Sentinel Building invoked the galley of a gentleman explorer's luxury schooner sailing the skies. There was a screening room and a bedroom, Coppola's sixteen-foot desk, and, up above, a cupola painted by Dean's brother Alex Tavoularis with characters from Coppola's movies. Beneath the cupola was a round table—whose symbolism was lost on visitors overcome by the grandeur—with egalitarian seating for as many as ten. "It was," production designer Dennis Gassner would remark, "one of the most beautiful rooms I think I had ever seen."

There was a price, however. Inundated with responsibility—to family, Zoetrope, and his own films—Coppola in 1972 was caught between Michael of *The Godfather* and Natalie of *The Rain People*, at once ennobled and divided by his obligations. "I now am as successful as I ever want to be, and I'm pretty rich, so I've got to change all my motivations." But he kept his sight lines clear: on communal cross-fertilization. Growing his North Beach compound, he added the Little Fox Theatre, a legit stage just around the corner from the Sentinel Building. As for work, he was equally expansive. He pressed forward on his script for *The Conversation* and directed Gottfried von Einem's *The Visit of the Old Lady* for the San Francisco Opera. ("I'm learning. I'm trying things here, and sometimes they don't work. This has been like a college extension course for me. Learning while you earn.") And he struck a king's deal with Paramount: a million dollars to write and direct *The Godfather Part II*, which made him the first director to get a million up front (plus gross points). Such was Coppola's power that Paramount also allowed him to team with directors Peter Bogdanovich and William Friedkin, powerhouses both—Coppola asked to include Lucas, but was turned down—in a courageous venture aptly called the Directors Company whereby each director was given the freedom to make, without script approval, any picture under $3 million. It looked like Zoetrope, except it was Paramount: "Part of my desire to get involved with them [the Directors Company] is revenge," Coppola said. "Part of me really wants to take control and own a piece of that film business, for lots of vindictive, Mafia-like reasons—because I'm so mad at Warner Bros. And I know that I can't do it alone. Billy Friedkin, Peter Bogdanovich and I are old friends, and we've all had a super-success this year"—Friedkin's *The French Connection* (1971), Bogdanovich's *What's Up, Doc?* (1972). "What if we all got together? We could really take over the business. In a company like that, for six years' work, you could make $20 million, and then spend the rest of your life making little movies that don't have to make money." For those movies, there would be Zoetrope; for the Directors Company, Coppola would make, finally, *The Conversation*—while he wrote, with Mario Puzo, *Godfather II*. "This year I've overcommitted myself," he told the press in 1972. "Next year I'll start doing things that I want to do, regardless of money."

About that money, specifically, the $300,000 Warner Bros. claimed he owed them: "Don't worry, Francis," his agent Freddie Fields assured him. "I'll handle it." And handle it he did, taking that very amount from Coppola's *Godfather* percentage and handing it over to the studio. "So Warner Bros.," Coppola concluded, "stole $300,000 from me."

In the meantime, his *Godfather* iron hot, he struck again, throwing his loyalty and support behind Lucas's *American Graffiti*, a script no one wanted—Lucas was no salesman, and the nostalgic tale was old-fashioned by New Hollywood standards—by a director who, everyone knew, hadn't fulfilled his early promise. Eleanor dissuaded Coppola from pursuing for Lucas a $700,000 loan—lucky number seven again—against future income from *Godfather*, and instead, he placed *Graffiti* with Universal and, cannily, Lucas with casting director Fred Roos, who had proven himself an invaluable asset to *The Godfather*. "I cast *American Graffiti*, three or four of them, almost all the roles, in my mind hours after I read it," Roos said. "I didn't tell that to George." But George came around to unknowns Richard Dreyfuss, Cindy Williams (Roos's former girlfriend), and Harrison Ford (Roos's former carpenter, who had first met Coppola and Lucas at Zoetrope's L.A. outpost at Goldwyn Studios, where he was working "American Zoetrope" onto the office door. Ford would even do some work on Coppola's Broadway house; "It was my first artistic experience," he said). As for Ron Howard, *American Graffiti* was something like his first starring role. The production he observed was "entirely unlike a Hollywood movie, the way it was crude, the vibe. Most people working on the film have been to film school, whether they were a sound mixer or a first AD or working in the sound department, as opposed to Hollywood, which was still highly unionized and highly nepotistic." The senior-most member, by far, was fifty-year-old cinematographer Haskell Wexler, "because he believed in George and Zoetrope and the spirit of it all," Howard said. "And he was also being allowed to experiment in a way that no Hollywood film would ever allow, because we were working at incredibly low light levels, with a lot of practical lighting. It was breakthrough stuff in terms of the naturalism of lighting, and the low light levels that we were working at were unlike anything I'd ever been around."

That same year, Coppola began filming *The Conversation*. It was a picture of his nightmare, a vision of himself as a lonely boy. "We all live in two worlds," he wrote in a book of notes for the film, "an internal private world—and an external or 'real' world. These worlds are always coming together for a moment, touching, one or the other dominating, and then moving apart. Some people live primarily in the real world, and never bother much to enjoy or suffer in the private world. Like teenagers who are so hung up on the fun [of] their popularity, their social activities, that they never really explore their personal world. As does the young misfit, an ill or weak or even diseased teenager, who broods and examines and develops to a greater and greater extent his internal resources. This is what Hemingway must have meant when he said all great writers have unhappy childhoods. The most interesting example of where the two worlds fuse is in the case of lovers. Here we have a strange internal-external thing—certainly being one of a pair of lovers is the most private thing in the world, and then again, it is TWO people, and therefore the opposite of true privacy. . . . Being in love and making love is the closest way to having a private and public moment at one and the same time."

In an early draft, Harry Caul's confession, given to a woman who doesn't understand, could easily be taken for Coppola's:

HARRY

I never did well; when I was younger I didn't do well at school.

MEREDITH

Huh?

HARRY

My father wanted me to apprentice to a printer so I would be assured a living. He had gone to college and was very disappointed in me.

And

HARRY

I was very sick when I was nine; I lost one entire year of school. I was paralyzed in my left arm and my left leg, and couldn't walk for six months. One doctor told me and my parents that I would never walk again. . . .

Coppola shot *The Conversation* in the fall of 1972, continuing to rewrite throughout production and very much on a deadline: the planned start date for his next film, *The Godfather Part II*. He cast *The Conversation* with friends and Zoetropeans: Robert Duvall, Cindy Williams, Harrison Ford, John Cazale, Frederic Forrest . . . He bought an interest in San Francisco's *City Magazine*, "and before you knew it," Mona Skager said, "Francis owned a hundred percent of the stock," and just as suddenly, a local radio station, too.

Coppola was once again met with the old charges of megalomania, but, he said, "I was seeing one day where there'd be a production that could be written for the theater, broadcast simultaneously on radio, that would become the basis of a screenplay that would be in the magazine and then be a film." He could see it all: highly lucrative were the possibilities of exploiting a single property across all media, and highly experimental, too. It was the sort of cross-pollination Coppola had conceived for the Coppola Company, his expanding creative conglomerate, of which Zoetrope, its film division, would be only a subsidiary. What would happen, for instance, if you mated magazine publishing with theater? Just think: *City* could hold its weekly closing in the Little Fox Theatre and open the event to the public! Editors would rush around onstage with galley proofs that could be simultaneously projected on a screen behind them big enough for the theater audience to see! The audience could even make comments! Comments they would publish in the magazine! "Publishing *City*," Coppola said, "is going to be like making a movie a week."

Adjacent to the Little Fox Theatre, at 529 Pacific Avenue, Coppola established the space they would call the Facility, an apt name for the nondescript (mostly) basement rooms Zoetrope manager Jack Fritz was charged with organizing into storage spaces for cameras, lenses, and a miscellaneous hundred or so other pieces of production equipment, "and it kind of grew," Fritz said. "Let's just say that if somebody needed a piece of equipment that it turned out we did not own, it became our responsibility to assess whether to buy it, or to rent it, or secure it."

To grow further, Coppola would have to delegate as never before. The responsibility of seeing *The Conversation* through to completion he gave, naturally, to Walter Murch, who, since *The Rain People*, had proven himself a sui generis and indispensably imaginative force. In the intervening years, their shared mission had not changed. "[Coppola] had felt that the sound on [*Finian's Rainbow*] had bogged down in the bureaucratic and technical inertia at the studios, and he didn't want to repeat the experience," Murch said. Since American Zoetrope began, the idea, their plan, was to elevate film sound the way great filmmakers elevated picture, the story *over* the story. Sound, the story *under* the story, would not merely be an appendage; for Coppola and Murch sound would be, as it had been for Murch and Lucas's *THX 1138*, *directed*, or, rather, *designed* by a single artistic force, the sound effects creator *and* mixer—in this case, Walter Murch. But the unions, as far back as *The Rain People*, weren't having it. On Murch's behalf, Coppola had argued fiercely with International Alliance of Theatrical Stage Employees boss Eddie Powell, until they finally reached a compromise: Murch could mix *The Rain People*, but he could not assume the union title of sound editor. On *The Rain People* and *THX 1138*, Murch was credited with "sound montage," a title new to film. On *The Godfather*, he was "supervising sound editor." "As I was writing [it]," Coppola said, "I had it in mind that Walter would do the sound. So I wrote many scenes to be sound-oriented . . ." For the sound of the door shutting on Kay, the final shot of the picture—Michael, literally and metaphorically, closes the door on his wife—Murch created a cue beyond the literal, a sound that "needed to give the audience more than the correct physical cues about the door; it was even more important to get a firm, irrevocable closure that resonated with and underscored Michael's final line: 'Never ask me about my

business, Kay.'" Or the rumbling screech of an elevated train outside the
Bronx restaurant where Michael, preparing to kill Captain McCluskey, per-
forms his baptismal act as mafioso; the cue conjures the image of a New
York train, but in pure, emotional sound, the screech describes the growing
anguish within Michael. "The result," Murch said, "is that we actually see
something on the screen that exists only in our mind . . ."

Strategically, Paramount's Robert Evans had at first insisted Murch work
on *The Godfather* in Los Angeles, away from Zoetrope and Coppola, leaving Murch to fend for himself and the picture (and the sound) against the
customs and culture of hierarchical Hollywood. "Whenever you go outside
this building," Paramount's department head of sound effects cautioned
Murch, "make sure you're holding something in your hands."

"But I was going to talk to Al Ruddy about the schedule . . ." Murch
countered.

"Doesn't matter. It could be an empty box. But make sure you have something in your hands."

"Why?"

"Because that son of a bitch"—the sound effects man pointed high up to
the office of Paramount's head of postproduction—"is looking at all of us,
and if he sees somebody walking around the studio lot without anything in
their hands, you're gonna get a phone call that's asking why are you wasting
time walking around the studio when you should be in your galley pulling
on an oar."

Mercifully, the undeniable victory of *The Godfather* won Zoetrope its
ticket back to San Francisco, where Murch, reunited with Lucas, was given
the happy challenge of making *American Graffiti* sound real. Lucas wanted
no fewer than forty-two popular songs of the period (that is, 1962), and he
wanted them played not as underscore, but on car radios, at drive-thrus,
and in stores. Universal thought he was out of his mind. What was this, a
musical? Murch and Lucas's first task was to record Wolfman Jack's fictional radio program, two hours of songs, deejay chatter, caller requests,
and commercials. They took that tape, with speakers and NAGRA, into the
backyard, the real acoustic world, and pressed Play. Lucas stood on one
end of the yard with a speaker, and Murch stood on the far opposite with
the mic. As they recorded, George would turn his speaker back and forth,

and Walter would do the same with his microphone, to simulate the erratic sonic elements of real life—a process Murch would call "worldizing." In thrall to music, the film has no score.

Murch mixed *American Graffiti* in the old Folsom Street building as Coppola shot *The Conversation*. It would be Murch's first job as picture editor, and quite rightly, for as Gene Hackman had been perfectly cast as Harry Caul, equally perfect was Walter Murch's casting as Harry's editor. "You work in sound," Coppola explained to him, "you're kind of like this Harry Caul character . . ." Murch would Method-edit, so to speak, *The Conversation*. As an actor might, he would focus his point of concentration to click into Harry's, tooth in sprocket. "There were many times while making the film that I had a sense of doubling," Murch said. "I'd be working on the film late at night, looking at an image of Harry Caul working on his tape, and there would be four hands, his and mine. Several times I was so tired and disoriented that Harry Caul would push the button to stop the tape and I would be amazed that the film didn't also stop! Why was it still moving!"

Murch thought cutting film was miraculous, transformative, the way changing the order and length of screen images changes an audience's mental image, momentarily reconstituting them themselves; the way dreams and daydreams, whose glory is instant transition through time and space, can reorder awareness. Film was, Murch said, like "the inertia of physical reality: 'I was in the middle of the jungle and then, suddenly, there I was, standing on top of an iceberg'—that can be a dream, but it can also be cinema. It is cinema! I believe that the secret engine which allows cinema to work, and have the power over us that it does, is the fact that for probably millions of years, we have spent eight hours a day of our lives in a 'cinematic' dream state, and so we are completely familiar with this version of reality."

Cutting *The Conversation*, Murch began to notice certain thought patterns—in himself and Harry Caul. He found, and kept finding, that Gene Hackman would blink very close to the point where he, Murch, had decided to make a cut. It happened too often to be coincidental. Was Murch so aligned with the character that he had lost his objectivity? Or, in losing himself, had he found Harry Caul? To test the integrity of his cuts, Murch would have to double-check; sensing a cut, he would run the film again to see if his body-mind stopped on the exact same "flinch point." When it did, he would know that his cuts were not arbitrary, that they were the soul of the character in his own fingers. "You get to a place where time is not an issue at all and [where] you're oddly at the center of things, but also you are not. You're the person doing it, yet the feeling is that you're *not* the origin of it, that somehow 'it' is happening around you, that you are being used by this thing to help bring it into the world." Sometimes, "the best times," he said, "this process reaches the point where I can look at the scene and say, 'I didn't have anything to do with that—it just created itself.'"

One morning, in August 1973, after another night spent gazing into *The Conversation*, Murch left the cutting room for a bite of breakfast. Passing the window of a Christian Science Reading Room, he caught the front page of the *Monitor*: an interview with John Huston. Film is like thought, Huston said in the piece. "It's the closest to thought process of any art." By way of example, he added, "Look at that lamp. Now look at me. Look back at that lamp. Now look at me again. Do you see what you did? You blinked. Those are cuts. After the first time you know that there's no reason to pan from me to the lamp, because you know what's in between. Your mind cuts [the scene]. You behold the lamp. [Cut.] And you behold me." It was happening naturally with Gene Hackman, a great actor; thinking Harry Caul's thoughts, he was also blinking Harry's blinks.

Murch started watching people's eyes. He saw that there was such a person so intent he didn't blink; there was also another kind of person, equally intent, who blinked continually. The unblinking person, Murch concluded, was held fixed by a single thought or emotion; the blinking person, by a rapid succession of related thoughts and feelings, each one a blink. But whereas blinks of the eye were always "right," cuts, when misplaced, could be "wrong."

The first cut of *The Conversation* was extremely long, close to five hours. "I was just kind of watching Walter," said Richard Chew. "All I needed to do was sort of watch and listen, and the lightbulb of recognition would go off in me." He would be a mixer in one room, recording tracks; and an editor in another, cutting picture on the KEM. "That's the kind of thing you wouldn't have in a studio space," Chew said. "You wouldn't have that flexibility, because of the rigid job delineations you would have in Hollywood.

So, Zoetrope provided for someone like Walter a way to fully explore what he was hearing, what he was imagining in his mind."

Murch was changing. He would live the movie; they would become each other. "It took many (many) years to get used to it," Aggie Murch explained, "but every film is a love affair. And it must be. And how you deal with them through the years is part of how you grow up. When a film would stop, Walter would refocus, and come back to me—for a while. I got a lot of gentle support from his mother; his father was a painter." Walter would be reconstituted by ecstasy, and Aggie, like Eleanor, would learn to wait.

Eleanor's own mother, she knew, had never managed the balancing act of her own internal and external worlds. Even in widowhood, "she never reconciled those aspects of her heart in her life," Eleanor said. "And so, I was determined to have a different sort of life." As her husband expanded his empire, she focused, became more selective. Her first short film, *Peeling a Potato Is a Work of Art*, was thirty seconds long. And her solo exhibition, *Eleanor Neil Coppola: Recent Drawings*, was "so fragile in its effect," to one critic, "that it seems that even the gentlest noise could shatter it."

On location in Lake Tahoe for *Godfather II*, Eleanor became, once again, Kay Corleone, charged with running the household, finding the grocery store, the dry cleaner, minding the children. That the Coppolas also lived in the Tahoe estate that doubled for the Corleone compound only enhanced their immersion in their roles; that the actors' memories were also their characters' memories blurred the lines further. "I was not happy," she would write. "I couldn't find myself, my place inside Francis's movie/world." Coppola, meanwhile, thrived. Kissing his ring at last, Paramount parent company Gulf+Western boss Charlie Bluhdorn promised to keep Evans out of Coppola's hair—and did. A bigger boy now, he got what he wanted. "I spent a whole day on the estate in Tahoe with every member of the [Corleone] Family present in their various houses, and for a day they just lived being a family. I wish I had had 16 cameras all over, because . . . one group would visit the other group, old stories began to come up . . . What I was looking for was for them to put on the clothing of the characters and really have bias: 'I like him but I didn't like her.'"

To add to his first Oscar for *Patton*, Coppola won another Oscar, for writing the first *Godfather*, and a Palme d'Or, the Cannes Film Festival's highest honor, for *The Conversation*. "To some extent, I have become Michael [Corleone]," he confessed, "a powerful man in charge of an entire production." Coppola had turned thirty-five and had "decided to view it as the end of Part I of my life. It could be considered a midpoint, you know, and certainly a good time to evaluate one's life . . ." Hence the *Godfather II*'s flashback structure, the means by which Michael, reviewing his and his father's parallel ascents, provided Coppola a venue to do the same. Both had fathers who loomed large, brothers who, at one time or another, hadn't fulfilled family expectations (Augie, a professor of comparative literature, was henceforth eclipsed by Francis), and both came burdened by the responsibility of tremendous power. The themes, characters, locations—they were memories, there for the taking.

Cutting *Godfather II* in the Sentinel Building, reunited with his (growing) family of Zoetrope craftsmen, Coppola increased his stature by achievement and community, "living a part of that *Godfather* movie in his own life," observed the film's assistant editor Lisa Fruchtman. As with the Corleones, the coalescence of work and family was mutually enhancing: tighter bonds created deeper work; deeper work, tighter bonds. "On *Godfather*, he was the godfather," editor Mark Berger concurred. "And every two weeks or so, we would have a big meeting, a big dinner at his house on Broadway. He would invite all the editors and sound people and assistants. He had a huge table set up with ham and spaghetti and salads and all sorts of Italian dishes. And there'd be twenty-five people there, and he would sit at the end of the table and invite everybody to sit down. And then he raised his hand and he'd say, 'Everybody, *mangia! Mangia!*' And it would be the Corleones having a big family dinner. Then there'd be espresso served around, and he'd have his kids come and sit on his lap." At one such gathering, Coppola polled his collaborators: "If you could go anywhere, anywhere in the world, where would you like to go?" When the film was completed, he awarded bonuses—not in cash, but in adventures: plane tickets to each person's dream destination.

In 1973, there was more than enough to go around. Scorsese had broken out with *Mean Streets* (for which Coppola had donated $5,000); Friedkin with *The Exorcist*; Bogdanovich hit again big with *Paper Moon* (a Directors Company win for Friedkin and Coppola as well); and coming up behind them, "little Stevie" Spielberg was shooting *Sugarland Express*, his theatrical debut, written by Zoetrope's Matthew Robbins and Hal Barwood. "Directors, the younger directors," Coppola said, "are no longer jealous of each other, they really like each other and like each other's work." But it was the announcement of that year's Oscar nominations—five for *American Graffiti*, including two for Lucas, Best Screenplay and Best Director; and one for Coppola as producer, Best Picture—that marked 1973's biggest win for Coppola. At long last, George Lucas's indisputable critical and commercial success—a box-office phenomenon, *Graffiti* took in an incredible $55 million, the biggest ever for a film made for under a million—not only signified Lucas's promise fulfilled, but also confirmed, finally, that the Zoetrope model could deliver a financial payoff for all involved. "Who was the star of *American Graffiti* when it was the *movie*?" Coppola explained. "It was George Lucas who created it, who was the star." Relative unknowns; a small, personal movie; personal challenge and growth; artistic innovation; excellence and fun—this was what American Zoetrope was all about. "The most significant fact of my brief career," Coppola said, "beyond any of the films I may have made is that I actively brought to some young directors the opportunity to direct. At home I have a lot of shiny awards, but . . . a Golden Globe for *American Graffiti*—in a way it's the best one I have."

Coppola was reinvigorated. Had he financed the picture himself, as he had originally intended to, he figured he would have been rich enough to buy Fox. Instead, in 1974, he bought up 72,000 shares of New York–based independent distributor/exhibitor Cinema 5, a move that granted him, a substantial stockholder under the aegis of the Coppola Company, the long-coveted ability to distribute independently financed films—his own films as director or his friends' as producer. No longer would he need, say, the muscle of a Warner Bros. to get his films to an audience. Instead, Coppola could circumvent fiascos like *THX*, and "bypass the kinds of movie deals filmmakers have to make, deals in which a filmmaker has to totally surrender ownership."

Who in Hollywood—indeed, who in America—could boast such freedom? John Cassavetes, icon of American independents, made the movies he wanted, but their distribution wasn't his. Roger Corman had the distribution, but without anything near Coppola's resources. But Cinema 5 owned and operated fourteen of the key theaters in New York.

In short order, Coppola and Fred Roos joined Cinema 5's board of directors and planned a "creative collaboration" with Donald Rugoff, Cinema 5 president, whom Coppola persuaded to rename the company "Cinema 7." Under Coppola, Cinema 7 would oversee development, production, and now distribution of three to five Zoetrope pictures a year, beginning with *The Black Stallion*, directed by Carroll Ballard and budgeted at $1.2 million; *Apocalypse Now*—still Lucas's to turn down—"best described [by Coppola] as a macabre comedy set in the midst of the Vietnam war"; and Coppola's own, an original musical, a *film à clef* based on the life of maligned car innovator Preston Tucker.

"Bergman is very high on you, Francis," enthused Rugoff, leaving a Cinema 7 board meeting with Coppola. "He's interested in giving his films to us."

"Good," replied Coppola. "Try for Kubrick."

Then he was off to London, Paris, Rome—where international distributors begged him for the right to distribute his next picture. In Rome, he dined with Fellini. The great director confessed that even *he*, who had just won his fourth Oscar, for *Amarcord*, still had to battle for financing.

"I am at the zenith of my opportunity to make big deals," Coppola said, correctly, in September 1974. "I have companies, I own a theater, a magazine in San Francisco and my own jet plane." But there was more to come: in December 1974, *The Godfather Part II* was released. If Francis Ford Coppola was godfather before, he was now simply a god. Making what many considered the greatest film Hollywood had ever produced—twice—he had achieved the unimaginable, to say nothing of *The Conversation*, another masterpiece seemingly tossed off in between.

"I've got to start paying attention to my kids and wife," he said in January 1975, a month after the film's release. "Too much attention to business destroys the family. Right?" Not necessarily: for just over $2 million, he bought them a dream 1,560 acres of the Inglenook estate in Napa Valley wine country. Inglenook was synonymous with the finest Cabernet Sauvignon, but the jewel of the vineyard was a sunny nineteenth-century mansion built atop the hill like a Winslow Homer rendering of Shangri-La. It appeared to Eleanor like a movie set, the Corleones' Tahoe compound in the country.

Soon came offers from expert wineries to buy 120 acres of Cabernet.

"Well, if they all want to buy our grapes," said husband to wife, "maybe they're good. Maybe we should just make the wine ourselves."

"What do you know about how to make wine?"

"I don't know anything about how to make wine. I don't know anything about how to make movies, but that doesn't stop me."

He "began to realize that the things you do out of truly loving it and wanting to enjoy your life are also the things that are sensible businesses." Welcoming tradition, the legacy and renewal of a family business where work and life were one, he could see, one day, his grandchildren in the vineyards, and though he wouldn't live to know *their* grandchildren, he could see them with the cousins, playing, cooking, and one day drinking the fruit of their old piece of earth. *Magari!* he would toast. *Magari, magari!* "It should be so!"

That year, Coppola became the first-ever director to be nominated by the Directors Guild of America twice in the same year, for *The Conversation* and *Godfather II*; the latter also received eleven Oscar nominations, twice as many as its predecessor; and *The Conversation* got three. Both films received Best Picture nominations. Further, Coppola's own father received a nomination (along with Nino Rota) for Best Original Dramatic Score, and his sister, Talia, for Best Supporting Actress (both for *Godfather II*). The night of the awards, April 8, 1975, *Godfather II* swept. (Backstage after accepting De Niro's *Godfather II* Oscar for Best Supporting Actor, Coppola tapped Scorsese on the shoulder: "This is good for your picture," he said, meaning *Taxi Driver*, then in the works.) Coppola himself won three Oscars, including Best Picture, but it was his father's victory that fired him literally out of his seat. "I want to thank my son Francis Ford Coppola for being up here," Carmine told the black-tie assemblage in the Dorothy Chandler Pavilion, "because without him, I wouldn't be here. *However*, if I wasn't here, he wouldn't be here, either, right?" His son Francis, in the audience, applauded with irrepressible joy. He had given his father the job; and his father had vanquished them both not simply with the win, but with the long-awaited affirmation of his wished-for self, Carmine Coppola, composer:

"Best Original Dramatic Score," the Oscar said. For all time, they had done it—and done it as a family.

Eleanor went home with Oscars, too. In those days, the Academy still engaged in the strange practice of handing out miniature statuettes on gold chains for the winner to present, presumably, to his wife. The idea was Eleanor might wear them on a bracelet or necklace. She didn't. Instead, she and Lynn Hershman invited the Society for Art from the L.A. Museum of Contemporary Art and the S.F. Museum of Modern Art to an exhibition at the Coppolas' house in San Francisco. Expecting to brush shoulders with the world's most famous director, visitors were surprised not to find him in the house. Instead, in the fabled glass case where his Oscars were kept, they found Eleanor's miniatures. ("Francis was furious," Eleanor recalled. "He thought I was making fun of him.") On the third floor Hershman presented Margo St. James, an activist organizing a union for prostitutes, nude in a bathtub. In the kitchen visitors were directed to peel a potato, then shown a quote by conceptual artist Joseph Beuys, "Peeling a potato can be a work of art if it is a conscious act," then they were asked to place it in one of two pots marked "Art" or "Not Art." In a second-floor bedroom with a velvet cord over the open door, Sofia and Roman played while a video of Sofia's birth was showing in the background. A plaque said, "Two of the artist's most important works expected to take twenty-one years to complete."

Looking down from his eighth-floor penthouse, Coppola set his sights higher and wider. "I'm getting to be an influential person in San Francisco," he said. "What if I and five other powerful guys with cigars got together in a smoke-filled room to decide who would be the next mayor of San Francisco? We'd do it because we're good guys and we really want the city to be wonderful for everybody. Then I thought, what's the difference between five good guys holding that kind of power and five bad guys? Just good intentions, and intentions can be corrupted."

Still, he had come this far. Why couldn't he go farther? "I'd like to start this place up in the North Pole . . . A sort of toy factory where all the toys were made by little people, children . . ."

He needed more money, much more, more than he could get directing.

"I've already made a million dollars for directing a film," he conceded. "So what do I do—ask for a million and half? Perhaps the wisest thing to do is to use all my energies to make a film that grosses some stupendous amount, then go out and buy a major company and change it from the top."

He would call Scorsese. "United Artists?"

"Yeah! Let's do it!"

Think of how much Universal had made on *American Graffiti*. What had it cost them? Only twenty-eight days of shooting, under a million dollars. Lucas made millions, but Universal made tens of millions *more*. The idea, then, was not to run Universal; it was to *be* Universal. To put all his money down on Cinema 7, to one day own the movie and control its distribution. So what if the ball bounced wrong? If he lost it all, he could always pick up another job. But what if . . . what if he won? *Magari!*

He reviewed the cache of American Zoetrope scripts Warner Bros. had returned to him after the *THX* debacle—they were mostly written for a tight budget, small in scope, like *The Conversation*. But this time, Coppola wanted to go in the opposite direction. Seeking nothing less than the jackpot, he was searching for a grand canvas, something culturally, even physically huge—like Milius's script, *Apocalypse Now*, for almost a decade betrothed to Lucas. But Lucas was elsewhere, writing his sci-fi movie and, if they started now and stayed on schedule, Coppola could get the movie out next year, 1976, in time for the American Bicentennial. Not a bad hook for what Milius had written: guns, girls, and rock 'n' roll. None of which Coppola could relate to exactly, but no matter. On this one, he was out to make money—a lot of money—and Milius's blockbuster glint could not be denied. Coppola would be an artist on the next one.

He fled to the penthouse of the Sentinel Building and turned his attention to rewriting, for maximum popular appeal, *Apocalypse Now*.

Eleanor was spending her days in her home studio, an octagonal perch on the third floor of the Broadway house, working before a window view of an old oak tree.

In June of that year, 1975, America's war had ended. The Coppolas' hadn't yet begun.

Everyone who has come out here to the Philippines seems to be going through something that is affecting them profoundly," Eleanor wrote, "changing their perspective about the world or themselves, while the same thing is supposedly happening to Willard in the course of the film. Something is definitely happening to me and to Francis."

Filming Francis directing at the Kurtz compound, she caught sight of him talking to one of the "Bunnies"—actual *Playboy* Playmates cast to play Bunnies entertaining the troops—and judiciously averted her eyes and camera.

There would be a short break in the production. Coppola and Dean Tavoularis flew to Hong Kong.

When Coppola returned he was bursting with forceful insight. While away, he told Eleanor, he had reviewed the entirety of his life. He could see it clearly now: he had always wanted to be gifted, just like his father and brother, and for years he had been thwarted in this by his limitations. What was he? He wasn't a writer, a director, not in the way he, or anyone, had thought of it; he was a conceptualizer, an engineer of events: the *Rain People* road trip, the *Godfather* family, and now this. He had been right to work this way. One could not contain what was real and mystical in life by trying to anticipate it in the script. Film was meant to be *lived*. To survive the movie, he told Eleanor, he would have to do what she, filming her documentary, did so naturally; he would have to cede control to the forces of nature and chance and disappear. Only then would the thing that needed to come out of him come out of him and onto screen.

Changing again, the caterpillar disintegrates happily in his cocoon. Everything is going to be all right, he told her. He knew what he was.

The Ifugao: the ceremonial slaughter of the carabao. There was something there for Coppola. Symbolically—for this was the function of ritual sacrifice—the animal's death forged the tribe's restoration. It was the theme of continuity, the awareness that nothing could be split from its opposite. Madness—as he was learning from his own mind—was pitting one against the other, trying to divide this from that, but you cannot. Kurtz understands this. A thing dies so that a bigger thing can live. "There's something really honest," Coppola said, "about the jungle." It was bewilderingly beautiful, the eternal truth: he had alighted on the sacred.

The night came, the night they were to film the ritual sacrifice.

Storaro set up and readied five cameras. Ifugao liaison Éva Gárdos enlisted Doug Madison to provide the carabao. "Sometimes a family will spend their entire earnings from the harvest or whatever just to provide the animals for a ritual that they feel they need," Gárdos informed Eleanor. "So this is kind of an insurance for them . . ."

Cast and crew gathered on the periphery. Eleanor saw a giant, eight-inch moth flutter through the beam of an arc light.

It started to rain.

Unsober, Sam Bottoms glared at the carabao. There were tears in its eyes, he thought. The animal knelt down, seeming to welcome what was coming, but was picked up and settled back onto its legs to die standing. Bottoms watched its eyes as the knife plunged in. Cameras rolling, the animal fell; the dancing began. Cast and crew, their faces painted, arms raised, joined in, twirling. Possessed now, Bottoms "started to get insane," he said. "I didn't really realize what I had done." He stole a chicken from its cage, as his character Lance would have, and threw it on the heap of bloody carabao meat. "It felt like you were in Dante's Inferno," said Frederic Forrest. He was, as his character, Chef, would have been, terrified and wanted to run. But he couldn't. "And the dreams you had during that time were, like, horrendous," he said. "I mean I had an awful dream, the end of the world and all kinds of shit during that." Attuned to the lasting impressions the unconscious made on his awareness, and how that awareness colored his waking experience, Vittorio Storaro regarded dreams as real.

Christmas 1976. Production paused for the holiday.

Returning to California, Coppola watched a five-hour assembly cut of *Apocalypse* and was overjoyed. Their work was tremendous. It might even be a masterpiece, he told Eleanor.

He was home, the children and their friends all around him.

"What do you think you're gonna be like when you're a big girl?" he asked Sofia. She was five and a half.

"I can make believe what I want to be like."

"Tell me what you want to be like."

"I am Sofia! When I grow up I want to be middle size, not fat and not skinny and I want to be a teacher or maybe I want to be a nurse and I like being Sofia because there's a lot of fun things that I know how to do. And my daddy just tickled me with his little nose."

Playing with the children, reorganizing the house, his office, singing and making music—it was as if the jungle Francis, Eleanor thought, had never existed.

He still had to destroy Kurtz's temple. Stormed with vivid intent, reinvigorated by the five-hour cut, he returned after a break in shooting to the Philippines a conqueror: writing, dictating, and rewriting urgent, exacting telexes in a hurricane of fire he sent around the world.

FEB 10
TO: TOM
FROM: FRANCIS
TOM, PLS RELAY THIS TELEGRAM TO WALTER MURCH:

DEAR WALTER, AM ABSOLUTELY COUNTING ON YOU TO MIX QUAD-
SENSURROUND APOCALYPSE NOW. AM BUILDING NEW STUDIO

JUST FOR THIS PURPOSE. I WILL NEVER ASK ANOTHER FAVOR
OF YOU, BUT THIS IS IMPORTANT TO ME. PLEASE SEND
TELEGRAM CONFIRMING SO WE CAN GO AHEAD WITH SPECIAL QUAD
COMPUTERIZED STUDIO. GEO. LUCAS WILL HELP TOO.

FEB 10

TO: MONA

FROM: DAVE

PLEASE HAVE DR. REISS BRING QUAALUDE, PERTINENT TO STORY.

FEB 10

TO: JODY POWELL FOR PRESIDENT CARTER

THE WHITE HOUSE

WASHINGTON, D.C.

U.S.A.

DEAR PRESIDENT CARTER:

ALL GOOD HOPES AND WISHES FOR YOURS AND THE NATION'S
SUCCESS. AM MAKING 24-MILLION-DOLLAR FILM ON VIETNAM.
WILL BE RELEASED BY UNITED ARTISTS CHRISTMAS 1977. IS
HONEST, MYTHICAL, PRO-HUMAN AND THEREFORE PRO-AMERICAN.
DEPT. OF DEFENSE HAS DONE EVERYTHING TO STOP ME BECAUSE OF
MISUNDERSTANDING ORIGINAL SCRIPT WHICH WAS ONLY STARTING
POINT FOR ME.
FILM ALMOST DONE. HOWEVER, I NEED SOME MODICUM OF
COOPERATION OR ENTIRE GOVERNMENT WILL APPEAR RIDICULOUS TO
AMERICAN AND WORLD PUBLIC.
WILL ARRANGE SCREENING OF EXCERPTS FOR ANYONE YOU
DESIGNATE, BUT NOT D.O.D.
NEED 1 CH-46 CHINOOK HELICOPTER FOR ONE DAY. WILL PAY ALL
COSTS AS PER D.O.D. GUIDELINES. ALL OUT COOPERATION WAS
GRANTED JOHN WAYNE'S FILM "GREEN BERET." WE WERE GIVEN
NONE, AND WERE HARASSED BY D.O.D.

ALSO, NEED IMMEDIATE APPROVAL TO PURCHASE 10 CASES EACH
SMOKE INCENDIARY UNITS OF ALL COLORS (SMOKE MAKERS)—THIS
REQUEST HAS BEEN DENIED US ALONG WITH ALL OTHERS.
THIS FILM TRIES ITS BEST TO HELP AMERICANS PUT VIETNAM BEHIND
US, WHICH WE MUST DO SO WE CAN GO ON TO A POSITIVE FUTURE.
SINCERELY,
FRANCIS FORD COPPOLA

"APOCALYPSE NOW"

FEB 11
TO: ROBIN
FROM: FRANCIS
MY TELEXES TO YOU DID NOT TELL YOU TO COME IMMEDIATELY—
THEY INQUIRED IF YOU COULD COME. YOUR ANSWER SHOULD HAVE
BEEN YES I CAN, FROM THIS DATE TO THIS DATE. I HAVE MANY
THINGS FOR YOU TO DO AND GET IN U.S. IF YOU LEAVE TOMORROW
YOU WILL NOT HAVE TIME TO GET THEM. THEREFORE PLS TRY TO
ANSWER MY SPECIFIC QUESTION AND WAIT FOR MY INSTRUCTIONS.
AT ANY RATE—THESE ARE THE THINGS I WANT FROM U.S. IF SUE
HAS ALREADY BROUGHT THEM, THEN FINE. IF NOT—DELAY YOUR
TRIP UNTIL YOU HAVE GOTTEN THEM.

1.   ONE CASE OF RUINART CHAMPAGNE
2.   ONE CASE OF WITCH HAZEL
3.   ONE CASE OF OZIUM [a bug repellant]
4.   ONE CASE OF ABADIE SMALL SIZE CIGARETTE PAPERS.
5.   ONE CASE BALKAN SOBRANIE CIGARETTES (MEDIUM NO
     FILTER)
6.   ONE MORE CASE (IF POSSIBLE) OF CHALONE PINOT NOIR.
7.   ONE CASE SMALL PERRIER BOTTLES.
8.   VARIOUS HIGH QUALITY, SMALL CUTS (INDIVIDUAL) FILETS,
     N.Y. STEAKS, LAMB CHOPS, ETC. WRAPPED AND FROZEN AND
     IDENTIFIED SO THEY CAN BE TAKEN OUT ONE AT A TIME.

9. ONE CASE OF GREAT WINE INCLUDING VINTAGE INGLENOOK AS PICKED BY MIKE BERNSTEIN.

10. 12 BOTTLE LEMON JUICE.

11. SEVERAL BOTTLES ANY EXOTIC STEAK SAUCES, SUCH AS PICK-A-PEPPER [sic], ETC.

12. GO TO THOMAS CARA AND GET ME VARIOUS GOURMET COOKING UTENSILS, FEW WOODEN SPOONS, HEAVY GARLIC CRUSHER (ALSO BRING AMERICAN GARLIC. THE STUFF HERE IS TERRIBLE.)

13. BRING THE <u>LARGEST</u> SIZE ESPRESSO POT—<u>MOKA</u> EXPRESS IT'S CALLED.

14. CASE OF MEDAGLIA D'ORO CANNED ESPRESSO COFFEE IN THE SMALLEST POSSIBLE CANS (ALSO CRUSHED RED PEPPER, WHOLE CASE IN SMALLEST, HUMIDITY FREE BOTTLE OR CANS).

15. 2 BOTTLE SAMBUCA, 1 BOTTLE KIRSCH, 1 BOTTLE GRAN MARNIER, 1 BOTTLE GOOD COGNAC, 1 LARGE BOTTLE LA TACHE WINE IN WINE CELLAR, 1 COCA-COLA OPENER LIKE IN S.F. IF NECESSARY, TAKE THAT ONE AND WE'LL BUY NEW ONE FOR THERE.

16. 1 COPY HEMINGWAY SHORT STORIES "IN OUR TIME," OR ANY OF THE "NICK STORIES," "THE KILLERS," ETC.

17. COMPLETE SET OF ALL BOB DYLAN RECORDS, JACKSON BROWNE, GRATEFUL DEAD—TOM STERNBERG MIGHT BE ABLE TO GET ALL THOSE FOR YOU FOR FREE BY CALLING THOSE PEOPLE.

18. COPY OF PAPERBACK "SHOGUN."

Et cetera.

He had another idea—something he called, mixing French and Italian, *La Bohème Povero* (The Impoverished Bohemian), a chamber adaptation of the Puccini opera set entirely in one location, a café. His father would modify Puccini's orchestration for a few instruments, and Coppola would have the libretto adapted by John Lennon.

Dear John,

We've never met, but, of course I've always enjoyed your work. I am
presently in the Philippines making APOCALYPSE NOW. I've been here
eight months, expect to be here another several months. I live inside
a Volcano which is a jungle paradise where there are beautiful mineral
springs and thought if ever you were in the Far East or if ever you would
enjoy spending a little time talking about things in general and some
distant future projects that I have in mind, please, I would love to cook
dinner for you and just talk, listen to music and talk about movies. If
coming to the Far East is difficult, then someday in the future, either in
Los Angeles, San Francisco or New York, I would like to meet you.

Sincerely,

Francis Coppola

Draft—Feb. 16, 1977

TO: BARRY HIRSCH, TOM STERNBERG, NORM WEBSTER, DAVE SALVEN,
RICHARD TONG, MONA SKAGER, NANCY ELY, JEAN AUTREY, FRED ROOS
FROM: FRANCIS COPPOLA
RE: PROJECTS

The following are the projects, film or otherwise, that
I am presently working on. I would like each one to have
some sort of easy code or account number so that any
expenses are fairly charged to those budgets. Since all
of these projects will have either partners or a financing
company (a Major), at some future time all costs will be
recouped. Therefore, to make your jobs easier now, I am
giving you these references:

1. "Apocalypse Now"
2. "Brotherhood of the Grape"

3.   "Tucker"

4.   "Elective Affinities"

5.   "Black Stallion"

6.   "Hammett"

7.   "La Boheme (Little Fox Theatre)"

8.   "The Escape Artist"

9.   "Desperados"

10. "Steve Alan / Jello"

11. "Lucie Bigelow Rosen"

12. Bob Towne—"Tarzan"

All of my activities, my strange requests, ordering film,
asking for people to come to the Philippines, or to go to
Tokyo, or any odd requests I may have are apportionable to
one or a combination of these projects. There is nothing
in my life that I will be doing, including my personal
life with my family, my children, that will not be
apportionable to these movies or theatre productions.
Each time I make a request of any nature that involves the
expenditure of money, I would like it to be automatically
apportioned to one or more of those categories.
For example, if I hire a part-time secretary in Japan, she
will be handling 75% in liaison with Tomita/"Apocalypse Now":

   75% "Apocalypse Now". #1
   25% "Elective Affinities". #4

Those rates will change. Sometimes, there will be 3 or 4
purposes for a specific request and I will give my best
judgment as to which productions should bear the cost.
Obviously, use any accounting numbering system that's
best, & you all agree on.
Obviously, I expect any current production, such as
"Apocalypse Now," to bear all costs which stem from my
being on location—such as telexes, phone calls, running

operating staff, etc., so the current production will
always be weighted the most heavily.
If I request Dick Lester's 3 films, "Hard Day's Night,"
"Help," "How I Won The War," the cost should be
apportioned 50/50 "Apocalypse Now" and "Tucker."
I will come up with the most extraordinary requests of you
and want to be sure that any expenditure of money goes into
the proper budget since it is all recoupable in the future.

To Eleanor, presently with the children in San Francisco, he explained the telexes as the plans of a new man. He was redesigning his life, he told her, "to live every moment magnificently." But she did not see magnificence. His frenzy disturbed her. For weeks, she elected to stay quiet rather than say something he would mistake for disloyalty, and if indeed it were true, as he had told her it was, that he was directing better than he ever had in his life, she decided it was cruel to interfere. But the telexes kept coming, her anxiety turned to terror, and she was, she realized, on her own. Who else would step in? Afraid he was becoming Kurtz, Eleanor sent out a missive warning he was "creating the very situation he went there to expose." She copied Storaro, Tavoularis, and other members of the crew, but because she naïvely sent it as a telex, as opposed to a letter, it traveled through several offices and was read not just by these intimates but by everyone. Coppola was humiliated, outraged, betrayed.

MAR 1
TO: ELLIE
FROM: FRANCIS

NORMALLY, I WOULD BE FURIOUS AT YOUR OUTRAGEOUS TELEX.
DON'T COMMENT ON WHAT I AM DOING UNTIL YOU UNDERSTAND
FULLY. REASON FOR EVERYTHING I AM DOING, AS USUAL. . . .
TALK TO BARRY HIRSCH. I UNDERSTAND YOU ARE CONFUSED, BUT
THIS IS A PRIVATE MATTER. FORTUNATELY, ONE OF US STILL HAS
SOME RESTRAINT. THANK YOU FOR EMBARRASSING ME IN FRONT OF
MY ENTIRE COMPANY WITHOUT COMMUNICATING WITH ME PRIVATE
FIRST. FRANCIS.

MAR 1

TO: L.A. AND S.F. OFCS

FROM: FRANCIS COPPOLA

MY MOST SINCERE THANKS TO ALL THOSE WHO HAVE SO PROMPTLY
RESPONDED TO MY VARIED AND APPARENTLY BIZARRE REQUESTS.
TO THOSE OF [YOU] WHO, AS MANY TIMES IN MY PAST, WONDERED
PUBLICLY WHETHER OR NOT I KNOW WHAT I'M DOING, INCLUDING
ELLIE, SUGGEST YOU READ LAST CHAPTER OF HOMER'S ULYSSES.

SINCERELY, FRANCIS.

MAR 2

SFO: TOM STERNBERG, JEANNIE AUTREY

RE: TELEX TRANSMITTED TO ME FROM ELEANOR COPPOLA

IT IS IMPOSSIBLE FOR ME TO CONCEIVE THAT MY COMPANY
COULD PUBLICLY TRANSMIT SUCH AN INSULTING, DEMEANING AND
DANGEROUS MESSAGE. EFFECTIVE IMMEDIATELY, THE FOLLOWING
EMPLOYEES ARE TERMINATED:

1. THE SECRETARY WHO TYPED AND TRANSMITTED THE TELEX.
2. HIS OR HER IMMEDIATE SUPERVISOR WHO KNEW OF AND
    AUTHORIZED THE TRANSMISSION OF THE TELEX.
3. ANY OTHER PERSON OF AUTHORITY WHO KNEW OF AND
    APPROVED THE TRANSMISSION OF THE TELEX.
4. MONA SKAGER, IF SHE KNEW OF AND APPROVED THE
    TRANSMISSION OF THE TELEX.
5. DOUG FERGUSON, IF HE KNEW OF AND APPROVED OF THE TELEX.
6. THE DOCUMENTARY PROJECT IS HEREWITH TERMINATED—
    ALL FOOTAGE IS TO BE CONFINED TO THE EDITING
    ROOM, LOCKED, AND NO ONE ALLOWED ACCESS. I DO NOT
    AUTHORIZE ANYONE VIEWING OR WORKING WITH FILM WHICH
    CONTAINS MY IMAGE, NOR THE IMAGES OF ANY SCENES,
    LOCATIONS, OR PERSONNEL FROM MY FILM, APOCALYPSE
    NOW. THIS IS TO REMAIN IN EFFECT UNTIL I CHOOSE
    ANOTHER DIRECTOR AND EDITOR. OBVIOUSLY, THIS MEANS

PAT JACKSON IS TERMINATED AS WELL, AND ALL WORK
CEASES WITH THIS DIRECTIVE.

7.   ANY AND ALL COPIES, XEROXES, ORIGINALS OF THE TELEX
      IN QUESTION MUST BE GATHERED AND SEALED, AND POUCHED
      TO ME IMMEDIATELY. THERE MUST BE NO COPIES OF THE
      TELEX IN EXISTENCE. ANY BREACH OF THIS WILL RESULT IN
      THE MOST SEVERE LEGAL ACTION FROM MY COMPANY.

8.   ANY OTHER MESSAGES WHICH CONTAIN DEROGATORY MESSAGES
      CONCERNING ME OR MY FILM ARE NOT TO BE SENT VIA THE
      TELEX MACHINE—ANY FURTHER BREACHES OF THIS RULE WILL
      RESULT IN SIMILAR ACTION.

I EXPECT THESE ORDERS TO BE COMPLIED WITH IMMEDIATELY.
THERE IS NO FURTHER DISCUSSION. PLEASE CONFIRM TODAY.

FRANCIS COPPOLA

What Eleanor sensed and what Francis, if he knew at all, could not have been but marginally aware of, was that his dialectical energies were always in cycle. First came generative conviction and enthusiasm—an idea. Then, like a scientist with a hypothesis, the period of uncertainty: testing that idea in the context of the larger story. Did it work? From that test, certainty would be restored again, but invariably, changes in his own life would at some point interrupt the cycle, change his story, and plunge him into the unknown once more. Did painters have this problem? "I guess this is the problem with film," he mused as early as *You're a Big Boy Now*, "it takes so long to get these projects written, and then even longer to get them off the ground, so that by the time you're there, you've passed it by." Rushing head-long into an imagined future of *Elective Affinities*, *The Black Stallion*, *Tucker*, et al., he was both recharging his depleted energies and also diverting himself from the terrible task at hand: finishing a movie that the new "he," unrecognizable to his former self, had never consented to make in the first place.

"F.F. Coppola let it be known through a spokesman that henceforth he wants to be called just plain 'Francis Coppola,'" *Variety* announced in April, adding, "[He] did not forward a definitive reason with his request."

Shedding "Ford"? He had always said he used his middle name because his brother, August Floyd Coppola, used his. But he was the bigger, badder boy now, maybe even a man. "Willard's journey up the river is also a journey into himself," Coppola wrote, "and the strange and savage man he finds at the end is also an aspect of himself." That aspect within Coppola he had unknowingly concealed, his whole life long, under the guise of "Good Boy." But to know, as he now did, tremendous artistic and fiscal power, while his father and older brother clung to his coattails, was to betray the stated order of the family hierarchy. It was "bad." "Italians that come from that little town mentality," Coppola said, "are very hard on their own and very cruel to those who don't quite cut the mustard at the same level that the star brothers or the star uncles do." His family's cruelty internalized, he whipped himself, on *Apocalypse*, not just as punishment for his success, but for gambling so much on the talent he and his parents decided, long ago, he didn't have. "My parents have that typical Italian-previous-generation thing that makes you doubt yourself and lose your confidence and feel guilty about being alive," Coppola said. "It's true that many of my complexes and embarrassments about myself, my insecurity about what I look like, come from that. My wife maintains that I've stayed overweight to 'fit in' with that idea. Because if I lost the weight, I'd be attractive, and I'm not prepared to do that." He said, "One of my prayers every day is that I could be more generous, because my nature is to be like my father, who was the opposite of that." And so it was that the very project of Zoetrope, premised on camaraderie and immoderation, struck at the very core of what Carmine was not.

"I was always in trouble with my father," Francis confessed. "So I was always depressed. And I think I started to become interested in projects to distract me from my state of being depressed. And I notice even now, if I'm just waiting for something like that, that depression comes back and of course modern treatment of depression is to give you drugs [but] I don't want an antidepressant. So instead, I invent another project and then I get all excited about it. So it's self medication."

Elective Affinities, Black Stallion, Tucker . . . But if success put him at odds with his family of origin *and* failure shamed him before himself, what kind of man was he? Michael?

The production had "gotten so crazy," Stephen Lighthill said, "that you didn't have to imagine being crazy or being driven crazy because you were crazy."

Kurtz?

"I didn't have any idea who the hell I was," Martin Sheen would say.

One day in the jungle, a bus found him on the side of the road at six in the morning. He had been crawling when it stopped for him. It was four hours by car—too far—to the nearest hospital. They lifted him onto the bus and drove off. From the bus, costumer Dennis Fill laid Sheen on a pile of shoes in a costume truck and raced him to the production office, where production manager Barrie Osborne emergency radioed Coppola's helicopter pilot: "I need you to go to immediately to these coordinates, pick up Marty Sheen and bring him to Makati Medical Center."

Sheen kept asking for a priest. The face he saw as they wheeled him down the hospital corridor was that of Janet, his wife. "It's only a movie, babe," she assured him. But it wasn't a movie; it was a heart attack. A heart attack and a nervous breakdown. "I completely fell apart," Sheen said. "My spirit was exposed. I cried and cried. I turned gray—my eyes, my beard—all gray. I was in intensive care." Janet slept on the floor beside him.

Sheen's translator, Delia Javier, prepared a funeral pyre; and a priest, at last, was called to his bedside.

Tom Sternberg strongly advised Coppola to keep shooting the film; he had to, "because if you stop," Sternberg explained, "it basically invalidates your insurance unless there is nothing else you can shoot." But there was nothing, without Sheen, to shoot. He was in virtually every shot. How long could they wait? "We didn't know if he was going to make it," Coppola said. "If he'd gone home to the U.S. for treatment, he might not have come back— his family might not have let him. I was scared shitless. The shooting was three-quarters done; it was all him, what was left." What if the studio pulled him, full stop, from the movie? What if Janet Sheen insisted her husband go home? Without a movie, how could Coppola pay back what he had borrowed?

In panic and haste, he telexed deputies Sternberg, Roos, and Hirsch with

"Coppola Cinema 7's official position policy": They would not suspend shooting, and it was *not* a heart attack. Sheen is resting in Manila, and "any speculation to the contrary is pure gossip. . . . Please be on guard to deny any other speculation. . . . I reiterate: any official and public word from us must first be approached by me." *They will not suspend shooting.*

Coppola felt himself, like Sheen, like Willard, he told Eleanor, as close to death as he had ever felt. But he had to keep shooting, using Sheen's brother Joe Estevez, his stand-in, for Willard, if only to keep up crew morale and the public relations charade of business as usual. "He is not dead until I say he is," Coppola decreed.

"There are a lot of emotional memories," Sheen reflected, "and they're the ones the soul hangs on to the longest. You have to find a place to let that go, and I think that belongs to God. I wouldn't share it with others that weren't there and don't know."

Eleanor was on the floor, seven thousand miles from home, crying. She had discovered he was having an affair, several affairs; there was, for starters, Playboy Bunny Linda Carpenter. . . . There was the kids' former babysitter, his assistant on *Godfather II*, Melissa Mathison. They had been seeing each other since then, the weekend, right before production began, he rewrote the script to Pacino's specifications. Melissa was there with him. In the penthouse. "Everybody I knew who cared about us," Eleanor explained, "everyone in the family who was aware of the conflicts that were going on in our experience—understood the situation." This new feeling, underneath the shock—what was it? "You go to the limits with your life and every possible aspect of it. You go to the heart of darkness in each of these different arenas, and why should I think I wouldn't go to the heart of darkness myself?"

MAR 11
TO: JEANNIE
FROM: FRANCIS
HAVE FULL RANGE CREDIT CARDS ISSUED TO MELISSA MATHISON
RE: AMERICAN ZOETROPE.

AMERICAN EXPRESS, MASTERCHARGE, TELEPHONE CREDIT CARD.
GIVE HER ACCOUNTING CODE SO SHE CAN APPORTION CHARGES
TO WHATEVER PROJECT SHE'S WORKING ON, I.E., TUCKER,
BROTHERHOOD, APOCALYPSE NOW, ETC.
HER SALARY IS 200 DLRS PER WEEK, PLUS FREE RENT IN L.A.
HOUSE AND CAR. SHE WILL BE DOING CERTAIN TRAVELLING, SO
MAKE SURE PETTY CASH IS AVAILABLE TO HER AS SHE NEEDS IT.
CONTACT HER AND CONFIRM TO ME.

The prop guy took Gray Frederickson to the big tent behind the mess hall and peeled back the tarpaulins revealing the source of the stench— real dead bodies. "Where'd these come from?"

"Some medical school gave them to us."

Frederickson had a fit. *Medical school?*

The military started an investigation and found out there was no such medical school.

Sam Bottoms, who ordinarily thought of himself as a peaceful man, discovered he had been robbed of two thousand dollars and went on a violent rampage, accusing everyone.

"After a while it was just like you were in a dream," Frederic Forrest said. "It just kept going on and on."

Dick White would see Coppola wandering outside his house at two or three in the morning.

Sofia, when they asked her at school what her father did, said, "He makes *Apocalypse Now*."

*　　*　　*

Walter Murch arrived as requested on March 11. Though Coppola, he saw, "was in unbelievable crisis," he still managed to lead a sound meeting with Murch, recordist Richard Beggs, and picture editor Richie Marks. George Lucas's *Star Wars* would be released in stereo; Coppola, inspired by the music of Japanese composer Isao Tomita, wanted *Apocalypse Now* to be presented with quadraphonic sound, a speaker in each corner of the theater. Ken Russell had used quintaphonic on *Tommy*, only provisionally, for the music, not dialogue and not effects. For *Apocalypse*, Murch said, they would need a single, central source for dialogue; that would necessitate *five* speakers, *five* tracks.

"Fine," Francis answered. "One other thing. When explosions happen I want the audience to *feel* the explosions, not just hear them."

Real explosions had frequencies down below the audible range. This meant an additional channel. "We need six tracks now," Murch said.

But why would the cinemas of the world reoutfit their theaters with new sound systems? Maybe, Francis thought, *Apocalypse* would be an event; it would play in one theater, one IMAX theater in the geographical center of the United States, and families from all over America would make the pilgrimage like they did to see Mount Rushmore or the Grand Canyon, to experience *Apocalypse*, a five- or six-hour movie with an intermission and dinner in between.

"Where are we going to mix?" Murch asked.

A former Chinese sweatshop, the Zoetrope storage space they were calling the Facility. "We can turn that into a mixing room."

"How big is this sweatshop?"

Coppola produced a floor plan. The space was small—smaller than their old mixing studio on Folsom.

Beggs said to Murch, "Work has already begun."

Sheen was still in the hospital.

They hadn't finished shooting.

The agreed-upon release date was nine months away.

Mounting daily, the interest on Coppola's loan was preposterously high.

He had no ending.

And he was now building *Apocalypse* its own postproduction studio in San Francisco.

"When are you going to finish this movie?" UA's Mike Medavoy asked Coppola over dinner in the Philippines.

"Never."

Coppola would deny succumbing, in the jungle, to what others described like convulsions, if indeed that's what they were.

His first episode had begun, just as mysteriously, in the final days of 1957. Coppola was at Hofstra, feeling scared and hard at work, when he was thrown down.

It would keep happening. Every few months, it would happen again. While at home a year or so later, his father berated him for not properly coiling the garden hose, and "an incident occurred in which [Coppola] suddenly became confused and began throwing things around," Queens Hospital psychiatrist Aaron Meister would report. "I threw myself on the floor," Coppola had written to one psychiatrist, "and although I knew and know it looked identical to a child's tantrum, it was a physical experience; like a sort of knotting of your muscles. I was very embarrassed and ashamed after I regained my control." Coppola surmised that the attacks were brought on by moments of incredible stress, "sometimes for important reasons, mostly for petty ones." He was prescribed tranquilizers. "I personally do feel it to be a sort of nervous fatigue . . ." he added, "recurring in an especially weak nervous system, and an especially overworked one, since I never stop feeling in a high pitched sort of way." Subsequently, Coppola's detractors would mistake his attacks for operatic bad behavior, hardly aware that a 1962 ECG reading had revealed to Dr. Meister a convulsive disorder and, obscurely, "an anxiety neurosis with underlying behavior disorder for which psychotherapy is needed." Eleanor had for years implored Francis to get help. He hadn't.

*   *   *

```
3/21/77
TO: FRANCIS
FROM: GEORGE LUCAS

GOING ON VACATION BUT SHOULD BE BACK BY JULY. EVERYTHING
GOING GREAT [on Star Wars]. START MIX ON MONDAY. HOPING
OPTICALS GET DONE IN TIME. WISH YOU LUCK.



3/21/77
TO: FRANCIS
FROM: ITALIA [Coppola]

THANKS FOR YR TLX. GLAD YOU ARE ALL SAFE. JOYCE JILLSON
ASTROLOGER WAS ON TV THIS A.M. AND SAID THAT SHE HAS
STUDIED YR CHART AND THAT YOU NOW HAVE DIFFICULTIES ON
YOUR FILM BUT IT WILL TURN OUT TO BE A GREAT FILM. AUGIE
TOLD ME THE SAME THING AND I WAS SO HAPPY TO HEAR HIM SAY
HE REALLY LOVES YOU A LOT. SO RELAX IN SPITE OF SETBACKS.
ALL WILL BE FINE. HOLD TIGHT.
```

April 1, 1977, marked the 200th day of shooting.

He would napalm the Kurtz compound the night of the 205th. "I want to create a big show," he had instructed Storaro—a visual war between high-octane American artillery and magnificent colored ribbons of flame and smoke. When they came, the booms were like body blows, and the conflagration so immense, the sky fire looked like daylight in the night. Outside a real war, the special effects experts agreed, there had never been anything like it on earth. And probably, Gray Frederickson thought, there never would be again.

"God," Dean Tavoularis murmured, "you couldn't buy a ticket to a show like that anywhere in the world."

```
APRIL 15
TO: TOM (TORONTO) AND NANCY [Ely]
FROM: FRANCIS
```

IN THE EVENT OF A TWO-WEEK HIATUS WAITING FOR MARTIN'S
RETURN TO WORK, I MAY RETURN TO S.F. FOR POST-PRODUCTION
PURPOSES. HOWEVER, I MAY RETURN VIA ROME TO GO TO
TECHNICOLOR WITH VITTORIO, THEN TO MADRID TO SEE JOSE
VICUNA, THEN TO PARIS TO SEE OUR DISTRIBUTOR THERE, ALSO
WOULD LIKE SOCIAL EVENING WITH ALBINA DU BOISROUVRAY
(THROUGH JACQUES BAR), THEN TO LONDON TO SEE WALTER MURCH,
THEN TO N.Y. TO SEE MALKIN AND NBC CENSORSHIP MAN, THEN
TO S.F. . . .
WOULD STAY NO LONGER THAN A DAY IN EACH PLACE.

Coppola, sitting on the bed in their home in the Philippines, called Gio in. Eleanor was seated at a table. "We're getting a divorce," he told his firstborn. "Your mother and I aren't happy together and we're getting a divorce."

Eleanor put on her bathing suit and took Sofia into the mineral pool. In time, Francis and the boys came in to join them. It could have been the late afternoon light, she thought, or the ancient power of the volcanic rocks; it could have been Sofia frolicking happily in the water, but Eleanor found herself relieved, restored, and, she could see, Francis did, too. Was this the real them?

"Well, kids," he said, "how do you like us now that we're divorced?"

"What's avorced?" Sofia said.

"I have wept over the impossible question of dual loyalties," Coppola said. "You feel loyal to your wife and your family, but you feel loyal to another person whom you have singled out for mutual confidence." Eleanor, he felt, had stopped encouraging him, but Melissa Mathison, he said, "was always on my side." Writer and muse and literary amanuensis, Mathison was bright and talented and also a midwife to Francis in transition, as he hid from shame, from his responsibilities to Eleanor and *Apocalypse*, in her, in the haven of Goethe's *Elective Affinities*, a novel that both dramatized Coppola's domestic crisis and reflected the kind of life-work continuum of Zoetrope. "[It's] about a husband and a wife," he said. "The former falls in love with a girl who comes to live with them, and the wife with another man. And what begins with a series of chemical attractions turns into an alchemical sense of relationships in which everyone and everything gets transformed." In Coppola's film adaptation of *Elective Affinities*—his next film, he decided—the character of Eduard, a scientist in Goethe's novel, he would change into a film director.

Waiting for Sheen to recover, *if* he recovered, Coppola applied himself to the future of Zoetrope, dividing his attention, conductor-like, over the various players in his movie orchestra—most pressingly, Carroll Ballard, instructing him via telex to stop rewriting his *Black Stallion* script ("I feel that this is a pattern of you as a writer") and to address, head-on, its "cliches and predictable characters and activities." By Coppola's count, Ballard had six first drafts—he thought now of changing the protagonist, Alec, a boy, into a girl—but with a start date looming, Coppola reminded him, with uncharacteristic harshness, "I intend to serve as executive producer on this film according to my best feelings as to what is best for the film, and I no longer care whether I am popular or have a million friends."

It was often like this: he went away to work on a movie and the people of Zoetrope lost course. They needed leadership, pulling back together.

MEMORANDUM

TO: ALL ASSOCIATES AND EMPLOYEES
DATE: April 30, 1977
FROM: Francis Coppola
I would like to clarify my hopes and plan, the nature of my Company, my various enterprises, and the way I would like to work with you in the future.
I realize that in the last three or four months I have been operating differently than I had in the past and that it must be difficult for the people who have worked with me and are working with me now, during this transition, to understand exactly what I expect of them. Let me take this opportunity to outline how I see the relationship.
. . . I have decided to reduce all the various companies and enterprises, wherever financially and legally prudent to do so, to one company. The

company will be known as AMERICAN ZOETROPE and, purely and
simply, it is <u>me and my work</u>.

. . . I would like to clarify this by saying that I am the person of authority
and would, for this period of transition, like to be kept abreast of all major
decisions be they financial or otherwise, and insist on giving my personal
okay on any expenditure (for obligations of $100 per week or a $500 one-
shot item) and any decisions which common sense would tell you would be
of importance.

About money in general—I know that the amounts of money I deal in seem
unreal to most people—they do to me as well; but please always remember
that I work in these amounts because I am willing to risk everything for
my work—very often, the money we are spending is borrowed by me—and
I must pay it back. I am cavalier with money, because I have to be, in order
not to be terrified every time I make an artistic decision. Don't confuse that
technique with the idea that I am infinitely wealthy. Many of you know
that is not true. Remember, the major studios and distributors have only
one thing that a filmmaker needs: capital. My flamboyant disregard for the
rules of capital and business is one of my major strengths when dealing
with them. It evens the score, so to speak . . .

This company is not a corporation with other stockholders. There is only
one person in authority and that is me. My wife has no interest in the
business or control and influence, other than what would naturally be so
through our marriage. Please remember, you are working for me . . .

Another area which is causing some problems is what I will call "jumping
the gun." I word my questions very carefully. Please act only on what I
have asked of you. If I ask you to order 12 Lalique glasses, please order
them. When they arrive, notify me that they have come in and ask me what
I want you to do with them. Don't jump the gun. Don't presume anything.
Check with me when in doubt or re-read my original Telex. $1,100 worth
of French crystal was sent to the Philippines unnecessarily because
someone did not read my Telex carefully. . . .

In the past, the nature of the company has been referred to as a "family" or
a club or hangout. In the future, I hope it will be none of these. My family
consists of my wife and three children. These people working for me and with
me are my Staff and Associates. I will pay them the respect of a courteous

and professional relationship and I ask that they do the same for me. My home, my personal possessions—automobiles, equipment, whatever—is my property just as your property is yours. Please do not assume the use of these things. I know in the past that I have encouraged this; but, simply, I have changed and I no longer see this as a viable way of working.

Please consider Zoetrope and the various other offices as your place of business. I expect people to dress and behave as they would for any other company. It is very important for me to dispel the seven-year ambience of a hippie hangout around the old American Zoetrope that attracted a certain group of young people anxious to work in the film business. I do not wish to attract these people. . . .

If I were to put one key statement as the source of my greatest trouble in the last two years, it would be lack of information—the reason my penthouse office is so expensive is because I never really knew or was told what it would cost. I know this is hard to believe, but it is true and, therefore, I must put it down. This is my fault and I accept the responsibility and the office . . .

When I am working in the San Francisco Penthouse, which I'll refer to now as my "studio" (I would appreciate it if you would refer to that in the future), I expect all telephone calls, messages and appointments to go through Nancy. I do not want anyone knocking on the back door or dialing me direct. Nancy will get you to me as soon as possible and will get your response back to you immediately . . .

Some other things on which I would like your consideration. Please remember, my name is Francis Coppola. I am dropping the Ford and would appreciate it if I am no longer referred to as I have been in the past. This comes from a statement I once heard which I feel is true: "Never trust a man who has three names." Also, my name is Coppola, the accent is on the Coppola. Please, if you aren't sure how to pronounce it, inquire— especially those of you who answer the telephone. Employees should certainly call me Francis unless there is some special reason of which you have otherwise been advised.

If you are dissatisfied with your job, conditions, salary and have received no results from your immediate supervisor, you may send me a short personal statement. I will answer immediately or I will talk to your boss.

The more concise your problem is stated, the more likely I will act on it. Obviously, the fewer problems I have, the better, but I don't want to feel that someone is dissatisfied or feels unfairly treated in my organization . . . Wherever I am will be considered the headquarters of the company, whether it be in the United States or somewhere else in the world. After that, what we now call the Columbus Tower is the headquarters of the company in San Francisco. I would like to change its name to what it has been known as for 60 years—"The Sentinel Building." As I mentioned before, I would like the 8th floor to be known as my "studio."

I hope that you don't regard this memo as a negative one. There are many fine people in my organization, people I want to continue with me and whose help has been invaluable in the past and with whom I look forward to a much more workable, pleasant relationship in the future . . .

My personal opinion is that "APOCALYPSE NOW" is going to be a very fine film, possibly even a great film. I have never worked on a film before that truly had the possibility and so I am very excited and exhilarated about thoughts of future productions, not only film, but in theater as well. I have very many ambitious plans for the future, and if things work out for me, I will have the capital and the staff to do them. However, the era of American Zoetrope being a Haven for young filmmakers or other directors and creative people to find a home is really not in the cards. From now on, I consider you my staff and to work on my films and my theater projects solely. Once Carroll Ballard finishes "THE BLACK STALLION" and Nick Roeg finishes "HAMMETT," there will be no future productions by any other directors. This will be a one-client studio and the sooner that we are able to gear ourselves to that fact, the better the company will run.

I've learned that success is as difficult to deal with as failure—perhaps more so. If this film is as successful as it could be, I will need your efforts and support more than ever.

Euripides, the Greek playwright, said thousands of years ago: "Whom God wishes to destroy, he first makes successful in show business."

With warm regards,

Francis Coppola

*   *   *

Returning to work after weeks in bed, Martin Sheen came to see that it was he himself, not Francis, who had given him the heart attack, "trying to avoid the interior pain," he said. The alcoholic "Martin Sheen" was merely a part he had been playing his whole life. "It was very simple," he said. Brando— Kurtz—had been right.

Vietnam veteran Doug Claybourne knew it was real; he would leap from dreams fighting the air above his bed. "I don't know if that was Vietnam or other things or who knows what," he said. Ten years later, there were times he still wouldn't make it through the night. In April 1977, he was holding a megaphone for Coppola on the river, filming a scene, as real as an improvisation, where Willard and the guys in the PBR shoot up a sampan of civilians. Filled with nonactors, the sampan carried an actual doctor and a lawyer and a young girl brought over that day from Vietnam—all meant "to die" in front of Claybourne as they might have ten years earlier in Vietnam. After a year of filming Filipinos standing in for Vietnamese, the actors were suddenly themselves, or closer to it: Americans and Vietnamese acting together. It took Claybourne's breath away. Not the terror or even the pain of reenactment, but, strangely, the calm. To bring into waking life what kept him from sleep, and collaboratively, with the Vietnamese, he felt he was for the first time "doing something" with the war. "I was getting it out there for the other vets."

Coppola called Claybourne into his houseboat on the 238th day of shooting *Apocalypse Now*. As he entered, Claybourne recognized the calm, philosophical look on Coppola's face; it was like his own the day they shot the sampan sequence.

"Let's pull the plug," Coppola spoke.

"What do you mean?"

"Let's wrap."

". . . Wrap?"

"I just realized today you can't make a perfect movie." It was May 21, 1977. "Let's wrap, Doug. Let's go home."

They wrapped.

Vietnam, however, came home with them.

The wilderness of the Coppolas' Napa estate was an ideal setting for combat. Staged for second-unit photography, the *Apocalypse* PBR was shipwrecked under an old oak tree visible from Eleanor's upstairs window; the helicopter was parked in the driveway. A gasoline bomb went off for the cameras, but the detonation was so powerful, it didn't ignite—it vaporized the fuel "into a giant opaque ball of gasoline," sound man Andy Aaron said, which just hung there, cloud-like, threatening to explode at any moment. "Nobody move!" Joe Lombardi was yelling. "Nobody move! Everybody just walk backward . . ." Beyond them, an olive grove, covered in military tents and bodies that looked like they had been dead for weeks, doubled as a battlefield. The sound of gunfire and flying shrapnel was continuous. "I heard the words no one ever wants to hear," Aaron said. *I didn't know it was loaded,* and a panicked housekeeper, not prepared for foley artists and sound recordists, forwarded Peter Dornbach an equally urgent call from the D.A.'s office. "Is this Francis Coppola's property?" they asked Dornbach. "We've been flying over that area and people are scared to death." They had been scouring the landscape for paramilitary groups.

Eleanor was different since her return to Napa. Her new knowledge she experienced sometimes as loss, other times as exhilaration. "I am emerging from my tunnel vision," she wrote. "I am in a clearing where I can see more, see the literal and the illusion both at the same time." Why were they, was *she*, living in a Victorian-era house? She saw herself living in a home of eucalyptus, glass, and adobe.

Determined to find restoration, she lost herself searching in tarot; in works by Lao-tzu; in Esalen, Zazen, dream analysis, meditation. In a dream, she was a mummy.

"More and more people you didn't know were coming to screenings, walking around in your house," she said. "One morning, I sat down in the breakfast room, and somebody came down the hall, sat opposite me, and said, 'I'd like an order of bagels, please.'"

"When George first showed *Star Wars* to me . . ." Coppola recalled, "well, the kid was a wreck. I saw it with one other friend and my wife. I was the first one to see it. It was a bunch of black-and-white stuff with lines crossing it, and then he'd have a stupid scene that looked like it was a Sunday morning English television children's show, and even though we were on George's side and we were saying, 'Don't worry, George, it's gonna be OK' . . . but even *I* thought the performances were terrible and, no matter what he did to it, the film would just barely squeak by, and no more. But then my wife caught it, when it was finished and with an audience, [and] she said to me, 'Francis, it's unbelievable. This is the greatest thing ever!' And when I saw it myself, I agreed."

May 1977 was the month *Star Wars* opened and made George Lucas rich beyond anyone's imagining. "We can do all the dreams we always wanted to," he told Coppola, "and I want to do it with you." They could buy Mann Theatres, all of them, including the Chinese on Hollywood Boulevard, for about $20 million. Or even Fox. "These were opportunities," Coppola explained, "that because of my appetite, I was not afraid of." Lucas, however . . . How committed was he?

"Well, George," Coppola assuaged him, "you wait until you get the dough, and then see if you still feel that way."

But George Lucas would get the dough. And more dough.

Coppola, meanwhile, was coming up short. All that he had to spend on *Apocalypse* he had already spent in production, leaving himself, on the brink of postproduction, strapped for cash once again.

The seismic, era-redefining impact of, first, *Jaws* and, now, *Star Wars* shredded the appetite for personal movies in Hollywood, the sort of director's cinema Lucas had longed for and achieved in *THX 1138* and *American Graffiti*. One could have imagined him, his pockets overflowing, renewing his commitment to the Zoetrope dream, taking a page out of Coppola's

Godfather book and using the Force to defeat the Hollywood Empire. But he, too, had changed.

It would be a sadness for Coppola—indeed, for the world—that the "Hollywood George Lucas" would never again be the George Lucas, glimpsed briefly, of USC or, briefer still, of American Zoetrope. But maybe those identities were detours, and he was, first and last, his father's son. For that matter, who in the post-*Star Wars* Hollywood would continue to wage the Oedipal war? BBS—the great production outfit of *Easy Rider* and *The Last Picture Show*, and an acknowledged inspiration for Zoetrope— had folded. Robert Evans, talent hustler of Paramount, had left his position as head of studio. John Calley, the director's best friend—even if not Coppola's—at Warner Bros., was in limbo. United Artists?

Hollywood, 1977.

"We were finished" is how Scorsese put it. He was speaking, of course, of his entire generation, their first dream—before money, before cocaine—to wrest Hollywood from the suits and change the way movies were made. What had been lost?

Lucas would say he based the character of Han Solo, his charisma and older-brother bravado, on Coppola, but the comparison is superficial. The true spirit of Coppola, if it's to be found anywhere in Lucas's comic book movie, is in Luke Skywalker, their first and only hope.

"Francis," Dennis Jakob told him, "it's all up to you now, you're the only one."

Apocalypse would be for them.

If it hit.

If he finished it.

But he was out of money.

"If you go under, Francis," George told him. "I'll buy the house and the personal things that you love, and when you make the money, you can pay me back."

Coppola didn't take him up on it. Instead, he sold his 72,000 shares in Cinema 7, divesting Zoetrope of its independent distribution arm. But that was only the beginning.

"COPPOLA HOCKS HIS PERSONAL FORTUNE"—*Variety*, June 8, 1977.

All his assets, including his homes, hocked to United Artists for *Apocalypse* completion funds worth about $10 million, bringing UA's total commitment to the neighborhood of $17 million and the complete bill, all in ($7 million of which had been advanced by foreign distributors), to something around $25 million.

United Artists took out a policy on Coppola worth $15 million. It was not lost on him that in weighing the dollar value of his death against potential box office, his death could be more lucrative. "I'm willing to die making this movie," he told John Milius. "And if I die making this movie, George will take over. And if George dies, you'll take over. And somehow this movie will get made."

From the Philippines, Coppola had flown directly to Toronto, where Carroll Ballard had begun, and immediately lost control of, *The Black Stallion*. Still in his black Vietcong pajamas, a surprisingly thin Coppola descended in a BAC-111 like a king, and with his entourage in tow, he regarded the quite obviously troubled production with a survivor's eye. Ballard was only a few days in, but already there was mutiny in the air. Crew members had quit, and Ballard openly disowned his own script, a dumb, *Leave It to Beaver* story, he thought, about a boy and a horse, which neither he nor Murch nor Melissa Mathison had improved to Ballard's satisfaction. They would try to think up scenes the night before, and sometimes Ballard would be handed a new idea in the middle of the scene, but Ballard still couldn't get his mind around the central concept. Nor could his star, Kelly Reno, a novice picked from among fifteen hundred young actors to star in a movie, maintain his concentration. "You could get fifteen, maybe twenty seconds out of him," Ballard said.

"I was having a terrible time," he conceded. "I was the most inept guy imaginable." He had, of course, made sensational documentaries and short films, but *Stallion* was, thanks to Coppola, his first scripted feature, and he was already vowing it would be his last. As director, he didn't know what to do with an outfit of seventy-five people, and even if he did, he was not a talker, not to crew, not to executives, and certainly not to actors.

And then there was Mickey Rooney.

"I want to do the scene with Mickey," Ballard announced to cinematographer Caleb Deschanel long after the lights had been set for the day's scene, which did not include Rooney. It was Deschanel's first feature, too.

"Mickey's an hour away."

"We'll just wait, then."

At this, the Canadian crew, mostly TV guys, went crazy. This is not how they did things—anywhere. In Hollywood, *The Black Stallion* could have cost the studio $40 million, and Ballard would have been fired long ago. "I have no illusions about the factory system," Ballard said. "Twenty-five-day shoots, a matte shot here, master shot, two-shot, single shot, bam-bam-bam. I'd be an utter failure at it because I'm muddleheaded and unorganized."

Disembarking from the BAC-111, Coppola surveyed the scene and put a hand on Ballard's back. "Good luck," he said, and flew away.

Later, in Sardinia, on what may have been the most beautiful beach ever filmed, Ballard and Deschanel started shooting the way no studio filmmakers could, following black horse and boy like documentarians. "The entire crew, I think, regarded me as a total moron," Ballard said, "because I wasn't doing anything the way it was supposed to be done." But in Italy, freed from union requirements and with a crew of about twenty, Ballard moved easier, at his own pace. For days, they would film the boy exploring the island, just discovering things to eat.

"Okay, Carroll," Deschanel said. "I think we got that."

Ballard sighed. "I got a few pieces." About two and a half hours.

He would think of the deepest core of the film, of any film, not as a script or even a story, but as a pebble he carried in his pocket. Each film had a pebble. You touch it when you get lost, and its surface tells you, though not in words, why you're there. On *The Black Stallion*, a Zoetrope movie, Ballard touched his imaginary pebble and remembered himself thousands of miles away and not so many years before, a boy in the woods, lonely but floating happily on Lake Tahoe, gazing into the water. That boy was free. Touching the pebble, he saw Coppola—in a similar show of freedom—throwing his hands in the air like Kelly Reno, the kid riding his powerful stallion. *We all have those friends*, Ballard thought—he had Francis—who would carry them stallion-like through life. "If it wasn't for Francis," Deschanel said, "I don't think Carroll would have a career at all."

The Sardinia sequence took up only a few pages in the script; they shot on the island for three months.

Returning with his hours and hours of footage to the Sentinel Building, Coppola planned to experiment with *Apocalypse Now* on video, dissolving between images, tape to tape, via an original editing system that he had hired Steve Calou, local video maven, to build in the penthouse. Calou had already developed Zoetrope's "film chain," the assembly line by which *Apocalypse* film dailies were transferred to video in San Francisco and sent to Coppola in the Philippines, but cutting video for a feature film—that is, going from film to three-quarter-inch videotape and then back to film again—had never been attempted. The cinematic equivalent of a sketch, Calou's system would allow Coppola to "previsualize"—his word—the cut without having to go through the cumbersome, costly, and time-consuming process of actually cutting film. "It was a little groundbreaking," Calou said modestly. They named it the Video Machine: three video screens, each with an image Coppola could then mix on the main monitor, layering picture on picture on picture as Murch layered sounds. "It was a one and only, a one-off," Calou said, "and I had no documentation, really, about how it worked if I had to fix it." It was a new technology perfectly suited to the liminal states of *Apocalypse Now*. Coppola could now cut as fast as he could think, and dissolving back and forth between images, as if between thoughts, he could also cut in a way that replicated the very process of thinking, or dreaming, or something in between.

As Coppola experimented with the film's opening sequence—Willard emerging into traumatized, drunk, and drugged semiconsciousness in his derelict Saigon motel—picture editors Barry Malkin, Richie Marks ("a poet with opticals," Coppola dubbed him), Walter Murch, Dennis Jakob, Jerry Greenberg, and their assistants toiled on their allotments of film on their traditional KEMs and Moviolas, splicing, taping, and grease-penciling in their basement rooms in the Facility underneath the Little Fox Theatre. The space was poorly ventilated, the air conditioners were old, and their rooms—rumored to have been part of a brothel for sailors and outfitted with tiny sinks for the care and cleaning of the girls—were dark virtually twenty-four hours a day; proof of sun was limited to one high little window that opened up to the alley behind the building. But spirits were up. Especially among the assistants—young, punk, and, for the first time in their lives, part of something important. One said, "There was a fair amount of partying going on, and the music at the time"—the Dead Kennedys, the Clash, X—"was kind of loud, angry, fast, up-tempo. Music very much set the tone for a lot of things." Less frisky were the editors themselves, charged with cutting into a "totally massive amount of film," Marks said, referring to the 1.5 million feet of exposed negative and a million feet of printed film.

Their spirit of accommodation Coppola returned with interest. They were all amateurs, he liked to say, including himself (the Latin *amātor* meaning "lover"), and so he wanted it to stay, because the second they started believing they knew what they were doing, they would lose the need—and it must be nothing less than a need—to discover things they didn't know. "I felt like it was the most exciting place on earth to be working," said Martha Cronin, who was hired into the clerical department with no accounting background. "They paid me so little, but I probably would have done it for nothing." Thus was the Sentinel Building populated almost exclusively by the passionately inexperienced. They'd all seen *The Godfather*. And *Godfather II*. Who on earth hadn't? "One time, I saw a piece of mail come into Francis's penthouse," Peter Dornbach recalled, "and it just said 'Francis Ford Coppola, San Francisco,' and it got to his office."

The Sentinel Building, artifact of his imagination, flew at the speed of a thousand parallel thoughts. Coppola gave the orders, but the youth of San Francisco interpreted and actualized them. Their only supervision was the limits of their courage and creativity, regenerated, it seemed, with each new idea poured down from the penthouse. If the Sentinel Building was his lab, they were his beakers, Bunsen burners, and—when yesterday's experiment ended, failed, or was just generally forgotten—they (running projectors, carrying KEMs up narrow stairs, edge-coating film) were merrily reshuffled, sent up the elevator to Tom Luddy, director of special projects, or down to Eleanor, reviewing the documentary footage she had shot in the Philippines . . .

"Zoetrope," Leana Lovejoy said, "was the promised land for anyone who was interested in filmmaking." Dennis Gassner, working in the art department with Alex Tavoularis and Angelo Graham, atop the Facility, said it was "like going to Mecca." "A Never-Neverland," Arthur Coburn called it. As they had on Folsom Street, they would come in literally off the sidewalk, some with no background in film. Like Holland Sutton, a chef looking for a job: she had run into her friend, Zoetrope's Arden Bucklin, while crossing the street near Russian Hill.

"Can you type?" Bucklin asked.

"*Type?* No!"

"They're looking for an assistant at the Facility. Just say you can type forty words a minute."

Sutton walked in her résumé, "which only had food stuff in it," she said, to Facility manager Karen Frerichs, and got the job. ("I think she thought I could teach her how to bake," Sutton said.) "When postproduction started gearing up," Frerichs recalled, "people from all over the place were calling for work." Word got around: Coppola, triumphant, was back in town. Folks would cluster outside the Facility just looking to be, somehow, a part of the next masterpiece. "It was that casual," Frerichs said. "And the kids who made an impression on me would leave their phone number, and we'd hire them. And then we'd hire their friends." Film editor Richard Candib said, "People just showed up and got hired, which just could not have happened in Hollywood in those days, because of the unions. That was the most important ingredient of Zoetrope, openness to anything and anyone."

You never knew when the phone would ring or who would be calling. Requests ranged from the sublime to the bizarre, Zoetrope's Trudy Hamm said, "like somebody would walk in and say, 'Francis called and said he left a rental car in Detroit, can we find it?' I'd say, 'Can you give me some more details?' They'd say, 'That's all we know.'"

No longer did the offices surge and slow at the erratic pace of a telex sent to San Francisco from across the world. Armed now with an internal telephone, Coppola fired his attention to his immediate left and right and eight floors below, and the scattershot evolution of his kingdom, its "rewriting," proceeded around the clock at an impossibly thrilling rate. The money—whether he had it or not—was never a question. They, he, were growing.

He needed more people—now.

Tess Haley was up in the penthouse interviewing with Coppola for the position of personal assistant when, in the middle of their conversation, he lit up. "Let's give everyone the day off," he decided, right then and there. "Let's give everyone a holiday. Let's call the Facility and tell everyone that Wednesday is going to be a free day," and he proceeded to ask Haley to make the necessary phone calls.

"Excuse me, Francis." She stopped him. "Do I have the job?"

(She had the job.)

The phone, the phone . . . Calls from Werner Herzog, crashing at the Broadway house; from Wim Wenders, pacing upstairs, toiling on the umpteenth revision of *Hammett*; calls from First Lady Rosalynn Carter; calls from the wacko woman who wanted to sell him Marilyn Monroe's soiled bra. Then there was the incessant Italia Coppola, described by one Zoetropean as a "very paranoid Anna Magnani, super intense, more intense than anyone you ever met in your life. And she started telling me some stories about things in her life with Francis, and I thought, *Well these are kind of personal. Why is she telling me?* She didn't know me, I'm a nobody here." There was filmmaker Stanton Kaye, who would wander in and out of the Sentinel Building in bare feet, let himself into the penthouse (when Coppola wasn't there), and, pretending to be Coppola, wave down at the people below. Or was that Stanton Kaye at all? "People would walk in off the street," Martha Cronin said, "and we wouldn't know whether this might be some derelict-looking person from North Beach or one of Francis's genius friends. It was like, 'Should we let this guy in?'" Dennis Jakob they called "the White Vampire." When he found out Zoetrope's Michael Lehmann knew German philosophy, he started popping in just to talk Hegel and Kant. "I didn't know how crazy [Jakob] was," Trudy Hamm said, "until I was told to go pick him up at the airport, and I remember him, in the backseat, saying very intensely that he only wanted me to drive in the middle lanes because he believed in moderation in all things."

As Hamm would explain, "What we were doing was dealing with people who were very artistic and not always practical and also needing things. You knew when you were talking to [Coppola] that he was a real artist, for good or for bad. That would mean that he needed to kind of pursue random ideas and [to] daydream, and all the things that artists need to do." What about buying a place in Belize? (It was rumored he meant buying the entire *country*.) What about buying the apartment up the street? What about buying a studio in Los Angeles?

"The mood swings were never negative for us," Hamm said. "He would go through months where everything had to be big big big, so that was sort of [what the] buying-Belize idea was. Then his money men would tell him, 'You're running out of money' or 'This isn't financially going to work,' and he would get very very angry, and then everybody had to go, except for us, because we were so lowly, we didn't even make much money, so we ended up being the ones who sort of surfed the highs and the lows. . . . And then, over the next couple of months, it would start building up again. There'd be plans, big, big, weird plans that he was going to do."

"The place was crazy," Jean Autrey said. "But that's what made it fun."

Why go home? After work, they would fill the Albatross, a maritime sa-loon up the street, for "drinking, drinking, drinking," one Zoetroper said. At any hour of the night at its long, beat-up wooden bar, you could find an editor or an assistant or an assistant editor exchanging can-you-believe-it tales from the day. "Everybody wound up at the Albatross having drinks after work," Frerichs said. "God we got drunk. We got very drunk." Though most hadn't been to the *Apocalypse* set, they somehow retained its spirit of freedom, anarchy, madness, community. "We were the cool kids," Leh-mann said, "not the corporate kids." It put them in a kind of friendly com-petition with their cousins up at Lucasfilm, who, by virtue of *Star Wars* and "Uncle" George, produced a more systematic, more focused working culture, pursuing similar if not identical goals in the advancement of post-production technology. But it wasn't Lucasfilm where, when a few women from accounting stepped into the elevator with Burt Reynolds, Francis, twinkling, sang, "Ah, the ladies from accounting and Burt Reynolds! Let's have a romantic ride down!" and then switched off the lights. All rode down to the street giggling.

Coppola took the editors—Murch, Jakob, Marks, Greenberg—for a Chi-nese lunch to warn them of "the law" of *Apocalypse*: anyone who works on the picture for any length of time, he said, "becomes insane." Pointing at himself, he added, "I'm the poster boy for the person who's the craziest sit-ting at this table because I've worked on the film the longest. The next per-son is Richie Marks because he's worked on it longer than Jerry. And then there's Jerry and then there's you, Walter." He turned to Murch. "You're the sanest because you haven't really started working on this film. Dennis, of course, is already completely crazy anyway." This was to be very much a part of the film's composition, Coppola explained: "I want the film to start normal and get crazier and more surreal the deeper you get into the film, so it's appropriate that Dennis is working on the very end of the film; it's appropriate that Richie is working on the lead up to the ending; it's appropriate that Jerry is working on the middle to early part of the film, and I want you, Walter, to work on the beginning of the film. Because I want it to be normal."

The editors sleepwalked into the Facility, still unfinished, around 9 or 9:30 a.m., put on the first pot of coffee, and gathered on the dormitoryesque couches in the break room. There would be jokes, perusals of Herb Caen's column for Coppola or *Apocalypse* gossip, and convivial talk of headlines, the ghastliest of which were gleefully posted on the refrigerator. "There were a lot of bus crash headlines," Karen Frerichs pointed out, tokens of the dark humor the editors held tight to to stay afloat. Keeping their minds fresh and objective in the face of so much footage required a steady, hard-won force of will, but down in their bunker, humor and bonhomie did not completely shield them from taking in a little madness themselves. Even Frerichs, at her post out front behind the reception desk, was not safe from the sounds of war coming from within nor from the *ca-chunk, ca-chunk, ca-chunk*, like an enemy approaching but never appearing, of the film chain running, always running, down the hall. "Oh my god, you went crazy," she said. "If I had to listen to one more 'never get off the boat, never get off the boat . . .'" Wisely, they made a game of it. Whenever an editor quoted a line ("Sell the house, sell the car, sell the kids"), he or she had to drop coins in the money jar, which would go toward financing their next party. But make no mistake: down there, they were in the jungle. "When you're editing," Murch said, "you're in an enclosed space for many, many hours a day. You're under a certain degree of tension and stress, and the same things are repeated to you over and over again, which Arthur Koestler once described, I think in *Darkness at Noon*, as being the three essential ingredients of brainwashing. So you become kind of benignly brainwashed into the methods by which the film will tell itself." The Tower Mentality, they called it.

With the editors unencumbered by stringent guild regulations, the traditional hierarchies of Hollywood cutting didn't apply. Richie Marks was a senior figure, father-like but never dictatorial; assistant editors were charged with creative responsibility and the mandate to experiment; there was simply too much to be done, too many questions unanswered and, with deadlines to hit, never enough time or hands. Michael Cimino was already making tracks on his own Vietnam film, *The Deer Hunter*, and stood a chance of releasing the first major American film about the war, filling the hole in the marketplace Coppola thought he had cornered for himself well over two years earlier.

Murch estimated they cut the film at the rate of 1.47 cuts per day.

Pushing the release date back once again, United Artists now wanted *Apocalypse* for June 1978. But Coppola was still talking about the ending. Stationing himself behind the video machine in his penthouse, he experimented with his dream sequences, slowly dissolving from image to image—and alone, as if he were once again a boy beset with polio discovering the power and freedom of remote control. The body of the film he left to his editorial deputies below. His ideas would be theirs to interpret. "He had something in mind," Andy Aaron said, "even if it wasn't fully formed. He was aiming at something. He had an encoded vision."

Panic was on a low flame, but the footage was so good, and their undertaking, they agreed, so honorable that for every terror, present and foreseen, there was an equally compelling promise—glory, take your pick: Oscars like those on a shelf in the Facility break room or, somehow, in cutting this story together, a making sense of the American trauma of Vietnam. Though he rarely appeared in the cutting room, Coppola—"a leader from the bottom up," Claybourne said, "not top down," and, by some accounts, too harried to lead at all—was continually collecting post-screening feedback from *anyone*, reassigning sequences, asking editor A to take a shot at editor B's footage. "I feel that it helps to give the film more of a uniform editorial sense," Coppola explained, "but it drives editors crazy." Dennis Jakob, already crazy, was mainly assigned to the crazy Kurtz compound sequence, a labor of Method editing Coppola had arranged to bring up what was underneath both artist and art—and did. To cut the helicopter battle—

some 130,000 feet; more than most feature films—Coppola recruited the soldierly Jerry Greenberg. "Francis saw I was the guy," Greenberg agreed. "I could live in that shit." Murch would trundle into the Facility, Candib observed, review all the footage, and then lower his head onto the KEM and, it seemed, go to sleep.

"What the hell are you doing?" Candib asked.

"I'm dreaming," he intoned. "I'm dreaming the scene."

Now there were, by some counts, only two Francis Ford Coppolas. By others, more. At work, he was a dervish. At home, he was unreachable, as depressed as Eleanor had ever seen him. They tried to find each other in discussions of the movie's themes, how there is no oneness, only duality, how there is no good without evil, and therefore, evil brings with it the possibility of good, and vice versa. Then he told her it wasn't just an affair; he was in love with Melissa Mathison.

He had promised he wouldn't see her again.

Outside her body, Eleanor watched herself throw a vase of flowers across the room. In the kitchen, she saw red walls crash into white dishes and one dictionary definition of *apocalypse*, she learned, was "revelation of hidden knowledge."

Staffers privy to his flings, the women zipping to and from his penthouse bedroom, were fraught with conflict and indecision. They knew they were complicit—often struggling to keep Eleanor, to the best of their ability, detained—but what else could they do? It was, they assured themselves, none of their business. Except, of course, Coppola frequently *made* it their business: he borrowed a Zoetroper's empty bedroom for a fling outside the city; he took off (with Melissa Mathison, one assistant editor speculated) without warning, going who knew where (Europe?); he invited girlfriends to Zoetrope parties at his own home and flirted openly; he flirted with journalists; he invited Mathison, instead of Eleanor, to a rough-cut screening of *Apocalypse . . .*

Coppola had never put much stock in keeping his private life private. Zoetrope, for better and for worse, was an extended family, and his immediate family, for worse and for better, carried into Zoetrope. They knew that Gio was having trouble at school, knew Carmine and Italia had to be appeased. They knew who Coppola's pot dealer was (his driver). Making no secret of his personal life, some surmised, even making an exhibition of it, Coppola engendered more exhibitions of intimacy in return, deepening confidences and family-like attachments that brought him increased loyalty, knowledge, and control. His own parents, many observed, operated in much the same way toward him, their Pinocchio, attached by an invisible umbilical cord. Theirs were bonds of love but also, as Francis was the family star, jealousy, anger, and need.

He would change the name of American Zoetrope to "Omni Zoetrope," that is, "OZ," casting him, in the minds of some Zoetrope staffers, alternately as the Wizard at his manic height, pushing buttons from behind his great curtain, and also, when the curtain fell, something like Frank Morgan's Professor Marvel, a great specter cut down to size—even if it was only he who was doing the cutting. Some speculated that the man in the penthouse, failing to end *Apocalypse*, swept his panic under the rug of new projects and plans for expansion; others said he was merely fulfilling Zoetrope's destiny . . . He would build Zoetrope a story department on the seventh floor. He saw a setup of writers and word processors on typewriter tables beneath giant reams of butcher paper (for outlining), hung on walls like white conceptual artwork . . . He would build an acting department; he would buy up properties around North Beach; there'd be buildings for each department; he'd have his own studio, a studio within a city . . . He appeared in Dennis Jakob's cutting room in the Facility, crawled under his flatbed, drew his knees into the fetal position, and sobbed. Jakob helped him to his feet, but Coppola turned away and began pounding his head against a wall. "Fool, fool," he muttered. "I don't know what this movie is about. I never did."

"A lot of people around me informed me that Francis was having a manic crisis," Eleanor said. Again, she would ask him to get help. Again, he resisted. His highs were too bracing, he maintained, and the lows too infrequent. Also, there existed the possibility—or, at least, the fear—that his abilities could vanish with the cure. One had to wonder, then, if "mental illness" was even an appropriate designation for a mind, however torrential, that produced *The Godfather*. "There's a kind of adrenaline efficiency," he said, "that's akin to madness. But it's not like banging your head against the wall. It's like maniacal purpose. You get extra good at what you're doing." Coppola had read enough of his own press to know the terms of his psychological well-being would be decided not by doctors, but by audiences and critics. If *Apocalypse* triumphed, they'd call him a visionary.

And if it didn't?

Eleanor arrived at *Moodswing: The Third Revolution in Psychiatry*, by New York psychiatrist Ronald R. Fieve MD, and read in his account of manic depression a complete portrait of her husband. It was freeing. To discover that *she* was not crazy, that her husband's behavior, however damaging, was not personal, and that her inability to alter him was not her failure, she reached out to Fieve for a series of consultations. They helped her further organize what she had felt and seen. Her husband's disparate selves (the gambler, the general, the writer, producer, director, boy scientist, salesman, showman, and rake) were all accounted for, as were their opposites (the paranoid, the enraged, the defeated). Lincoln, Churchill, and Theodore Roosevelt had suffered similarly; the number of artists afflicted was legion.

The Coppolas were entertaining Warren Beatty in the screening room of the Broadway house: Coppola was telling Beatty of the new world he envisioned, the coming of a completely digital cinema, a *video* cinema, wherein a single actor could play every character, man, woman, giant, dwarf, the way an electronic keyboard could be programmed to sound like an oboe, a bassoon, a violin, a whole orchestra . . .

Beatty, something of a medical gourmet, looked to Eleanor. "I think we should take Francis to a doctor."

They did. The prescription, lithium.

In her book *Touched with Fire: Manic-Depressive Illness and the Artistic Temperament*, which she would send to Coppola, Kay Redfield Jamison characterizes the condition as "a singularly cyclic disease" inherently aligned with ideas of regeneration, a central preoccupation of Coppola's work, a defining quality of his Icarian career and Zoetrope's own revolutions, its new beginnings and ends. Jamison quotes Edgar Allan Poe, himself a manic-depressive:

"I come of a race noted for vigor of fancy and ardor of passion. Men have called me mad; but the question is not yet settled, whether madness is or is not the loftiest intelligence—whether much that is glorious—whether all that is profound—does not spring from disease of thought—from *moods* of mind exalted at the expense of the general intellect. They who dream by day are cognizant of many things which escape those who dream only by night."

"You know, my wife and children don't enjoy the opera," Coppola told Dennis Jakob, "but I have these tickets."

Jakob took the tickets and invited Nancy Jencks, assistant editor on *Apocalypse*; Coppola had his eye on her, too. But "Dennis was in love with Nancy Jencks," said someone close to the production, and Coppola knew it. He met Jakob and Jencks at the opera, and Jakob watched, with growing rage, as Coppola, quite benignly, started flirting with his date, and Jakob "fucking hit the roof." Coppola had planned the whole thing, Jakob decided. He had staged it.

The next morning, sound effects editor Tim Holland and a colleague walked into Jakob's cutting room and found that both Jakob and his reels, the Do Lung Bridge sequence and all the trims, had gone missing. "Word got out quickly," Holland said. "People were running around, and it was very crazy." A full week later, Jakob and the film were still missing, but the real alarm didn't sound until the plastic bags started arriving—full of ashes. The first appeared with a note to the tune of "Francis, this is reel one. I've got a fireplace. It made a real nice fire." Then came the next bag and "Francis, this is reel two. We've got eleven more reels to go. It's a lot of fun seeing it go up." But Holland wasn't buying it. To be absolutely sure, they tried to set some discarded film on fire and—they were right—it wouldn't light. What had been burned wasn't film. So, they met with Jakob for a surprisingly sedate lunch in Berkeley. "He was really affable," Holland said, "but exactly what he wanted was a little bit unclear." Seemingly vindicated, Jakob had exacted his pound of flesh from Coppola—"Boy, did that guy *sweat*," Jakob said—and the Do Lung Bridge sequence, along with Jakob, contentedly humming "Back in the Saddle Again," returned to the Facility.

But Jakob didn't like running his sequence in the Facility's little screening room, so Holland would lug the work print to Coppola's spacious home theater, in the basement of his house on Broadway, where Jakob could analyze his progress on the big screen. "He would occasionally scream at the picture," Holland said, then rush upstairs to debate changes with Coppola. In November, a sudden boom so powerful that it could be felt through the soundproof projection booth walls had Holland and a colleague racing upstairs into the Coppola family kitchen, where they found Dennis and Francis, sitting contentedly at the dining room table, enjoying a drink as if nothing had happened. Outside, it was raining heavily. "What was that noise?" Holland asked. Jakob pointed behind them to a giant palm tree that had crashed through Gio's room and the breakfast room below, "like a knife through a wedding cake," as Coppola put it. Now its crown sat there in a chair, as if it had been invited. Coppola decided to acknowledge the miracle—"an act of God," Richard Candib said—with a celebration. "We have to have a party!" he rejoiced to Candib. "We survived!"

The workday was just ending at Zoetrope when phones started ringing with an invitation that spread, person to person, from the Facility to the Sentinel Building. "What had actually happened," Coppola said, was he "was sitting at a table with a young Sofia in rear of house, looking with her at a sea-horse-filled aquarium there. The phone rang, and it was from Ellie, who was visiting New York. I went to the phone by the entrance to the kitchen, and called little Sofia to come and say hi to her mom. We were both on the phone about fifteen feet away from the aquarium when there was a sudden, unexpected crash almost as if a grenade had gone off. The large towering palm tree in the garden had fallen on the house, slicing through its three floors and landing where we had just been sitting." Coppola would not recall whipping up an enormous pot of a pasta and pouring wine into overflowing Lalique glasses, passing them in handfuls to editors and secretaries and carpenters called forth to eat, drink, and fix the sunroom, but leave the tree, which lay there in the middle of the revel like a sacrificial carabao as music and laughter filled the house.

Clamming season. The winter king tides came to Walter and Aggie Murch in Bolinas, and the families Murch, Coppola, Ballard, Robbins, Lucas, and

Barwood took to the shoreline to harvest mussels. For years, it had been their tradition. "Those who didn't mind stealing and getting caught would go to the reef and 'thin' the mussels," Aggie wrote, "while those of us who were too chicken dug for clams." Eleanor would go for the mussels. She walked with Gio and Roman and Carroll Ballard out past the tide pools, to where the waves were breaking.

Francis, barefoot, caught up with them. He was lost in his film's ending.

Eleanor was as desperate as he was. She had been wrong to think that leaving the Philippines would bring them back; Francis wouldn't return until he had his ending. It was like he was sick with it; when he saw *Apocalypse* completed on-screen, outside his mind, he would be healthy again, she thought. Until then, they had to wait. The longer they withstood the pressure to define themselves, the more they could—if they could—evolve.

For instance, just weeks earlier, they had been driving with the children in Napa when Francis, the old Francis, started singing. It had been so long since they were in a musical.

In May 1978, Eleanor and Francis flew to New York. They had lunch with Bernardo Bertolucci; there were bags under his eyes. At Elaine's with Nan and Gay Talese, she noted that Bob Fosse was seemingly unwell; and at another table, Woody Allen sat alone. Reminded of their friend Martin Scorsese, his trials with his musical, *New York, New York*, his divorce, she wondered if what was happening to Francis was only symptomatic of a greater change. They were the most gifted, the most celebrated filmmakers of their generation, but something was taking them.

Francis was thirty-nine. Bertolucci was thirty-seven. Scorsese was thirty-five.

She went downtown—to the gallery Paul Mazursky had used in *An Unmarried Woman*—to see an old boyfriend. He had children now; they lived part-time with their mother in California. He was, of course, an artist.

Mostly, Walter Murch dreamt in silence. In dreams, he noticed, he moved slowly, deliberately, as if subject to the physical laws of waking life; whereas, in his waking life of cutting film and sound, where his imagination was free to defy physical laws, time and space sped by as freely as if he were in dream.

Encircled by trim bins, Murch was dreaming standing up at his editing table—a KEM raised to his height by apple boxes—when he was interrupted by a young man's voice. Awoken, he turned.

Dan Gleich had come for a job.

Murch felt him out with a round of standard questions. "You know," he offered. "I think we can hire you." He walked over to Gleich, who sat down as Murch came near, sat taller as Murch came closer still . . . until Murch was close enough to look intently into Gleich's eyes, as if inspecting them for tells.

"One last thing . . ." Murch leaned in. "One last thing we have to do before we can hire you for this job. You have to agree that you will stay on the job and do this job until the movie is finished . . ."

("And then," Gleich recalled, "he just *looked* at me.")

". . . No matter . . . *how long . . . that takes.*"

They began mixing *Apocalypse Now* on December 18, 1978.

Immersed in ancillary endeavors, Coppola in his absence demanded their total presence. They ran free. Mark Berger said of *Apocalypse*, "The picture, the vision, became bigger than Francis's imagination." Facing the big screen in the Facility's basement mixing room, Murch and Berger worked side by side in a pair of squeaky black leather chairs at their brand-new computerized mixing board—adapted from music industry technology specifically for *Apocalypse*—of six thousand dials, buttons, and switches. "We were living in a quest to explore new boundaries and create new ways of presenting sound," Berger said.

"Team spirit," Richard Beggs said, "would be putting it lightly. We all knew, from the highest to the lowest, that we were involved in something special and different. The stuff that we got into was amazing and hair-raising both creatively and technically. And I have to say, if I was a hard professional who was doing it for years, I would have said, 'Let me out of here.' But I didn't know any better." For Beggs, the experience was terrifyingly expansive, like dropping acid. "There were a lot of personal damages along the way," he said. "There were divorces, there were families that were neglected for months on end." Beggs's wife used to joke about Apocalypse chicken. "It was the chicken that was always dry because I said I'd be home in another hour, another hour, another hour . . ."

They needed helicopter pilot chatter for the attack on Baler—"It had to be real," Beggs said; "no actors"—so they brought in four Vietnam veteran helicopter pilots, and Beggs went down to an army surplus store on Market Street, bought a barrel of noise-canceling headsets and wired them into his console. In his studio in the basement of the Sentinel Building, he set up four chairs, no microphones, "just these headsets, which were like what they wore when they were flying"; the biggest screen he could possibly find, to screen for the vets the raw footage shot inside the helicopter from the pilots' perspective. There was no audio on the film, but Beggs had set up heavy-duty JBL studio speakers to play "interior helicopter noise with a lot of variation [and] at earsplitting quality, the way [it] would really sound inside one of those helicopters with the doors and everything open." When the moment came, Beggs sat the vets down in chairs in front of that screen. "You be the pilot," he directed them. "Take me back. I want to be there. Show me what it was like when you were in the air." The vets joked through the first ten or fifteen minutes of footage, "but over a relatively short period of time," Beggs said, "they transformed themselves into these guys, the men they were. You could hear it in their voices. They were screaming at each other. One of these guys had brought his wife—like, 'Hey, honey. It's showbiz.' Anyway, she came. And she was sitting behind me a few feet away, in the control room. And at one point, we stopped and took a break. And I heard something behind me. His wife is sobbing. She never heard her husband behave this way. I'm sure he had forgotten she was even there."

Randy Thom, on postproduction sound, said, "When Willard murders the young woman with the pistol, all of us dreaded going through that sequence every time we had to go through it, and we went through it thousands of times. You can't watch a sequence like that without being affected by it, even if you are a filmmaker, even if you know it's a movie, even if you know it's all fake, because, in a way, it's *not* fake." To mix a section of characters sloshing around in the muck, Murch came to the Facility basement in knee-high rubber boots and "was so in the zone," machine room operator Andy Moore said, "we didn't speak the whole time." Ordinarily, it was just one or two intercom words to Moore—"Put up reel two" or "next reel, please"—but as night came on, and the hours got longer, the immersion deepened, sometimes troublingly. "I think if you are fully invested in working on a movie like that, you are in danger of sinking into all of those things," Thom said.

The dominant means of presentation, until then, was Dolby stereo, speakers just left, center, right. Murch's team upgraded surround technology to 5.1: three channels in front, two in the back, and a low-frequency subwoofer that would make those bullet sounds—recorded expressly for the film by actual soldiers on a munitions range—"Francis wanted even the foley to be life-changing," said Thom—feel like body blows. It was a perfect setup for the helicopter *whomps*; with 5.1, the choppers would now circle, sonically, the movie audience. Feeding helicopter sounds to the synthesizer, they deconstructed and then embellished individually articulated sounds to achieve maximal familiar-strangeness, the feeling of semi- or hyperconsciousness. "You'll hear five or six different things going on when you get into different spatial relationships to it," said Thom. "Sometimes you'll hear just the rotor, then you'll hear just the turbine, then you'll hear just the tail rotor, then you'll hear some clanking piece of machinery, then you'll hear low thuds." The Ghost Helicopter, they called it. It was in them. "Walter was using his emotion," Thom observed. "He's very quiet, and the sense that you get when you're around him is of absolute focus. He is able to ignore the world and focus on this moment that he's working on. For him, I think, it is like a dream." The moment Murch, at the KEM, made a sonic connection between the chopper blades and the ceiling fan *whomping* over Willard's hotel room bed, Murch said, "was like one of those moments when Kennedy was shot"—he could never forget it. It hit him like a bullet to the solar plexus. "I, therefore, had become Willard," he said.

"*Apocalypse* was tough," Aggie Murch said.

Coppola brought in Michael Herr, author of the celebrated Vietnam memoir *Dispatches*, to produce a voice-over for Willard, and worked him like a screenwriter: draft after draft after draft. "And Francis fucking loved that," one Zoetroper said. "It was as though he wanted every single person working for him to be crawling on the edge of a straight razor." Herr and Coppola wrote together and wrote apart, and when the writing wasn't helping, Coppola enlisted others, Murch, Ferlinghetti . . . Milius, armed with a gun in a shoulder holster under his jacket, wrote with a serial killer gleam in his eye. "Everyone was exhausted, demoralized, could barely look at the problem in front of them," Herr said. Stripped down to raw delirium for energy, he saw his own eyes in the eyes of the editors, their "'thousand yard' stare. They were, you know, sittin' in front of their Moviolas, but it was almost like they weren't seeing anything." He came to consider the possibility that no book, no film, no channel of known human expression could achieve an understanding of Vietnam. Despite years of Coppola's sincerest efforts, the reckoning could not happen on the cultural scale; it had to happen one individual at a time. "What happened in Vietnam is not 'other,'" Herr said. "Everyone's got it in them. Everyone's got that shadow in them."

Herr would return to the Sentinel Building to rewrite Willard's narration off and on for a year and a half. "Sometimes," he said, "I would be working thirty-six to forty-eight hours, barely sleeping; almost ruined my health." Martin Sheen was no different. He came to town to record the voice-over, went out to Enrico's with Tony Dingman, and, finding himself back in the jungle, relapsed. Dingman bailed him out of jail and, the next morning, ushered him to the basement of the Sentinel Building, hungover, a mess of crumpled narration pages in his hand. Coppola, meanwhile, stayed up in the penthouse. The night Sheen spent in jail, electricians had spent yanking cables up the side of the building and into a custom box on Coppola's desk: now, with the push of a button, he could direct the basement editors by intercom, Oz-like. A full six hours later, they were still going, Coppola soaring the sky, Sheen down in hell. Returning haphazardly to discarded voice-overs, adding new ones, and combining them piecemeal on the fly, Coppola's voice was everywhere—directing Sheen, directing the sound crew, imploring them to add new and old narrations. New pages for Sheen came elevator-rushed down.

Coppola hadn't stopped, hadn't slept for three days. He sent one typist to the pharmacy to pick up his lithium prescription. The name on the label was Colonel Kurtz.

The screenwriter Armyan Bernstein just wanted to write a sweet, small, personal film. His last, *Thank God It's Friday*, had been mangled studio style; this one, based on his own breakup and set in his hometown of Chicago, he would spec.

"When am I going to read it?" MGM's Lucy Fisher kept asking him.

"No, no. This one is different. This one I'm just keeping for myself."

"Got it," she said. "It's one from the heart."

It was a love story. Hank and Frannie, regular folks, reach a dull patch in their relationship. They split, find the lovers of their dreams—or so it seems—and in the end, reunite. Fantasy is only a fling, the story says; the real thing is forever.

Fisher and Mark Canton ended up buying Bernstein's script for a tremendous $350,000. That's what CAA, gatekeepers of the new, post-studio Hollywood, could do for a writer. And for even more money, they could also make the writer a producer. Who did Armyan Bernstein, writer-producer of *One from the Heart*, want to direct his (no longer little) movie?

"Francis Ford Coppola."

MGM slumped in their chairs. "You're dreaming."

"Let's just send it to him. Let's just see what he says. Okay?"

"Every writer in the world wants Coppola to make their movie. You won't even get a reply. We'll be waiting for who knows how long . . ."

Bernstein sent Coppola the script anyway and, like every other screenwriter in the world, heard nothing.

Months later, as if in a movie, Bernstein saw the actual Francis Ford Coppola at JFK, apparently about to board a plane to San Francisco. Eleanor was with him.

"I'm sorry to bother you . . ."

Coppola turned.

"I—I'm a writer. I wrote a script called *One from the Heart*—"

"*One from the Heart?*"

"Yes, I—"

"Ellie, this is the kid who wrote *One from the Heart*."

Coppola pulled Bernstein into a hug and held him there. ("It seemed," Bernstein recalled, "he wasn't going to let go.") The call came for boarding.

"I love your script," Coppola said, moving toward the gate. "It's great—"

"Can you direct it?"

"No, no, no, no. You wrote it. It's your story. Get some friends and go make it. You should make it yourself."

"MGM owns it," Bernstein protested.

"Tell them you want to do it. They'll let you do it. Have you ever read *Elective Affinities*? Been trying to figure out a way to do it. It's like your script."

MGM offered Coppola a million dollars to direct the picture. He said no. At three million—thinking something "entertaining and popular" would guard him from the imminent disaster of *Apocalypse*—he said yes.

One from the Heart, like its thematic predecessor, *Elective Affinities*, was to be the story Coppola hadn't yet completed with Eleanor: lovers drawn apart by their fantasies, reunited by deeper acceptance and love. His rewrite of Bernstein's draft would be made of memories, one Zoetrope typist said, "about innocent romantic confusion," stories of growing up, girls and first heartbreak. "By his own admission," she said, "he was a little frozen in time," the polio kid intent on the girl he couldn't have, Gatsby chasing the dream . . . It had stifled him, in script form, before . . . how to convey love visually, in cinematic terms? Among the solutions he had discussed, nearly a decade earlier, with *Gatsby* director Jack Clayton, was Gatsby's remembered image of Daisy's face—elicited from Fitzgerald's own description—superimposed by languid dissolves over Gatsby's real life in the present. But as for intimate man-woman interactions, scenes set in the real world between two nondreaming lovers, he confessed to coming up short. Less artist to artist than man to man, Coppola asked Clayton, "Do people in love talk about it?" The time had come to find out.

In the penthouse, as far away from Vietnam and Kurtz and *Apocalypse Now* as his imagination could take him, rewriting *One from the Heart*, he was trying to remember how he began, who he was *before*.

There was the girl. The ocean.

He was four or five.

Long Island. Standing on the sidewalk in his winter coat. Holding his mother's hand. She was speaking to another woman, the wife of a navy officer, mother of the blond girl, about his age—Carolyn? Marjorie?—standing opposite him. Francie matched her face to pictures in the fairy tales he read before bed. She was the Little Mermaid.

"She can't cross the street by herself," her mother had explained to him. "She's only four years old. It will be your special job to take her across the street. Will you do that?"

HARRY CAUL

I remember a girl named Marjorie who kissed me on the lips and told me she loved me on the day her family was moving back to Virginia because her father was an officer in the Navy . . .

And then he was seventeen.

Wendy was sixteen. He kissed her in her parents' house—a mansion full of books and topped with a turret, a library castle on Long Island—his first kiss. "It was for me a transformation," he would say. Moments after the kiss, they reappeared in real life on the sofa in her living room, under a giant Tschacbasov painting, and he told her his soul had gone up into the picture, or the painting had dropped into his soul. Wendy was a writer but was going to be a ballerina and dance for Balanchine, and he was going to be a director; they joined their high school's dramatic society, they sneaked into Birdland, and he sang her "I Talk to the Trees" by Lerner and Loewe.

He never brought her home. "I wasn't allowed to bring girls to my house," he said. "My mother would have had a nervous breakdown." She had been quite clear with him: making a pass was a show of disrespect—and much of his boy and young-adult life he spent in yearning: "I slept in beds all night with beautiful women and didn't do a thing because I was trying to show them what a gentleman I was." One invited him into her bed, and he preemptively turned his shorts around, so the fly was in the back, and slept as close to the wall as possible. "I have done amazing things in that respect," he said. Perhaps almost as amazing as the fantasies such deprivations tilled in him.

Arlene was beautiful, fascinating, nutty, an artist. She drove over in her Ford Convertible after his mother had left the house. Backing Francis into his bedroom, she closed the door behind them and zipped open her jeans down to her blue underwear—"and the next thing I knew, the wood of the door is being kicked in, flying across the room." It was his mother, screaming.

"You have a girl in here! I'm going to call your father!"

His one satisfaction was that his mother never knew whether Arlene was taking her pants off or putting them back on.

He was nineteen or twenty.

At Hofstra, he met Emy. "Francis was the king at Hofstra," she said. "He ran everything in the theater and had everyone's respect, and they all did what he told them." She fell for his charisma. They went to movies, to Chinese dinners in Manhattan, and stayed up talking about Brando. It was always Brando for them. "It was a real romance," Emy said. "We thought we were actually going to get married." He gave her a charm necklace with a tiny golden camera dangling from its chain and brought her home to meet his father and mother, "who was not too crazy about her son getting involved with anybody." But he was a Hofstra boy now.

Then she met an older guy, an actor. He lived in the Village. "Francis was so mad," she said. "He demanded I give him the necklace back." He cast her as Stella in his production of *Streetcar*, and to play Stanley, Bob Spiotta, imported from the football team. Coppola designed, built, and painted sets and even the makeup in black and white and shades of gray to create the effect of a living movie. He ran the Izenour lightboard, and of course he directed, rehearsing the actors after classes ended, sometimes as late as two in the morning. "Everybody just lived and breathed *Streetcar*," Emy said—so much so, in fact, that her Stella and Bob Spiotta's Stanley fell in love. They were engaged soon after.

There was that feeling—the feeling, so common in the show world, of falling in love with the character, and mixed in with it, the innocence of those Hofstra days, the refining charge they all shared generating theater together, and the life-or-death flings that came and went. That feeling—he would put it into *One from the Heart*. "I'm a big consumer of things and people," Coppola acknowledged to *Playboy* in 1975. Perhaps that accounted for his attachment to Eleanor, he speculated; she was, if not immune to his devouring, inconsumable. "I do a lot of things and live in the same fantasy spirit that I write in," he confessed. "It's all make-believe to me. It's a fairy tale and I get to do all the things I can imagine. But I find that as I actually do them, I don't need them anymore."

April 9, 1979: Coppola brought his pal Bill Graham to the Oscars, and Bill Graham brought along cookies, which Coppola, nervously hungry before joining Ali McGraw onstage to present the award for Best Director—

"Francis! No, no!"

"What?"

Pot cookies. Too late.

". . . Italians call him *regista*," McGraw teleprompted beside Coppola moments later. "It translates 'the realizer.' The one who realizes the dream."

"Actually," Coppola answered, "whatever you call it, the job is to make dreams come true, so that audiences can see them and hear them and be part of them." And then, seemingly not reading from the teleprompter, he started speaking directly into the camera, to the many millions at home. "You know, I'd like to say that we're on the eve of something that's gonna make the industrial revolution look like a small-town tryout out of town. I'm talking about the communications revolution. I think it's coming very quickly and that the movies of the eighties are going to be amazing beyond what any of you can dream, just a couple years away from now, and I can see—I can see—"

McGraw's eyes were darting.

"—a communications revolution that is about movies and art and music and digital electronics and computers and satellites and, above all, human talent."

McGraw, adrift . . .

"And it's gonna make things for the masters of the cinema, from whom we've inherited this business—wouldn't believe the things that are going to be possible.

"And in the spirit of this wonderful new spirit of the future, we're very, very honored to announce the nominations for the Best Director of 1979 . . ."

The Oscar went to Michael Cimino, for the Vietnam epic that had beaten *Apocalypse* to the theaters, *The Deer Hunter*.

A week later, Coppola celebrated his fortieth birthday—"That was *old* to us," said Karen Frerichs—on Easter weekend, inviting seven hundred to his Napa estate for three days of music, food, and, above all, relief—the collective sigh from the ragbag entirety of Zoetrope, its friends and family, of having come this far through the jungle and survived, just over a month before the film was due to preview—all these years later, the film's ending still unsettled—in Los Angeles.

All were welcome to camp on the grounds or the forest hills behind the big yellow house among the unexpected rivers and tree clusters and fairy rings. "It was kind of like *Midsummer Night's Dream*," Martha Cronin said. "There were these big barrels of Francis's wine all over the place, so people were very drunk, kind of wandering around." And music everywhere, all kinds of music: there was Carmine, leading an ensemble on the veranda of the big house, and there was Zoetrope's own punk rock orchestra in the barn, the "otherwise talented" (Coppola's introduction) Zero VU and the Meter Needles (Jean Autrey on flute, Jack Fritz on drums, sound mixer Dale Strumpell on keyboard, and about ten others . . .), still burning off the steam of *Apocalypse Now* with lyrics, "Hey hey hey / Do mau may / Shut up slope / Shut up slope . . ." and snare hits for machine gun fire. And throughout the evening, Dennis Hopper's laugh echoed up the mountains.

In front of the big house, eyes looked to the sky, at a low-flying plane trailing the banner "Happy Birthday from One Yenta to Another." Then came horn blasts and drum rolls as the San Francisco Gay and Lesbian Marching Band stormed up the driveway. A parachuter jumped from the plane and, landing at Francis's feet in a black tuxedo, clipped off his parachute, produced from his bag a bottle of champagne and two glasses, and wished Coppola a "Happy Birthday, from Bill"—Graham. The cork popped, he poured for Francis and Eleanor, and all joined in a round of "Happy Birthday to You." No one present that day would ever forget it. Set decorator Gary Fettis, who had come through the jungle and survived, was among them. "All that is good in life," he said, "is what Zoetrope was."

Later, when things quieted down, Zoetrope sound folk, some in baseball caps bearing the tagline "Apocalypse Now: Release with Honor," were on hands and knees at Coppola's pool, recording water laps for the movie; out in the bushes, it would be amphibians and insects for jungle noise—as counterparts from Lucasfilm, in khaki shorts and sandals (with socks, it was noted by the Zoetropers), looked on in bemusement. With the exception of Walter Murch, equal parts Lucas and Coppola and an inimitable world unto himself, there was an unspoken rule that Francis wouldn't poach George's "Droids" if George didn't poach Francis's "ANdroids" (the "AN" for *Apocalypse Now*). When employees did move from one camp to the other, it was largely due to changes in lifestyle, often because the mover "had to grow up." The general idea was that Zoetrope—in the city, up late, in perpetual and vigorous revolution—was for the young, while out in San Anselmo, Lucasfilm made family movies by family people at a family pace. "They were all quite clean, and most of them were married," one Zoetroper said of the Lucasfilmers, "and had some small children that they were lovingly looking after, and they might have had expressions of consternation or intensity, but, I mean, they weren't losing their minds." Both sides came together for "the Droid Olympics," hosted—for the first time that summer—at the Murches' place in Bolinas. With Moviolas, splicers, rewind tables, and other editing gear, teams from Lucasfilm, Zoetrope, and elsewhere around the Bay Area would compete in "Bobbing for Smitchies" (a race to find a marked frame in a bin of 35 mm film), "Rack Arranging," "Speed Rewind," and so on.

They played together, but Lucasfilm and Zoetrope pointed toward different futures for Hollywood. One had been inaugurated by the economics and special effects of *Star Wars*, the other would be so by the artistry and independence of *Apocalypse*. On that score, it really was a race: George versus Francis. "If I ever got the bucks that, say, George Lucas got from *Star Wars*," Coppola would say, "I'd put every penny into changing the rules. . . . People like myself and George, who's building his own production facility, are going to turn the studios into dinosaurs."

Lucas had a vision for "Skywalker Ranch," the filmmaking think tank he planned to build not too far away, where once he hoped to found Zoetrope, in Marin County. He had his sights set on Bulltail Ranch, a nearly thousand-acre spread located, coincidentally, off Lucas Valley Road. "It was really an extraordinary dream," said Irvin Kershner, one of Lucas's former USC professors and the appointed director of the *Star Wars* follow-up, *The Empire Strikes Back*. "All the billions of dollars ever made in the film business, and no one has ever plowed it back into a library, research, bringing directors together, creating an environment where the love of films could create new dimensions." San Rafael was the latest setting for Industrial Light and Magic, Lucasfilm's special effects team of miniature model makers–photographers. They were already hard at work on a digital film printer, a computer that would replace the slow, cumbersome process of creating analog effects photographically. "It took eight months to do the opening shot of *Star Wars*," said producer Gary Kurtz. "[With digital compositing] you could see that overnight. Or immediately." In 1979, there were computer people and there were movie people; it would be Lucas's project to merge them.

Lynnea Johnson, Gio's teacher at the Athenian School, who had just given her notice, was at the Coppolas' that weekend, drinking in the view—children, parents, families in ritual celebration. "These kids," Coppola said to her, "are going to be in my school." She wasn't sure what he meant.

On Monday, she was working out her final days at the Athenian School when the phone rang. It was from Zoetrope. "We got these kids here," someone told her. "What do we do with them?"

Two days later, she appeared at the Sentinel Building and was introduced to August Coppola, the new head of the Zoetrope Film Academy.

"Where are the kids?" she asked.

"They're at the Broadway house," he answered.

Johnson met them—there were maybe half a dozen students: Dean Tavoularis's girls, Allison and Gina Tavoularis; *Apocalypse*'s Laurence Fishburne; Mickey Hart's son, Creek, and others—upstairs at the Coppolas' (Italia Coppola was downstairs cooking pasta). Gio, already Johnson's student, would soon be among them. Since returning from the Philippines, "he didn't want to go back to school," said Zoetrope's Linda Phillips-Palo. "He was delightfully floaty, quieter than a lot of the kids, and very introspective. It would have harmed him, I think, to be thrown back into high school. He would have been left behind." His father sympathized.

Working alongside August Coppola, Lynnea Johnson hurriedly improvised a curriculum for the remaining two months of the school year. On the fifth floor of the Sentinel Building, she taught French, hired a friend to teach social studies, and brought in Frank Oppenheimer of the Exploratorium to teach a weekly science class. But, mainly, the students' education would be work-study apprenticeships with Zoetrope artists and craftspeople in the Facility and the art department. At least, it was supposed to be. "It turned out to be Gio and Larry Fishburne hanging out and smoking dope in the little back room behind the screening room at the Facility," Karen Frerichs said. "They would think they were hiding."

The Zoetrope Film Academy lasted for a few months. "It was a wonderful idea," Johnson concluded, "but it wasn't really feasible. It was more like a dream. Like a vignette of a movie in Francis's head."

Eleanor showed him the notebook and back-of-envelope writings she had kept throughout *Apocalypse*. Painfully candid—brutal, even—they exposed the dark trough under their marriage, his insecurity, her paralysis and despair. That she gave them to Coppola to read, and that he read them, was an act of mutual courage. That he encouraged her to publish them and that Fred Roos introduced Eleanor to editor Nan Talese would be a salvation, perhaps, for both husband and wife.

Only weeks away from its preview date in L.A., *Apocalypse Now* was still waiting on a completed score.

It had been in the works, Richard Beggs recalled, for almost a year. "Francis had asked me who the heavyweights in the world of electronic music were," he said. "So I came up with a list of five names, submitted them to Francis, assuming that he would hire one of them. He actually ended up hiring all five of these individuals, which created this sort of amazing musical circus." Each brought his or her own distinct synths to the score: Bernie Krause and Don Preston, primarily their Moog; Patrick Gleeson, his 16-Voice E-MU, a 4-Voice E-MU, and two 10-Voice Prophets, "tied together in a bastardized analog-digital set-up"; and Nyle Steiner, his original EVI (or "electronic valve instrument"), the first practical wind-controlled synth, modulated by human breath pressure. Each would interpret the orchestral compositions Carmine Coppola had written for the film.

"On one level, the creation of the score was like our involvement in Vietnam," said Shirley Walker, a composer hired to play the synths. "We have these classical military concepts of how you fight a war—that's Carmine's writing, which is grounded in the best European tradition. Then you take those ideas and apply the most advanced technology we have: the scientists have their input and come up with missiles and weapons you've never even *heard* of. That's the synthesis." The hallucinatory effect would be achieved in the mix, as musical sounds, like the synth, would be enhanced to emulate natural sounds: rain, wind, thunder, and explosions. Likewise, a helicopter would become the bass in a piece of music, its rotor whirring like a cello line. Said Krause, "The demands of this score pushed me—pushed *all* of us—to our creative limits, and I honestly feel that this music could trigger a re-birth in the potential of synthesizers. What happened here was, in a sense, the first 'new' thing to happen in the field for a long time."

Percussion sessions at Club Front, the Grateful Dead's Front Street studio, in San Rafael, would last for ten days straight. Backed by the Rhythm Devils, Mickey Hart's ensemble would improvise to the movie on bamboo, stone, water-filled crystal glasses, and a giant drum set known as the Beast. "We laid out the instruments so we could walk through the room without stumbling, and make the music flow—like the river," Hart said. "Sometimes we got lost in it, just like Kurtz got lost in it. Just about everybody involved with *Apocalypse* got 'Kurtzed' at one time or another."

Les Blank came to film their percussion sessions, "every primitive sound known to man," Hart said. For five nights, Blank shot video, with four cameras. Outside the warehouse studio, tech director Clark Higgins manned the mobile unit—the only broadcast-quality production truck in the Bay Area.

Higgins gave Coppola a tour inside the box truck. He gazed childlike at the little monitors, each with its own live camera feed, a mini studio on wheels. "I can see what the cameras are shooting in here?" Coppola asked, amazed.

"Yeah. In fact, press this button, and you can talk to each cameraman. You can direct them. Try it."

Coppola took a seat at the console, toggled switches, called directions to Blank's cameramen shooting in the warehouse, watched the monitors for the results. It was a live version of what he enjoyed at his video suite in the penthouse, what he had enjoyed, imagining remote control, from his boyhood bed. "This is what I've always dreamed of."

"You can cut live. Like television."

"It's like being inside my head, you know?" Coppola ignited.

"You could shoot and cut a movie almost as fast as you can think it." It was true. Cutting live, a filmmaker could work as quickly as John Frankenheimer directing a *Playhouse 90* . . . "Cuts down on production costs, postproduction . . ." And working fast cuts down on interest . . .

A *live* cinema. With all the delegating and self-dividing Coppola had to do as a director, now, just sitting there, in the video van, he could be everywhere at once. If he could solve this film-video-film problem and work from a van like this, he could, with the press of a button, save money and multiply his artistic influence immeasurably. Could they broadcast movies the way they did television and beam them, somehow, to theaters and living rooms? Surely that would cut down on distribution costs, too . . . "We'll make media out of pure energy," Coppola would say, "and distribution becomes a matter of pushing buttons for where you want it to go and in what form."

"This," Coppola said to Higgins that day in the mobile unit, "is what the future is going to be."

He didn't just mean the movies.

In those last days before *Apocalypse*'s L.A. preview, Coppola was in an agitated state. Galvanized by Higgins's mobile unit, he was brimming with ideas . . . building, for Zoetrope, a "digital skyscraper" analogous to the Sentinel Building but in New York City where everyone would be working exclusively on video . . . buying, in Los Angeles, a fully operational movie studio, his own, *their* own—a costume department, casting department, a commissary where employees would eat for free, with soundstages big enough to service several productions at once . . . and they could all move there, *live* there, even . . . "in a little factory, like a Republic or an RKO, making one movie a month in the old style and at an intelligent price. . . . We'll use the full magic of technology, we won't shoot on film or even on tape, it'll be on some other memory—call it electronic memory. And then there's the possibility of synthesizing images on computers, of having an electronic facsimile of Napoleon playing the life of Napoleon. It's almost do-able right now; it just takes the wisdom and the guts to invest in the future." Digital wasn't just a medium, it was a means; what allowed them to work faster and cheaper would help them work better and happier . . . working all day and feasting all night . . .

It was technology. That was the answer. It always had been.

Many at Zoetrope rolled their eyes at the vaguely discernible form and function of this live, electric cinema. Many sighed at the notion of picking up and moving the operation down to Los Angeles, scene of the Hollywood crime. Wasn't the whole Zoetrope ideal premised on working intimately, artfully, away from the center of industry life? Zoetroper Sherry Rogers said, "It was over the top. He was trying to buy a studio in L.A. I think he was trying to buy up parts of San Francisco, parts of Broadway. He was on a roll. He was going to take over the world. But he didn't seem to have any regard for the fact that he might be in debt up to his eyeballs." Afraid to lose their jobs, some kept their mouths shut. ("Just let the train get out of the station!" Coppola liked to say of incipient dreams. "If anyone says stop, it's already over!") "I saw him lose his patience with people who were telling him no," Michael Lehmann said. "I saw crazy, and I saw creativity, and sometimes together and sometimes apart. The way he spoke when he talked about creative things was both grandiose and extremely perceptive and wide-ranging in his references. He had great knowledge of literature, he had some knowledge of history, and he would weave all these things together when he talked about the work that he was doing. The plan kept changing, but the goal was always the same: to create and have a good time doing it."

"In the future," he would say, "making movies will be like writing poetry is now . . . Anybody can sit at home and do it . . ." Or sit in a van, calling the shots . . .

Coppola was smoking more weed to deal with the stress. "Cinema's all going to be electronic . . . We're just going to manipulate photons . . ."

Francis Ford Coppola's brain was a wheel, a Zoetrope, "spinning very fast. In that state I can do everything," he explained. "I can concentrate on twenty things. I can come up with solutions. But if you jam that wheel with a stick, if you stop it, if it is disturbed by some left hook I wasn't expecting, I fall apart. It's like an internal combustion engine. It has the power when it's up to a certain RPM, but if you interrupt it, there's a moment where I'm just incompetent to do anything. And that's what the temper is. When you interrupt that inertia. But when I'm in that state, I'm amazing. I can do things that are not human."

He was in the penthouse working on the ending, spinning, sometimes all night. Sitting nearby was David Macmillan's wife, equally absorbed in her task, knitting. Her presence was calming to Coppola. "I was scared," he said. "And I think the fact that I wasn't alone meant something. Just that she was there." He was deep into the footage of Brando, Kurtz's bald head coming in and out of the light. That always amazed Coppola, how Brando, improvising, worked with that beam of Storaro's as if it were another actor. If he placed his cuts when Brando's face was out of the beam, in darkness, he could reorder the scene. He could cut in other elements—flickers of the carabao sacrifice, echoes of the succession and regeneration myths gleaned from Dennis Jakob, death and life. Accepting his place in the great cycle, Kurtz would, in the end, welcome his own sacrifice, and Willard, his assassin, would succeed him as Michael Corleone succeeded his father. Within the society and within individual souls, the transformation would be complete. It could work.

French film critic Gilles Jacob was calling and calling and calling Tess Haley, Coppola's assistant, begging her to beg Coppola to please let them have the world premiere of *Apocalypse* in Cannes. But it wasn't finished, she told him. There was no way it would be Cannes-ready when they needed it, just a week after the Los Angeles previews. But Jacob kept calling, and Haley kept telling him no. The L.A. screenings were just *previews*, she said. Cannes meant *premiere*. As it was, they barely had enough time to make the L.A. deadline.

"Well . . . *what if* we took the movie to Cannes?" Coppola mused aloud. He was flying to New York with Tom Sternberg and assistant editor Tracey Smith to show the latest cut of *Apocalypse* to UA.

"Francis . . ." Sternberg almost choked on his lunch. "UA's not going to like that. What if we're destroyed?"

"What if we're not?"

It was a grand showman's gamble. Debut the movie at the most prestigious film festival on the planet . . . as *a work in progress*. And with only domestic rights to distribution, UA couldn't stop Coppola from doing it. Nor were its executives, under Arthur Krim, the most compassionate in the business, inclined to resist. Consider the recent Seattle test screening—after two full years of postproduction on *The Black Stallion* (which still didn't really have an ending). Following the screening—a very good one—those who had been with *Stallion* the longest had repaired to a nearby restaurant to wait for the results. With them was UA's David Field. As soon as Field produced his own envelope of notes, Coppola held up a hand. "David, wait one second. You've got to understand something. If this is how Carroll wants the movie to go out, David, this is how the movie's going out." Field folded up his envelope and returned it to his pocket. That's how they did it at UA.

Apocalypse Now, therefore, would go to Cannes. In whatever shape it was in.

All eyes turned then to the Facility, the small, airless mixing stage under Pacific Street. It was down to them.

"Walter would come in exhausted," Karen Frerichs said. "You could see it in his face. His eyes were hollow." To get Cannes-ready, the mixers upgraded their schedule to three shifts, with crews of two or three each, rotating day and night. More than once, Frerichs watched Walter get on his motorcycle for a 1 a.m. ride back to Bolinas and thought, *What if he went off a cliff in the middle of the night?* That's when she had the rollaway bed brought in.

Murch had specifically requested the graveyard shift. Nights suited him as much as they suited *Apocalypse*. Deliberately courting his own deprivation, he insisted on mixing with the black-and-white work print of *Apocalypse*, his idea being that whatever visual information he lacked in color he would make up for in sound.

Just to watch Murch work, machine room attendants Doug Hemphill and Paul Broucek volunteered for his hours, from seven at night to six the next morning. Their first pot of coffee went on at around three a.m.

"Walter, it's time for lunch. You've got to eat."

Nine months after they had begun, *Apocalypse Now* was, by most people's count, the longest, most intricate sound mix ever attempted in or outside Hollywood.

"Walter, breakfast . . ."

The mixture of exhaustion and concentration simultaneously contracts and dilates time. This interested Murch, as did many things. To Hemphill, he said, "The car has replaced the hat to contain the personality in Western civilization."

He went for walks. He parked his motorcycle over in the marina, to give his mind more space and time to get to the Facility.

He was wearing the same ski sweater every day.

"Reel two again, please," he would say to the machine room. "Thank you."

He slipped a strike of bowling pins into an exploding bridge.

His ears would get less and less sensitive as night wore on. There was no room tone, just the grinding, spinning noises of exhausted technology. "The machine room ran twenty-four hours a day," Andy Moore said. "There was at any point between one and five engineers. Not only were they working constantly on all this equipment which would fail all the time, or need to be tweaked somehow, [but] they were building it, they were soldering things."

In the remaining days leading up to the L.A. preview, Randy Thom put in 172 hours. "We never left the building," he said. "You work for eight or ten or twelve hours and then go lie on a couch somewhere for a couple of hours and try to go to sleep and then come back and work for another eight or ten."

Laying a hand on Walter's shoulder, Mark Berger would come in to relieve him. It was always startling, his hand, another person, real life.

In that final week, Aggie Murch would appear at the Facility to physically remove her husband from the mixing stage. He returned eight hours later.

Francis Ford Coppola was a supercharged Santa Claus of cinema, personally greeting and engaging Westwood audiences outside the Bruin and Village Theatres, as if welcoming them into his home. He was a scientist, and this L.A. preview was his experiment; strangers, children, college students, filmmakers, critics, grandparents, and Vietnam veterans, even those who didn't like the film, he would attend with the spirit of fraternity and learning, assuring them he meant it when he said he wanted their honest opinion. But dissenters were few. Westwood audiences, tastemakers, were knocked over by the scope and daring and sensual surplus of Coppola's vision, and UA representatives were bragging, "Told ya so." At last, the papers reported actual good news from the *Apocalypse* warfront, and four years of rumored waste and indulgence evaporated.

The goodwill trailed Coppola to Cannes, aboard Kirk Kerkorian's plane with his friends, real estate maven George Altamura and his wife; Tess Haley; Eleanor, Gio, Roman, Sofia, Carmine, Italia, and Augie and his girlfriend; the Kerkorians; and also a chef, Yoshiko, who served Armenian lamb in honor of the Kerkorians and followed it with a birthday cake for Sofia, who was turning eight. "We took off our shoes and flew all through the night," Haley said, "eating and sleeping."

From the airport, they were limousined to a gigantic (forty-person), bright white yacht, the *Amazone*, rented from the Renault family—"I was in the navy," George Altamura said, "and that wasn't a boat; it was a ship"—sitting proudly off the Côte d'Azur. *Apocalypse Now*—the only work in progress ever to be screened in festival competition, described by UA's Steven Bach as "the most public sneak preview in the history of motion pictures"—was of course the talk of the Croisette.

"Are you nervous?" Haley asked Coppola.

"I don't get heart attacks. I give them."

The day of the premiere, May 19, 1979, at 10 a.m., Coppola, tuxedoed, sat with his family in the front row of the balcony of the Palais des Festivals, surrounded above and below by the most important, most intelligently vengeful and adoring film figures in the world.

The "work in progress" version of *Apocalypse Now*, presented without opening credits, began in darkness, in silence . . . a silence dreamily infiltrated, from five directions, by jungle sounds . . . birds and mosquitos filling the audience's imagination with a location of the mind . . . Then, into the ambience came strange, unnatural electronic tones, the whir of helicopters, and smoke, and the gravelly, close-mic'd voice of Captain Willard: "Saigon. Shit . . ."

. . . and after he assassinates Kurtz—the start to an ending Coppola would change, once again, for the film's release—Willard, wide-eyed, if not deranged, then stunned at his own violence, absently directs the PBR away from the shore, unresponsive to the radio. ("PBR Street Gang? Do you read me? Over . . .") His disembodied face, menacing now, half-shadowed in close-up like Kurtz, passes through a sinister shift of unreal imagery, a great statue deity, the fire and choppers of the opening scene, the sound of rain, a drone, and the whisper "The horror . . . the horror . . ." And *Apocalypse Now* ended as it began, in silence.

Inside the Palais, the silence persisted. For one beat. Two beats. Three beats.

Then an eruption, a standing ovation, disbelief, a swarm, frenzy, arc lights in the sky, a private party in a little restaurant—Coppola was soaring—and the next day was spent fielding journalists so aggressive for a moment of Coppola's attention that he was nearly edged off the top of a building. Andrew Sarris, still grumpy that his editors at the *Village Voice* were having him cover *Apocalypse Now*, "to the virtual exclusion of every other eminently worthy film at the festival," heard that Coppola received something in the vicinity of nine hundred requests to meet. Roman Polanski, Gilles Jacob, Andrei Konchalovsky, Sergio Leone, Roger Ebert—Coppola invited them all, and more, to the yacht for conversation—about the impending electronic revolution, his persistent trouble with the film's ending—and for a feast Coppola had prepared with the freshest ingredients, purchased by Haley at seven that very morning. Somewhere along the way, he lost his lithium.

"Find Bob Spiotta," Coppola instructed Tess Haley.

She had never heard the name before, but she found him. In Italy. Spiotta was living with his wife and children in Rome, where he was head of Mobil Oil; he had barely been in touch with Coppola since the two were at Hofstra together so many years ago—Francis, director of *Streetcar* starring Bob as Stanley and Emy—Coppola's former girlfriend, now Mrs. Spiotta—as Stella.

"Are you drunk?" Emy asked Coppola on the phone.

No, he wasn't drunk, he said. He was in Cannes. And he was inviting the Spiottas and their three kids to join him on his yacht. It took the Spiottas "all of two seconds," Emy said, to get on the next plane. Spiotta's daughter, Robin Supak, said the whole gambit, the suddenness and adventure, "was a magical, magical dream."

On the yacht, Coppola asked Spiotta to move his family to California to run the newest and, as of yet, most ambitious incarnation of Zoetrope: Zoetrope Studios. Yes, an actual studio: sound stages, costume shops, screening rooms, writers' offices, the whole thing. Spiotta had never worked in the movie business, let alone run a Hollywood studio, but Coppola, a believer in amateurs, had a feeling. Spiotta also hit Coppola's older-brother chord. "And don't think for one second that Francis wasn't perennially pissed that Bob Spiotta married [Emy]," Haley said. "That was always in the back of his mind, always. Francis was no longer the schlubby little kid who was dating Emy. He's Francis Ford Coppola, with Oscars in each hand, and he's gonna hire Emy's husband who took her away from him. That was always in the back of his mind, that Bob Spiotta took his girlfriend away from him."

"What do you make now?" Coppola asked his old friend.

Spiotta told him.

"I'll double it."

Spiotta—"definitely a fake-it-till-you-make-it kind of guy," his daughter Robin said—accepted the offer to work for Coppola and asked Haley to buy him books "on how to run a movie studio." No such book existed. Nor was there anything written, Haley said, "on how you handle an absolutely extraordinarily talented, slightly crazy, manic-depressive, wonderful Italian man."

Coppola didn't have the real estate yet, but he had heard, from Gray Frederickson, about a studio for sale. It was Hollywood General Studios, at Santa Monica Boulevard and Las Palmas, the very lot Francie Coppola used to pass by when he and his father were living in L.A., on his lonely way to and from school, wondering, at the gate, mere steps from where they had made *The Thief of Bagdad*, what magic was on the other side. The rightness of the undertaking, the precipitous arrival of the elements, the sweetness of the future: like a cloud curtain opening the view to Shangri-La, the vision—Zoetrope Studios—was fairy-tale perfect.

Apocalypse Now would win the Palme d'Or, Cannes's highest prize, splitting it with a completed film, *The Tin Drum*.

Coppola brought all the children—his own and the Spiottas'—up with him to the microphones for a press conference.

"C'mon Sofia," he said, urging her ahead. He turned to the press. "I'm protected by an army of kids. My kids are tough. Where's Roman?

"In my opinion," Coppola said to the room, "cinema is the most potent . . . I don't choose to use the word *weapon*, but the most potent force in modern times. Especially when you begin to consider that cinema as we know it is going to radically change. I mean, I see twelve cameras over here with little movements shuttling film through it, and I see one"—directly in front of him, a video camera—"that doesn't need that over there. . . . And we must realize that cinema is going to be—whether you argue and say, 'No, it'll be five years; it'll be three years'—it'll be electronic. It will be electronic, it will be digital, it will bounce off satellites. And it will create the dreams and hallucinations of the future of the world.

"This film just presents a very extreme case where one man goes off, as the line is, beyond the pale of normal human restraint. He goes too far. He's destroyed by it. But, in a sense, it's a sacrificial thing, because I wanted to kill Kurtz *for* America. I wanted America to look at the face of it"—he took little Sofia's smiling face in his hands—"to look at the face of the horror and to accept it and say, 'Yes, it is my face.' And only then could they go beyond to some new age."

He flew down to Los Angeles with Tess Haley and George Altamura to have a look at Hollywood General Studios, his destined incubator for the new age. Aware of Coppola's enthusiasm, Altamura counseled him aboard the plane that they were going to play it close to the vest. A show of interest could raise the asking price. If Coppola liked it, he was to say, covertly, "I like Coca-Cola," and let Altamura handle the rest.

From the airplane to the limo, and from the limo to the lot: acres of illustrious Hollywood history, soundstages and offices, room for a commissary, and a little grass pasture for young and visiting filmmakers, and—if Zoetrope moved in—hundreds of years of future. Alight, Coppola threw his hands in the air. "I'll take it!"

II

THE APOCALYPSE

If a man could pass through Paradise in a dream, and have a flower presented to him as a pledge that his soul had really been there, and if he found that flower in his hand when he awoke—Ay! And what then?

—SAMUEL TAYLOR COLERIDGE,
ANIMA POETAE

pocalypse Now is not, as Coppola began it, a film about Vietnam. It isn't even about war. Nor did the philosophical play of good and evil Coppola had so arduously engaged survive his years-long reckoning with self and story. But where the film muddles, the psychic toll of Coppola's quandary is felt throughout. For all its spectacle, the venue of *Apocalypse Now* is interior. An impression of Coppola's private battle and Willard's spiraling semiconsciousness, it is, at its best, a holy madness of sight and sound. Coppola never would find a worthy ending—indeed, there is no ending in the field of philosophical inquiry; at least, after thousands of years of searching, there hasn't been yet—but the passions of the filmmaking ensemble, of Vittorio Storaro and Walter Murch, their pounding miasma of soaring color bombs and hypernatural audio environments, elevate the foundering Big Ideas of *Apocalypse* to what may even be a higher plane, rapture.

And so, for all the agony, the story of *Apocalypse Now* ends in ecstasy: Coppola's dream of Zoetrope really did come true, and on a scale only he could have imagined. More than just a production company, it proved to be a heightened awareness for all, a path to new frontiers of life and film.

For audiences, that is, *Apocalypse Now* is a film; for its filmmakers, a life. But for Francis Ford Coppola, it was a rite of passage. In his book *From Ritual to Theatre*, anthropologist Victor Turner locates the moment of ritual transformation in the juncture between chaos and order, what he calls "liminality," the intermediary state of consciousness between one's old self and the new. The trancelike state of liminality can be literal or figurative, psychologically or socially evoked—as among the Ndembu of Zimbabwe, whose royalty are made to assume the role of commoner before they can assume the crown. But like any rite of passage, it is a grief, for it necessitates a killing of the old and dying self. In much of the psychological West, it's called a nervous breakdown. Not everyone emerges intact, but those who do speak of being re-created. The same can be said for Coppola's creative process: literally, a process of self-creation. For only in losing himself in *Apocalypse* could Coppola be—and was—reconstituted, found.

Looking back from the vantage of *Apocalypse Now*, it is evident that each of Coppola's personal works, his Zoetrope or Zoetrope-affiliated films, was likewise a rite of passage. *You're a Big Boy Now*—its very title literalizing the first rite of passage—preceded the first incarnation of Zoetrope, where Coppola was already beginning his processes of artistic and self-experimentation. In *The Rain People*, he retraced similar narrative territory, leaving home and family, this time with Natalie Ravenna, no longer a girl, married and with child: *You're a Big Girl Now*. The rites of passage to follow, each lived by Coppola in tandem with his creation, proceeded, basically, in chronological sequence from young adulthood to midlife crisis: Michael Corleone, *You're a Man Now*; Don Michael Corleone, *You're a Big Man Now*; Captain Willard/Colonel Kurtz, *You're a Broken Man Now*. Only *The Conversation*, hearkening back to Coppola's earliest nightmares, breaks the chronology—but then again, those nightmares, resurfacing in the crisis years of *Apocalypse*, never fully abated—and never will. Harry Caul, *You're a Little Boy Now*—alone, still; always.

Released in the United States on August 15, 1979, *Apocalypse Now*—which cost, all in, over $40 million, approximately half of which was billed to Coppola—would gross, in its original theatrical release, more than $80 million worldwide. "It started very slowly," Barry Hirsch said, "but it kept building and building."

Coppola could take his first deep breath in four long years: the financial forecast indicated that he could repay his debts to United Artists and his foreign investors; he could furnish the banks and Marlon Brando with their participants' share in the multimillions; he could retain his property, his filmmaker's credibility; and he could even, astonishingly, with patience, anticipate profits for himself. In seven years' time, he knew, ownership of *Apocalypse* would be his in perpetuity.

His streak—*The Godfather*, *The Conversation*, *The Godfather Part II*, and now *Apocalypse Now*—was beyond compare. *Godfather* alone had marked him a master; but his subsequent films, testaments to his range, depth, and vision, made Coppola something of a miracle. They do still.

With glory, the rush of success in his sails—and *Apocalypse*'s future well on its way, and *The Black Stallion* debuting to rave reviews—Coppola went to Tokyo to cool off and think: about his marriage, about the sudden glow of Zoetrope, about the next chapter of his work.

Despite his astounding reversal of fortune, the trip, which he took alone, was not an easy one. Heavy with regret and resolutions, he was determined to make it work with Eleanor. "I'd just as soon keep my family together," he would say, "and stay married, because . . . if you leave your partner and marry someone else you may very well leave the next person and go somewhere else, and you've disrupted one of the most important things you can have, which is a continuous family."

Eleanor's book, *Notes*, a diary of her *Apocalypse* reckoning, had been published late in 1979 to coincide with the release of the film. The book was a critical sensation. Pauline Kael called it, rightly, "the most lucid account of the strain of epic moviemaking that we'll ever get." A singularly candid and intimate chronicle of the personal cost of filmmaking, *Notes* laid bare the Coppolas' private weaknesses in life and art in crisp, clear prose that would raise Eleanor's diaries, beyond confessional or reportage, to the realm of literature. Even Francis, when first presented with the manuscript, the portrait she had painted of him in darkness and in light, agreed with her friends that their story had universal value, and he bravely endorsed the publication. But for Eleanor the book brought visibility. People in Hollywood began to address her not just as the quiet wife they approached as a conduit to Francis, but for her perspective.

It was the feeling of embarrassment Francis hadn't anticipated, the friends and associates who, in reading the book, hinted at having mistaken his struggle in the Philippines for artistic paralysis. That hurt him. At his insistence, Eleanor withdrew from her press tour. That hurt her. As for the hours of material she shot on location, she put it in storage.

He walked the Tokyo streets at night. "I was lonely and trying to stay afloat," he said, sifting his mind's rubble inside the small room he took in a small inn, reading (Goethe and Yukio Mishima) and writing about how Goethe, in *Elective Affinities*, turned love into science, and Mishima turned his life into art. Months before his ritual suicide, Coppola read, Mishima rented a department store and mounted an exhibition of the artifacts of his life.

He was also, like Hank and Frannie, the warring lovers of *One from the Heart*, trying to square the dream of romance with the real thing. "When I was first married," Coppola would say, "I couldn't say I thought it would be forever. I didn't know. I could have thought of many other romantic eventualities if I had become an important director—I could have married Rita Hayworth! But I was crazy about that idea of having kids. I loved the little boys, taking them out, and it was just in my nature to like kids. My marriage has obviously gone through a few strains, but quite honestly I know that if I ever left my wife, and especially if I got involved with some other woman, then I might very well be in the same spot six years later except that I would have broken everything up . . ."

So, this time, he already had his ending, and unlike that of *Apocalypse*, it would be a happy one—happy and simple: Hank and Frannie, after their respective flings, would be reunited. "I didn't want to lose my family," Coppola said. "I didn't want to lose my children. A lot of men can do that. But I was just not the kind of person who could go and wipe out my family like that and do a second family or something. I'm just not that kind of person. I never will do that. I just can't."

He thought about the future of Zoetrope, about the coming digital revolution, how technology and the arts could free people, how freed people could reconstitute the world.

There was in Japan, he noted, as so many others have, a regard for form and custom, for perfection of being, that didn't exist in America. He tasted it in the food; he gleaned it in the symmetry of the buildings, the eloquence of the design, the pervasive regard for ritual that elevated everyday behavior almost to theater.

In the future, he decided, his new Zoetrope Studio—populating itself in Los Angeles one ramshackle office bungalow at a time—would be, like Kyoto, a living work of art, paradise now.

He went to Kabuki. Complete immersion in the abstract elements of theatrical expression, so far from the photographic realism of cinema, overcame him. Kabuki spoke in a highly codified dream language rich in metaphor and historical palimpsest. There was nothing like it in the West, not even the musical. Not even opera. Watching, he felt "the desire to work in a musical-cinema form that was sort of like Kabuki, where you had many elements, you had the actors, you had dance, and you had song, and you had image and you had scenic elements, and that each part would tell that part of the story that it could tell best."

Outdoing *Apocalypse*, even the *Godfathers*, his film version of *Elective Affinities* would be such a work, not one or even two, but four films wide, "my superproduction," he called it. He would make it after he made *One from the Heart*, and it would be about a filmmaker and his wife; in the film, the filmmaker would be in Japan, in production on a film of *Elective Affinities* while simultaneously editing another movie within the movie, which would be *One from the Heart*. Coppola said, "One [*Elective Affinities* film] will take place in the period when the Americans and the Japanese first met, another in postwar Japan, another during the period of the Sixties—the business-Mishima-gay-bar scene—and the fourth time period will be the future. This last part will deal with an enormous space telescope the size of the Graf Zeppelin that America and Japan send out into the universe because of its incredible capacity to witness the birth of the universe. And the last ten minutes or so of the movie, at the moment that it gets to that point, will be what it sees."

This was why he was building Zoetrope Studios, where no one could tell him "No, you can't make a twelve-hour movie of four parts based on a classic of nineteenth-century German literature that spans ten centuries and incorporates narrative styles from theater, literature, film, and dance." Toho had made the same mistake: the film company had said no to Kurosawa, telling him, after it had green-lighted *Kagemusha*, that it was pulling out. "It was like telling Michelangelo, 'All right, you're 70 and we're not letting you paint anymore,'" George Lucas said.

Lucas literally couldn't believe it. "I contacted Kurosawa," he said, "and asked him if it was true that they didn't have enough money to do it, and he said yes. I said, 'How much do they need in order to finish the movie?' It was about two or three million, or something like that. So I turned around and went to Laddie [Alan Ladd Jr.] at Fox, and I told him that I wanted him to buy the international rights to the film and pay them the difference between what they had and what they needed to finish the movie—about two or three million." Laddie said yes. "Then I went to Francis and said, 'You're a friend of Kurosawa's. Would you like to be the co-international producer on this picture with me?'" Of course he would.

But who—when he turned seventy—would do the same for Coppola?

With Zoetrope Studios, they wouldn't have to. Coppola imagined a movie studio that was about more than even movies; if they pulled it off, it would be, like his vision of Japan, a new land of beauty and ritual, a kingdom of creativity. "We have the tremendous talent in this country and in the world to redesign the world," he explained. "Redesign it in every possible way. Even our ethics systems. So that the new world that will be designed from our *talent* will be our best chance for operating as human beings in some sort of joyous and enlightened way. I mean, it's so preferable to what is being offered us that it's hardly not worth the risk." The plan—as all good plans are—was premised on a simple, historically sound notion, one that had proven instrumental to the artistic and economic stability of Hollywood's golden age: volume.

In 1940, the Hollywood majors produced 348 feature films. In 1949, the number was 224. The output declined steadily from there. In the years following the Hollywood antitrust action of the Paramount Decrees, the rising costs of production, the declining profit margin, and increased competition from TV meant less money for Hollywood to spend and fewer films to make. With fewer films, each one became a roll of the dice for the studio, meaning fewer chances at the craps table, more conservative rolls, further restraints on creativity. Volume had also meant job security; it meant opportunity to practice and, therefore, improve art and craft, and distributing the risk over more films meant, also, security of a kind and a better quality of life. In the old days, your studio was your home.

How to turn back the clocks? How to lower the cost, up the volume, reduce the risk, improve the art, save the future?

Video.

He said, "I'm interested in an area that is perhaps so radical that people don't even see it as political yet."

In Japan, Coppola caught up with the latest in video technology, the impressive advances made in high-definition television, far ahead of any video format that was being shot or broadcast in America, where motion picture research and development was, and always had been, an afterthought, if that. Let someone else reinvent the wheel, Hollywood would say. We'll buy it when it's ready. Which always put the industry, Coppola knew, on the wrong side of the cutting edge.

Video was most certainly not yet ready for feature film production and exhibition anywhere in the world, but Coppola was a boy scientist. He would make it ready. The economic and artistic incentives were there. With video, he could significantly reduce the costly element of time. If he could shoot a feature film on video, the way they used to make television—the way, say, John Frankenheimer had made *The Comedian*, in Television City in Los Angeles, cutting, live, between cameras, the sort of setup Clark Higgins had shown him in the mobile unit rigged for Les Blank's documentary—Coppola could shoot *and* edit a movie, basically, in the time it currently took to shoot it. Imagine it: the length of the traditional months-long production period would be reduced to a couple of hours, the length of a performance. As the movie would be edited practically as it was shot, in real time, the many months of postproduction could be seriously mitigated, if not eliminated completely. Reducing the time it took to make a movie would also diminish interest charges on investment capital. The major time investment, then, would reside in preproduction, when the actors, director, and principal technicians rehearsed the movie like a play. It was win-win, a boon to movie actors who were only rarely given sufficient rehearsal time; a boon to the screenwriter, who, attending those rehearsals, would be able to revise his script accordingly; and a boon to the director, who, like everyone else, would have the time to learn about and "practice" his film, and comfortably, in the least expensive way possible.

He would call it Electronic Cinema.

Working with maximal efficiency, Zoetrope Studios could achieve the high volume of feature film product a studio needed to thrive financially and artistically. "My idea of the perfect studio was: You make one film that has a real shot to make a lot of money and then you make another one that has no shot to make a lot of money, but one protects the other."

There were, of course, challenges. Until high-definition video had been perfected and an international standard agreed upon, video would not meet the aesthetic standards of film. But for this, Coppola had a solution: he would fit the viewfinders of his film cameras with television cameras and photograph his movie on film and video simultaneously. He could then review, edit, and mix the video footage live and then, later, just follow the same recipe with the exposed film. *Voilà!* A film cut speedily on video and released theatrically on beautiful film. Naturally, he would have to build the necessary equipment—another challenge—but, again, hardly a problem. If there was a challenge that posed an actual problem, it was the adversity he was sure to face from Hollywood. Should he succeed, he and his Electronic Cinema technology could and probably would supplant the entire industry—not a position Hollywood would welcome. But this—how to spread the good word—was merely a public relations problem. His Zoetrope Studios would be the proof of concept.

Hollywood, the studios . . . To speak to them, he would have to speak in their language. What did one think of first when one thought of, say, MGM, the greatest studio of them all? What did they make so well, so proficiently then, that they didn't make now? The musical, of course. There was a kind of serenity in that thought, of making, at Zoetrope Studios, a tender musical, in letting himself drift backward to innocence and virtue, values *Apocalypse* had blown out of him, as if going backward in time, to the studio era . . . to a younger age in the heart of America, before cynicism, before Vietnam, when it was not yet considered naïve to dream. He needed that.

He had been Kurtz. It had almost destroyed him. He needed now to live in a musical. One could say his life, and the lives of those he loved, depended on it.

Walking through the Ginza district, in the center of Tokyo, he had been struck by how similar it was to Las Vegas.

"Army, what is love?" Coppola would ask Armyan Bernstein in their conversations about *One from the Heart.*

"That's a great question, and I don't know the answer."

"Love is a gamble."

"Yeah. Okay."

"Where do people gamble?"

"Vegas.

"That's what we should do. Let's set this in Vegas."

* * *

Coppola's experiment with Electronic Cinema began late in March 1980. He had been appointed by California governor Jerry Brown to create a live television broadcast of Brown's presidential primary campaign rally, in advance of the Wisconsin primary on April 1, outside Madison. In honor of H. G. Wells's utopian novel and the 1936 Korda film adaptation, Coppola would call his broadcast *The Shape of Things to Come*.

He arrived in Madison with his "little Zoetrope SWAT team," including assistant Tess Haley, Dean Tavoularis, Caleb Deschanel, Bill Graham, Gio, Roman, Eleanor, and video mavericks Steve Calou, who had set up the video editing platform in Coppola's penthouse, and Clark Higgins, whose gear truck inspired the improvised mobile unit from which Coppola would be directing the broadcast—live. There would be crisscrossing searchlights in the sky, fires in steel drums, six television cameras, helicopter shots— "Holy shit," someone yelled, "Francis is going to napalm us!"—cranes, and three thousand servings of chicken soup to keep the night crowd warm. But it would begin simply, like the beginning of *Patton*, with Governor Brown appearing before the capitol building, in front of a blue screen on which Coppola would project prerecorded electronic imagery via a process known as chroma key. And all of it live. "If something goes wrong," he confessed, "I'll have to show it."

Coppola agreed to forgo rehearsals. "Jerry didn't want to rehearse," Tess Haley recalled, "because it was just giving a speech." It wasn't. Checking in on Brown a few hours before he was scheduled to appear, Haley found him not in the agreed-upon white shirt, but in blue, a color that would blend in with the giant chroma key blue screen behind him, effectively "dissolving" Brown, who was supposed to look presidential, into his own electronic background. But Brown had cut himself shaving in his white shirt, he told Haley, and couldn't get the blood out. Haley tried, but she couldn't get it out, either; nor could she find, with the clock ticking, another white button-down. And then, before they began, Coppola's intercom went out.

"LIVE FROM MADISNO, WISCINSIN" the big screen in front of the Capitol erroneously announced, and Brown, hands inside his pockets, took the stage unintroduced. But his microphone didn't work. He started sweating. The sweat caught the light, "and a little hole appeared in his forehead," Calou said, "because the other thing they didn't test was the lighting; there was no way to test the lighting. So, here they had a Super Trouper, which is like an arc light, which are very, very blue, and the blue reflected off Jerry's forehead and burned a hole in his head electronically." Nor had the images Coppola was live-mixing in the mobile unit been synchronized to the speech; when Brown addressed urban decay, Coppola mistakenly cut to green pastures. An unchecked zoom overshot Brown's close-up and ended on the giant screen behind him.

Exasperated in his mobile unit, Coppola threw a shoe at the monitor.

Four days later, Brown withdrew his bid for the nomination.

As television, *Jerry Brown: The Shape of Things to Come* was a failure, a fiasco, a public humiliation that Clark Higgins called "probably the worst production experience of my life." The press jumped on Coppola.

And yet, as an experiment, a test that wants only to teach, this first venture of Electronic Cinema was a success. "When I came back to California," Coppola said, "I thought, if you had a truck with all those buttons, and if you said, 'Do that,' and it would do that, and if you could also edit electronically, you could make a movie by staging an event. . . . So why not then stage *One from the Heart* by going to Las Vegas with this new super-duper video approach, just as if it had worked in Madison? Go to Las Vegas and pull up on the street, and, instead of just directing a moment, which is to say a shot, set up a situation, sort of like taking theater and actually putting it on a street in Las Vegas—and shooting it not like a movie, but like a baseball game."

Vegas was only one of many. Coppola could take his mobile unit anywhere. Imagine a world in which the quirks of *The Shape of Things to Come* were ironed out and he made his mobile unit into an international mini-electronic studio on wheels . . . the humble beginnings of an Italian Zoetrope, a British Zoetrope, Mexican Zoetrope . . . Zoetrope Belize . . .

He had read it in the paper: British Honduras was becoming Belize, "and it sounded exciting," he said, "a new nation means it can be Utopia." One day, he thought, South America and North America would be connected culturally and economically, and right there was Belize, a fresh start between them. Fondly recalling Hidden Valley, his Philippine oasis for a stretch of *Apocalypse Now*, and thinking of Plato's *Republic*, of starting "a school of the arts, but also zoology, botany—all the things that pertain to an area like that.

But ultimately, a telecommunications center. A satellite address. . . . The first pan-American, bilingual superstation," he flew south with Gio to look for the future site of what he was calling The Creative States of America. He knew, of course, that Belize was a troubled area, but it had miles of beautiful, untouched coastline, was only three hours from New York, and with its new independence, perhaps a government inclined to embrace the new industry of telecommunications . . . Coppola said, "I would turn the young people of that country and the young people of the Caribbean and young people in general to video. Give them the tools to do it and then make it a little national industry." Upon their arrival in Belize City, Coppola and son started looking for an island.

Around three in the morning, Gio rushed him out of bed. "Dad, dad, c'mon! Get up!"

"What? What is it?"

"I found draft beer and fresh lobster!"

Entering the shack, they encountered Chef Ramon, boiling—just as Gio had said—lobster in the middle of the night. "You won't find an island of the type you're describing," Ramon told them. "But there is, up in the mountains, there is a place in fact known as Hidden Valley." The coincidence! "It's very beautiful, a forestry preserve . . ."

Through the jungle, they came to an improbable pine forest ("How did *that* happen?" Coppola asked), a river, an airstrip, and a short distance away the abandoned Blancaneaux Lodge. Enchanted, Coppola bought the property for $40,000. Although the local government would decline his plan for the young nation ("There's just one little thing," they told him. "We don't have TV sets yet"), Coppola's portion of the rainforest would remain their own Swiss Family Robinson hideaway, he thought, for years to come.

Leaving the Northpoint Theatre in San Francisco after an early screening of *The Empire Strikes Back*, Coppola and Eleanor were seen openly fighting on the street. "It was a blowout," said one Zoetrope employee, watching from a distance. "Francis was screaming and yelling, and I went, *Wow, that guy's out of his mind*. Then I thought, *This is really interesting. His protégé has just made a follow-up to his hugely successful movie that's also going to be hugely successful.*" (Gene Siskel: "*The Empire Strikes Back* joins *The Godfather Part II* as one of the rarest of films—a sequel that lives up to and expands upon its original.")

Lucas's Skywalker Ranch, the biggest-yet undertaking in all of Bay Area Hollywood, was already in construction not too far from the city. "We both have the same goals," Lucas explained, somewhat misappraising himself and Coppola, "we both have the same ideas and we both have the same ambitions. . . . [We have] a disagreement in the way it should be done . . ." Lucas openly discouraged Coppola from moving the better part of Zoetrope to Hollywood, "because you're trying to change a system that will never change." Instead, he had focused his sights on the comparatively manageable problems of special effects. Eminently practical, Lucas was also now fantastically rich, and if wealth decided the future, then the future of Hollywood was looking more like Lucasfilm's than Zoetrope's. "Lucas has a bank called *Star Wars*," their mutual friend Spielberg said. "Coppola doesn't have a bank—only courage and fortitude."

That summer, Coppola invited two dozen of the world's leaders in digital art and technology to an Electronic Cinema summit he held at the Broadway house in San Francisco. "It is my hope and ambition," he told them at the top of the weekend, "that [Zoetrope Studios] will be within five years an Electronic Cinema movie studio, so that all the work that we do, all the films that we do will be made electronically . . ." They would pool their knowledge, discuss collective next steps in the evolution of a digital cinema, and agree upon what impossibles needed to be made possible. "It was like a mind meld," said attendee Louise Ledeen.

Many at the summit were already working for Lucas, making terrific advances at top speed. But unlike Lucas's plan for the future, with its emphasis on postproduction, Coppola's would be on preproduction. In fact, his and Lucas's visions were, or would be, compatible, complementary even, but with the field as small as it was, there was only a small number of experts to split between them. They had no choice but to compete.

"George has many applications [for digital film]," Coppola explained to the group. "He really needs to synthesize sequences—maybe whole films. My interest is more in an electronic armature to plan films by constructing them in simulated ways just like a wind tunnel test, [in] which I could make the whole movie before it's shot, to design the actual shooting of the production more efficiently. Then shoot the film in, say, ten minute increments, ten minutes because that's how long the stock is. Then develop, but transfer the negative to video without printing it onto film. And handle all the post-production, all the editorial, all the way down to the end in video. My gamble is that the money we spend on it will be saved by the fact that we'll shoot it that much quicker. So it's an experiment that Zoetrope is doing to start getting into more video style production, even though right now we're wedded to film. So that when we go to all high resolution video, we'll have the methods down. . . .

"Then the other side of it," he added later, "if you can get the economics down to a certain point through technology, then the subject matter can get more ambitious, and more unorthodox. So if we can get to the point where we can make a movie in four weeks, then we can make a lot of movies, and they can be of themes and subject matters that we wouldn't be able to finance otherwise."

High on his unorthodox agenda was *Interface*, a feature script that experimental filmmaker Scott Bartlett was to direct for Zoetrope Studios, about an impaired war veteran whose mind is hooked into a computer that translates his thoughts into action. *Interface* was to approach subjectivity through all planes of consciousness, part live action, part digital effects, to simulate "psychological realities, image tunnels, metaphors for consciousness, and dreams," Ledeen said. But they had not been brought to the symposium that weekend to discuss special effects. As Coppola presented it, the Electronic Cinema promised to speak in a new language entirely; as with cinema, it would be a universal language *above* language, but unlike cinema, its tools and technologies would one day be made available to all.

"I guess, in one sense," Scott Bartlett told the group, "we have, on a technical and tactile level, a film that would run the full range of everything imaginable!"

"The full range of everything imaginable," echoed Coppola. "I like that."

He would build at least six parks around Zoetrope Studios. He would develop a training program for under-represented Zoetrope employees of the future. He would rent out space with no overhead charge to producers. He would offer two acting tracks, one for contracted actors in his repertory company, the other for freelance talent. He would do the same for writers and directors. Instead of giving out percentage points in individual films, he would give his contract players a share in the profits of the entire studio. Should they want to work elsewhere while under contract, he would, within reason, encourage them. For Zoetrope workers and their families, he would enlist Hollywood professionals to lead free studio workshops in the art of filmmaking. He would open a Zoetrope Studios restaurant, several restaurants, so employees and their families would eat—and for free. He would open a library. He would screen, night and day, favorite films. He would sign directors emeritus to serve as artists in residence. While at Zoetrope Studios, they would develop their own dream projects and act as ubiquitous mentors to Zoetrope artists. Zoetrope artists, in turn, would mentor high school students; under the aegis of August Coppola, the studio would become "a living high school" alternative for young artists like Gio, who struggled to learn the scholastic way. In addition, Coppola would develop Zoetrope Studios' nonprofit arm. He would open the lot to the greater community, like a museum or public park, and host film festivals, dance festivals, and drive-ins. He would lease the Pilot Light Theatre, on nearby Santa Monica Boulevard, for Zoetrope rehearsals and auditions by day and ticketed performances by night. He would expand to New York and develop a Zoetrope theater division. They would hold an annual new play festival. The theater division would feed new talent to the film division, and the film division would feed seasoned talent to the theater division. He would connect them by satellite. He would computerize the entire studio and, to reserve the predictable claims of waste and indulgence, make budgetary statistics available for all employed. He would oversee fifteen modestly budgeted films a year. His name and reputation would earn him a healthy line of credit from Chase Manhattan; European and domestic distributors would provide the rest. He would devote a staggering 50 percent of Zoetrope's profits to research and development. He would have parties. He would keep his bungalow door open, even while he worked. He would nurture a creative ecosystem that would keep everyone happily employed forever. No one would have to go to the jungle again.

*　　*　　*

Nine soundstages, a few office bungalows, a mill, two projection rooms, editorial facilities, executive and production buildings, grip and electrical storage, a paint shop . . .

They weren't in great shape, but in those early days of Zoetrope Studios, they didn't have to be. It would be an exaggeration even to call the few kids schlepping and fetching in their shorts and Chuck Taylors production assistants; at that stage, there were no productions to assist. Save for them, the lot was empty. The kids were there because—why not? They loved film, and because film school, if they were lucky enough to get in, and then lucky enough to advance, would not likely get them a job, let alone a potentially life-changing introduction to Francis Ford Coppola. It happened to George Lucas on *Finian's Rainbow*. Why couldn't it happen to them?

Ed Rugoff, whose father, Donald Rugoff, had partnered with Coppola on Cinema 7, was there with his pal Robert Kensinger. They were moving furniture into offices with a few other guys, like August Coppola's son, Nicolas, soon to be Nicolas Cage. At a certain point, realizing they hadn't settled the matter of the paychecks, so they could afford things like food and rent, the kids innocently approached Fred Roos and Ron Colby and, after some embarrassment from both sides, were swiftly paid. Which gave Roos an idea. Now that the furniture had been moved, how did they feel about reading scripts and writing coverage? For a job as cool as that, they would have said yes to any offer, but none could have anticipated anything as good as a hundred dollars a script.

They were twenty, twenty-one, and twenty-two; they were reading scripts for Francis Ford Coppola; and they were getting paid, probably, better than their friends at Paramount or MGM or Warner Bros. "The optimism, the bursts of creativity, the sense of remaking Hollywood," noted young Zoetroper Dan Attias, was a feeling echoed by all.

Mitch Dubin had been sent down from San Francisco to make an inventory of the camera, lighting, and electrical gear. He found them stacked high in a forgotten soundstage, a neglected pile of outmoded VistaVision cameras and giant blimps for the noisiest of the old cameras, aging in the smell of old mold and wood, the bouquet of studio Hollywood. Not too far away, Dean Tavoularis—"You're going to be the director of design!" Francis had decreed—alighted on the perfect setting for Zoetrope's art department and drafting room. He had the place drywalled, varnished its wood floors back to their chocolate shine, and dispatched his niece to find antique oak drafting tables for his incoming coterie of production designers young and old. Their first project, he decided, would be the studio itself, perhaps even the design and construction of a twelve-foot-long pencil that would read "Writers' Building," the first of many lusciously pop art signs that were to hang outside each of Zoetrope's stages and office buildings. Maybe a giant music stand for the music department? Ask Francis? No need—he'll love it.

Where *was* Francis?

Everywhere. Split among *One from the Heart* rewrites, sundry producing duties (Scott Bartlett's impending *Interface*, Wim Wenders's collapsing *Hammett . . .*), overseeing the development and installation of Electronic Cinema technology, and promoting the studio to the doubting press, Coppola himself would appear only sporadically in those first months, glimpsed bicycling up and down the long studio streets (named for heroes Fellini, Kurosawa, Buster Keaton, Nino Rota, Dorothy Arzner . . .) or ambling proudly between soundstages in his white Panama hat, hands tucked into corduroy jacket or kimono, leading this or that journalist, potential investor, or representative flown in from Sony Japan on a tour of the lot. He was bursting with enthusiasm for the studio's history, pointing up at the storied yellowed walls, explaining that this is where they shot *I Love Lucy*, this is where they shot *Ozzie and Harriet.* . . . He was engaging young Zoetropers, goofing off on their way to execute some menial task, about their favorite movies, what they had seen lately, what movies they wanted to make, befriending them as he, when he was young, so wished to be befriended. He crossed paths with Bob Spiotta's daughter, Dana. She was reading. They had talked often about books and stories; he would always ask her *What do you think of . . . ?* and *Have you read . . . ?* and knew the girl was serious about becoming a writer. "You shouldn't be reading that," he offered.

"What should I be reading?"

"A book called *The Courage to Create*, by a psychologist named Rollo May."

For a man of his stature, Coppola could facilitate the new world just by engaging people in conversation. He was creating, Armyan Bernstein observed, "a world that was, to many people, like Camelot. It was like Camelot meets a circus." "It was the Camelot of the movie business at the time," agreed Barry Hirsch. "It was all about creating a place and an environment that facilitated youthful expression."

"This is a story about a little girl who is six years old," Sofia Coppola, nine years old, wrote with a friend. "Her name is Lucy. She lives in L.A. in a movie studio her parents owned. She was an only child in this studio where Harold Lloyd and May [sic] West worked. (They are actors.) They are not alive right now, but every afternoon she has tea with the ghost of May West and Harold Lloyd . . ."

Sofia was a goofy, inquisitive, sprightly, big-toothed little girl, dressed up in weird and glamorous costumes, grossed out by but crushing on boys, roller-skating the sunlit lot with her girlfriends, sisters Jenny and Jilian Gersten—daughters of producer Bernie Gersten, who had been called in to Zoetrope Studios to bring Coppola the same magic he had brought to Joe Papp and the Public Theater—the girls called themselves the Ding-bats. "We were troublemakers," Jenny Gersten said, "the young Dadaists of Zoetrope Studios," giving silly names to the grown-ups and their movies ("Fracas Flop Cucamonga" had directed *The Oddfather*, *The Johnversation*, *Acockoroach Now* . . .), making up stories about Fred Roos or a romance for Bob Spiotta (which ended up being true), scheming and snooping for dish for the "Zoesoap" page of their studio newsletter, *The Ding-bat News!*, written, illustrated, and collaged by Sofia and the Gerstens. The charge: one cent (their motto, "You pay a cheap price for a cheap paper"), but once you read the paper, you had to give it back because they only had two copies.

A life lived on the periphery of a film set is a life spent waiting, at a remove from the communal spirit of collaboration, and often on location far from home. For a child or even an adult close to but not a part of the production, it can be a life lived a distance from love, alone. But for Sofia Coppola—as with her brothers and her friends—growing up Zoetrope, waiting in the ongoing company of Dean, Vittorio, Walter, and other colleagues elevated to family, it was a sandbox of fun. No part of the studio was off limits to them.

"Because we lived nearby," Sofia said, "I don't remember any world out-side of our house on June Street and the studio. It felt like our whole world revolved around this fantasy world." For her birthday, her father gave Sofia a costume box stocked with glittery tube tops and fishnets and boas taken from the Las Vegas wardrobe of *One from the Heart*. "That era was so glamorous," she would say, "the neon and eighties style," the first Go-Go's album, her first brush with Chanel, French braids, white linen jackets, and giddy fashion shoots with Jenny and Jilian Gersten inspired by French *Vogue*. "We were little rascals," Jenny said, "and we would just go around taking pictures of people's desks when they weren't sitting at them and, you know, put them in our newsletter and say, so-and-so hard at work. Everything was satirical to us." Dustin Hoffman paid a visit to Coppola's bungalow and looked with the girls at beautiful pictures—men transformed into the most stunning women—from Coppola's collection of Kabuki books. "I want to make *this* movie," Hoffman told them. "I want to make a movie where I get to do this . . ." (He would—but with Sydney Pollack.) "It was so inspiring to be around [the studio]," Sofia recalled. "Everyone was making stuff." The miniaturists at the model shop gave her projects, the makeup artists showed the girls how to apply rhinestones to their faces. "All the people working there were like my aunts and uncles because my dad always worked with the same people," Sofia said. "It was a child's world, and we had the keys to the castle," Jilian Gersten said. "We would just roller-skate around, and we just knew if there was a closed set or whatever, if the red light was on the studio door, you couldn't walk in. But other than that, we would go in and out of spaces to watch scenes being shot and play on the props. It was all like a fantasyland, like living in a movie."

What are you working on? Coppola, peeking into this or that office bungalow, would ask. "Francis was interested in what I thought," said Fred Roos's assistant, and later story editor, Jill Kearney, who was hired at twenty-two with no experience in the film business. She was, by her own estimation, not even a film aficionado. But she was interested. That interested Coppola. "Francis was interested in everyone. He was interested in what the guards at the gate thought. When he asked their opinion about what movie he should make or what they thought, he really asked it." Kearney heard he wanted to build a day care center for the children of Zoetrope employees; she heard he wanted to teach Zoetrope assistants to adapt novels into first-draft screenplays—a responsibility far from the purview of any other assistant in Hollywood. "Zoetrope was filled with these kinds of utopian exercises," Kearney said.

"The atmosphere," Gary Fettis said, "was like a Roman chalice overflowing with the birth of new ideas." George Burns would still drive his big Cadillac through the studio gates, cigar in mouth, his head barely above the wheel. Though he was only putting in half days, Burns kept the office he'd had for the last thirty years, since *The Burns and Allen Show*; now his floor was amiably trafficked with the young people of Zoetrope, and the aroma of pot where there once was cigar smoke. The afternoon Burns signed his will, he needed a witness quickly and called in Jill Kearney, who just happened to be near. "I thought it was adorable," she said. He thanked her with a cigar and a signed headshot. She went back to work, and he took off to Hillcrest to play poker for the rest of the day.

Casual cross-pollination, Coppola knew, paid artistic and spiritual dividends to both sides, old and young. Continuity: that was how you built a family and sustained a community. Born in 1909, Zoetrope Studios publicist Max Bercutt had been a publicist on *Gone with the Wind*. "Max was a real old-timer, a colorful character," his younger counterpart, publicist Anne Diamond, said. "Everyone adored him." He walked around the lot gushing with a lifetime of tales from *Giant* and RKO and Jack Warner (to some, it seemed Coppola kept him on the payroll for the stories alone), which he offered up on request, like a disc jockey of Hollywood history. Crossing paths with Doug Claybourne on the lot, Bercutt insisted that the young fellow take his tickets to that year's Academy Awards ceremony. *Apocalypse Now* was a front-runner, and the movie, obviously, meant more to Claybourne, who had worked on it, than to Bercutt. *Please, I insist! Go, have fun!* "That's the kind of people that were there," Claybourne said. "They really cared about the movie business."

Oh my goodness, Kearney thought. *This place is so cool.*

Studio manager Ben Cowitt had come by way of MGM, "where everybody was always nervous about the shareholders," he said. "But [at Zoetrope Studios] it was just Francis." Cowitt and his wife, helping him set up the place, went to buy benches and placed them outside Coppola's bungalow. Francis, they knew, wanted to take all his meetings outside. Was Barry Diller doing that?

An old generator building, formerly the site of Harold Lloyd's personal handball court, was transformed into what they would call the War Room. Here is where Zoetrope movies would be conceived *cinematically*, where a "draft" of a movie could be seen well before the film was shot. Step one: scenes, arranged in traditional storyboards, were hung along the War Room walls like panels in a hundred-foot-long comic book, "because," Tavoularis explained, "if you were doing a mural or a movie, which is hard to see all at once, you need a sketch." It had never been done before. "It became apparent that a movie was actually just a giant database," said electronics expert Thomas Brown, "and we were technologically a long way from that, so it needed to be created." "Previsualization," Coppola called it, and they hung a sign to that effect over the front door. Inside, Coppola could "show" the unmade movie, panel by panel, as he imagined it might unfold, enlisting comments and ideas from actors, musicians, writers, designers. Shooting video of the storyboards, he would move from the wall to the video monitor, and run through the movie in a kind of digital slideshow form, gradually adding elements as they were captured—music, prerecorded dialogue, videotaped rehearsals—which could be reconceived at low cost before they were finally committed to film. It was an added step in the production process, but learning now would save them time and money in the long run.

"Francis was making a think tank," said Dan Attias, "and there were so many ideas, you couldn't be sure which ones were crazy and which ones were genius," in part because "when you invent something, it doesn't always happen in a straightforward order." One could lose the long view, especially as all of Zoetrope Studios was a work in progress, evolving to meet the changing assumptions of possibility.

At the center of the War Room, folks gathered at the bespoke video editing console adapted from the pilot model Coppola hired Steve Calou to devise for his Sentinel Building penthouse. Significantly, it was centrally placed on a long table ceremoniously covered in green felt, as if it were a gambling table. One couldn't ignore the metaphoric pileup: making a movie was a gamble, making a movie about falling in love in Las Vegas was making a movie about gambling, and doing it all at Zoetrope Studios—to Steve Calou, itself a kind of Vegas, one where they didn't bet with chips, but with passions and ideas—was Coppola's biggest gamble of all. Calou mentioned the analogy to Coppola. "I become my characters," Coppola answered him. "When I did *Apocalypse*, I was Kurtz."

More than just an innovative filmmaking tool, the War Room—a fascination to artists and innovators of all stripes—was a gathering place. Debbie Harry, Ralph Nader, Martin Scorsese and Isabella Rossellini, Ray Davies of the Kinks—all came for tours . . . And then there was madman/visionary Zoltan Tarczy-Hornoch, the science world's answer to Dennis Jakob. An extension of Coppola's additive imagination, the War Room, Tavoularis said, "brought everyone together." Twenty-four-year-old Michael Lehmann had the honor of giving the War Room tour to Robert Wise, esteemed director of *West Side Story* and *The Sound of Music* . . .

"I don't know how knowledgeable you are about the details of the editorial process . . ." Lehmann offered to Wise.

"I edited *Citizen Kane*."

"Oh. Okay, good."

Friends and employees of Zoetrope Studios were invited to gather early one morning in the parking lot. Coppola didn't say why. But they did as requested, and at the designated hour, giant speakers blasted "Ride of the Valkyries," and all beheld the entrance of a gleaming silver trailer: Coppola's "Image and Sound Control Vehicle," a digital command center on wheels modeled after Clark Higgins's mobile unit. It was mysterious, beautiful; a what and also a wow. Outfitted with source monitors corresponding to film cameras, dubbing boards for sound, an offline editing system complete with instant optical effects, and an intercom feature that would pipe Coppola's voice through the studio soundstages (and a kitchen and a Japanese hot tub), the trailer—one of only two Airstream made that year, the other for the Apollo mission—offered Coppola the Oz-like ability to direct his film remotely as well as to make a "first impression" edit of what had been shot, as if he were directing live television. With this rudimentary cut— further grist for the War Room—he could learn about his movie fast and cheap, without having to wait for dailies or even editors. "In the trailer, all the creative elements of filmmaking were in Francis's control," said Clark Higgins. He and "Video Rangers" Murdo Laird and Thomas Brown, assisted by Michael Lehmann, oversaw its construction. "I think where Francis was headed was 'I sit. I view the screen, I talk to the screen, and the screen does what I asked it to do,'" Brown surmised. "You tell the blank canvas what to paint." Brown got the equipment; Higgins made the technology work. "I want it to *be* me," Coppola said to Higgins. The whole unit was to be an island apart but "connected to every aspect of the studio," Coppola said. "I want images and sound to flow through the studio like hot and cold running water" had been his directive to Brown. Brown could do that. For Coppola, he could do it all. "It was springtime at Zoetrope," he said. "Anything was possible. We started at infinity."

Walter Murch—in the midst of postproduction work on *Dragonslayer*, written by Zoetrope's Barwood and Robbins and directed by Robbins—had his reservations about Coppola's new invention. *There is something crazy about all this*, he thought. Roger Corman smiled at it, shrugging.

They were not alone. To the dubious in and outside the inner circle, Coppola would explain that he was just adapting music recording technology to film. "If you were in a recording studio," he said, "and someone was recording an orchestra and the producer was using a booth announcing device to tell them to do something a little different, it wouldn't have been regarded as anything unusual." Still, Coppola's mobile unit met with widespread suspicion, even hostility. Was Coppola getting high in there? (Zoetrope's Dorothy Meriwether said, "The Zoetrope drug policy was something like, 'Please confine your marijuana to your office; please don't do it in the hallways or the parking lots.'") Some spoke of Coppola's trailer with a sneer of almost moral disgust ("How much did he *pay* for this thing?"); others sniffed a Howard Hughesian eccentricity. "There was a lot of resentment and kind of nastiness directed his way for doing what he was doing," Lehmann said, "which was interesting to see, because I think it was mostly misplaced. Francis's attitude was an artist's attitude toward technology. There's no such a thing as a 'no.' Eventually, if time runs out, you take it as a 'no,' but until time runs out, it's something to work on." But to those—like most of Hollywood—who fearfully lived by "no," perversely seeking it out in order to curb their own anxieties, Coppola's "yeses" were a strange dialect.

"This technology shouldn't exclusively be in the hands of the professionals," Coppola told Clark Higgins, sitting beside him at the monitors. "Soon everyone will have their own. Maybe not on wheels. Maybe it will be smaller, in their homes. But everyone will have the ability to make movies, like every poet has paper and pen. And what will the studios do then?" Higgins had no doubt. It was only a question of time. "All the elements," Coppola would explain to the press, "information technology, video technology, audio technology—have one thing in common in that they're electronic, they can all work together. And that can give us an audio-visual instrument—so that, really, groups of artists could come together in the studio of the future and use this audio-visual instrument almost as performance artists. You go in [the Image and Sound Control Vehicle] and you stay locked up in this configuration for a month and out comes *Lawrence of Arabia*." To Higgins, he said, "All these advances in communication are going to put the world in the hands of artists." *Art*, he thought, *not for the popes and the Medicis, but for all mankind.*

Mankind—at least their representatives at Zoetrope Studios—would cross paths at the studio library, the first bungalow you saw after passing the guard off the Las Palmas entrance and conveniently close to the story department. Zoetrope readers would hang out on the library steps, snacking on cookies that librarian Lillian Michelson (always laughing, with a "honey" for everyone) kept out in the library's little foyer. It was a relief to have any home for her wandering research library, but to have it out of boxes and in the service of one who prized learning as highly as Coppola was Michelson's dream deluxe. ("And he didn't even charge me rent," she said.) At Paramount, her previous home, they had put Michelson's collection in the basement—no small indication of their esteem for research, let alone for Michelson's library, one of the largest independent motion picture research collections in Hollywood. Since she bought it from Goldwyn Studios in 1969, she had amassed thousands of periodicals, an estimated three thousand books, and millions of clipping files. Before Zoetrope, Michelson had been paid to research on a project-to-project basis, but "I never charged my home studio," she said. "I always felt guilty when they paid me, and so I always used the money to go out and buy more books." At Zoetrope, she gave away her expertise freely and to anyone who asked. Tom Waits would bashfully shuffle in from his office across the courtyard to sing the songs he was writing for *One from the Heart*. Filmmakers Andrei Konchalovsky and Michael Powell came with a bottle of vodka and, "within twenty minutes," Michelson said, "Andrei was dancing on my desk."

Seemingly fresh off the screen of an Ealing Studios comedy, Powell was a jaunty and twinkling presence on the lot. Coppola had first encountered him—one half (with Emeric Pressburger) of the production company the Archers, whose musical Technicolor fantasias of theater and cinema Coppola had adored since childhood—one evening at the Plaza. The New York Film Festival was screening Powell's *Peeping Tom* and Zoetrope's *The Black Stallion*. But the two didn't get to talking until the next evening, when they met for dinner. At the restaurant, Coppola came skipping toward Powell singing, full-throated, Abu's theme from *The Thief of Bagdad* ("I want to be a sailor sailing off to sea!"), and they talked half the night about how to build an independent film studio in Hollywood.

"Why don't you come along and help?" Coppola asked.

Powell was then working on his autobiography, biding his later years of inactivity while he sought financing for his next film, another theater picture, this one about ballerina Anna Pavlova. But he was running out of money and, Coppola knew, time. "What do I come as? Consultant or something?"

"Oh, no. We'll think up a fine title for you. How about senior director in residence?" It was not a title native to Hollywood (or the British film industry, or any film industry for that matter). What would it entail? As senior director in residence, Coppola proposed, Powell would read scripts, look at rushes, mentor the young, develop his Pavlova project—and be paid.

To all of Zoetrope, Coppola announced Michael Powell's arrival by letter: "I hope you will feel free to consult him, get to know him, go to him for advice and comfort, learn to expect no quarter from him and that best use of him will be to overwork him mercilessly." But Coppola, endlessly distracted, had not yet arranged a place in Los Angeles for his senior director in residence to reside. "Can Michael Powell stay at your house?" Coppola asked Dean Tavoularis, who lived in Hancock Park, not too far from the studio. Tavoularis was delighted to oblige, and for several weeks, he drove Powell, who couldn't afford a car of his own, to the studio every day. At seventy-five, he hadn't directed a feature film in nearly a decade. "It was absolutely wonderful to me," Powell said of his new studio position. "I felt as if I had come home again."

When Tavoularis got Coppola's call about hosting Jean-Luc Godard, he gave the same answer, but this time it was Tavoularis's girlfriend, French actress Aurore Clément, who drove the guest around L.A. ("He was crazy about tennis," Tavoularis said. "He wanted to see tennis courts.") Godard's association with Zoetrope had been brokered by Coppola's international film liaison and director of special projects, Tom Luddy, who was instrumental in winning Zoetrope U.S. distribution rights to Godard's *Sauve qui peut la vie* (*Every Man for Himself*). In addition, it was agreed that Zoetrope would coproduce Godard's first American film, to be shot at Zoetrope Studios. *The Story*, a movie set against the backdrop of Bugsy Siegel, starred, tentatively, Robert De Niro, as a film critic, and Diane Keaton, as his ex-wife, a movie star. Characteristically, the film "is something of an experiment," Luddy explained, "an experimental parasite on *One from the Heart*." Godard, who had already begun his own experiments in video, would make extensive use of Coppola's Las Vegas locations from *One from the Heart*, perhaps even filming the production of the film itself.

Still reeling from the effects of Vietnam, America needed Zoetrope Studios, Godard thought; it needed a digital revolution. "I always wondered why Italy invented a new kind of cinema after [World War II]," Godard said. "In my opinion, Italy was such a weak country, even during the war, that by the time the fighting had ended, the country had lost its identity. I think a really new cinema, a new image, emerges when an identity is lost . . ." He also said, "I think all good American directors—Scorsese, De Palma, all the famous ones, they are as lost as I am," Godard confessed. To that list, he would add Kubrick and Coppola. "They can't work against the system," he said.

That was the beauty of Lucy Fisher, Zoetrope Studios' head of production. Though she was recently *from* the Hollywood system, she was most certainly not *of* the system, not by character and not by training. Having started smart, as a reader for Mike Medavoy and Marcia Nasatir during "a golden era of UA," Fisher moved upward but not onward, from UA to MGM (where, as an executive, she had first set up *One from the Heart*) to Fox, where she endured four administrations in four years. *Fame*, which she got going at MGM, was good business and a good time, but what made her ideal for Zoetrope Studios was her youth (only thirty!) and enduring cool. "My life was not like a studio executive's life," she said. "My boyfriend [Peter Ivers] was a rock musician–composer, and I was not in the mainstream, even though I had a mainstream job and my friends were the artists and creators."

Fred Roos put Coppola on to her. Run a studio? For Francis Ford Coppola? Fisher flew up to San Francisco to meet Coppola and was terrified when he, point-blank, offered her the job. "How will I know how to do this?" she mustered the courage to ask him. "And how will I know that you're going to be reliable? You know, how do I know that I can do the job *and* that you can do the job?" It was the right question, given that neither had done the job—run a studio (Fisher) and own a studio (Coppola). Coppola responded by getting on his knees: He begged her. He wanted a woman to be his head of production.

It was tempting. But she had heard the stories. "If you want me to do my job, we have to be clear what *your* job is," Fisher answered him. "You can't just act crazy and only care about your movies. We have to have a *company*."

He said yes.

"You have to be available," she continued, "to have meetings and make decisions on other things . . ."

He said yes again, and then he said: "What's the worst that could happen? You'll know more about making a movie than any other studio executive, and I'll go bankrupt?"

After she accepted, Coppola loaned her a baby-blue 1957 Thunderbird—as if to announce to Hollywood that *this* is how they would do it at Zoetrope Studios—a car she was so nervous driving onto the lot that she protectively parked it across two spots, which she did the first day on the job, then walked into her own bungalow (a few steps from the library), which had been painted, at Tavoularis's order, in shades of confectionery pink. Waiting on her desk was a pink orchid beside a gift of Japanese sea pearls and a note of greeting: "Looking forward to our collaboration, Francis." Yes—as anyone who saw the Thunderbird knew—they did do things differently here.

Between Fisher's bungalow and the library, there was the venerable Bernie Gersten, easily the most esteemed and well-liked theatrical producer in the country, grinning on the phone. New to Hollywood by way of the Public Theater—happy home of Shakespeare in the Park, a utopian venture he and Joe Papp had made one of the greatest arts traditions in America—Gersten would be Coppola's tie to Broadway talent. He had brought Gersten and his considerable New York muscle aboard "to keep [his own] nose to the grindstone." But Gersten's daughter Jenny called her father a "dreamer-enabler."

To succeed, he would have to have it both ways. Protecting Coppola meant shielding him from the vengeful press, delivering the truth with a light touch, and, mostly, as Gersten put it, "protecting Francis from himself." *Frantasy* was Gersten's word for it, the six hundred ideas coming at you from a single source. "If only one affirmative idea develops or is encouraged by my having been here," Gersten wrote at the beginning of his association with Zoetrope Studios, "it will be worth it."

They were beginning with a musical. Who better than Gene Kelly to lead Zoetrope's musical unit? "The way Gene Kelly would walk from the gate to the bungalow," Tess Haley recalled, "was like watching him dance. His walk was as beautiful as his dance." As Kelly's former boss Arthur Freed once had at MGM, Kelly would oversee all musical film activity on the lot, beginning with *One from the Heart*, advising Coppola on how to direct numbers choreographed by Kelly's protégé Kenny Ortega. ("If Gene likes you, I like you," Francis told Ortega. "If you want the job, you've got the job.") Kelly would assist also in the development offices, checking on director Martha Coolidge's emerging musical, *Sex and Violence*, to star actress Cindy Williams (with music by Sting?), and also Coppola's upcoming, long-planned tragicomic musical *Tucker*, with songs by the authors of *Singin' in the Rain*, Comden and Green. In the future, Kelly would develop new Zoetrope composers, lyricists, writers, directors, and choreographers; audition children for the untitled children's musical Coppola had in mind; and train dancers in the singular—and nearly lost—art form of dancing for the camera. "What I'm saying with this [Kelly] unit," Coppola said, "is that I think that musical films and the possible ways music and film can go together are just a part of the future, and part of the past [that] film shouldn't have lost in the last 20 years."

And then there was Coppola in his bungalow, welcomingly situated at the very front of the lot, to the right of the entrance guard gate, a bowl of fresh strawberries perpetually set on the living room table. He was still trying to figure out love, trying new *One from the Heart* scenes on typewriter paper or thinking aloud, musing notes to himself on audiocassette. His rewrites were personal, lusty, regretful, erotic, and fairy-tale tender; dreams from a kinder world of broken hearts. But they were corny. He had been drawn to Bernstein's script for its guy-meets-girl modesty, its universality, but thinking *One from the Heart* would be easier to nail than *Apocalypse*, Coppola had been fooling himself. Where *Apocalypse Now* needed metaphor, *Heart*'s "simplicity" demanded frankness and ease. Most audiences hadn't gone mad killing in the jungle, but they had loved. They had been there with Frannie and Hank, fighting, making up, fighting again. There was a kind of form to that, wasn't there? A kind of natural, even archetypal cycle? But how to go for archetype without getting generic? Or was that another unresolvable, like loving one's wife and one's mistress? What would Goethe say?

Elective Affinities, of which *One from the Heart* would be only a single part, would have to be sixteen hours long. "I hired two court stenographers when Francis was writing [*One from the Heart*] because he talked so fast," Tess Haley said. "One stenographer would signal to the other that he couldn't type fast enough, and the other stenographer would take it up." They sat on either side of Coppola, at the long table in his bungalow dining room, and would work sometimes until three or four in the morning. "There were times when he just slept there at the studio," assistant director Arne Schmidt said. "We'd get there in the morning, and he'd be there."

Passing the bungalow one night, Gray Frederickson would catch Coppola's eye. "Gray! Gray!"

Frederickson pulled up a seat.

"What is it, ultimately, that keeps a man and a woman, after everything that could pull them apart, together?"

Frederickson took a deep breath in and a long breath out.

"Is it luck?" Coppola asked.

Eleanor only rarely appeared at the studio. She had no desire to move to Los Angeles, and after the ordeal of *Apocalypse*, she conscientiously guarded herself from joining Francis's next adventure. "But he's an artist," she decided. "He should have his freedom to do what he does and not feel like his family is dragging on him." She moved with the family to a home on June Street, near the studio in Hancock Park—and kept her distance. With her friend, costume designer Marjorie Bowers, she started making and selling fabrics and contemporary kimonos. "Francis's whole thing was a little bit in my sideview mirror," she said. What was that line of Cheever's? Something about "my wife and I": two weeks never pass without our seriously talking about divorce.

In the War Room, Coppola would look down at the future, a table-size model of the unbuilt Zoetrope Studios, each of its structures, like dollhouse furniture, moveable. Stage 9, the biggest on the lot, he would raze. In its place, he would build a tower, modeled after the Chrysler Building, all of it soundstages and of them rigged for Electronic Cinema. A permanent War Room in skyscraper form, the tower would rise to his penthouse office and be topped off with a satellite dish, he explained to onlookers, "shooting out our message." The studio restaurant would go next to the park. There, in the evenings, they would set up chairs for outdoor screenings for whoever wanted to come.

He liked to walk around the lot, his lot. There still wasn't much at Zoetrope Studios, but like the Stage Manager in *Our Town*, he guarded his world, patted the walls reassuringly, kicked debris off the roads, found a burnt patch of grass outside the empty cutting rooms and watered it back to life. He wasn't out to supervise the various studio departments or even to monitor his *One from the Heart* artists' progress—he wouldn't want to make them feel self-conscious. His bungalow rounds were meant only for encouragement. Naturally, Coppola, the conductor, set the tempo; he'd say, *Louder here, What if you tried this here?*—but it was their playing, their satisfaction, he wanted to ensure for them.

On one of the soundstages, he proudly visited his father at work, conducting an orchestra rehearsal of—at last—his own original composition, a new score to Abel Gance's 1927 silent masterpiece, *Napoleon*. Tom Luddy had turned Coppola on to the film, but it was Coppola who had seen the chance to simultaneously bring *Napoleon* back to life, give the eighty-two-year-old Abel Gance new life, and grant his father his lifelong wish. "My dad told me that when he was a kid the thrill of his life was to go to the movies"—*Thief of Bagdad*, Douglas Fairbanks, Radio City Music Hall, second balcony—"and the movie would be accompanied by a symphony orchestra, and I thought, 'Gee, how wonderful to be able to hear that.'" Coppola called Radio City.

Could he and Zoetrope present a restored *Napoleon* with a new score by his father? That they said yes brought Coppola the further satisfactions of not only renting what may be the greatest theater in the world but supplying it money it so desperately needed to stay afloat.

"Kenny, Kenny, Kenny!" Coppola sang to Ortega as he entered a dance rehearsal. "I want to introduce you to Michael Powell!"

Ortega, born a lower-middle-class kid in Palo Alto, was now creating his own dances in the company of Michael Powell and Gene Kelly. "I was becoming me," he would say. "I was learning from the greats. We all were." The egalitarian atmosphere of Zoetrope Studios was so euphoric, Ortega thought, that an emerging artist could feel that merely by being there, he had already succeeded. "That came from Francis. It was the environment he created for us to be creative."

This went for all departments. "Janet [Hirshenson] and I have always referred to it as the University of Zoetrope," said casting director Jane Jenkins of her partner. Under the tutelage of Coppola, who taught patience, and Fred Roos, who taught scrupulousness, Jenkins and Hirshenson learned what casting was about: encouragement. In his interviews with actors, Jenkins said, "Francis would not ever ask, 'Tell me what you have done lately or where have you studied?' He would say, 'What did you have for breakfast this morning?' 'When you were growing up, did you and your family eat in the kitchen or in the dining room?' And he really could get a sense of who this person was by asking them, you know, 'How do you like your coffee?'" It took time. "It was a different mind-set," Jenkins explained. "At Zoetrope, you'd sit and talk to somebody for a half an hour. It wasn't like slam-bam-thank-you-ma'am, in-and-out auditions. We got to meet people and actually talk." The job was not to say no, but to try to find a way to say yes.

"Zoetrope Seeks Unusual People"—the signs went up all over town with a phone number. That's it. The studio was holding open casting calls, a strategy so quaint by contemporary standards, with their star-driven projects and agency packaging, that greater Hollywood would react to Zoetrope's policy with a mix of derision and curiosity. Francis Ford Coppola? What was he doing over there? The line—the *long* line—formed every week outside the Las Palmas gate: "It was a cattle call the likes of which I had no idea even existed," recalled Rebecca De Mornay, who called the number on the poster hung up in her acting class, "like five hundred people. It had whole families there. I couldn't tell if there were even any actors." De Mornay would be cast as an understudy in *One from the Heart* (an understudy in a *film*?). "Anybody who wanted to come to Zoetrope Studios and bring their picture and résumé could come, and you'd be considered," said casting associate Aleta Chappelle. "Actors were calling us asking to work for Francis for free," Jenkins recalled. "I would say, 'I don't think SAG would like that . . .'"

Nowhere at Zoetrope was the exploratory approach more evident than in the extras-casting department run by Elisabeth Leustig. "Francis wanted extras interviewed," Chappelle said. "He wanted people to know who they were." Roos gave Susie Landau a Polaroid and installed her at extras casting under Leustig; Coppola told her he wanted no one over the age of forty-five in the background of *One from the Heart*, and he charged her with finding specialty performers—jugglers, contortionists, stilt walkers, magicians—to color the streets of singing and dancing Las Vegas. "The job was way past what I knew," said Landau, only nineteen at the time, "but Fred had a vision that I could do it." Her "intern," Roman Coppola, was only fifteen.

"Nastassja's here," Roos announced to Landau one day. Nastassja Kinski, who had come to star in *One from the Heart*. "I'm going to send her to work with you."

"Work—? With me?" *Tess*, Kinski's film with Roman Polanski, had been released a year earlier.

"She wants to learn."

Kinski, who had arrived in Los Angeles a week early, was also nineteen. "What do I do?" she asked Landau the day she turned up to intern. ("She was the most beautiful thing I've ever seen in my life.") They sat together on the floor and sorted, by sex and age, the hundreds of Polaroids Roman Coppola had taken of the extras.

For the part of Leila, Hank's fantasy girl, Kinski had to learn to walk a tightrope. Between acting and singing rehearsals, she trained at Zoetrope Studios with teacher Roy Johns for three months, an hour a day, five days a week. When word spread that Kinski was ready, that she could walk the tightrope without a harness, twenty feet in the air, her rehearsal studio became the most exciting place on the lot. "You were welcome," Johns said—so everyone came: Michael Powell, Gene Kelly, Ortega, gobsmacked

men, women, boys and girls. ("It was magical," Sofia Coppola said.) Zoetrope's Louise Ledeen found her attention turning from Kinski, dancing
on air, to Gene Kelly, standing below. She didn't think he knew she was
watching him, which is probably why he did, when no one was supposed to
be looking, what he quietly did next: step off a low curb and give that kick
from *Singin' in the Rain*.

This is another world, she thought.

All this—the family, the flexibility, the fun, as film historian Jeanine Basinger
would characterize studio culture of Hollywood's golden age—returned to
Coppola the good life of writing and directing plays at Hofstra. Which is
exactly what he had wanted Zoetrope Studios to be, a student-run film and
theater department on a Hollywood studio scale. And it was happening.

In a soundstage with the film's interiors and exteriors delineated in tape
on the floor, Coppola was rehearsing *One from the Heart*—which he was
still rewriting—like a play, running it through in continuity, beginning to
end. He and the six principal actors (Frederic Forrest, Teri Garr, Nastassja
Kinski, Raul Julia, Harry Dean Stanton, and Hofstra's Lainie Kazan) would
talk, improvise, generate dramatic ideas about how these characters fell in
and out of love with their domestic partners and romantic fantasies. "Francis was constantly rehearsing, taping, editing, and rewriting," said second
AD Dan Attias, who estimated that the script was rewritten over a dozen
times. "It just kept evolving, but it never felt like he wasn't getting what
he wanted." Combined with "previsualization," the process would carry on
for six months. Once they had squeezed the coal into diamonds, the company would be able to "play" the whole movie like a Broadway show, which
Coppola could shoot and edit live from his electronic trailer. "It's the ideal
situation," said Raul Julia, who came from theater.

One day, Coppola looked up and said, "I wonder how Tom's doing?"

Tom Waits and Coppola, like Coppola and his actors, had been trading
musical ideas for months. "I usually get Francis to tell me the story over
and over again," Waits said. "Seems every time he tells it, he adds something different." The concept they finally settled on—that Waits's songs
wouldn't be sung by the characters, as is traditional, but by unidentified off-

camera male and female voices—Waits described as "Zeus and Hera somehow peeking through the clouds and commenting on the action in Vegas," singing the archetypal drama of boy meets girl.

Coppola and AD Arne Schmidt crossed the lot to Waits's studio, which was squeezed between George Burns's offices and those kept for *Interface*, and knocked. Waits, looking like he had just woken up, opened the door to find the director and his AD staring back at him. "It looked like he was crashing there," Schmidt said. Behind Waits, newspapers were spread on the couch almost like a blanket. Foam coffee cups and bent cigarette packs littered the piano.

"How's it going?" Coppola asked.

Waits groaned, shrugged. He was disarmingly shy, surprising all who knew him only as the rascally troubadour of nighthawk L.A. When he did talk, he spoke quietly and to the ground, scratching the back of his head or tapping out a cigarette.

Waits had come to Zoetrope at a low. His last albums hadn't been up to par; he'd had it with the music business and had tried and failed at a life in New York; and he'd split with singer-songwriter Rickie Lee Jones, who had been hired to sing the Hera to his Zeus. Before her, Bette Midler had fallen out, and they still didn't have a replacement. In April 1980, Waits had come back to L.A., to an empty studio on the lot, drawn the curtains between him and Santa Monica Boulevard, and woken up late every day. The job overwhelmed him. He'd never had to compose so much music before— music and lyrics *and* score—never had to answer to a story, and a changing one at that. "Something might have happened perhaps last night that will change the entire emotional geography of this picture," he explained. "So everybody works under those circumstances."

One day, Waits was spotted by young Zoetropers sitting alone in a nearby diner, looking like he was trying to stay sober; the next day, he opened his studio door, and there was Kathleen Brennan, Zoetrope Studios story analyst. Waits fell in love with her, and the entire emotional geography of *One from the Heart* changed again. "Kathleen had heard some of the jazz-flavored tracks on Crystal Gayle's albums and played them for Tom and me," music producer Bones Howe explained. "We made a tape of the songs and played them for Francis, and he thought the all-American quality in her voice would be perfect for the film." The couple's own love story spread through the lot. "You could see it happening," Ed Rugoff said, "this really incredible attraction, the look in their eyes." Rugoff, Robert Kensinger, and Jill Kearney were enjoying a late-afternoon smoke out on the library steps when Tom and Kathleen approached, as if lit by Storaro, in sunset silhouette. "You know when the sun goes down in L.A.," Kensinger said. "You know how it gets kind of orangery. It was that kind of beautiful, beautiful evening sun." So thick was the lovers' halo, it held the library gang an awestruck moment before it dawned on them that they should "probably go back to work." Two hours later, and the sun had disappeared completely, but Waits and Brennan were still talking on the library steps.

The next time Coppola and Schmidt walked into Waits's studio office, the singer took a seat at the piano and out came a tango as if played by a deranged, drunken roué. "He played the hell out of it," Schmidt said, "and no longer exhibited any shyness."

Regularly described as magical, the alchemical climate of Zoetrope Studios was in fact not supernatural, but the effect of very terrestrial community building—the sudden announcement, for instance, of a screening of *The Thief of Bagdad*; or regular showings of Orson Welles and Preston Sturges pictures, sometimes spontaneously at midday. "I didn't really know who Preston Sturges was," said dialogue director Jeff Hamlin, "and I fell in love with these movies. It was a great education." After work and without much notice, Coppola filled a van with half a dozen studio folk and pizzas—they were going to see a three-and-a-half-hour movie, they were told, and would miss dinner—and drove them out to MGM to watch a rough cut of Michael Cimino's new picture, long in the works and preemptively attacked by the press, *Heaven's Gate*. Coppola could identify.

One day, he called together the *One from the Heart* understudies—six, one for each of the film's leads and supporting players—to explain that they, more than mere stand-ins, were a part of the Zoetrope repertory company. He felt terrible, though; as he explained it, he had just discovered he couldn't afford to pay them their SAG minimum. Going forward, this would change, but on *One from the Heart*, he could pay them only as "interns slash stand-ins," Rebecca De Mornay explained. But the six were so excited to be working with Francis Ford Coppola, they barely minded. Once the production began, they were to come every day to work (whether their character was in the scene or not), stand in where necessary, and when not working—per Coppola's mandate—they were to "talk to every single person in every single department and find out about how it's done." Which is what they did, and were paid something to do it.

Field trip! Just down the street from Zoetrope Studios, Coppola; his brother, August; and Zoetrope actress Cindy Williams sat in little blue school chairs on a gymnasium stage. Called to assembly before them were the 950 pumped-up kids of Bancroft Junior High School. Coppola was appearing per L.A.'s new adopt-a-school program, as the Bancroft students' "adoptive father," as Williams introduced him.

Coppola took the stage to a roar of whoops and applause and presented for the students' contemplation what looked like a small bowl. "The reason I brought this to show you is because I knew two questions were going to come up when I saw on the bulletin board that Zoetrope Studios has adopted Bancroft Junior High School. One is, 'What is a zoetrope?' and two is 'What does adopting Bancroft Junior High School really mean? What are we going to do?' So, the first answer: This is a zoetrope. And it probably looks like a hatbox with holes in it. Of course, you can't really see what it does. There's a little kinda cartoon figure, and when you spin it and look into it, it moves. And this was the first motion picture. This is how it started. . . .

"Twelve years ago, when we were not really a lot older than you, but just out of school, myself and my friend George Lucas, who was working as an associate of mine, we wanted our own company where we could do things the way we saw it and the way we wanted . . ."

Coppola told them Zoetrope had prepared a list of the thirty-five greatest films ever made, and they were going to show them, one a week—on 35 mm projectors donated by Zoetrope—to the members of the newly formed Bancroft Movie Club.

Bancroft was the very school a lonely Francie Coppola had attended years ago, when he had been relocated to Los Angeles with his father. "I went here when I was a kid," Coppola told the students. "And I was a new kid. I wasn't allowed to be in the drama club. But I would go across the street to the gate of the studio, and it was locked, and I wanted so badly to get in. But now I own the studio. It's called Zoetrope Studios. And I want to promise you that not only will I let you in, I want you to learn with us. You will learn all the aspects of moviemaking. You will learn writing, directing, photography, acting . . . Do you want to go?"

A roar of yes!

"Let's go!"

With a great cheer, the entire student body and their befuddled teachers followed Coppola from the assembly hall out onto North Las Palmas Boulevard. Bullhorn in hand, he led them ("like the Pied Piper," publicist Anne Schwebel said) across the street and up to the Zoetrope Studio gates. The guard was not prepared.

"Now this is yours," he declared to the students.

("You should have seen the look on the guard's face," said Arne Schmidt.)

Coppola marched the rowdy nine hundred through his studio departments and busy soundstages. These were sets for *One from the Heart*, he explained, the movie he was making. On Stage 9, the biggest stage at the studio, they were building Fremont Street, a copy of the big street in Las Vegas. On another stage, they were building the street where the main characters, Hank and Frannie, lived. Over on another stage, they were building the junkyard where Hank worked . . .

"Why not make the movie in the real Las Vegas?"

It was a good question. Coppola had just made a movie in the Philippines—not in a studio, like this, but a *location*—and had had a hard time getting real life to look the way he wanted it to look. But shooting at a studio, in these nine soundstages, it was easier to control all the elements of moviemaking—color, light, scenery, actors—the way a painter has to control every brushstroke on his canvas, or a writer has to pick every word on the page. That's what a director does, he explained. But he doesn't do it with paint or words; he (or she) does it with real life. And that's what Zoetrope Studios was for—to make real life.

What the children may have not understood—but one day, hopefully, would—was that in building Las Vegas, Coppola was trying to achieve "truly one of the objectives of my life . . . the attempt to reconcile theater with cinema," and to shoot *One from the Heart* "in ten-minute live cinema units, completed, edited, mixed, finished. All that would be necessary would be to splice those ten-minute sections together and you'd have the finished movie"; *this*—made possible by the experimental ingenuity of his mobile cinema unit—would point the way toward a new cinema, "in better condition," Coppola said, not just for him, but for them, the children, the new generation, and the future.

Interested and uninterested middle-schoolers swarmed in all directions. All over the lot, Zoetropeans popped heads around doors and stood grinning (some in annoyance) on stairways; pressed against a wall, Tess Haley passed out introductory brochures to every young person that reached toward her; others, like Gio, were given megaphones to lead groups of a dozen or so kids on a walking tour.

On their way out, each student was given their own strip of film. "Use 'em as bookmarks!" Coppola suggested, stationed at the gate to shake a hundred, maybe two hundred little hands goodbye. Thank you for coming, he said to as many as he could, and please come back and see you soon.

Nearly seventy of the nine hundred applied, though there was room for only thirty-five in Zoetrope Studios' apprenticeship program. "You're lucky to have this training, this preparation for going in," said Michael Powell at the microphone at their welcome party on the Fremont Street set. "When I got into pictures, I *crept* in." For the rest of the school year, three days a week, Zoetrope apprentices would be assigned to a studio member who worked in their particular field of interest, whether Gene Kelly, Fred Roos, or Lucy Fisher—and once a week, all apprentices came together to hear speakers talk about their jobs making movies at the studio. Otherwise, they worked. Art department apprentice Andrew Lasser built three-dimensional storyboards for *Sex and Violence*, a movie he would be too young to see; Joey Tintflas sat at Dean Tavoularis's feet, watching. "Joey is already frustrated, like art directors everywhere," the department administrator observed. "He had all these grandiose ideas, and found out that the budget wouldn't permit them." Kenny Ortega taught his apprentices to tango, cha-cha, and jitterbug. Storaro, newly arrived from Rome to shoot the movie, told his apprentices to sit very still and observe the world by moving only their heads, like a camera on a tripod.

Coppola brought his own apprentice, a nerdy, precocious twelve-year-old Michael Cohen, with him into his Image and Sound Control trailer to watch rehearsals on the wall of little video monitors, and to the soundstage with Teri Garr and Raul Julia to observe the actors working up close. Coppola gave Cohen his viewfinder and, with it, permission to comment directly to the actors.

"What's he doing?" Coppola, eying Cohen, asked the actors between run-throughs.

The kid was rearranging props, condiments, and tableware—apparently to help Coppola reblock the scene. "That is Frannie," Cohen pointed to one prop. "That is you," he said to another prop, meaning Raul Julia. "And this," he said, indicating an empty space, "would be paradise."

"Who?" Coppola asked.

"Paradise!" Frannie's dream.

Coppola grinned. "Oh. Gotcha."

"And this would show that you're closer to paradise than she is and that the thing that is standing in the way is Hank."

"Yes," Garr deadpanned, charmed and annoyed. "Perfectly clear."

"I think sometimes [Coppola would] rather have the kids around than the adults," Anne Schwebel said. "These kids are letting him act out *his* fantasies, too."

There were still kinks in the program—the kids, being kids, of alternately high or low energy, could detain the filmmakers—but like everything else at Zoetrope it was a work in progress. August Coppola, appointed head of education, talked of developing a Zoetrope magnet school, which would teach young students linguistics, philosophy, art, political science, economics, and, he said, a "professional education [in filmmaking], encouraging teamwork in communication arts and developing mental logic through image visions as well as introducing the young generation of filmmakers to the new software technology." Graduating, they could then bring projects to Zoetrope Studios, even get a job working there.

The future—it wasn't perfect, but it was happening. "I don't want to be minister of culture," Coppola would say. "But I could be the secretary of youth."

One midsummer weekend, they were all up at the Coppolas' in Napa: Storaro at the stove, stirring a sauce of tomatoes from the garden; Nastassja

Kinski with Tom Waits and Kathleen Brennan at the piano; the Gersten girls and Coppola children running across the lawns to the pool; Fred Forrest and Teri Garr taking in sunset on the veranda; Eleanor snapping pictures; and Dean and Aurore, in love. At dinner, Waits told the story of his and Brennan's elopement. The way it happened was they just opened a phone book one night and called a justice of the peace. "Why don't *you* get married?" Coppola asked Dean and Aurore. Right then, Dean proposed. Before Aurore had time to answer, Coppola was skimming the phone book. Kinski ran to the garden for roses, and Sofia and the Gersten girls raced Aurore upstairs into Sofia's room for white calico dresses for the bride and bridesmaids. Around one in the morning, a justice of the peace arrived. Waits played "Here Comes the Bride" on the library harpsichord, then Aurore, in makeup by Kinski, appeared in white at the top of the stairs. She was wearing a crown of roses tied for her by Sofia. Dean, waiting for her below, stood quite solemnly beside his best man, Francis Ford Coppola. There were candles everywhere, and throughout the ceremony (Eleanor's wedding ring—something borrowed), the Ding-bat girls, huddled together in nervous excitement, giggled behind their hands.

The next day, Forrest drove down to a phone booth, dialed, and proposed to *his* girlfriend, Marilu Henner. She said yes and they married three weeks later.

At the annual harvest party that year, Coppola called an informal meeting of the studio brain trust. He gathered them not after or before the party, but amid the revelry, at a table of half-empty wine bottles on the veranda, the vineyard valley horizon showing half a golden sun below.

Coppola was at the head of the table, excitedly leaning over his elbows like a boy in the front row of the mezzanine. "We have achieved buying the television station on the corner of the property!" he told them.

It seemed that some there had never realistically considered the possibility.

Fred Roos was cool. "You've arrived at a price, or—?"

"No, we've made a deal. We're buying it."

The incredulous exchanged looks.

Tavoularis was the first to ask. "To do what with?"

"Nag, nag, nag!" Lucy Fisher laughed. "That's all you ever do!"

They all laughed at that. Save for Coppola.

"Number one, you get their mill," he persisted. "So your whole mill gets twice as big. Number two, you get a whole little parking lot which could become a day care center for little kids. Number three, you get the whole building. And I think that should become the new casting department."

A day care? "Like at Japanese factories?" Tavoularis asked.

"It'll be nice because they'd be kids in little costumes, and they can do little plays. It'll be like a theatrical day care center."

Someone chimed in, "Yeah, I think it would be great . . ."

"We need to put some obligation on all of us here to start having some babies!" Coppola said.

Tents went up around the fire, sleeping bags opened on the grass, and Coppola, laughing, stomped grapes with the others. How long had humans been doing this? The tradition stretched back eons to the Bacchus festival in Dacia. Was that also the beginning of theater? When someone got tired of winemaking and sat down to watch the stomping—and the first audience was born? Such traditions would never end. Most things in life, Coppola thought, would only get better. Technology would bring us more leisure, more time to become and enjoy ourselves, and the true nature of people was kindness. It had to be. How else, after so many thousands of years on earth, could we have come so far together and learned so much from each other?

Coppola, up to his knees in Cabernet Franc, waved to Gio up ahead. "My son, my son!"

"Pack tonight," Tess Haley told those in the rehearsal room at Zoetrope Studios. "And this is your call sheet for tomorrow. Do you have animals, or kids to take to school?"

Script supervisor Joanie Blum looked up from her call sheet. "What's happening?"

"You're going to Vegas."

"What?"

In a flash, they were on the plane: Francis, the actors, Attias, Schmidt, Blum, Haley, Bernie Gersten, Ron Colby, and Jeff Hamlin, with Gio filming it all on video. "I need you guys to get the feel of Vegas," Francis had explained, but the trip was about more than just research. "Francis had this goal of making all of us collegial," Blum said, "and he wanted us to work on one movie after the other."

"Come on, everybody!" Coppola called out as they walked into the Desert Inn. "Take your per diem and let's go to the crap tables! This is Vegas! This is what life *is*! This is what we've got to experience!"

In ten minutes, everyone had lost their per diem. Then they checked in.

"This is great! This *is* the experience!"

Coppola, it emerged, wasn't after the glitz culture of Vegas but the ordinary locations, the highway motels and desert RVs, peopled by those, like Hank and Frannie, who hadn't hit the jackpot, "the everyday life of people who had the fantasies," said Lainie Kazan.

By day, they improvised in public. They rode around in a video van and stopped to shoot—a scene for Hank and his coworker Moe (Harry Dean Stanton)—at a wrecking company, a Laundromat . . . "Wait!" Coppola said. "Stop here! Stop the van!" He reached into his pocket and pulled out a few hundreds. "Jeff," he said, putting the bills in Hamlin's hand. "Go in and tell them we want to use the Laundromat for an hour."

They would all return to Vegas for more work and play. "Francis lives in a kind of a fantasy of all these people getting together," Blum said, "because he thought this was going to be a very romantic experience for everybody."

"Wouldn't it be great if Nastassja and Gio got together?" Coppola whispered to her.

The two young people had sat across from each other at dinner the night Coppola took everyone to Caesars Palace. Everyone could see there was something there: they sat in the back rows of theaters, they strolled together, poking one another, around the lot.

Kinski was the most beautiful woman any of them had ever seen, and Gio was charming, sweetly odd, and, with his first mustache, almost dashing. Their futures were decided; she would be a star and he, the oldest son of Francis Ford Coppola, a filmmaker, and one day the head of Zoetrope Studios, giving his father work as his father gave work to his father.

No one can create love, but the writer-director-producer Francis Ford Coppola could create worlds. "We were in a musical making a musical," Ortega said. "We might as well have been singing our hearts out."

The world inside the studio gates—in full swing now—was teeming with artisans, matte painters and model builders, masters of forced perspective and trompe l'oeil. Their expertise in illusion and stagecraft, belonging more to the theater and the bygone age of studio filmmaking, would be the perfect complement to the romantic fantasy of *One from the Heart*—and, costing far less than special effects, it would be economical, too. But with all those empty soundstages, Coppola thought, it seemed a shame not to expand. The entire studio was theirs to remake, and Tavoularis's sets, scrupulously detailed, bejeweled in rainbow light, were already exceeding everyone's expectations. With all that neon glittering—and with Storaro, like a conductor of colored light, preprogramming the Izenour board, which had been borrowed from theater to mix light live, recoloring, blue to red to green, the actors' skin to convey subtle changes in their hearts—more would be more. This was to be the fantasy, was it not?

It was an expensive and unforeseen addition to the budget—but as the sets grew, Coppola's vision for a "live" Electronic Cinema became even more feasible. As soundstages could connect to soundstages, the stage world would expand; actors would be able to walk from set to set, and with cameras rolling continuously—several cameras rolling at once, that is, including Garrett Brown on his own creation, the Steadicam—Coppola could film more pages faster. "You could film *One from the Heart* every day," he said. "Even film it with different casts, a black one, a white one." Hitchcock's *Rope* became a frame of reference; Coppola, too, would cut only when the reel ran out.

Even Tavoularis's own construction workers were astonished by *One from the Heart*'s monumental centerpiece, Tavoularis's Fremont Street, an entire living intersection many believed improved upon the real thing. In grandeur and artistry, it was an inspiration to all departments on the lot. "These guys would come and get me," Zoetrope associate Sondra Scerca said. "They would say, 'Come look at what we did today.'" Tavoularis's creation was so beautiful that studio employees would turn down the fresh air and take their lunches on the soundstage just to enjoy the view. Before long, the electric city street became the talk of Hollywood. "People would come to the set," Armyan Bernstein recalled, "and it was like they were entering a cathedral. They would just stand there and they would just stare at it. And they would watch Vittorio hold the light and they would look at the set. And it became almost like they were in the temple of movie-making that was created by his genius."

Storaro could make *One from the Heart* even more beautiful, however, if Coppola agreed to shoot the picture with the traditional single-camera. Completely controlling the elements of the frame would not be possible for Storaro—or any cinematographer, for that matter—under the conditions of Coppola's live, multi-camera arrangement: the practical necessity for general lighting would impede Storaro's painterly imagination. A film as dreamlike as *One from the Heart* could come across only with dreamlike imagery, Storaro argued, and with Tavoularis's awe-inspiring sets going up all around them—the sound of construction, of hammers, saws, and drills, was constant—it would be folly not to honor their labor and artistry (and the studio's expense) with the perfect photographic setting for every distinct shot. And with one camera, Storaro reasoned, he could go faster, the whole production could. Then Tavoularis came to Coppola with a complementary request, as Coppola explained it, "that we not do it as I planned and had prepared for, but rather allow [them] to shoot essentially in a more conventional movie way, which of course was really the only way he knew how to and since yes, I loved both Vittorio and Dean and couldn't say what I knew I should say, which was 'No, we must shoot the way I planned and if you don't want to or don't know how to, you're fired and I'll bring replacements who do know how to.' Clearly that is not something I could say to collaborators I loved . . ." Coppola conceded. One camera. But what would that mean for Coppola's Live Cinema, Zoetrope Studios' core experiment, the plan that would sustain them, artistically as well as financially, into the future?

"There was not one iota of motivation to make money at Zoetrope Studios," said story editor John Solomon. "The motivation was to make films you wanted to see." Solomon's days were spent in passionate pursuit of movie material, reading scripts and watching films by recent film school graduates, sitting in the screening room with Michael Powell ("Mr. Powell" dressed always in a shirt and tie), Solomon splitting his watch between the screen and the old man's reaction, waiting for a spark from either. "Next please," Powell would say after a few minutes of film. "Stop the film. Next please." Powell liked *The Loveless*, by Kathryn Bigelow and Monty Montgomery. Should they make a movie with them? They could.

They could do anything.

"It wasn't a job," Solomon explained. "It was something else."

Elsewhere in the story department, Coppola had assigned one reader the classics. She read everything by Orwell, Chaucer, Dickens; *Pride and Prejudice*; and, curiously, *Scaramouche*, and would report her findings to Coppola in their weekly meetings. "Tell me about the book," he would begin. "Tell me what you thought, tell me about the characters, the story . . ."

Lucy Fisher, whose boyfriend had written music for *Eraserhead*, introduced David Lynch to Zoetrope Studios. He took an office across from George Burns. With his twenty-five-year-old assistant, Steve Martin ("not *that* Steve Martin"), Lynch began prepping his (hopefully) next feature, the netherworld freakshow *Ronnie Rocket*. "*Ronnie Rocket* was a dream for a long time," Lynch said, the most improbable film, by general consensus, in any Hollywood pipeline, so improbable, in fact, that even a former Omni-Zoetrope story executive had passed on it. But Zoetrope Studios wasn't in the executive business. Fisher had picked Lynch, and Lynch had picked *Ronnie Rocket*: There would be no stopping now. While Lynch was budgeting the script (approximately $8 million), his phone rang with an offer to direct the next *Star Wars*, then called *Revenge of the Jedi*. Lynch turned it down, stunning his young assistant.

"It wouldn't be my film," Lynch explained to Martin.

"But you could get paid like millions of dollars, and then you could make whatever you wanted from that day forward . . ."

"No. I can't do it."

In an office nearby toiled Martha Coolidge, developing *Sex and Violence*. Downstairs was Franc Roddam, director of *Quadrophenia*, casting Clair Noto's science-fiction script (for adults), *The Tourist*. Across the hall from

Lynch were Wim Wenders and Jean-Luc Godard. Godard would go everywhere with this camera.

Susan Rogers stopped him on the stairwell. "Jean-Luc. Your camera's on."

"Yes. That's how I make all my movies."

Ed Rugoff was chosen to drive Godard wherever he needed to go, often to the tennis shop and to the movies.

"Could you take me to see *Raging Bull*?"

Off they went in Rugoff's Alfetta to the matinee at the Village Theater in Westwood. (Godard didn't love the movie.) Then Rugoff drove them back to the studio. A day's work for both.

The "other Steve Martin," meanwhile, reviewed a stack of résumés— all from forty-year-old PhDs wanting to work at Zoetrope Studios. He was supposed to choose? "I kept thinking, like, *I don't belong here*," he said. "Like, *When are they going to discover that?*"

"Hiya, kid," George Burns would say, pointing his cigar into the open door.

Was this really happening? "It was the sort of magical feeling of optimism about the way films could be made," Martin said. They just didn't say *no* here. He could call anyone to come in for a meeting. Who did he want to call? He called up Lou Reed. "I didn't know him," Martin said. "I just thought Lou Reed should be making movies," and they talked about making a film of Reed's album *Street Hassle*. Martin called Devo: Did they want to make a movie? Yes, in fact they did (who didn't?), a musical version of *Animal Farm . . .*

Most studios got their material from agents; then again, most studios didn't have open casting calls. "We were more talent based," Lucy Fisher explained. "People came to work with people that they knew." Carroll Ballard, for instance. *The Black Stallion*—that rare thing, a family movie so beautiful it really *was* for everyone—had made his name a blessing in Hollywood, and his next project, an adaptation of *The Secret Garden*, was shaping up to be even better. Ballard submitted to Fisher the first four pages of the script. "They were the best four pages of anything I've ever read in my life," Fisher said. "It was magical." Robert Dalva was developing *The Black Stallion Returns*; Fisher and Roos were taking a musical *Peter Pan* to Paramount; novelist Jim Harrison was adapting James M. Cain's *Serenade*; there was *Intrusive Burials*, a script by Walter Murch and Gill Dennis; Linda Feferman's *Seven*

Minutes in Heaven; *Lionheart*, by Menno Meyjes; Robert Towne's script of John Fante's novel *The Brotherhood of the Grape*; Broadway director Michael Bennett's Hollywood debut, *Our Father*; *Mishima*, by writer-director Paul Schrader; an adaptation of *On the Road*; and there was, closer to ready than most, the computer-consciousness drama *Interface*, a script Fisher deemed "brilliant, ahead of its time."

Fisher looked up from her desk. Coppola was pushing into her office an old man in a wheelchair—King Vidor, born in 1894.

"We have to find something for Mr. Vidor!" Coppola exclaimed

It was obvious to Fisher that Vidor was already half blind and, needless to say, wasn't walking.

Coppola had another idea for her—a little panel of red lights, each light representing a soundstage. She could have it on her desk. When the light was on, they were filming; when it was off, she would know she could go over to tell them to get to work. But how would she tell Coppola, her boss, to get to work? "This is how democratic [Zoetrope Studios was]," Lucy Fisher recalled. "A janitor comes into my office, and says, 'You know, I've been reading Francis's rewrites, and they're not very good . . .'"

In his bungalow at night, when the lot emptied of everyone but nine-teen- and twenty-year-olds stealing last smokes with friends and crushes they had smuggled into Neverland from their waitress and retail jobs, Coppola would light a joint and imagine Hank and Frannie into his micro-phone. Forgoing the mother who taught him not to "disrespect" girls with lustful feelings, Coppola would drift through the bedrooms of *One from the Heart*, improvising erotic scenes to the coyote voice of Tom Waits howling out a stereo in the background. "A general note to those of you in the various areas," he had announced to an outdoor meeting of *One from the Heart* department heads late in 1980. "Wardrobe, make up, casting, this is a very idealized reality, this movie. The people in it all look really good and their clothes are beautiful, so that, in general, when in doubt, if you're sitting there and you have to make a choice, should something be beautiful or should it be realistic, make it beautiful." Sometimes, after his night's desiring, Coppola would walk the lot at sunrise, singing up the soundstage walls the music from *La Bohème*.

*   *   *

Thanksgiving—Michael Cimino, the extended Tavoularis family, and others were feasting at the Coppola house in Hancock Park.

"How's your turkey?" Dean Tavoularis's mother asked Cimino.

"I'm still cutting it."

His turkey had opened in New York only days earlier. At three hours and thirty-nine minutes, *Heaven's Gate*—as *New York Times* critic Vincent Canby expressed, repeating a widely held opinion—was "an unqualified disaster." United Artists had withdrawn the film from distribution, and Cimino was indeed back to cutting it.

Cimino and United Artists had tried, as Coppola had on *Apocalypse*, to keep the financial details of their production from the press. But they could only do so much: the debacle of the making of *Heaven's Gate* had been a public laughingstock for over a year.

Once upon a time, box-office information was of limited or no interest to readers outside the trade. But in the years following the David Begelman–Columbia Pictures embezzlement scandal—made national news by the *Washington Post* and, quite memorably, David McClintick in the *Wall Street Journal*—"hard" Hollywood reporting had infiltrated the mainstream media. With Watergate hangovers, reporters and readers were now inclined to suspicion and retribution, and with Wall Street creeping into yuppie Hollywood, tales of Hollywood "excess," "extravagance," and other rebukes generated by a largely uncomprehending public could be enjoyed like the gossip pages. Throughout the country, journalists and readers alike—none of whom had seen *Heaven's Gate*, let alone read the script—delighted in Cimino's disastrous production, self-righteously tsk-tsking Hollywood for its megalomania, venality, and decadence. Welcome to the new American pastime: armchair mogul. Where audiences would review the numbers *before* they reviewed the film—if they ever seriously reviewed the film at all.

True, the financial details of *Heaven's Gate* were staggering, in many ways more dramatic than the film itself. In the first twelve days of production, for instance, Cimino shot a daily average of ten thousand feet of film, practically an entire feature every day. Over the course of the entire shoot, it was reported, he shot no less than 1.5 million feet and printed an extraordinary 1.3 million feet, enough to cut well over a hundred feature films. How had this happened? In 1978, with *Apocalypse* in the throes of postproduction, advance word on *The Deer Hunter* was so strong that United Artists, proudly a director's studio, had practically signed its life away to get *Heaven's Gate*, granting Cimino no budgetary restraints on his projected $7.5 million Western. Over $30 million later, both sides, the artist and money, were quick to deflect the shame, giving the press one of its greatest rides in Hollywood history. And though it is impossible for anyone, even the professionals, to define the concept of artistic excess, American audiences sanctimoniously drew the line at Michael Cimino. Thirty million for *Moonraker* was fine, but thirty-plus million for *Heaven's Gate*?

Auditors now, audiences had seen the receipts. The studios were spending more, making more, losing more—on fewer movies. In the inflationary climate of the 1980s, with so much riding on a picture, the change spelled trouble for every serious filmmaker in Hollywood. "*Heaven's Gate*—the phenomenon not the movie—has been a long time coming," Canby noted accurately, "but to blame it on any one director or corporate management is vastly to oversimplify what's been happening to commercial American movies over the last several decades. . . . The cost of making a movie, even a modest one, has soared even faster than the cost of everything else in the economy. . . . The hits make more money than ever, while people won't even go to see a flop if it's free." The year's biggest moneymaker, George Lucas's *The Empire Strikes Back*, returned $120 million to Universal. Runner-up *Kramer vs. Kramer* returned only half that.

Once merely a crazy business, Hollywood had become a losing business. For the big studios of the 1980s, it was either merge or die—and merge they did (Universal with MCA, Warner Bros. into Warner Communications Inc. . . .). But in contrast to the wave of corporate acquisitions that took Hollywood in the 1970s, conglomerates in the 1980s era were multinational media giants out to exploit their film properties across hybrid markets. A Hollywood movie of the eighties was no longer just a movie; it was (potentially) a book, a soundtrack, a Happy Meal, a VHS tape, a television show, a theme park ride, a T-shirt. Thus was filmmaking per se deprioritized and debased throughout the industry. The oligopoly replaced the auteur; the new watchword was *synergy*, and "the great crafts," Coppola observed, "the great traditions [were] systematically dismantled while no one noticed."

The fix was in. When *Heaven's Gate* finally opened and bombed, Transamerica, the parent company of United Artists, would suffer only a momentary stock loss of three-eighths of a point. *Three-eighths of a point* for the biggest "disaster" in contemporary American film? Crying crocodile tears, Transamerica swiftly dumped United Artists, selling it to Kirk Kerkorian-owned MGM. But MGM/UA bore exactly no resemblance to the venerable spirit of United Artists, Zoetrope's partners in *Apocalypse Now* and *The Black Stallion*. "Henceforth, it would be corporate suicide to fund an expensive production that lacked the potential for generating multiple revenue streams across the range of entertainment markets," wrote film historian Stephen Prince. "The death of United Artists certified this principle."

In 1981, Coppola would concede, "There really is no film business in Hollywood."

There was Zoetrope Studios.

A studio that—as *One from the Heart* approached its first day of filming—now had a publicity problem. The little love story that became, first, a $15 million musical had now increased in size and spectacle to the tune of nine soundstages, not the intended two, and at a cost of $23 million.

For Coppola, who had bet big and scored big on *Apocalypse Now*, the additional millions were the cost of doing artistic business, and with the new budget backed by Chase Manhattan and certain foreign presales, he could safely say his investors agreed. But in December 1980, mere weeks after the release of *Heaven's Gate*, only weeks before cameras were set to roll on *One from the Heart*, Coppola was notified that $8 million of that foreign tax shelter investment had been unexpectedly withdrawn. Instantly, panic set in.

Eight million dollars—gone.

There was no recourse. "If that occurred in a [Twentieth] Century–Fox or Paramount, they would reallocate eight million from someplace else and solve the problem," Bob Spiotta explained. But Zoetrope, being a private corporation, 100 percent owned by Francis Coppola, there was no "someplace else." The timing simply could not have been worse; had the eight million dollars been withdrawn earlier, before set construction began, Coppola would have sought new financing or reconsidered the late-in-the-day addition to his studio's multimillion-dollar replica of the Las Vegas Strip and its surroundings. At such a late stage, however, Coppola couldn't pause the film to raise additional funds; he had cast and crew schedules to account for. Nor was MGM, who had paid Coppola his $3 million directing fee in exchange for a piece of *One from the Heart*'s gross, willing to swoop in to lend a hand. Why? "We expected our partners would step in and be helpful when the production date was imminent, to help me on a short-term basis," Coppola said. "But MGM wouldn't even float our payroll for two weeks. Yet they couldn't cooperate enough when we had a tax shelter to make it possible." Nor were other studios willing. Again, why? Did they know something Coppola didn't? Or did they, Coppola wondered, *want* to see him imperiled or, worse, fail? The way corporate interests had wanted Preston Tucker to fail?

Coppola had no more distribution rights to offer any new financier. Instead, he offered to exchange a piece of his gross percentage for money up front, but at its $23 million price tag, *One from the Heart*'s break-even point was already too high, it seemed, to make further investments worthwhile. Lucy Fisher put it simply: "We had too many bed partners."

Coppola had, then, two choices: he could either fold up his tent or, seriously in debt, figure out a way to proceed, as planned, with *One from the Heart*, which now represented—more than *Apocalypse*, far more than any love affair—the gamble of his life.

He chose to proceed.

"Anyone in this business with any kind of experience has got to evaluate that as being at least reckless," Spiotta said, "because we didn't have the funding to last one week." Zoetrope did have nonliquid assets of $55 million, but they were tied up in studio real estate and equipment. How could he sell off his studio as he went into production *at* his studio? They couldn't shoot the film without sets and cameras.

Coppola shifted into action. He put up $1 million of his real estate holdings in San Francisco as collateral against a loan from Security Pacific Bank set at 21 percent interest—high. And he knew it would not end there. "To get through each week of shooting," he told the press, "I will have to put up $1 million week by week from the real-estate package that represents all my personal assets, until I've put up the $8 million."

February 2, 1981—the first day of production. "We had so much light," Gray Frederickson said (by one estimate, $300,000 worth of neon alone), "that, when we turned it on for the first day of shooting, it browned out Hollywood."

When at last they made the first shot, Coppola gave the signal, and champagne was passed around for all. Coppola held up his glass. "We've begun!"

He then disappeared back to where he had come from: his Image and Sound Control vehicle.

The next day, he was forced to lay off Zoetrope's entire story department. "Basically," Lucy Fisher told the press, "we are changing our orientation from that of a financing organization to a production entity that will concentrate on the pictures we already have in development, so we may not be able to support a large staff of story editors and readers." They would now hire development personnel on a picture-by-picture basis.

If he shot fast—and given his months spent in "previsualization" and in rehearsal with the actors and the time-saving editorial techniques of live-cutting in his video trailer—he could conceivably shoot the entire movie in a month and have it released almost as quickly (saving considerable interest payments) in July of the very same year. In fact, there would be no better proof of concept. The electronic technology some said would sink Zoetrope Studios would actually save it.

To spread the word, he would throw a party—a $13,000 press conference and luncheon (pasta al dente, chocolate-covered strawberries), a commercial intended to attract additional financing, fast.

Very fast. Only two days after his champagne toast marking the first day of shooting, he stood under the marquee of Tavoularis's Lady Luck Casino and addressed a soundstage packed with two hundred members of the Hollywood press, assuring them in high showman fashion (white Panama hat, pink shirt, and tie) that he had not lost faith in the Electronic Cinema he said would make "the process of motion pictures much more efficient" and allow filmmakers to "approach subject matter or works of art that perhaps would have been too costly."

He narrated a video demonstration of the process. "The Motion Picture technology that is used today is the first technology that we ever came up with. And the cameras that were made in 1920, in 1940, or ones designed just like it, are still turning in every studio today. Editors still take pieces of celluloid and glue them together and then break them apart. Sound cutters take sound and build separate reels like some sort of enormous handiwork. And the answer to that comes very simply that the cinema will become electronic, whether it becomes electronic now, as I'm going to try to show you, or in five years, it *will* become electronic . . ."

The film industries of Japan, Italy, the United Kingdom, were nearly washed up, he warned them. Pinewood Studios may even go on the block. "There is only one cinema," he declared, "and it's here. We have to stay at the vanguard of our industry."

He added: "I'm trying to hold something together. I have options open to me. Some of them are very painful."

The situation was, in fact, even worse than Coppola was willing to discuss. As the press knew, Zoetrope's long-stalled *Hammett*, directed by Wim Wenders—which Coppola, ordering the whole movie reshot, shut down on location in San Francisco late in its production—was an additional threat to the studio's, and therefore his own, financial life. But paying prime interest rates on $4 million of a $9 million production was only half his crisis; Coppola still had to account for the fact that *Hammett* had to be completed in some form, either finished as written or, he feared, worse, reshot completely from page one—a page they were still fighting over, two directors, four writers, twenty drafts, and five years later. But as long as Frederic Forrest, the titular Hammett, was also starring in *One from the Heart*, *Hammett* would have to wait, and Zoetrope's exorbitant interest payments would continue to mount. So would the antipathy of the public, already resentful toward Coppola for spending the kind of money they would never have on dreams they didn't share, and the attendant hostility of the press. In collusion, they would fan the flames of expectation. As Walter Murch knew, "The longer a film takes, the more you think that to explain *why* it's taking longer, it has to be *more*. It's like a note that you should write in one day. If you put it off for two days, you say, 'Well, I can't write a note, now I'll have to write a letter.' And if you put the letter off for a week, now it can't be a letter, it has to be an essay. And if you put it off for six months, it has to be the Meaning of Life."

Zoetrope's Hail Mary made national news, and investment offers came in from all corners—save one, Hollywood. Again, why? Didn't they realize he was doing this for them, too? "I don't think Hollywood was out there rooting for Francis or for us to be successful," Gray Frederickson reflected.

"We were interlopers in their world." Their wrongheadedness drove Coppola wild. "How many times do I have to be laughed at?" he raged to the *L.A. Herald Examiner*. The technology he was testing, *his* risk, could end up saving every studio in the long run, but the gatekeepers were so fearful Coppola's own studio might get out ahead of them that they eyed Zoetrope as the competition. It was Warner Bros. and American Zoetrope—the *THX* debacle—all over again. What would a few million dollars of a research and development write-off be to Paramount?

As for the outside offers that did come in, none was enough.

Without an influx of capital immediately, it would not be possible, Coppola realized, to proceed with *One from the Heart*.

Peeling off one million of his own real estate dollars every week and shouldering the guilt of disbanding Zoetrope Studios one department at a time, he could hardly become the person he needed to be to make the movie he needed to make, a sweet, charming musical love story. Even under ideal circumstances, the questions he was asking himself about love would be difficult to answer. But given the persistently rocky state of his own marriage, his eyes that still roved and the body that occasionally followed, Coppola could not confidently say he, in his own life, was in the right frame of heart and mind to make *One from the Heart*—as he had made and lived *The Godfather, The Conversation, Godfather Part II, Apocalypse Now*—truthfully. Attempting and failing would undoubtedly bankrupt him and the studio and sink the nearly four hundred Zoetropeans who had been counting on him. Or he could cut his losses and get out now.

Increasingly, he would be found—when he was found—in his video trailer.

Days after the press conference, Zoetrope couldn't make payroll. Bernie Gersten helped Coppola draft his letter to Bob Spiotta and Barry Hirsch:

> After considerable thought and assessment of an untenable situation, I have decided to resign my position as Artistic Director of Zoetrope and my positions as Director of all Zoetrope motion pictures either in development or in shooting, as well as the writing and directing on *One from the Heart*.

I do this with a clear understanding of the consequences but I have reached the point where the emotional strain, the constant harassment just at a moment when I am to begin directing a motion picture make it impossible for me.

I leave the entire management, decision-making and authority to act in my behalf in the hands of Bob Spiotta.

The letter was premature. Vulture-like, Paramount landed on Coppola's shoulder, sniffing the air around his assets. The *Interface* script took their interest. They made an offer of $500,000 and threw in another $500,000 loan to Coppola, an advance against *One from the Heart*. But Coppola did not want a partner, let alone a corporate influence such as Paramount, in a project as transgressive as *Interface*. But of all the scripts in his bank, none was further along. The picture could even begin shooting at Zoetrope Studios (renting facilities to Paramount) in two months' time. "Francis shouldn't be shut down," Paramount's Barry Diller proclaimed with dubious magnanimity. "He is a national resource."

A national resource without resources, Coppola accepted Diller's offer. It bought Zoetrope two weeks of paychecks—one for the week outstanding, the other for the week upon them, February 10, 1981. What would they do then?

They had been shooting *One from the Heart* for only one week.

Following a period of extensive deliberation, the decision was made to have Spiotta deliver the message—that living from hand to mouth, they would invariably run out of money again (and again . . .)—to the cast and crew and all remaining Zoetrope Studios personnel, "because," Spiotta explained, "Francis being the emotional guy and dedicated guy, and sometimes impetuous, might get involved in saying, 'Hey, I guarantee all of you people and your children's education and everything,' and that would have been a disaster." Spiotta would do it in three meetings.

He would be direct. "I simply told them what the situation was," Spiotta said. Sweating, he faced the 155 Zoetrope Studios staff people who had gathered in the screening room. "Imagine a lifeboat," Spiotta explained to them, "and it's full of people, and there's x amount of bread. We're going to go on half rations." Some would be laid off, he said, beginning with those not essential to the production of *One from the Heart*. "Rather than lay off a great number of people and shut this down and make this production impossible, our attitude was we would try and trim as few people as possible." Worst-case scenario, they'd work for two weeks at half pay. That's what he was asking. Would they be willing?

To Spiotta's astonishment, they would be. Francis had bet so much; why shouldn't they? "The mood here is one of hope," said one Zoetrope worker after the meeting. "We're all behind him. We all support him. People with all their hearts want it to go. The studio is a baby, and it's going to take nurturing and care before it's going to blossom."

One meeting, two to go.

Spiotta faced the Zoetrope Studios construction staff: tough guys, mostly. They had come to "Fremont Street," Stage 9, to hear the bad news. Just how many there were—several hundred, Spiotta guessed—was a terrible surprise to him, and "all of them had mortgages to pay and car payments and whatever else people do with their money." As briefly as he could, Spiotta tried to explain how Zoetrope had gotten into this situation. He said that while it might look like Francis was being irresponsible, he was doing what he had been doing all along, what he believed was best for all of them, as artist and businessman, the 100 percent owner of the company and studio. "The bad news," he proceeded, trying to hide his embarrassment, "is that a comprehensive package resolving this has not been put together. It's still alive, but it has not been put together. The good news—good for us and bad for Francis—is that Francis went out and, by hook or by crook, bummed some more bucks . . . Essentially, Francis borrowed more money. Enough to cover the payroll for *last* week . . ."

They—all these union guys—listened quietly. That in itself was a shock to Spiotta. He had expected a vengeful scene out of *On the Waterfront*. And then, "almost in unison," Spiotta recalled, "they responded in an incredibly supportive way." He wasn't sure if they were being sarcastic. But then they started asking questions. Some, Spiotta said, were even "saying kind of corny, non-jaded things that you don't expect to be said in this town" . . .

"Can we help?" was one question.

"Maybe we can chip in," said someone else.

"Can we invest?"

"How about everybody putting in a hundred bucks?"

"We'll work anyway."

There was applause, a *round* of applause . . . it grew . . .

"We'll keep working . . ."

Spiotta was amazed. *This isn't* Waterfront, he thought; *it's* The Pajama Game.

Looking around the room, he began to cry. All these faces, suddenly all in agreement. "What they simply said is that they would be patient," he explained, "and 'Get us the dough as quickly as you can.' And then, just as the meeting ended, somebody came in and said the union called and they are willing to support whatever the people want to do, and the support is 100%." Some approached Spiotta after the meeting, hats in hand: "We really appreciate what Zoetrope and Francis are trying to do. We're proud of it and we want to help you." Said Al Price, business agent for Local 44, "If a man's a friend and he gets in trouble, you don't kick him when he's down. Mr. Coppola came to this town. He bought a dilapidated studio, rebuilt it, and extended a hand of friendship. As a goodwill gesture on our part, I asked our members to stay on the job, and I think it was the proper thing to do." Construction foreman Al Roundy said, "Coppola has treated us right, like human beings. The union gives us a 30-minute lunch break. Coppola gives us 45 minutes. Hell, yes, I'd work for him for nothing, and so will a lot of the rest of us. He's a hell of an improvement over any of the other studios."

It was a Thursday. Union officials permitted members to continue working on *One from the Heart* with the understanding that the production's cash problems would be resolved over the weekend, by Monday. "Francis was literally in tears when I told him about it," Spiotta said.

Dan Attias was the one to knock on Coppola's bungalow door before the third and final meeting, this one for the cast and crew of *One from the Heart*.

"Are they ready?"

"Yeah."

Inside projection room one, Coppola stood by quietly—few, if any, had seen him silent before—as Spiotta carefully reiterated, one last time, what most already knew: Zoetrope had come up short both on its $600,000 payroll and on the $600,000 due to outside vendors. Unions were prepared to grant them a waiver through Monday; until then, he and Coppola would be meeting with bankers and financiers around the clock . . . But then, wrote the *Herald-Examiner*, reporting on the scene, "something that has never happened before in the history of Hollywood movie-making occurred": instead of walking off the job, all present agreed to forgo salaries and stay on until Coppola got the money. "I've never seen anything like what happened," Frederic Forrest said. "As in a scene from a Frank Capra film," film critic Todd McCarthy wrote, "over 500 employees at Zoetrope Studios yesterday afternoon voted unanimously to continue working without pay after being told that management would not be able to meet this week's payroll." The decision, wrote Dale Pollock in the *Los Angeles Times*, "is virtually unprecedented in Hollywood labor annals." "This type of loyalty has no price," echoed Gerald Smith, business representative for the cameraman's local. "It hasn't existed in this town for years." Zoetrope publicist Max Bercutt went further still: "Never in forty years in the business have I known employees to come to bat like this for a troubled producer. This is a first."

When at last it came time for Coppola to speak, he managed only a few words. His voice cracked. He looked at the floor. McCarthy reported, "Coppola was unable to restrain his emotions, crying openly in the wake of an action unprecedented in the memory of industry vets." Bernie Gersten would write, "What was interesting was that all of us seemed to share—at least at that moment—a common belief in the work we were engaged in and the conviction that somehow the film and the company would pull through." The crowd broke into hugs and cheers, and Teri Garr said, "Time isn't money anymore. Time is just time." Kenny Ortega would speak for most: "For those of us that were, like, really month to month, like myself, it was, like, I don't care. I'll sleep in my car rather than not be where I am today." Carpenters, painters, electricians, dancers, stars, executives—they, not just Coppola, were all gambling together now.

"By risking all, you risk nothing," Bernie Gersten would say. "That's Francis's paradox." Existing, as Zoetrope always did, on "the sharp edge of panic" is precisely what made the community strong, Gersten thought. Danger *was* its life. At Zoetrope, "you're feeling all the time," he said; it was like Vegas, or being on drugs. "The excitement that generates is quite tremendous," far more sensate than living by the bottom line. "All [bottom lines] tell you is how much money you've spent. Not what you've made."

What had they made? So far, only a world.

Coppola and Spiotta had no time to celebrate. They spent the next forty-eight hours—their union-imposed deadline—in search of an angel investor. They found none.

"Most everywhere you go in Hollywood," wrote *LA Weekly*'s Michael Ventura,

> surprisingly, many an agent, producer, director and studio-wig is quietly and a little sardonically satisfied to have Coppola in trouble. My guess is that this is so because Zoetrope is truly a revolution in filmmaking as it is now practiced. It foretells an economic revolution and—more to the point, perhaps, for the people who represent what we mean by "Hollywood"—it foretells a revolution in power. . . . The weight of the town, the momentum, is to resist what Coppola is doing, because it is going to turn the business of moviemaking upside down. It is not a conspiracy, only a state of mind that makes it very difficult for Coppola and his agents to ignite a fire of enthusiasm for his innovations that would bring him the money and good will he needs.

United Artists appeared with an offer of $22 million for all of it, everything, the works. Under their terms, Coppola would still run the studio on *his* terms and would retain the Zoetrope banner; UA asked only for a couple offices on the far end of the lot. Coppola turned them down flat.

In came an offer from Jerry Perenchio, billionaire partner of writer-producer Norman Lear: $18 million for the studio that Coppola had purchased only ten months earlier for $6.7 million. It meant Coppola could survive—and with a juicy profit. But he turned the offer down. Said producer Jon Davison, "You don't sell the dream of a lifetime."

Meanwhile, a total of fifty-one people, both from Zoetrope Studios and the Sentinel Building in San Francisco, were let go. Remarkably, only one from the studio had quit voluntarily—an upholsterer. To stave off further sacrifice, the remaining community got creative in a hurry. Nonunion employees, nearly half the studio, took 50 percent pay cuts, effectively helping their unionized cohorts to their full salary, "like taking from Peter to pay Paul," Bercutt said, vowing the former would be reimbursed. Coppola alighted upon the idea of approaching actual Las Vegas hotels to see if they wanted to advertise on *his* Fremont Street—say, a billboard for $5,000—and some employees volunteered to arrange a telethon and hold a cake sale. Further offers came from outside the studio. USC's Delta Kappa Alpha, the college's honorary cinema fraternity, proposed two campus screenings of *Apocalypse Now* whose proceeds they would donate to the studio. "As cinema students," said Katherine Morris, director of the USC film series, "we very much admire Mr. Coppola and want to support his efforts." And from all over the world, ten- and twenty-dollar checks arrived daily at Zoetrope Studios with notes of gratitude, admiration, and support. They were returned with notes of thanks.

If the studio folded now, would they say he had failed? Would they say he was reckless, selfish, stupid, blind? Or would they say: It *happened*. If for only a moment, it existed.

Bernie Gersten fortified himself with history. He was reading about Paris, "and how Paris must survive because Paris has the history of art contained within its walls, within its being. And I thought, Nobody remembers the crises that Paris may or may not have gone through in terms of its municipal budget. Everyone who knows Paris, everyone who cares about Paris, everyone who loves Paris, as every civilized person I think *must*, loves Paris for what it has achieved in art. And the same thing is true of New York. Long after the threat of bankruptcy New York faced a few years ago has been forgotten, New York will be remembered for all that it has achieved, not by what it cost to achieve what it has achieved."

"Would you get on a plane now, tonight, and go, if you were offered this amazing, once-in-a-lifetime trip?" Coppola, at the craft services table, asked Rebecca De Mornay. "Would you go?"

"What?"

"If you had to leave tonight? Would you get on the plane?"

It took her a moment to adjust. Get on a plane? "Well, I—I think so . . ."

"No, no, really *think* about it. Would you? *Could* you?" He wasn't inviting her, but he *was* asking. If she could visit paradise—now?

"Well . . . I—" Would she be allowed to pack?

"Here's the thing: Most people, they say they would want to do it. That they'd love to do it. That they love spontaneity and excitement. But they won't actually do it. There's too many things that they would think get in the way, that they need to do and get ready for and take care of and they wouldn't be able to do it. They say they want the dream, but when it comes, they actually find ways not to be ready."

Still, Coppola charioted little Sofia, laughing in mock fright, around the lot on his bicycle—"while Rome is burning," John Solomon recalled. Perched on the handlebars in her white leather lace-up sneaker skates, careening around Fellini Avenue at one in the morning while older girls of Los Angeles slept, she knew only this life.

Every Friday night, the line of black cars inched bumper-to-bumper up Las Palmas, waiting to be directed to the soundstage, where the blowout was this week. Come Friday night, that's the way it was. Money or not, Zoetrope Studios partied. Only the soundstage changed. "There was no more incredible place to be," said Martha Cronin. "Hot set? Who cares?" One night, she returned from the buffet with a full plate to find her seat taken . . . by Jean-Luc Godard. "But that's how it was," Cronin said, "every time you turned around." Spielberg came. Sophia Loren, Kurosawa. ("I sat on Rutger Hauer's lap," Holland Sutton said.) Dressed in his white jumpsuit and the white fringe jacket from *Missouri Breaks*, Brando appeared. "Holy shit, Marlon fucking *Brando* . . ." As Coppola introduced him around, news of Brando's arrival tore through the Bora Bora stage. "You're such a nice little girl," dancer Javier Grajeda overheard him cooing to Sofia.

No one was turned away. "You'd bring your whole family," said Lainie Kazan. "Nobody ever did that in Hollywood. It would just spill out into the alleys and between the stages. Every Friday." Money was tight, but certain caterers, as if part of the team, donated their food and services. If the bar went dry, people brought their own. Anyone with a song or a band would perform. Ronee Blakley, the Doors, sans Jim Morrison . . . Lainie Kazan would sing, almost every week, at Coppola's request, "The Impossible Dream."

"It was a huge waste of money," Mitch Dubin would say. "The whole lot would fill up with people from every studio in town, and it was certainly a lot of fun, and I had a great time. But there's only so many parties and drugs and sex and whatever that you can tolerate before it starts to, like, wear your soul down. And especially with the financial crisis that was going on at the studio. And there were times when we actually didn't get paid . . ." Others speculated Friday nights were Coppola's way of saying thank you. "Friday night was like a cheerleading party, so everyone would come back Monday," Sondra Scerca said. They took to calling them, not unironically, wrap parties. Hookers and executives started showing up. But not everyone was happy to see the executives. "It was like, are you kidding me?" Michael Lehmann said, "All these people coming to our party? It just felt really false. We were all about *rah-rah!* We're not about Hollywood. We're about movies!" But the fun at Zoetrope was Coppola's best advertisement; setting the table for the whole town, he could lure investors, and even if he didn't . . .

"If we're going to go down," Coppola told actress Cynthia Kania, "let's go down in a blaze of glory and share this with the rest of Hollywood . . ."

There were premieres and, one night a year, the Oscars, but Hollywood, despite its reputation for social decadence, has always been, above all, hard at work, early bed, early to rise. In any such a competitive, high-stakes, publicly scrutinized, fearfully imperiled community, recreational health and goodwill are not prioritized. But Coppola, a consummate student of history and culture, understood there is no community without celebration, even if the impetus for that celebration was as secular as: we survived another week. "The parties were celebrations for having done the work," Dennis Gassner said. "It was Francis's tradition. That's family. That's the Italian way. It was about celebration and 'Isn't this what life should be?'" Hence the incredible rarity and industry-wide popularity of Zoetrope Studios' Friday nights.

"In filmmaking and in life," Coppola would say, "extraordinary things happen to you, and it's up to you to make them be positive, because the good news is that there is no hell, but the quasi-good news is that this is heaven. So, make it be heaven. Because it's up to you. Don't waste heaven. And the same with the movies."

Save for the looming threat of extinction, it was ideal. They weren't shooting long days. They weren't on location, far from their loved ones, dealing with the numberless unforeseens of filmmaking in the real world. They were home. "[At a studio] you don't have to load in equipment in the morning and take the lights in and start lighting from scratch," Arne Schmidt said. "And at the end of the day, you don't have to take everything back on the truck so it can be at another location the next morning . . . It's very painless." To many, this was Zoetrope Studios' best gift of all: the opportunity to make a movie in comfort, without losing one's personal life. And to be under contract—to "have the confidence," Schmidt said, "that we didn't have to work to find our next job, we could just be relaxed and focus on our work and be part of the family"—was not an obligation, but a promise of support.

On certain Monday nights, free acting workshops for writers, directors, and, of course, actors in and out of Zoetrope were held on a vacant soundstage. Anybody working on a play or a film could bring it in to rehearse. Rotating weekly, workshop leaders included friends of friends, actors Sally Kellerman, LeVar Burton, Bill Macy from *Maude* . . . While over in the War Room, Fred Roos put together a screenwriting seminar, inviting legends like I. A. L. Diamond and new stars Robert Towne, Terry Southern, and Mardik Martin "just to talk to us about their process and answer questions," Michael Lehmann said. "It was like nirvana," Steve Martin said. "Theoretically, it was that we would all be working on screenplays and we would all get feedback and learn from these people and could ask questions. And I don't know how many screenplays were actually written, because we were all working, but listening to them talk and discuss film with Francis Ford Coppola . . . it was a master class." To Armyan Bernstein, the workshops formally transformed Zoetrope Studios into "the small college we all wanted to go to."

Coppola's *One from the Heart* dailies, a nightly tradition at Zoetrope Studios, would begin as the shooting day ended, around seven o'clock, as the people of Zoetrope—really anyone was welcome—tiptoed in and found a seat. Coppola's was the place down in front, on the ratty couch beside assistant Tess Haley, who was ready with her pad and pen, should any idea occur to him. Any idea at all: "Tess, can you get a hamburger for . . ."; "Tess, you know, I think we should call Cher . . ."; "Tess, can we get a jet available for tonight?" It was only pieces, but what they saw in that theater of *One from the Heart*—its colors, Storaro's lush greens and purple-blues, his camera gliding high circles over Tavoularis's neon cityscapes in lusty long takes up to six and seven and eight minutes in length—enthralled them. "We thought we were making the best movie ever," Michael Lehmann said. "We would applaud in *dailies*. They were like nothing any of us had ever seen." There, whatever artistic or budgetary terrors that carried over from the shooting day were banished, and by eight o'clock, the theater would be packed. Warren Beatty came just to see what the town was talking about.

But Coppola still hadn't figured out the script. Which meant the leads hadn't completely figured out their characters. "This is the hardest job I've ever done," confessed Teri Garr during a break from shooting. "You grasp an idea, you dive in one hundred percent and he goes, 'No, wrong idea.' You go, 'Okay, okay, we're back to square one. I'll go with you. What is it?' I mean this has happened fifty times. That's the exhausting part." Like the other leads, Garr was called every day, whether she had a scene or not. Just in case Coppola had an idea. (He would protest, "Did they tell Van Gogh he only had *green* on certain days?") "I don't have any life other than this," Garr said. "I go home and go to sleep." She missed Christmas at home. "I've been here since the middle of December and every day I've come to work," she complained to Fred Roos late in February 1981. "What is this, EST? I mean what *is* this?" Was she supposed to be acting—or posing? To Storaro, Frannie was red; to Coppola, she was Woman. But how do you play an archetype? The direction Garr needed, Coppola wasn't providing. She felt he saw the actors only as he imagined them, through his camera. "I feel like I've fought with Francis a lot about this character, although I haven't really," she said. What did Frannie really want? Fantasy or the real thing?

Storaro, on the other hand, understood his part. All of Las Vegas—the *actual* Vegas—had been built on the psychology of color. Where there were no windows, and where the neon lights were always bright, time became suspended. Entirely his to control, Zoetrope's soundstages were likewise a world apart, conducted through "day" and "night" by the Izenour dimmer box that gave Storaro a freedom with light and color he had never had. The slow pull of a lever could bring the sun up or down; it could make light "follow the characters around like shadows or like the long train on a wedding dress," Coppola said; it could turn opaque scrims transparent and divulge silhouettes, like ghosts, or thoughts from distant lovers. Shooting in a studio, there was simply no end to the photographic possibilities. In the words of Steadicam operator Garrett Brown, Storaro was "infuriatingly self-confident, unswerving, willing to take chances based on careful thinking as well as impulse; he is a phenomenon," and Coppola gave him everything, as much freedom as he had ever given anyone. "Tommy, I no-like-a this wall," Vittorio would murmur in his Italian accent. "I imagine a wall different to this . . ." Storaro's light was so wondrously moody that set photographer Peter Semel felt he could confidently take his pictures without the actors and even, it seemed, without the physical set itself. He could just shoot the light. "There was never light like that in my life," he said.

When lunch was called and cast and crew left for the sun, Storaro would remain on the stage to be alone with the light and further study the physiology of color. It was not always conscious: color, he told Peter Semel, transformed bodies and minds. He would demonstrate. First, a manila envelope. Then a volunteer. He had done so at parties: he would begin by placing the envelope in Sofia's hands. She would then disappear to a corner, where out of Storaro's view, she would pick one of the colored sheets of construction paper and slip it in the envelope. She would then return it and watch, smiling, as Storaro laid his palms upon the envelope a moment before announcing the color he felt within. "Green." He had eyes in his hands.

Once, the maestro had opened his hands for Armyan Bernstein. "You a-see what I'm doing?" His palms changed color. "I am a-holding the light in-a my hands."

Meanwhile, construction on the *One from the Heart* sets still moved slowly, at the stop-and-start pace of unraised money.

"Talk to Ray about that airport glass," Tavoularis advised an associate.

"Oh yeah. As soon as I get that check they'll start cutting. The girl in the office says she should have a check by four o'clock. Minute we get it we run it over there, the minute they get the check they start cutting. They won't even cut a piece of glass until they get a check."

Tavoularis chuckled. "They're wising up fast."

Coppola was everywhere and nowhere to be found, both in person and as a disembodied voice, addressing actors and crew either as an ensemble, through loudspeakers that boomed his directions from the video trailer through the stages—Teri Garr, squinting, trying to hear through the reverb—or one-on-one to, say, Arne Schmidt, via their headsets. "He [would tell] me what to tell somebody else so most of what he said to the actors came to my ears and out my lips and I tried to quote him exactly." Schmidt would stare into the camera lens—its video feed piped directly to Coppola in his trailer. "How was that for you, Francis? Should we go again?"

There wasn't always a response.

"All right," Schmidt decided. "Let's go again."

Did they have the money to wait around like this? Or was all this trial-and-error, as Coppola had repeatedly assured them, going to be a money saver in the end? Cast and crew had to take it on faith that with Coppola increasingly MIA, directing from the trailer, his experiment was still worthwhile.

"Francis, please come in . . ." script supervisor Joanie Blum, sitting beside Storaro at the monitor, called in after a take. There was no answer.

She looked to Storaro, too gracious to contradict his director. "I don't understand why he wants to do it this way."

There were times, Dan Attias said, "when even staging the actors, Francis wouldn't do it. He would let Vittorio stage it." Storaro naturally staged them in accord with his light. "The way it was shot," Frederic Forrest said, "meant that sometimes you were more accommodating the character than living the character. You had to stand in a certain way because of the lighting."

"I would like for you, Freddie, to a-start here," Storaro directed. They, with Kinski, were on the junkyard set under the tightrope. Starlight sprinkled the black canopy above. "This is-a your mark one. I would a-like-a you to walk along the fence and when you get to a-mark two, I want you to turn to your left. I want you to keep your head up and to look like this, toward this a-direction . . ."

And then, suddenly, the big voice from above: "Nastassja, your expression. Make it like you're walking a tightrope."

Her answer was tiny by comparison: "Okay, Francis."

"Action."

A hundred feet away, outside the darkened stage, Tony Dingman stood guard over Coppola in his video trailer. Why, some wondered, did the mobile unit need a guard?

The voice: "Freddie and Nastassja, face the camera so I can see you when I'm talking to you."

They did as directed.

"Nastassja, be real haughty." Her first language was German. "Do you know what 'haughty' means? You don't, do you?"

"No."

"It means willful. Be more forward."

"What does forward mean?"

Was this working? Like jungle ivy, rumors grew larger and twined together. What was he doing in there, really? Was remote directing, as Coppola had foreseen, just a part of the Electronic Cinema experiment, or was it—as the press had decided—one big *Heaven's Gate*-style power trip, Kurtz redux? (Murch: "It was no way to run a railroad.") Through the process of previsualization, Coppola had, by one count, "made" the movie five distinct times: first, as sketches hung up around the War Room; then as Polaroids; then on tape in Vegas; and again on tape in the studio; and finally, now, on film. "It actually became rather comical," said Dan Attias, "because so much resources were spent and so many rehearsals were done and runthroughs and everything else, and so much money was thrown out, and so much time was thrown out . . . It was—I don't want to say nuts—but kind of nuts." Was this whole Electronic Cinema experiment not really about what Coppola kept saying it was about? "Honestly," Mitch Dubin reflected, "I got the feeling he was petrified to come out of the trailer." They had said he was crazy to make *Apocalypse* as he did, and he had proved them wrong there. Was this time different? No, Coppola insisted; no, it was not. He was directing just as John Frankenheimer had—from within the control room. "I was very actively directing the piece that way I had originally conceived to," Coppola explained, "and why I just didn't shoot it in Las Vegas like a regular movie. To some it was weird, it was *not* weird. It was an essential part of the concept." Why didn't they understand that? He had so carefully explained his intention and process to everyone. Were the naysayers preemptively setting him up to be their fall guy?

"Francis could be told there's a better way," Michael Lehmann explained. "He could be told, 'Let's be patient.' He could be told, 'You're looking in the wrong direction' or 'This could be very difficult,' but he never wanted to be told no." Indeed, those whom he had installed in positions of power—foremost Spiotta and Gersten—had been hired to say yes; hired, that is, to transform "nos" into "maybes." How else to create creativity? "Francis turned to the people that he thought could help him," Lehmann elaborated. "And when he thought you couldn't help anymore, he turned to somebody else. The guy who had all the creative ideas and all the creative interest could overrule all the people who were involved in being financially responsible." Since the founding of Zoetrope, that had always been the dream. "No," Lehmann said, "he was not always reasonable. He was enchanting and enchanted, and he was focused on making his movies. But those of us who worked there, we knew full well that he was on a collision course for disaster unless the movie was amazing and became a huge hit."

This can't keep going on like this, Lucy Fisher told herself.

Up in San Francisco, in the Sentinel Building all but vacated by the exodus to Los Angeles, those who had been with Zoetrope the longest were the most skeptical, the most disheartened. One view held that, by moving to Hollywood, Francis hadn't so much achieved his dream as betrayed *theirs*. Another held that he had gone off his lithium. "I went down there one time," accountant Jean Autrey recalled, "and nobody knew what the bank balance was. I mean, how hard is it to keep track of the bank balance?" Whenever she met with producer Gray Frederickson to do a cost report on *One from the Heart*, he would ask, with surprising concern, if she was sure *everything* had been entered. "Because apparently the production accountant didn't know how to enter all the neon bills," Autrey said. "He had a million dollars' worth of bills that had never been entered into the system."

When the Sentinel Building would call down to Los Angeles asking for Coppola, "Ask Gio" was the regular response. "Find Gio"; "Check with Gio"; "Gio said . . ." At his father's side throughout, Gio knew more about Coppola's whereabouts than most anyone else. When push came to shove, he would be made to delegate, uncomfortably, sometimes, for both sides. "Gio was sort of thrust into this position when things were getting bad," Lehmann said. "He would communicate what Francis needed and wanted to people around the studio. There would be times when we wouldn't get really much direction from Francis, but Gio would come in and say, 'My dad wants you to get this or wants you to put that together. He has an idea about this . . .' So, there was a lot of 'my dad says.'"

"Do you have any petty cash?" Gio asked Tess Haley.

"Yeah, what do you need?"

"I just need about forty thousand dollars."

"What for?"

"Well, my dad said he wants to buy Uruguay. Or was it Paraguay?" He paused. "You know, I have to go back and ask my dad which one."

With what money? Would-be director of *The Tourist* Franc Roddam hadn't been paid, nor had his assistant, Ceci Dempsey. The excuses "were becoming more and more scary," Dempsey said. "Like, what do you mean, only come to you with an *emergency*? It had gotten to that point. How do you define an emergency? Is making a car payment an emergency?" Development on *The Tourist* had, of course, stalled, and Roddam spent his days in a fog. Were they just supposed to wait? Wait doing *what* exactly? Walking across the parking lot, Roddam spotted Gene Kelly. It was raining, Roddam recalled, "and he wasn't singing, and he wasn't dancing."

To break up the monotony, Roddam invited Godard to lunch. Godard, equally stalled, accepted. When the hour came, the two walked in silence from their studio offices to Roddam's parked car, spoke not a word through the ten-minute drive to Musso and Frank's, not a word as they parked and entered the restaurant, arrived at their table, ordered, not a word as they waited for their food to arrive—then: "You know," Roddam chanced, "I thought I'd be doing this film, but nothing is happening." Godard's reply was a paraphrase from Chairman Mao: "If you are one and they are ten, retreat. If you are ten and they are one, go forward." The remark would constitute the entirety of their conversation that afternoon.

Eventually, Roddam stormed Lucy's Fisher's office. "You have to give me the money now! I cannot live! I'm in trouble! I've got a new baby!"

"I can't, Franc. I can't . . . It's the lawyers—"

"The lawyers work for *you*. Get on the phone right now. Get on the phone and call them!"

"Franc . . ."

You can't kidnap an executive, he thought. "Pick up that phone, call the lawyer, and release that money to me immediately . . ."

Money was released to Roddam. Not all of it, but some.

"I was stuck," Fisher said. For her, the fun was over.

She had been submitted *Fanny and Alexander*, an epic eight-hour family drama/fairy-tale by Ingmar Bergman. It arrived, bittersweetly—care of legendary agent Paul Kohner—with a box of strawberries. Fisher kindly protested Zoetrope was out of money, but Kohner was a gentleman, and insisted she treat herself deal or no deal. "It was beautiful, a fantastic script," Fisher said, "and I ate the strawberries while I read." They were among her last tastes of Zoetrope Studios. Forcibly shifting her attention from script development, the job she had been hired to do, she was now spending her days trying to grin, leading investors around the lot, showing off the Vegas set, Zoetrope's crown jewel . . .

No longer could Coppola afford merely to borrow money; in no place to negotiate, if he wanted to keep the studio, he needed a partner—fast.

Described by one Zoetroper as "this weird little arthritic midget with these crawly little hands," Jack Singer was also, conveniently, an oil tycoon horny for celebrity access. "I really came to get his autograph," he said of Coppola. "That's stupid, but that's true." Singer had almost zero experience in show business: just a tax shelter investment in a Canadian picture called *Surfacing*, yet to be released in the United States. What he did have was a crisp check for a million dollars, made out to Zoetrope, February 20, 1981, worth an estimated additional two weeks of payroll. He dangled an additional $2 million in completion funds, plus another $5 million, "committed as long as I am happy," he bragged; all that would buy Singer gross participation in *One from the Heart*, an office on the lot, a first-look deal with Coppola via the newly formed Jack Singer Productions, and the right to lord it over the studio. They needed him now. "Suppose I drop dead tomorrow," he told the press, almost smiling.

Singer purred with sudden power. He received visitors in his own studio bungalow, drinking gin at any hour, laughing at his own jokes, dropping names (Eva Gabor, Patty Duke) while claiming not to be impressed by fame. He chatted up the girls of *One from the Heart*, and mused that he would one day come completely to Coppola's rescue and buy up half the studio.

In truth, Singer wasn't about to buy anything. His proposed second financial installment of $5 million was subject to the approval of Chase Bank, which had already loaned Coppola $16 million. And the bank would not approve the deal, depriving Coppola of Singer's additional $5 million and Singer of his hoped-for gross participation in *One from the Heart*, leaving, in its place, Singer's $3 million completion guarantee—secured against a lien on Coppola's studio property. "What I did was save the movie," Singer boasted. "I saved the movie, okay?"

Spiotta hated him. Coppola suffered him. Tony Dingman called him the Bogeyman. "He was such a cliché," said Cynthia Kania. "I mean, you just couldn't believe the tan." Or his gold chains and tracksuit. Or the drunken swagger. But Bernie and Cora Gersten, doing their part, had to take him to dinner. They had only sat down at their table at Michael's in Santa Monica when Singer, "fifty-five sheets to the wind," Cora Gersten recalled, put his head down on his plate and fell backward off his chair.

Singer's formal introduction to the Zoetrope family was no better. All had been called to the soundstage—a full-scale Las Vegas motel—to welcome their new benefactor with a song in his honor, performed by Raul Julia, and a flashy dance number from the company. "Ladies and Gentleman . . ." Julia began, extending an arm. "Jack Singer!" The name brought a swell of obliging cheers and applause, and the small man sauntered up, drink in hand. "Thank you everyone," he slurred, and then fell forward into the audience.

Throughout, Coppola kept confident. As head of the studio, he was also head of morale. Appearing on the set with Gio to watch a round of dance rehearsals for the camera, he picked up a horn between takes and tried an impromptu song. Gene Kelly at his side, Coppola burst into a verse of "Almost Like Being in Love"—a tribute to Kelly in *Brigadoon*—nervously watching for Kelly's reaction. Kelly outstretched an arm and joined in.

"I need a helicopter right outside in five minutes!" Coppola joked aloud to the crew. "To the Philippines!"

Hidden somewhere on the Bora Bora set, Jean-Luc Godard (with cinematographer Ed Lachman) would film, his Ray-Bans pressed to his viewfinder, the activity on the stage. This documentary footage Godard could use in his next scripted film (if he ever finished it): Coppola, Kenny Ortega, and Gene Kelly standing at the monitor, watching with careful concern as Raul Julia and Teri Garr twirled before the ocean backdrop.

"Straighten the leg . . ." Ortega implored the monitor.

"CUUUUTTTTTTT!" Kelly yelled, loud, the old-fashioned way, as if still directing at MGM when there were no headsets.

Coppola stood by as the choreographer and his mentor discussed the take.

"It's all right," Kelly assured Ortega. Vigorously chewing gum, he pointed to the monitor, all business. "We'll bring this. They'll make a frame cut between the two arabesques . . ."

Coppola was there to see to it that *they* were getting what they wanted. What *he* wanted was the dances to look real, even messy by traditional standards. So he would remind Ortega to "dirty it up" here and there, "so the audience could put themselves in the head of the characters," dancer Miranda Garrison explained, "and fantasize they were them." It would be Ortega's job to bridge the gap between the hoped-for and the actual.

They ran the number again. Again, Coppola, Ortega, and Kelly huddled at the monitor.

"That's it . . ." Kelly said to the screen. "That's it. She's got it. CUUUTTTTT!! PRIIIIIINT!"

There was a wave of relieved applause. Garr and Julia joined the celebration at the monitor to review their work, and peeking over a tall shoulder, Michael Powell jostled in for a better view. They watched, rapt, smiling at intervals, sharing praise and amazement. This is what it was all about, wasn't it?

Across the stage, Coppola would spy a stagehand huddled flirtatiously with a woman in a cocktail dress. "Who's the guy with the girl on his lap?"

"If he's an electrician," returned the production manager, "he's going to get his pink slip."

"Nah," Coppola said.

"I'm taking care of your money, Francis. You don't want him doing that on your time."

"Leave the guy alone."

Coppola would wearily, cheerily, plop down on a chair in the production accounting office. "Can I have some money?" he would joke. Given that he wasn't really joking, they couldn't really laugh. (Still, Martha Cronin got a kick out of payroll's Norma Smith, who changed the paychecks—what was left of them—to read "One Through the Heart.") Magician Ricky Jay, advising on the Zoetrope production of *The Escape Artist*, would stop by accounting with a trick; David Lynch, coffee in hand, would drop in from his office across the hall. "He was bored," Cronin said.

Accounting didn't have that luxury. "The boots-on-the-ground people who were trying to control the production like you normally do," Cronin said, "if they would start putting the brakes on spending, then it would come to a head, and they would get fired." Her job was to negotiate with unpaid vendors, not to ask, when she got the bill, why the department store set had been stocked with the highest-quality imported lingerie. But she had asked anyway. "Couldn't we just put the expensive stuff on the ends of the racks and fill it in with Macy's?" "No," a set dresser had answered. "Because you never know when Francis is going to come in and say, 'I want to do a shot through the middle of the rack.'"

At ten o'clock one payday morning, production accountant Jim Turner's phone rang with a request from Bob Spiotta's assistant. "Could Bob get his check *now*?"

It was becoming increasingly clear that Spiotta, in the words of many, "did nothing." Dodging blame, he called Tess Haley into his office one day, admonishing her, she said, "for something—he didn't know what he was talking about." It was bluster, cover for inadequacy and terror. Spiotta's wife, Emy, was coming to see this version of him, too. "Bob thought he could make movies on his own," she said. "At a certain point, he got sick of being a businessperson. He wanted to be valued more for his creativity." ("He got hit with a palm tree," as Haley put it.) Spiotta's daughter Robin saw vanity, plain and simple. "It was the glamour and the whole every-thing . . . that went to my dad's head," she said, "and then eventually, things went sour . . . Francis responded to it, like, 'Wow, that's not what I hired you for.'" In his defense, Spiotta was also observed trying to slow Coppola's spending, but "Francis was not a person who took criticism very well," said Emy. "He had some illnesses he was dealing with. So we had to respect that. He was taking medications and all that kind of stuff." Spiotta would show up on the stage for serious financial discussions with Francis—"There were a couple of points where he'd see me and duck," Spiotta joked. Once, Coppola was heard over the loudspeakers shouting back at him, "You guys are all the same! 'We can't have *this*!' 'We can't have *that*!'" To Michael Lehmann, Spiotta admitted, "I can't deal with this crazy guy anymore." But the very last straw broke for Coppola when he heard that Spiotta was leaving his wife and three children for—just as the Ding-bats had predicted in their newsletter—his Zoetrope secretary. "Francis was not happy about that at all," Robin Supak said. "He super lost respect for my dad."

Coppola had also lost his oldest associate. Midway into *One from the Heart*, Mona Skager fled Zoetrope and Coppola. So did, for a time, Dean Tavoularis. "Dean and Francis had a falling-out," Alex Tavoularis said. "Francis was feeling the financial pressure. And he wanted to blame somebody for how much the sets cost for *One from the Heart*. There was a lot of neon. Dean didn't even say anything. He just disappeared."

Murch and Lucas were occupied elsewhere, by their own projects.

Francis's mother and father were seen berating him outside his bungalow, screaming at him for destroying his own studio. "Going against Italia was going against a brick wall," said Tess Haley. "They were nightmares," Zoetrope's Sonia Socher said of Coppola's parents, "always wanting something, being torments." How else would Carmine become the musical genius he was destined to be when it was irresponsible Francis, not August, with the power?

Blame was omnipresent. "Toward the end of *One from the Heart*, it just felt kind of sad," said Martha Cronin. "It was out of control. Francis would yell at people. What he said was, 'The production assistants are there for me if I need to yell at somebody, because it would be very destructive if I yelled at Vittorio.'" ("True, those times I lost my temper I'm sure I expressed it," Coppola would reflect, "but it is not typical of me to yell at people, especially collaborators. The many kindnesses I am known for on some occasions is balanced in part by frustration, losing my temper, and shouting.")

To the best of his ability, he hid his lowest self from others. "There was nothing you could do to pull him out if it," Haley said. "You just had to wait." Sometimes it would take days. Sometimes it was not clear what had made him cry, even after it was explained. "He was happiest when he was directing, and he had huge amounts of people around him," Haley said. His closest allies remained, as always, the children, his own and others', but none stayed closer than Gio, heir apparent. He was nearly eighteen, and his interest in filmmaking had matured with increased responsibility.

The video trailer was, of course, both Coppola's dream machine and his childhood bedroom; an electronic appendage, like the computer consciousness of *Interface*, lost now to Paramount; the polio sickbed across from his television—in this case, many televisions, his to control. "There's no doubt," Coppola confessed, "that it goes back to that year I spent in bed." Lucy Fisher pictured him this way, as the little boy in the illustration "Sick Day," from *A Child's Garden of Verses*: alone in bed, surrounded by toy figurines. "We were little puppets," as Teri Garr put it. One day, with a tug on a string, he would be able to transform Las Vegas into Dusseldorf or, instead of recasting, press a button and swap Harvey Keitel and Martin Sheen. He wouldn't need Spiotta to tell him yes. Beaming his movie through the satellites, he wouldn't need the philistines at Chase Bank to approve his distributor. He could—the way a writer would—remake the world instantly and on his own, the way he did when playing puppets to the children's voices on *The Horn and Hardart Children's Hour* and *Let's Pretend*. "There are Francis Ford Coppola films, and there are Francis Coppola films," his brother, August, who probably knew him best, said, "but there's only one *Francie* film, and that's *One from the Heart*. 'Francie' is the name that we used when he was young. When he had done everything that he wanted to do, he made a Francie movie. He wanted to do the thing that delighted him as a child."

Francie Coppola was sixteen . . .

"King God," he typed. "A Tale for Children."

There was once a king, and although he was the ruler of a very large and powerful land, he was unhappy. His was a wealthy kingdom, so every person in it had plenty. The people were as happy as any people had ever been, yet the king was unhappy. He thought: "I have given my people as much as I can. They all have enough food, clothing, and shelter, but it isn't enough. Old men still die, little babies still get sick, people still get killed in accidents. All this misery and I cannot do anything about it." Of course, there really wasn't anything for him to do, yet he worried and worried. Then finally he decided.

"Of all the kings on earth I have been the best. But I am not the most powerful, there is one, this King God. He may be more powerful than I, but he isn't as good a king. All sickness and deaths and accidents are under his control. He doesn't know how to run things. I had better go and show him how to do a proper job."

And so the king left the happy land and began his search for King God. On his way he passed through less fortunate kingdoms than his own. Places where the kings would use up all the food for themselves and let the people starve.

"Ahhhh! If I were King God there wouldn't be any of this."

He passed huge churches where the bishops would take most of the money and land.

"Even his nobles are evil. . . . If I only had a chance to control the world, then things would be different."

The King discovered King God in heaven sitting at a giant desk.

"Well at any rate," says the King, *"let's get down to business. As King God you have fabulous power. Yet you let people die and all sorts of horrible things happen. Why?"*

King God was about to speak but was interrupted by a ringing black box on his desk.

"Hello."

"Dear God, my name is Suzie. Please make daddy president of the bank and get Momie a mink coat and please Dear God, Get me a baby sister to play with. Amen."

God looked pleased.

"That was a little girl. I can't make her daddy president of the bank because hundreds of other little girls want their daddies to be president, I can't go around giving away free coats because then the furriers will start praying for better business. But . . . As far as little baby sisters go, I think I can manage . . ."

Just as God was about to push some buttons, the black box rang again.

"Hello."

"Oh God, our father, This is Suzie's mommy, uh ... I don't do this very often but ... now it's important ... uh ... I really need a new mink coat, why, it's absolutely freezing outside ... and uh ... one more thing, I'm still a young woman, I'd like to enjoy my youth, please God ... no more children ..."

God's hand was trembling.

"You see my friend, it's not as easy as you think."

But the king was still not convinced.

"I still can't see why you let certain things happen, why if I were God I'd ..."

"So you want to be God, eh? ... Then I'll let you. For an hour or a year or a century ... or even forever ... I don't care. When a phone rings just lift up the receiver and you'll hear the prayers. Over here is the Master Wheel. If it's turned to the left: Evil, to the right: Good."

The king scratched his head.

"If it's as easy as that, why not keep it on Good all the time, then you'll have no problems."

Which is how King God left the mortal King alone with the controls.

At the far end of the board there was a row of buttons marked: Death, and then another row ... Marked: Life.

"I'll never push a button marked Death, instead I'll push twice as many marked Life."

So the king went down the row of "life" buttons ... 1—2—3—4—5 ... he pushed and pushed. Meanwhile, back on earth, millions of babies were being born. There was a milk shortage ...

"Ha" he thought to himself, "I'll make more cows."

And he pushed and pushed ...

Back on earth: millions of cows, and not enough grass. The king snapped his fingers.

"No problem at all," he muttered ... "more grass."

And he pushed and pushed. On earth it was getting more and more crowded, until the king thought: "All I have to do is make more earth, I'll make a bigger world."

Which he did, bigger and bigger, with more and more life ...

. . . and BOOM . . . He ran to the window and looked to see what had happened to the earth. He looked . . . and saw blue . . . only blue. It was gone, there was no earth anymore, he had destroyed it. He had been worse than any sickness or war. He had killed everything, everyone . . . there was nothing. The king sat on the floor of the huge room and cried.

"Look what I've done . . . I can never forgive myself."

Then God walked in and put his hand on the shoulder of the crying mortal.

"I forgive you. You were a good king and only tried to make the earth better . . . but I'm afraid the earth will have to have a little evil and some deaths . . . The trick is to enjoy what good there is."

The sobbing king looked up.

"But . . . there is no more. . . . I've destroyed the earth . . ."

God smiled.

"Look."

And there, hugged by a blanket of blue, spun the most beautiful earth the king had ever seen.

He was somehow not there. "While making *One from the Heart*," as Thomas Brown put it, "he's living *Interface*." As *One from the Heart* was the antidote to *Apocalypse*, so would the world of *Interface* be the antidote to *Heart*. "Francis was hiding from his debtors or his creditors," Murch contended. "He couldn't go onto the set for fear of being hit with a lawsuit or something." So, too, was he hiding from the very subject of his movie. Eleanor, his primary creative sounding board on *Apocalypse*, maintained a conscientious distance throughout, their own love story less a Vegas gamble than a long game of double solitaire. Quoting Tom Waits, she would say, "Family and art eat each other."

The affairs he had sworn off he resumed. The gamble of love—as he had once described it to Armyan Bernstein—he was losing nightly. He did not transform making *One from the Heart* as he had making *Apocalypse*, he did not launch from the spiritual cliff and discover, on the way down, the secrets of his story. He had died out there in the jungle, but death he could do; it's done alone. Love, as Harry Caul knew, was another apocalypse entirely.

Always a challenge to Coppola, love scenes—the very heart of *One from the Heart*—he often oversaw from his trailer monitors, where the emotional core of Hank and Frannie, why they leave their fantasy lovers and why they reunite, lost out to remote control. But how else was he try to work as John Frankheimer had, directing live from "the booth"? "Try not to anticipate the kiss," his voice barreled over the stage. This was aimed, though everyone else could hear it, at Teri Garr. "And try to appear more happy that he's kissed you, Teri . . ."

"It is true," he confessed in 1982, "I am more interested in technology than I am in content." On his copy of Armyan Bernstein's first draft, beside its title, *One from the Heart*, on the first page, he had written, "*You're a Big Boy Now*, 15 Years Later."

A letter came to Coppola from a librarian. She had written it on behalf of her students, imploring Coppola to make a film of the book her class loved: S. E. Hinton's novel of growing up, *The Outsiders*. Coppola, likely in need of another distraction, better still, one that would return him to the company of young people, said yes.

The option on the book would cost Zoetrope five thousand dollars.

"Can we pay it incrementally?" Lucy Fisher asked Barry Hirsch.

Principal photography on *One from the Heart* ended. Cast and most of the crew were dismissed.

"*Laaaaainie* . . ." Jack Singer drunkenly croaked to Kazan on her way out. "Sing it for me . . . Sing 'The Impossible Dream.'"

"It's not impossible," was her reply.

In April 1981, Coppola, withdrawing more from his Singer account, added to *One from the Heart* thirty-two additional days of reshoots, additional special effects photography, and an elaborate opening title sequence of miniature Vegas signs, the smallest neon models ever built, 160,000 miniature lightbulbs in all, some smaller than the head of a pin and soldered in place by medical tweezer.

Walking by the model stage, Coppola had another thought. "Wouldn't it be fun if we had different kinds of typefaces for the signs? We could use a kind of Panavision typeface for Vittorio's sign and for me it could be like the Ford logo . . ."

"Francis was completely emotional," said visual effects editor Kathy Campbell. "He had no idea what goes on in an effects department. He was all heart." When Coppola left for New York to attempt further negotiations with Chase, pressure was applied to rush special effects, and certain crafts-people were let go. "Wait till Francis gets back," Gray Frederickson assured Campbell. "It'll all be back to the way it should be." And it was.

In June 1981, with principal photography of *One from the Heart* finally complete, Lucy Fisher realized she could hold out no longer. "I stayed to fire most everybody, and then I fired myself."

The lot emptied, save for the flailing production of *Hammett* and the frenzy in the editing suite. Inside, they were cutting, cutting, cutting *One from the Heart*, trying everything, trying *bad* ideas, which could be future good ideas in disguise, as Coppola, seemingly unfazed, barbecuing with his shirt off, served midnight dinners on real china. "Make it beautiful," Coppola would tell the editors. Randy Roberts, cutting video, and veteran Rudi Fehr, cutting film on a Moviola, had been let go—test screenings had disappointed Coppola—and in came Anne Goursaud to edit her first Hollywood feature (on a flatbed KEM). "Francis never gave me anything specific to do, ever," Goursaud said. "He wanted me to dazzle him, dare him." Along with everyone else in the cutting room, Chris Lebenzon, on his first feature as assistant editor, was working "passionate, unlimited hours," cutting after dinner, during dinner. They'd run a cut and then go back and cut some more as Sofia, sometimes at one in the morning, ran video tapes back and forth from her father in his trailer to the editors in their cutting room.

No idea would be denied. Between age and youth, man and woman, film and video, they would find *One from the Heart*. They had to. And when they did, when they turned this multimillion-dollar film, its slight story, its humble musical numbers, into a multimillion-dollar hit, Coppola could pay off his debts, and Zoetrope Studios would be saved.

If the film was anything less than a hit, he would lose the studio to Jack

Singer. Factoring in the exhibitors' and distributors' shares, "*One from the Heart*," Coppola said, "will have to earn from two and a half to three times its cost, or—according to a broad rule of thumb—about sixty-eight million dollars, before we break even." Or, in other words: *One from the Heart*, given the box-office trends, would have to be at least the second-highest-grossing film of 1982.

Eleanor paid a rare visit to the cutting room and found Gio there, lending a hand, hard at work on the cut. "Look what your son has done," Coppola said to her, beaming.

Frederic Forrest, back to playing Dashiell Hammett once again, waved over Joanie Blum. The set, he wanted her to see, was even more incredible than she knew. "Now here's a closet." He smiled at her. "Open up the closet door . . ."

She did.

"Open up these drawers . . ."

Her jaw dropped. Each drawer was filled with "Dashiell Hammett's" clothing, pressed and folded; the drawer itself lined in cedar. This was Tavoularis, his tribute to the actors.

"What do *I* need to do?" the actor asked Blum rhetorically. "Just remember my lines."

The beauty of the craftsmanship, the consideration of costume and décor—even if it never registered with audiences, let alone made it to the screen—showed nothing but the highest respect for the artists and artisans. *Hammett* would be a disaster, but running her hand along the drawer's cedar lining, Blum thought, *This is why I fell in love with movies*.

And then even the editing rooms at Zoetrope Studios emptied.

Postproduction on *One from the Heart*—finishing the picture edit, the sound mix, finessing the completed Tom Waits score—continued back in the Sentinel Building, and Coppola "immediately made everyone change offices," said Gary Weimberg. "And in the Francis Ford Coppola way, it created chaos. His belief was that it would inculcate us with the creative spirit and out of it would come productivity and brilliance as we raced against Doomsday."

They worked all hours.

"Francis," Weimberg said. "It doesn't make sense to work us this hard. Our efficiency goes down. You're wasting your money."

"Gary, you don't understand. If every single sound person worked around the clock for a year and that shortened the production deadline by three days, the interest on the loan would pay for double your salaries." There was always the possibility that he could maximize their postproduction time if he borrowed Jerry Perenchio's jet and flew the editors and their equipment from screening to screening, showing the film to test audiences, learning from their reactions (he had tasked Weimberg with counting instances of audience fidgets) and then recutting the film in the air en route to the next audience. "We've been through tremendous crises," Coppola would say, "but this company will always be in crisis. Because the company will always be remaking itself. And whenever you remake yourself, it's terrifying."

He was sleeping in the Sentinel Building, Lebenzon said, "so he was always two doors away." Announced by a cloud of marijuana smoke, Coppola burst from a cutting room flush with joy. "You won't believe it! Listen to this! I just got a bank loan so big they forgot to ask for collateral!" And then he skipped down the hall.

There were still nights of parties downstairs in the Zoetrope café, formerly Zim's. Coppola had changed the name to Wim's in honor of the beleaguered director of *Hammett*. There was still dancing to the jukebox on Formica tables and twirling on the barstools. There was also the night Coppola woke up alone in the Broadway house with a panicked dream "and decided the thing to do," Weimberg said, was "to throw a party." By 3 a.m., there were fifty people in the house. The party went till dawn.

"Gary," he said to Weimberg, "you know, you can borrow anything you want."

They were browsing Coppola's personal library of 16 mm prints.

"Can I borrow *Godfather*?"

"Of course. You can borrow anything."

Weimberg brought the print home to the little projector he kept in his apartment bedroom and, onto the white wall he had left bare for moving pictures, he projected *The Godfather*. He watched the print, he estimated, a dozen times, "and this was when nobody, other than Hollywood zillionaires, had screening rooms," he said. "I felt like I was the richest man in the world."

England's Pinewood Studios, the biggest and best studio in Europe, covered almost a hundred acres—a giant water tank, fifty cutting rooms, six screening rooms, and, among its fifteen soundstages, the single biggest in the world, built for James Bond. Backed by Spielberg, Scorsese, De Palma, and Michael Powell, Coppola made a bid to buy Pinewood "right out of the blue," said the Rank Organization's Rodney Rycroft. The offer was rejected, and Coppola returned to the image of the Chrysler Building, "an idea center," he thought, "an experimental thing. Not really a story department, but . . ." the beginning of a new kind of city . . . a megacity for a new kind of world, a communications world, a world unified by cinema . . .

It began a rumor. Spiotta's son, Christian, heard Coppola was buying the world. "I want to run Africa," he requested.

Coppola thought a second. "I'm okay with that."

Block booking: it was the old Hollywood studio system's ace in the hole. Outlawed in 1948 by the Supreme Court, the practice of forcing theaters to take multiple films as a unit, as one would buy a carton of eggs, rather than take them individually, was a handy and economical way for the studios to exploit films of lesser appeal. It meant also that theaters were forced to take movies sight unseen. Under the 1948 ruling, however, studios were required to hold anti–blind screenings for theater owners; it was their chance to look at a movie, albeit in its uncompleted state, before they committed. But as of August 1981, the cut of *One from the Heart*, which Coppola likened "to a three-legged coffee table"—the majority of Waits's numbers were not yet in the film—was raw even by anti–blind bidding standards. But Paramount, the film's distributor, proceeded anyway, screening a work print of *One from the Heart* with bad color and sound in a tiny screening room for exhibitors in San Francisco.

San Francisco Chronicle reporter Judy Stone was on hand to poll the exhibitors for their reactions to the film. One called it "probably one of the ten worst films I have ever seen"; another said "the scenery was real pretty, but the parts that did not work at all were the dialogue, the acting and the directing"; and another: "I almost think the film is unreleasable. How can these very talented Big People be so wrong . . . Does Francis have people all around him mesmerized so that they can't even tell him the truth?" It wasn't so much the humiliation. "It makes my relationship with the bank very tough," Coppola said. "They read the papers like everybody else."

Paramount's callousness "was like being rejected from your lover," Coppola explained. "It gives you an excuse to call somebody else." As the $1.6 million in *One from the Heart* completion funds Paramount owed him remained unpaid, Coppola argued that the film still belonged to Zoetrope. But, Spiotta said, "Paramount felt there was no obligation for it to put up *any* money, because we had exceeded the shooting days allowed in the contract. We felt strongly, and still do, that, despite the extra shooting days, Paramount had an obligation to provide completion funds. As a consequence, Chase Manhattan Bank had to provide further funds in the form of personal loans guaranteed by Mr. Coppola and his wife and utilizing as collateral just about everything they have, including his seventeen-hundred-acre estate in Napa Valley and once again, of course, Zoetrope Studios."

Coppola wrote to Barry Diller: "Due to Paramount's failure to comply with its completion obligations for *One from the Heart*; the considerable damage done by Paramount's slovenly handling of an unauthorized screening in a non-bid city, San Francisco, resulting in considerable negative publicity and general negative comments of Paramount executives to the press and industry professionals; Paramount's pressure to release the film in 1982 so as to not compete with its self-financed films; and the general disregard and lack of confidence in myself and *One from the Heart*, I have decided to withdraw the film from your release schedule."

"Then they sent out a news release that they'd dropped the picture," Coppola said. "They hadn't. We dropped them."

Either way, *One from the Heart*—unfinished, unliked, notoriously $25 mil-lion over its original budget, prematurely decreed self-indulgent by the press, shouldering Coppola's entire livelihood and the future of his vision for an Electronic Cinema for all—now had no distributor.

Premiering earlier that year at Radio City Music Hall, Zoetrope's presenta-tion of the restored *Napoleon* with a new score by Carmine Coppola was such a triumphant success ("the film event of the year"—Vincent Canby) that Carmine's intended single weekend of performances was extended to a na-tional tour. "I'm predicting we'll march down Italy with this film, following in the footsteps of Napoleon," Carmine told Roger Ebert. "You know, Napo-leon was a Corsican? To the Italians . . . that doesn't mean he was French."

Carmine proved correct. Facing bankruptcy, the Coppolas flew to Rome for the Italian premiere of *Napoleon*, Carmine Coppola presiding. There, Eleanor signed documents preparing the family for her husband's almost inevitable defeat. To stymie creditors, half his holdings were transferred to her. "Deep inside," she wrote, "I know I hide the fear that if something happened to Francis, I would be responsible for those debts, with no possible way to repay them."

Coppola had no distributor, bad word-of-mouth, and no leash left with banks. But *Napoleon* . . . The triumphant feeling of watching his father lead his orchestra before a giant screen hung outside the Coliseum as spectators watched from trees and hillsides—in the rain . . . What if they previewed *One from the Heart* at Radio City Music Hall? There would be press coverage; there would be goodwill. There could even be another loan.

At a cost of $24,000, Coppola secured Radio City for an evening, and at a cost of $27,000, he took out a full-page ad in the *New York Times* Sunday Arts and Leisure section announcing the event. Programs, posters, and but-tons cost him $15,000. The party after—in the Tower Suite of the Time-Life Building—$19,410. "I knew that if I were going to pull this off, I'd have to do it fast," Coppola said. "If I'd delayed a week, someone would have talked me out of it." Ticket prices to the screening were $10 for reserved seats and $5 for general admission. There would be two showings, at 7:30 and 10 p.m.

"On Friday, January 15," the *Times* ad announced, "at Radio City Music Hall, Francis Coppola presents the final preview of his new movie."

Let the public decide. If they hate it, it could die. But if they love it . . . "This is my reaction to the system by which movies are usually released," Coppola said, "the system of blind bidding, exhibitors watching the film in smoky rooms, some critics seeing it way ahead of time and others mad because they haven't seen it yet."

He also did it for himself, for the people who had made the movie. To show them their film in a proper theater, in its proper aspect ratio, significantly 1.33:1, the way they did it in the old days, before it was sent to "all those modern shoeboxes," Coppola said, referring to the glut of cramped cineplex cinemas in malls and shopping plazas, "and they cut the top and the bottom off the frame."

Buy your plane tickets to New York, he told his cast and crew and remaining studio personnel. I will reimburse you.

"I brought the color-corrected silent print back to New York to run for Radio City Music Hall," Chris Lebenzon said. "We didn't even have a composite print. They were mixing, doing the sound mix in San Francisco while the picture itself was locked and getting color-corrected in Rome, halfway around the world, and they met in New York. So, it did work out. But it could have gone either way." The day of the screening, Coppola finished the final sound mix at dawn.

It was New York City cold outside Radio City Music Hall the evening of January 15, 1982. Bundled tight, moviegoers had come early to wait in line. Despite freezing gusts down Sixth Avenue, some had been waiting since morning. They greeted Zoetrope's documentary video cameramen with enthusiastic shouts of "We love Francis Coppola!" "Coppola is a genius!" and "Break a leg, Francis!" as they passed cups of piping hot pea soup with sausage, provided by Coppola, from mitten to mitten. Five thousand of them would get in.

Coppola, in a green beret, shared a limo to the theater with Eleanor, Dean Tavoularis, Bernie Gersten, and *New Yorker* writer Lillian Ross. "Here's a movie that cost a lot of dough," he explained to Ross, "that even before it was finished had this terrible reputation, so all of those things make me say what the hell I'll just show the god damned thing instead of having people snipe or guess . . ."

The limo pulled up outside Radio City, and Coppola glanced through the window. The line was around the block. Calmly, he looked to Bernie Gersten. "When are the people going to convene? The Zoetrope people?"

"For the Poowabah? Seven fifteen."

The Poowabah, a tradition since Hofstra. ("It exorcizes the evil spirits and invokes the good spirits.") On the first day of production, cast and crew had chanted it three times—"Poowabah! Poowabah! Poowabah!"—and they would come together that evening, before the curtain went up, to chant it again, closing the circle.

Surrounded backstage by friends, family, colleagues, and three ten-year-old Ding-bats (in white tie and tails, prepping their after-party performance of "One" from *A Chorus Line*), Coppola was not thinking about money, his or anyone else's—he was elated. Radio City Music Hall was still the most beautiful theater he ever saw, and the crowd, he already felt, was completely his. The present screening had sold out, and it looked like the ten o'clock screening would sell out as well. That meant fifty thousand dollars right there, back in Coppola's pocket. "You'd just look at him," Gary Fettis said, "and think, *How could a human being take this on?*"

Backstage, Coppola hushed the gathering. It was time for the Poowabah, he announced, and the Zoetropers formed a circle. Hand in hand, they lifted their arms in the air: "Poowabah! Poowabah! Poowabah!" they chanted, then cheered. As the show was about to start, Coppola hurriedly reminded everyone once more about the after-party. "And when the movie is about to end," he told them, "I want everybody to come down to the front of the stage. And we'll walk up onstage, and we'll take a bow."

Someone asked, "What if people don't like it?"

"We'll take a bow anyway."

The house lights dimmed, the gang dispersed. Some embraced till there was no more light. Then they ran off, too.

Coppola fled to the lobby and tossed his coat on the floor. He'd wait out the movie here, where he could pace.

Then—coming from inside the theater—there was the applause, and the movie began.

Coppola started pacing.

At intervals, he cracked a door to listen for the audience reaction, then paced again.

Halfway into the movie, he couldn't stand it any longer. Snapping his coat off the carpet, he slipped inside the theater and took a seat on the floor, at the back of the center aisle. On-screen, Teri Garr and Raul Julia were dancing a tango.

He clocked the audience. *They don't seem to dislike this*, he thought. *In fact, they like it. Maybe this is working. Maybe this is good. Maybe*—millions of dollars and years and one very endangered dream later—*they understand.*

The movie ended an hour later in a wave of warm applause that lasted through the end credits. It waned as expected as the house lights came on, and the theater fell silent again. It swelled one last time as Coppola and his company were announced and took their bows before the screen. Then it died down for good as Coppola raced to a rehearsal room backstage for the press conference. He took his place smiling. Seventy reporters, their hot lights blazing, were waiting for him, pens out:

"Mr. Coppola, What is the arrangement for the distribution of this movie? Do we know whether Paramount is going to do this?"

"Well, I don't really know," he answered. "What we're talking about, I suppose, is what the reaction of the audience was to the picture. And I can only speak as someone—and you correct me if you wish to—who was there. They seemed to laugh throughout the picture. They stayed pretty motionless and attentive throughout the picture. There weren't very many walkouts; at the end, there was a play of emotions and enthusiastic applause, which lingered throughout the titles and even after the titles. That's what I saw. If someone saw it a different way, then maybe that's so."

Bernie Gersten stood at Coppola's side, guarding him.

"Have you, in your opinion, accomplished your purpose?" a reporter asked.

It was then that Coppola got the first hint, and by no means a small one, that *One from the Heart* was not going to be embraced. "A lot of people who spoke to me before said, 'That was a very unusual and beautiful picture,'" he replied. "Perhaps other people didn't. The question is that when I make a film, I take a jump into something I'm interested in. In this, I was inter-ested in showbusiness and I was interested in gambling and I was interested in love. And I was interested in fantasy and I was interested in music. Those are the things I worked with in my film. And I'm very proud of it. And I imagine that years from now, just as with my other films, people will see something. It's an original work. It's not a copy of anything. It's not like anything. It entertains people, and it's innocent."

"But will it be commercially successful?"

He almost laughed. "Well, I mean, how do *I* know? I mean, how many seats did we sell tonight?"

Gersten: "Twelve thousand."

"How much did we gross today?"

"One hundred fifty thousand."

"What other film grossed that today?"

Another question: "How important is the success of this movie to your future movie productions and moviemaking ventures?"

Why were they always against him? Was it always going to be about money?

"If this film doesn't succeed, will the studio stay viable? Will it be alive?" another reporter shot out.

"No."

"Everything lives on the success of this film?"

"Yes."

"You helped create George Lucas. Why hasn't he—"

"I don't need to be bailed out. My friendship with George is such that I know that that's not his style of doing things. He would help me in other ways, maybe driving to the airport when I needed it." They laughed, but Coppola didn't. "Everybody's a different human being, and George is a good friend; we were having dinner for Thanksgiving. We played Risk."

"Mr. Coppola, do you love this movie as much as Hank liked Frannie?"

Another question: "After tonight, when are people gonna get to see it again?"

He would arrive late to the after-party at the top of the Time-Life Build-ing. By then, the first guests—Andy Warhol, Norman Mailer, Martin Scor-sese, Robert Duvall, Joe Papp, Robert De Niro—had already begun to pour in. Earlier, stepping from the elevator, the very first arrivals had found the doors to the Tower Suite locked shut. "Because the check had bounced," miniature and visual effects photographer Robert Eberlein recalled, "and a bunch of folks there had to pull out credit cards."

An uncomfortable week passed.

"Daddy," Coppola asked his father, "what did you think of *One from the Heart*?"

"I think it's a piece of shit."

A knife in Coppola's heart. Despite Carmine's world-conquering tour of *Napoleon*, Coppola knew his father was angry he hadn't been asked to compose the movie, but it was a knife nonetheless. "He sort of thought he in his mind was Napoleon," Coppola said.

After New York and Los Angeles previews, and the rainy Los Angeles premiere, for which Coppola reserved an exceptional four hundred seats for union members—grateful for their patience in forgoing pay through *One from the Heart*—the word of mouth on the film was still inconclusive: "It was a lot like having dessert for about eight courses" went one exit interview. "It was beautiful, it was *beautiful*, and sometimes you wanted to *diiiiiiie* . . ." Pauline Kael and Andrew Sarris ("Coppola has thrown out the baby and photographed the bathwater") were negative. Warner Bros. and Columbia were distant.

Alone among critics, Sheila Benson, film critic for the *Los Angeles Times*, gave Coppola the early review he needed. "A work of constant astonishment," she called *Heart*. "Francis Coppola's new film is so daring it takes away your breath while staggering you visually."

In due course, Spiotta and Columbia continued their negotiations. Reluctantly, it seemed, Columbia picked up the picture—a Valentine's Day release—then dropped it, on February 11, 1982, into forty-one theaters in eight American cities. The studio would go wider, one assumed, if they found they had reason to. But they did not. In the *New York Times*, Vincent Canby called the film "unfunny, unjoyous, unsexy, and unromantic."

The press saw *One from the Heart* only as an indulgence: too much money spent and lost. But as *Apocalypse Now*, and every other misbudgeted success, proves, artistic waste can be argued only in retrospect. Other (better and worse) films had cost more, much more. What might have saved Zoetrope Studios, ironically, would have cost Francis Ford Coppola exactly zero dollars to budget into *One from the Heart*: love, the truth, as he and Eleanor knew it.

Coppola had begun with a simple love story, one that could accommodate dance and music and flights of fancy. But love, real love, is not a dream. Nor are soft changes of light and color, no matter how luscious, equal to human emotion. Nor theatrical gestures, no matter how grand, nor Tom Waits's music and lyrics, no matter how beautifully broken, enough to compensate for the heavy lifting of story and character. Had Coppola lived the film through its making, he might have called his own bluff. But divided between soundstage and trailer, exterior and interior worlds, he had not wrestled with the reality of fantasy unresolved within himself.

However.

To eye and ear, *One from the Heart* is a utopia. Coppola's appetite for film and theater, his inclusion of the various art departments of studio film-making (production design, model making, original score, etc.), his delight in their efforts and innovations, the sum of its many passionate parts, even if they never cohere, are rampant and abundant, a sufficient 107 minutes of evidence that Francis Ford Coppola, on the earth between Las Palmas and Santa Monica Boulevards, made what could be thought of as better world. If only briefly. Once upon a time.

After five weeks and four days in the theaters, *One from the Heart* managed only $982,492. "I pulled it out of distribution thinking I could sit on it for six months and get a second chance to release it," Coppola said, "but what happened is when I pulled it, it went immediately to home video. I was stupid." He was angry and he was heartbroken. Its final showing, on April 1, just down the street from the Radio City Music Hall at the 450-seat Guild Theater in New York, played to only forty-three people.

That month, Coppola put Zoetrope Studios up for sale. The asking price was $20 million. He owed Chase Manhattan over $30 million.

But money was money; it came and went. It was the lost opportunity, his decision to shoot *One from the Heart*, as Storaro and Tavoularis had suggested, the old-fashioned way, with a single camera instead of many—one of the few regrets he would hold for the rest of his life—that was the most painful of all. "I had bought a studio," he reflected, "and filled it with nine stages with sets of Las Vegas (when the real Las Vegas was only a forty-five-minute flight away). I had done all of this so I could shoot *One from the Heart* live—to fulfill my life's dream to do Live Cinema. And because I cared so much for Vittorio and Dean, and probably because I was so frightened of what I was attempting to do—I caved in."

To escape, he threw himself into his next production, *The Outsiders*. "I like being with kids rather than adults," he said, "so it turned into a way for me to soothe my heartache over the terrible rejection at that point." Budgeted at $10 million and only weeks away from the start of production in Tulsa, the picture had yet to receive backing.

Dear Mr. Coppola,

Just a note to tell you how much my wife, Christine; my friend, Jason and I loved *One from the Heart*. The rest of the audience did too; it's the only film at which I have ever seen a Toronto audience vigorously applaud.

We know the dire financial straits Zoetrope Studios is in so we thought we'd make a contribution (check enclosed).

Thank you,
Elliot Harper

There were others like it. Each check was returned uncashed, with a note of thanks.

In Tulsa, Coppola made a world for the cast of *The Outsiders*. "From day one," C. Thomas Howell said, "Francis created this competitive environment." Separated into their fictional gangs, the scrappy Greasers and the uptown Socs, Coppola booked his actors into the Excelsior Hotel by class: the Socs got the top floor, and Greasers the third. The Socs were given beautifully engraved leather-bound scripts, a cushy per diem, and cool sweat suits. "It worked brilliantly," Howell said. "They treated us like scum, so when we started filming, the animosity was already there." Coppola, a former camp counselor, gave the Soc guys a long leash: they sweet-talked housekeeping into getting keys to all the hotel rooms; they short-sheeted beds, put honey on Diane Lane's toilet seat and "REDRUM"-ed her mirror in lipstick, and all of it, Lane said, "was being nurtured by Francis."

He was spending less time in his video trailer, which the cast had memorably named the Silverfish. "After the experience of *One from the Heart*," Coppola said, "I decided that I preferred being right in front of the actors so they could see me."

It worked. Life happened. "We would have walked through fire for each other," Rob Lowe said. "We were absolute brothers."

One night in the hotel, Lowe and a few others caught *The Godfather* on TV. "I know you hear this all the time," Lowe told Coppola, "but I have to tell you, we all got together and watched it in my room. And it's just amazing."

"Ehhhh. Robbie, you know what *The Godfather* is to me? *The Godfather* is to me the experience I had while I made it."

He had transformed a cluster of classrooms allotted to him by the local high school into the next incarnation of Zoetrope Studios' War Room, setting up what he called an electronic blackboard for the storyboards he captured on video. As he had in previsualization, he then replaced those storyboards with video of the actors shot before a blue screen and invited the cast to come watch. "We got to sit on the floor together and watch our best efforts on the screen," Lane said. "I doubt I was the only one who saw mostly room for improvement: more emotional courage, less safety against 'looking uncool.' Had we not gotten to do and watch that embryonic, school play version, Francis would not have gotten as much trust from us as he got."

Tavoularis said one day to Coppola, "We could make a studio here . . ."

Coppola smiled and sang, "Zo-klahoma . . ."

A mere two weeks after he wrapped *The Outsiders*, figuring that "as much production as I could get would be good," Coppola began *Rumble Fish*, also based on a novel by S. E. Hinton, with most of the previous film's cast and crew—quite suddenly, a small repertory company.

Rumble Fish—which ranks with Coppola's most exciting work and most successful adventures in filmmaking—was, he said, an art film for kids. "I find, as I am now pushing forty-five," he said, "all the more precious to me is to make sure that the young people inherit the cinema."

In October 1982, holders of the fourth deed of trust on Zoetrope Studios, Security Pacific National Bank, filed a notice of default on Zoetrope's $8,162,881.45 in unpaid loans. The bank gave Coppola until January 14 to find a buyer for the lot, or it would commence foreclosure.

Coppola wrote, "I feel once again paralyzed in a room watching *The Children's Hour* and listening to *Let's Pretend*, and yearning to be with the children." Cocooning in Napa, at his writing desk, he faced the failure of Zoetrope on a scale greater than it or he had ever known.

In December 1982, he opened a new notebook and wrote under "Central Idea," "Energy Art Death Rebirth"; and under "The Times," "A world on the brink of destruction and rebirth."

He saw a character who is himself destruction and rebirth, apocalypse and dream; a character like Catiline, a story like the Catilinarian conspiracy of 63 B.C., a man against the system. Coppola scoured his library, his books of Roman history, Tennyson ("For I dipt into the future, far as human eye could see, / Saw the vision of the world, and all the wonder that would be"), *The Shape of Things to Come*, Hesse's *The Glass Bead Game*, *The Power Broker*, Oscar Wilde ("A map of the world that does not include Utopia is not worth even glancing at"), imagining "an epic about today that deals with the theme of utopia . . . a word whose time has come. We used to make fun of it, and we all know that the word utopia in Greek means nowhere."

Come February 1983, with the banks waiting outside his door, he was discovering his character Catalina. He was a builder of cities. Catilina, he dictated, "goes to a number of friends who would be in a position to guarantee his loans. And right now at that time nobody wants to extend themselves. He goes to Coleman King, who can't help him at this time, so that slowly in the course of the film [Catilina] literally goes broke and is filled with a tremendous amount of bitterness as to the nature of the debt and how he came to be stuck with it and about the subject of debt in general. He feels in some way you are cultivated for debt and you are made a casualty of the system. So he does become something of an Iago or evil force for part of the way this thing is going to be set up. At one point he kind of walks out on some type of negotiation and basically expresses himself regarding the subject of debt and walks out at the middle of [the] negotiation, which is a surefire indication that he's going to lose everything. But he has his good name."

In Los Angeles, they were packing up Zoetrope Studios.

"Everything in his life is in transition," he dictated. "It's being put in boxes, and the people who have the boxes weren't getting paid so the boxes are sort of where they were."

Items would be auctioned.

"But kind of, it takes on a *Sullivan's Travels* tone in that rather than be upset about the bankruptcy or the loss of his luxuries, he still sees it as a game. And what a wonderful opportunity to see the world from another point of view, that perhaps he's failed so dramatically it will get—it isn't because of the—maybe the late nights and orgies and the drugs as so many of his close friends suggest—he thinks it's not that, but perhaps that he . . . designing out of poverty will be the opportunity."

The Cotton Club. He would do it—with old Paramount foe Robert Evans, also down on his luck—for the money.

"He sees it now almost with a wrath or an anger at the city, at the society that he would redesign or die in the trying. Of course, he's sort of disturbed and has this obsessive, manic personality that more and more believes that he can do it and pursues it as if it were a secret plot. In fact, there are things about it that become attractive to people at that time. And there begins to be something of a following."

The bank granted Coppola a reprieve. He had until February 28, 1983. Then—reprieved again—to March. Then to April.

The day came: still, no buyer had stepped forward. Coppola, in Santa Fe for *The Spirit of Zoetrope*, a three-day retrospective of films and symposia, now had until May to sell the lot. "Obviously genuine support and admiration expressed by a capacity audience so won him over and buoyed his spirits," reported film historian William K. Everson from Santa Fe, "that he remained the proverbial pussycat for the rest of the festival, launching into his assigned lectures and intros with zest and enthusiasm, and making himself available beyond the call of duty to anyone—reporter and fan alike—who collared him in a theater lobby or restaurant." Heading toward a festival party at two in the morning, Coppola was glimpsed soaring a Jeep down a one-way street in the wrong direction.

On May 23, 1983, he received his tenth reprieve. He now had until May 27, four days, to find a buyer for the lot.

On May 26, a day before the next scheduled auction, Coppola bought an electronic editing system, Montage Picture Processor, for Zoetrope Studios.

As Coppola's loan, its interest growing with every reprieve, rose to $10 million, he won Zoetrope its eleventh reprieve. He now had until June 16 to find a buyer. On June 1, a Zoetrope spokesperson told *Variety* the studio "is very optimistic."

His eyes trained on the horizon, Coppola would executive-produce, for Zoetrope Studios, Paul Schrader's *Mishima: A Life in Four Chapters*. Mishima Coppola saw as "the ultimate artistic hero. Everything you always wanted to define, he tried to define once and for all. . . . And on that final day of his life"—a suicide Mishima directed like theater—"he turned it all into an act of art." But Coppola was in no position to make the movie on his own. That's why they called George Lucas; and why Lucas, more comfortable lending his name than a dollar, stepped in. "What attracted me to *Mishima* was friendship," he would write, "a group of friends were having a problem getting the film off the ground." He'd *command* a studio to make it.

"I have one idea," Lucas told *Mishima* producer Tom Luddy, "which is Warner Bros."

"Aren't they the Evil Empire?" Luddy asked, invoking the studio's pummeling of *THX 1138* and the subsequent first death of American Zoetrope.

"That's the reason. I think they'd like to bury the hatchet with me."

At Warner, he met with old faces Ted Ashley and John Calley. He asked for $2.5 million.

"If we do this, George, will we be doing you a favor?"

"Yes, you will."

"It's funny," Lucas wrote, "because the kinds of films I was doing early in my career, like *THX 1138*, are much more like *Mishima*, directed towards an avant-garde, adult audience." *Return of the Jedi*, top box-office film of that year, would gross, in 1983 alone, over $300 million.

Coppola's twelfth reprieve was set for July 1, the thirteenth for July 8, the fourteenth for the twenty-second, the fifteenth for the twenty-eighth.

Coppola began production of *The Cotton Club* in August in New York.

It was after the eighteenth reprieve that Jack Singer, fearing the sale of the lot would not be sufficient to return him his investment, filed an involuntary Chapter 11, despite Spiotta's claims that this time Zoetrope was "very close to consummating a sale" to an unnamed individual or individuals outside Hollywood for just below Zoetrope's original asking price of $20 million. In fact, Zoetrope did have buyers: financier Robert Sonnenblick and producer Jerry Kramer, for $17.5 million. "There's no deal," Singer countered. "I'm not accepting the deal as of now. Zoetrope can accept it, but that doesn't mean that I have to accept it." The $17.5 million sale—to Sonnenblick and Kramer—went into escrow.

The phone rang in an empty Zoetrope office on the lot. Michael Lehmann, good to the last drop, happened to be nearby and picked it up. "Hello?"

"Who is this?"

"Michael."

"Good. Michael, it's Francis. I want you to take every bit of equipment. And I want you to rent a truck. And I want you to take it off the lot and drive it up to Napa."

"You want me to do what?"

"Take everything."

"But they've already started putting inventory stickers—do I take those too?"

"Fuck yes."

Lehmann did as requested. Late at night, it was Gio who gathered up his father's Zeiss high-speed lenses. When they made their own movies, Coppola thought, he wanted those for his children.

Bob Spiotta resigned in October 1983. A week later, Sonnenblick and Kramer failed to meet the agreed-upon terms, and the sale fell through, and on February 10, 1984, Hollywood General Studios, appraised at $16.8 million, was once and for all put up for auction. The starting bid was $12.2 million, and the studio was sold—for $12.3 million, insufficient to cover Zoetrope's debts—to Jack Singer. His son Alan renamed the lot Hollywood

Center Studios. "We're not going to be making movies ourselves," Alan Singer announced. "It's going to be a rental lot, basically."

Two weeks later, at the door of the Harold Lloyd Bungalow, Jack Singer put up a brass plaque with his name on it, and the last Zoetrope employees vacated the lot. They left behind equipment and props, wardrobe, Matt Dillon's leather jacket—the one with the bullet hole—from *The Outsiders*; fictional *Time* magazine covers with Brando as Colonel Kurtz; back issues of *City Magazine*; street signs for Raoul Walsh Alley, Piazza Nino Rota, and Dorothy Arzner Avenue; 35 mm prints of *The Conversation*; a *Godfather II* work print; neon miniatures from *One from the Heart*; and furniture originally meant for Francis and Eleanor Coppola's Hancock Park home on June Street, a few blocks from the studio.

The Coppolas' apartment at the Sherry-Netherland in New York was put up for sale for $700,000, and the starting bid for the Sentinel Building was set at $1.7 million.

A month later, on March 12, 1984, Coppola completed his first draft of *Megalopolis*.

The Shape of Things to Come

"You speak of the city whose foundation we have been describing, which has its being in words; for there is no spot on earth, I imagine, where it exists."

"No," I said; "but perhaps it is laid up in heaven as a pattern for him who wills to see, and seeing, to found a city in himself. Whether it exists anywhere or ever will exist, is no matter."

—PLATO, *REPUBLIC*

Mnmnmnmnmnmnmnnnnnnnnnnnnnmnmnnnnmnm

There is a hum in the studio, miles from Atlanta, ten thousand feet in the air over "New Rome," imagined city of *Megalopolis*; it is the hum of millions of LED lights, nearly 360 degrees of computer-generated sunset in heavenly pinks and blues and far-off city skyscrapers shining gold beneath the clouds.

The year off camera is 2023. Francis Ford Coppola is eighty-four. Sitting alone, to the side of the stage, he wears a suit and tie and, in his lapel, a rose as pink as the sky over New Rome. This is how he begins each day: arriving on the set early to think more about *Megalopolis*, the movie he had been thinking about for forty years. It was never too late a for a new idea.

"I'm not making the film," he says. "It's making itself."

Mnmnmnmnmnmnmn. The sound of thinking, or savoring; of waiting for "the volume," new filmmaking technology created to create, with a click, a heaven or hell or new world in between.

So, Coppola waits. Having waited for forty years and spent over one hundred million of his own dollars, he is in no rush. That's why he's sold the winery and footed the bill himself—so he didn't have to call Action for the executives, but for his movie, for *his* future; so he could, at last, sit alone and gaze out at the digital firmament, nodding at the ideas as they passed through his awareness at their own pace. He is in no rush.

"I'm so happy," he says, showing his open palms, "which can get me in trouble."

After he lost Zoetrope Studios, Coppola, in terrible debt, was forced into directing for hire, working for money. All the while, he kept notes on the destruction of his dream. By December 1985—the year his Niebaum-Coppola Winery released its first vintage of Rubicon, almost seven years in the making—he had amassed five volumes of notes; they would form the emotional foundation of *Megalopolis*. "What little fortune they had, [Catilina] lost in those tempestuous years from 1972 to '79," Coppola wrote. And it had been true of Zoetrope: ". . . That was when [The Design Authority] was at its most ambitious. There was a school interconnected with the design studio and architectural firm. [Catilina] had modeled it on Walter Gropius' Bauhaus. Except the students' garden and cafe, and the screening rooms and library began to take up more of his time and energy and money than the jobs that theoretically were going to pay for it all. . . . He ran the company like a summer theater company where everybody loved everybody and loved working with each other."

And: "There were no friends now. . . . Oh there were those architects, doing well now. He'd run into them at Mortimer's or the Oyster House, and there'd be the obligatory embrace, extra hard so he'd feel how much he meant to them. They were all trading on his association now, rich and written about everywhere, while he was scratching in the dirt for a job. How exotic the feelings they produced in him. Trying not to sound like he was down, or hurting. They were so patronizing, railing at the press for the unfair treatment of [The Design Authority] . . . But the more they consoled him, and treated him as though he was not a 'has been,' the more he felt like one. It filled him with an acidy shame, the shame a little boy feels when he pees in his pants in first grade. Everyone looking at him, laughing at him, even overreaching, society's worst sin, punishable [by] everything, everywhere. Ten worst lists, snubs at banquets, cooling bank credit, mistreatment by former subordinates. But he could endure the insults, the professional demotement [*sic*], the boos and bad reviews. What he couldn't stand was the drying up of the money."

Nineteen eighty-six, *Peggy Sue Got Married* . . . ; 1987, *Gardens of Stone* . . . He was lost. "I would say, even though I don't understand it 100 percent or even 50 percent, that those movies made after my attempt to found my studio very much show my desire to find out my own place. Where should I go? What should I do?"

Memorial Day 1986, early in the production of *Gardens of Stone*.

"The telephone rang," Eleanor would write. "Sofia answered it downstairs and I picked up the extension. We both heard the strange, strangled sound of Francis's voice, as if he were speaking without breathing. 'Ellie, we've lost our beloved son. Gio is dead.'"

On location with Coppola, supervising the Electronic Cinema division, he was killed in a boating accident.

"That night Sofia and I flew to Washington, D.C.," Eleanor wrote. "The next days are memory fragments."

The film—set among the ceremonial burials of fallen soldiers, about "a man," Coppola would say, "mourning his son"—would continue, though Coppola, its director, was no longer directing as himself. His every experience, his every thought, he could not complete. Still, he insisted on working. But with what life? For the first time, he could not bear to use his own. "After that, I realized that no matter what happened, I had *lost*. That no matter what happened, it would always be incomplete. The next day, I could have all my fondest dreams come true: Someone could give me Paramount Pictures to organize the way I would do it and develop talent and technology. And even if I did get it, I lost already." He would wake up dreamless, staring at his walls, wanting nothing. Nothing but Gio. He was a very serious kid, Coppola would say, "a serious kid of the cinema."

Like George Lucas on *Finian's Rainbow*, the young apprentices of *Megalopolis*, some from Europe, another from North Carolina, were asked to add something of themselves to the film and its satellite projects. One had shot and edited a music video; another was acting; others, pen pals of Coppola's for years, were assisting filmmaker Mike Figgis on his documentary about the production. Between takes, Coppola leaned on their eyes and ears and filled them with thoughts and images from the film.

"Would you rather have a million friends or a million dollars?" he asked them. "Really *think* about it. There's a lot you could do with a million dollars . . ."

Encircled by the digital heaven of pink and blue, he told a new young friend the story of *Megalopolis*, why he was making it. He invited her to ask him questions about the story, the future, how we could build cities to better secure the essential human priorities, learning, creating, developing, celebrating . . .

"Would people work in the future? Would there be war?" She was asking, it turned out, the same questions he was asking of himself.

"Have you ever been in love?"

She had, yes.

"Look up there." He motioned up to the high-hanging beams where the characters would kiss thousands of feet over the city of dreams. "This is what it feels like to kiss someone you love for the first time. In other words, even if that kiss happens on a subway, you're still ten thousand feet in the air . . . metaphorically . . ."

The man, played by Adam Driver, is Catiline, master builder. The woman, played by Nathalie Emmanuel, is Julia, daughter of his enemy.

"It is important," Coppola adds, "that they don't wear harnesses when they're shooting so they can have the feeling when they kiss that they really can fall . . ."

In 1987, George Lucas and Coppola were contemplating the giant oak tree in front of Coppola's big yellow house in Napa. Lucas "was at the height of his success," Coppola said, "and I was at the height of my failure . . ." when Lucas came to his old friend's rescue to produce *Tucker: A Man and His Dream*, written and directed by Coppola.

"Now *that*," Lucas said, "is a great tree."

"It's between 300 and 900 years old," Coppola said. "I think it likes to be talked to. I talk to it." He embraced the tree, his arms failing to take in the entirety of its impossibly large trunk. "Hello, tree"—and with hardly a pause—"what would you do if somebody gave you $2 billion?"

Lucas grinned at the question and allowed Coppola to proceed.

"I'd use it as leverage to borrow $30 billion, and do something *really* big. Maybe build a city that really works. I went to see Brasília once; I was fascinated by what I'd read about it. And here were all these dead, monumental buildings. Nothing for *people*. Cities have to be built for people."

Lucas laughed. "Yeah, Francis, and then it would go bust and this time you'd *have* to go into bankruptcy and lose it all."

"Yeah, maybe. But . . . maybe *not*."

In 1988, he declared that Zoetrope was "a solvent company totally out of debt."

That year, he was in Cinecittà, in Rome, a city that reminded him of his old studio. Could the future be found back here, at the birthplace of Western civilization?

"We want to cooperate with Coppola in helping him carry out the important experiment he started with Zoetrope Studios in Los Angeles," said Ettore Pasculli, director of technology.

That first $35 million version of *Megalopolis* Coppola would shoot on Cinecittà stages in Sony high-definition video. The story was of "a vision of the future," he said, a utopia "in which the priorities of life are ritual, celebration and art."

The film was not made.

He said, "I do not think that dream of mine is ever going to be given me—that dream of having a company along studio lines . . ." Maybe, he thought, Sony "could make a dream studio from the old MGM lot." After all, Sony had the technology. "That's what the human fate is," he said. "The technology's gonna do all the work," so we can create.

In 1989, Coppola reconstituted Zoetrope, and Jack Singer reappeared with a vengeance. Coppola, he claimed, owed him $6 million—that is, payment on 1981's $3 million loan with interest. Coppola, caught, agreed to a deal he said he never would, to cowrite, with Mario Puzo, coproduce, and direct *Godfather III*, for $6 million and a percentage of the gross.

"I just made *Godfather III* the way I felt about things," he said, "and in a way, put myself in Michael Corleone's shoes." He was, he thought, evermore Michael, not as a criminal, "but as a person who had gone really from a sort of innocent guy, just loved movies, into something involving power and influence," adding, "as with all characters—Mr. Kurtz, Mr. Tucker, Mr. Corleone—I have tremendous personal feelings myself that I might be like them." In the case of *Godfather III*, it was the quicksand of debt, personal and otherwise. "Just as Michael feels anxious to want to get on with your life and to mature and to try to be a better man, a better artist, you get pulled back into something of your youth," he explained. "The past is always having a war with the future. I find I try so hard to be in the future and to think of new things, and new thoughts, and always I'm pulled back by the past." When, if ever, would the debt be paid? The film would end with the murder of Michael Corleone's daughter, Mary. "For Michael just to die for his sins—it's gotta be worse than that. Worse than that would be to put some innocent kid in the position of being the hope of the family, of getting out of the mire of the parents and going on and having a beautiful future—the death of a daughter would be a far worse punishment."

The decision to cast Sofia to play Mary—a last-minute replacement for Winona Ryder—was immediately a controversial one. On location in Rome, Coppola, sitting in the Silverfish, turned to face Richard Beggs. Friends and coworkers for fifteen years, both had lost children.

"You know why I did it, Richard," Coppola said.

In January 1990—with Coppola in Italy filming *Godfather III*—a Los Angeles Superior Court judge ordered him to pay Singer $3 million; he also set a hearing to settle the matter of interest owed to Singer, which would raise Coppola's liability to $8 million, and required Coppola to post a $12 million bond in order to pursue an appeal.

"*Godfather III* will give us a great shot in the arm to subsidize our operation," Francis declared optimistically, "and when it is finished we will return to *Megalopolis*."

Coppola and Zoetrope Productions—a new venture launched in 1984 after Coppola sold the studio to Singer—filed for federal bankruptcy protection. According to the filing, Zoetrope Productions had $28.8 million in debts and $22.1 million in assets. In February, Coppola was ordered to pay Singer $4.8 million in interest, which brought the total owed to nearly $8 million. The *Variety* headline read, "Apocalypse Now, Chapter 11."

In September, to celebrate the completion of *Godfather III*, George Lucas invited Francis, Eleanor, Sofia, Roman, Al Pacino, Talia Shire, Carmine, and others to his ranch for an all-day screening of the entire *Godfather* saga. "It was very emotional to see the movie again on a big screen," Eleanor wrote after the screening of Part I, "to watch film events so interwoven with my real life, and especially to see Sofia, the baby baptized at the end." Her own real-life film, the forgotten sixty hours of footage and forty hours of audiotape she amassed during the filming of *Apocalypse Now*, had that year gone to filmmakers George Hickenlooper and Fax Bahr. They would make her material into a documentary, *Hearts of Darkness: A Filmmaker's Apocalypse*, using for voiceover selections from Eleanor's book *Notes*, read by the author herself. It had been Francis's idea to incorporate the book—previously an embarrassment to him—into the film. Visiting the editing room, watching the footage she shot ten years before, Eleanor recalled the ways in which, despite everything, she treasured the *Apocalypse* experience, "a time," she wrote, "when the boundaries of my thoughts and feelings were stretched in ways I had never imagined possible." With Hickenlooper and Bahr she would win an Emmy for directing. "I could hardly separate my own memories from the drama of the film," Eleanor wrote of watching *Godfather II* that afternoon at George Lucas's ranch. "I felt an ache seeing a forgotten moment when I was an extra on the boat of immigrants headed for Ellis Island with two-year-old Sofia on my lap and Gio and Roman beside me." After the screening of *Godfather III*, she wrote, "I felt Francis's deep relief."

Weeks earlier, he had at last settled with Jack Singer and had already begun to settle his debt—approximately $7 million—with funds Paramount had advanced him against future profits from *Godfather III*, "a story," Coppola said, "about an old man who is dying and is asking to be redeemed to some extent."

"I was *dying*," he had confessed, while making *Godfather III*.

In Atlanta, living *Megalopolis*, he was building—a few miles from the studio where his character Catilina was building the future—a small hotel for movie people. Its every facet was, like Catilina's dream of the perfect society, novel and evolving and ideal; there would be the requisite bedrooms and restaurant, postproduction facilities for editors, fitting rooms for actors and costumers, and a screening room for all. Though the project was incomplete—hard hats were still required in what was going to become the lobby—Coppola and his inner circle, including Zoetrope's Masa Tsuyuki, Anahid Nazarian, and Roman Coppola, would live and work there throughout *Megalopolis*.

*   *   *

According to one headline, Coppola's follow-up to *Godfather III*, *Bram Stoker's Dracula*, would "raise Zoetrope from [the] dead." Released in 1992, only months after he, Eleanor, and parent company Zoetrope Corp. filed for bankruptcy—a third time for Coppola—*Dracula* was an enormous, spectacular hit: $35 million in its first five days, a Columbia record, earning a total of $200 million worldwide.

"Maybe," he said, "I can buy back my studio."

Instead, Coppola transformed his private hideaway in Belize into a public resort—his first of many—and reincarnated Zoetrope. It was smaller this time, perhaps truer to Coppola's original inclination, not as an alternative to Hollywood, but a complement. Solvent again, he now wanted "to be improving my base with Hollywood and the film industry in general."

His films *Jack* and *The Rainmaker* did not approach his potential; it was the films of filmmaker Sofia Coppola, first with *The Virgin Suicides* in 1999, and then *Lost in Translation* four years later, that reinstated Zoetrope to the cultural fore. Working economically and intimately, with a premium of personal and creative freedom, Sofia Coppola thrived as her father stood proudly by.

Growing all the time, his Niebaum-Coppola Estate Winery had become a multimillion-dollar success, but what Coppola most wanted was to return to his beginning, to shed dead skins—director for hire, showman, communications chief—and salvage, through cinema, an innermost self. Come the new millennium, and annual wine profits estimated at just under $100 million, the film he really wanted to make, *Megalopolis*, was, he felt, still out of his range; perhaps, like utopia itself, better left to the imagination. So it was that the cycle of *Youth Without Youth*, *Tetro*, *Twixt* (2007–11), he said, "ended a certain period . . . where I was going to 'destroy myself.'" Casting aside all his so-called "knowledge" of film, he did: the cycle was unsuccessful by some counts, but as a personal experiment, reviving his love of experimentation, it was a triumph, reviving him. At last, he was, once again, Francis Ford Coppola, amateur.

Like a film student, he was making his living not on art, but on his businesses, wine, food, hospitality, and passing the profits from one hand to the other, fulfilling the original dream of Zoetrope, to make personal films outside the system. Forty years later, he continued to admonish himself for his "fatal mistake: to set up an ambitious change to how movies are made, and ultimately not doing it, which is why that, truthfully, as I am *vicino-morte* now, I only have one regret, one real personal decision I regret, which is not making *One from the Heart* the way I had planned to," as Live Cinema. "The other regret," he said, "isn't mine alone but my amazing generation which didn't leave the Cinema in better condition for the next generation."

In 2015 and 2016, while Hollywood, as he had predicted decades earlier, became electronic, he made good on the original promise of *One from the Heart* and conducted two successful proof-of-concept experiments in Live Cinema. His findings he published in 2017 as *Live Cinema and Its Techniques*, a primer, one hopes, for successive generations.

Adam Driver and Nathalie Emmanuel were called in to block their kiss, to negotiate, like tightrope walkers, the crisscrossing beams hanging over the digital skyline. She was to approach, timidly, with flowers; he was to take her up into his arms; and with feeling commensurate to the LED sunset, they were to passionately kiss. But there were unexpected problems. Her high-heeled shoes, the cables, his height, their balance. Do they lower the beam? Hurry their lines?

After an adjustment to the beam, the actors ran the scene again. Clumsily encumbered, they stumbled and, distressed, looked down for direction. *Mnmnmnmnmnmnmn . . .*

Coppola, sitting against the digital clouds, was looking up. "I don't care if it takes three hours to block this scene," he answered calmly. "If we don't get the shot today, we don't get the shot today."

Everything they needed was at hand.

"We're not going to hurry," Coppola assured them. They would get there. *Mnmnmnmnmnmnmnmnmnmnmnmnmnmnmn . . .*

How long had he waited? Giving more than he had to give, how far had he gone? In his half century of Hollywood, none had adventured farther, experimented and become more. None had battled as completely. In victory and in defeat, he was the map of history, the next idea. Heaven, he held its compass for those who dreamed the furthest. What wonders lay ahead, they would find together.

Acknowledgments

Paradise—

"For the artist," August Coppola wrote, "the process is an approach to life, a mystery, a sacred human experience." The audience, ideally, finds them in the product.

The painter enjoys his paradise alone, and his audience is restricted by access to his product. But for the filmmaker, whose process invites a veritable studio of personnel, the paradise is actual, and his product, reproduced and disseminated to a mass audience worldwide, can spread his sacred experience to more and farther.

By no means have I finished interviewing those who have worked for or with or observed Zoetrope. But the process can't go on forever. Or can it, Andy Aaron, George Altamura, Dan Attias, Jean Autrey, Carroll Ballard, Peter Bart, Ronee Blakely, Jeff Berg, Mark Berger, Richard Beggs, Armyan Bernstein, Jim Bloom, Joanie Blum, Peter Bogdanovich, Benjamin Breslauer, Adrienne Brodeur, Paul Broucek, Thomas Brown, Arden Bucklin-Sporer, April Calou, Colleen Camp, Kathy Campbell, Richard Candib, Randy Carter, Aleta Chappelle, Richard Chew, Doug Claybourne, Aurore Clément, Arthur Coburn, Martha Coolidge, Gary Copeland, Eleanor Coppola, Francis Ford Coppola, Gia Coppola, Roman Coppola, Sofia Coppola, Roger Corman, Ben Cowitt, Martha Cronin, Larry Cuba, Robert Dalva, Rose

Deleon, Stel Deleon, Ceci Dempsey, Caleb Deschanel, Tony Dingman, Bob Dolman, Wendy Doniger, Peter Dornbach, Teri Dovidio, Mitch Dubin, Kevin Dwan, Bob Eberlein, Donald Elmblad, Robert Evans, Linda Feferman, Gary Fettis, Mike Figgis, Susie Landau Finch, Lucy Fisher, Sue Fox, Nancy Foy, Gray Frederickson, Karen Frerichs, Jack Fritz, Lisa Fruchtman, Fred Fuchs, Eva Gardos, Miranda Garrison, Dennis Gassner, Crystal Gayle, Bernard Gersten, Cora Gersten, Jenny Gersten, Jilian Gersten, Aaron Glascock, Dan Gleich, Carl Gottlieb, Anne Goursaud, Javier Grajeda, Sandra Gray, Jerry Greenberg, Gary Gutierrez, Jeff Hamlin, Trudy Hamm, Tess Haley, Douglas Hemphill, Marilu Henner, Lynn Hershman, Werner Herzog, Clark Higgins, Barry Hirsch, Janet Hirshenson, Dustin Hoffman, Tim Holland, Richard Hollander, Ron Howard, Ann Humphrey, Anjelica Huston, Pat Jackson, Nancy Jencks, Jane Jenkins, Roy Johns, Lynnea Johnson, Cynthia Kania, Jay Kantor, Pam Kaye, Lainie Kazan, Jill Kearney, Harvey Keitel, Patricia Ward Kelly, Robert Kensinger, Michael Kirchberger, Colin Michael Kitchens, Kathy Kloves, Ed Lachman, Alan Ladd Jr., Clifford Latimer, Chris Lebenzon, Louise Ledeen, Sharon F. Lee, Michael Lehmann, Stephen Lighthill, Leana Lovejoy, Tom Luddy, David Macmillan, Colette Madison, Michelle Manning, Jim Mansen, Steve Martin, Mike Medavoy, Dorothy Meriwether, Lillian Michelson, Andy Moore, Rebecca De Mornay, Aggie Murch, Walter Murch, Anahid Nazarian, Rick Nicita, Kenny Ortega, Laura Parker, Alexander Payne, Linda Phillips, David Picker, Dale Pollock, Yoshiko Poncher, Matthew Robbins, Janet Robbins, Bobby Rock, Cecilia Rodarte, Franc Roddam, Aggie Rodgers, Sherry Rogers, Susan Rogers, Fred Roos, Jerry Ross, Edward Rugoff, Sondra Scerca, Arne Schmidt, Paul Schrader, Anne Schwabel, Talia Schwartzman, Stephen Semel, Michael Shamberg, Jennifer Shull, Frank Simeone, Mona Skager, Alvy Ray Smith, Sonia Socher, Peter Sorel, John Solomon, Christian Spiotta, Dana Spiotta, Emy Spiotta, Roger Spottiswoode, Tom Sternberg, George Stevens Jr., Sara Strom, Dale Strumpell, Dan Suhart, Robin Supak, Holland Sutton, Bob Swarthe, Nan Talese, Alex Tavoularis, Dean Tavoularis, Stacy Thal, Randy Thom, Serena Tripi, Masa Tsuyuki, Jim Turner, Harry Ufland, Gary Ventimiglia, Jack Walsh, Steve Wax, April Webster, Gary Weimberg, Wim Wenders, and Karen Wilson? Thank you all for letting me in and showing me around. It was, if you can believe it, even better than I imagined.

And I always did imagine. Ever since Michael Lehmann and Holland Sutton first told me what sounded like fairy tales of Zoetrope Studios. Looking back, it seems I've spent a large part of my life gathering and fact-checking their memories. Could such a place really exist? What is the path? (Have we lost it?) To anyone who recognizes the artistic, social, cultural, financial, and political value of a movie studio, these are essential questions. Answered or not, they must be asked, and—by some of us, religiously—asked again.

This book is dedicated to two people who, while researching and writing it, I thought about constantly, whose influence guided me even when they themselves weren't physically present, like the *One from the Heart* singing voices of Tom Waits and Crystal Gayle: they are my friend and editor Noah Eaker and my friend and Ding-bat Jenny Gersten (thank you for Jenny, Rick Pappas). To Noah and Jenny I owe the happiest writing experience I've ever had, what felt to me like a feast-day parade four years long.

Every parade must have a drummer. Mine was Anahid Nazarian, producer and Zoetrope librarian-archivist. In addition to making a home for me at the research table, she gave me what she may not have known I needed, the trust and therefore the confidence to face a subject as sprawling and wondrous as Zoetrope. By her side (and mine) were Courtney Garcia, Masa Tsuyuki, and James Mockoski. Thank you all for your patience and expertise, and on more than one occasion, lunch.

Apropos research: To the team at the Margaret Herrick Library in Los Angeles, thank you, foremost, essential accomplices Louise Hilton and Elizabeth Youle. And thank you, Maitlyn Fletcher, for your assistance and great company. And Edie Astley for lending a hand and saving the day.

More than thank you to my agent who is more than an agent. David Halpern, your greatness sets you apart. And alongside David, thank you, my pals Kathy Robbins, Janet Oshiro, and the gang at The Robbins Office.

To those close to me who lent their time, passion, and minds to this undertaking, Jeanine Basinger, Maria Diaz, Lynne Littman, Brandon Millan, Lorraine Nicholson, Cindy Wasson, Jeffrey Wasson, and Sophie Wasson.

To Eleanor Coppola, whose *Notes: On the Making of Apocalypse Now*, written with the wisdom and poetry of an artist-teacher, has been a North Star to me long before I started this or any book. So admiring am I of that work, its candid approach to some of my life's own themes, I was embarrassed to meet her in person. But over the course of our conversations, rather than acclimate to her startling clarity and openness, I found myself increasingly speechless at her willingness to proceed into waters I myself was afraid to swim.

To Francis Ford Coppola, who said, "Any friend of Jenny's is a friend of mine," and waved me into his office, who made me espresso, poured me tequila, ice water, and wine, served me dinner, thoughtfully answered my every question ("Ask me something you think no one has ever asked me before"), implored me to ask more, take more, come back, speak further, think further, think bigger, think for myself, who sang old Broadway songs, who smiled as I sang back, who sang to his grandchildren, who sang to Roger Corman when he came to celebrate their joint birthdays, who played the ukulele, who mused harmonically on Hesse, Kerouac, Proust, *A Dream of Red Mansions*, who beamed when I accidentally called him professor, who sat beside me at the library and asked if I had discovered anything interesting, who made *Apocalypse Now*, *One from the Heart*, and keeps making American Zoetrope, who emailed (on April 27, 2020) when I asked him where does the Zoetrope story begin and where does it end, "My one word of advice is to try to make it about a company or idea rather than a person. After all, all I ever really wanted was to be one of the group which required that the group be born!," whom I first met (though he could never remember) when I saw him, in scarf and fedora, just sitting there outside his café at the bottom of the Sentinel Building over twenty years ago. Then I knew him only as the director of *The Godfather* and the Hollywood Ahab of *One from the Heart*. Like a fool, I interrupted him at his dinner. Like a fool, I asked, though I asked with my whole heart, "Zoetrope Studios—what happened?" I hadn't even said hello. But without hesitation, without even a question back, this semi-imagined man I had never met set his real wine on the bistro table, looked up to a memory in the sky, and said, as if to me, "It's an interesting story . . ."

Sam Wasson
Los Angeles, 2023

Notes

THE FRANCIS FORD COPPOLAS

1   "The friends that have it": William Butler Yeats, *The Collected Works in Verse and Prose of William Butler Yeats* (Charleston, SC: BiblioLife, 2009).

3   "I am *vicino-morte*": Francis Ford Coppola, author interview (henceforth AI).

4   "My technique for making film": Francis Ford Coppola, AI.

4   recognizes his new self in the mirror of the movie: Eleanor Coppola, AI.

5   "Ready!": Masa Tsuyuki, reported by author.

6   The world had changed suddenly: Francis Ford Coppola, AI.

7   "This is a wonderful plum": Francis Ford Coppola, reported by author.

7   "Here is the architect": Francis Ford Coppola, reported by author.

7   "What do you think?": Francis Ford Coppola, reported by author.

7   "What is that *book* you're reading?": Francis Ford Coppola, reported by author.

7   That wasn't the way: Francis Ford Coppola, reported by author.

I: THE DREAM

9   "The Modern Utopia": H. G. Wells, *A Modern Utopia* (New York: Charles Scribner's Sons, 1905), 5.

12   *O bella età d'inganni e d'utopie!*: *La Bohème*, libretto by Luigi Illica.

12   Coppola's "influence over people's minds": Joseph McBride, "Coppola, Inc: The Director as Godfather," *American Film*, November 1975.

13   "in a format that's incredibly inexpensive": James Harwood, "Coppola's Media Crossing," *Variety*, August 6, 1975.

13   an unusual TV idea: Francis Ford Coppola, AI.

13   "I don't need more power": McBride, "Coppola, Inc."

13   "I'm at a Y in the road": Maureen Orth, "Godfather of the Movies," *Newsweek*, November 25, 1974.

14   "a little too early for a Vietnam picture": Peter Cowie, *The Apocalypse Now Book* (New York: Da Capo Press, 2000), 6.

14   "Coppola's commercial touch": Richard Albarino, "Coppola, Top Money Filmmaker, Entering Distribution-Exhibition," *Variety*, August 21, 1974.

15   "That gave us the opportunity to go out": Barry Hirsch, AI.

15   "Whose fault is it that": Jim Harwood, "Wanted $3 Mil for 3 Weeks Work on 'Apocalypse Now'; Director Eyes Term Contracts," *Daily Variety*, February 5, 1976.

16   "Ten percent": *Apocalypse Now*, on-set transcript, American Zoetrope Library Archive.

16   "I began to see": Harwood, "Wanted $3 Mil For 3 Weeks Work on 'Apocalypse Now.'"

17   "I feel very strongly about term contracts": Harwood, "Wanted $3 Mil for 3 Weeks Work on 'Apocalypse Now.'"

17   "Every studio in this town": Harwood, "Wanted $3 Mil for 3 Weeks Work on 'Apocalypse Now.'"

17   "It won't be too long": Harlan Jacobson, "Coppola's Casting Via Term-Pact Offers for 'Apocalypse' Not Suspicion-Free," *Daily Variety*, March 10, 1976.

17   "is to develop stars": Mary Murphy, "Movie Call Sheet," *Los Angeles Times*, March 10, 1976.

18   "It's not a baseball team": Jacobson, "Coppola's Casting Via Term-Pact Offers for 'Apocalypse' Not Suspicion-Free."

18   "I think it's the right concept": Jacobson, "Coppola's Casting Via Term-Pact Offers for 'Apocalypse' Not Suspicion-Free."

18   "is mad, Marlon": Cowie, *Apocalypse Now Book*, 24.

18   "Willard starts to come apart": Cowie, *Apocalypse Now Book*, 28.

19   "We sat around in my office": Cowie, *Apocalypse Now Book*, 2.

20   "I was really thinking of [*Apocalypse Now*]": Francis Ford Coppola, *Apocalypse Now* interview, undated, American Zoetrope Library Archives.

20   "It wasn't that the script": Francis Ford Coppola, AI.

20   "an L.A. war": Francis Ford Coppola, AI.

20   "I wanted to remember it like a dream": Cowie, *Apocalypse Now Book*, 5.

20   "Best wishes for a great picture": George Lucas, March 22, 1976.

22   "With my helicopters": Michael Schumacher, *Francis Ford Coppola: A Filmmaker's Life* (New York: Crown, 1999), 207.

22   "lose a helicopter": *Hearts of Darkness: A Filmmaker's Apocalypse*, directed by Fax Bahr, George Hicken-looper, and Eleanor Coppola (1991), Triton Pictures, Paramount Home Video, 2007, DVD.

22   "if a helicopter rotor": Schumacher, *Francis Ford Coppola*, 208.

22   "burned the socks off the guy": Dick White, *Apocalypse Now* interview, undated, American Zoetrope Library Archives.

23   "I was responsible": Francis Ford Coppola, AI.

23   "lost souls": Ric Gentry, "Dean Tavoularis," *Post Script: Essays in Film and Humanities* 29 (Winter/Spring 2010): 93–100.

23   "Black smoke or white smoke?": Gentry, "Dean Tavoularis."

23   "What gets me so berserk": Francis Ford Coppola, Fred Roos, and Leon Chooluck, conversation transcript, undated, American Zoetrope Library Archives.

24   "go over there for three weeks": *Hearts of Darkness: A Filmmaker's Apocalypse*.

24   "What I do": Francis Ford Coppola, AI.

24   "Yeah, but that's fine": Francis Ford Coppola, Fred Roos, and Barry Hirsch, conversation transcript, un-dated, American Zoetrope Library Archives.

25   "I mean it'd be very easy": Francis Ford Coppola, Fred Roos, and Barry Hirsch, conversation transcript, undated, American Zoetrope Library Archives.

25   "Marlon put a very restrictive condition": Francis Ford Coppola, letter to Arthur Krim, unsent, April 10, 1976, American Zoetrope Library Archives.

26   Harvey Keitel, was miscast: Harvey Keitel, AI.

26   "His style of acting": Francis Ford Coppola, AI.

26   "sort of outward symbol": Eleanor Coppola, *Notes: On the Making of Apocalypse Now* (New York: Limelight Editions, 1991), 34.

26   most satisfying director: Silvio G. Gutierrez, "Duvall Loves the Smell of Directing," *UCLA Daily Bruin*, May 23, 1983.

26   "only do two": Francis Ford Coppola, AI.

27   "our pilots": Gray Frederickson, *Apocalypse Now* interview, undated, American Zoetrope Library Archives.

27   Coppola imagined some kid wandering: Francis Ford Coppola, AI.

27   "There's got to be a better way": Francis Ford Coppola, *Apocalypse Now Redux* interview: Peter Cowie/ Francis Ford Coppola, undated, American Zoetrope Library Archives.

28   "It's really, really Vietnam": Dick White, *Apocalypse Now* interview, undated, American Zoetrope Library Archives.

28   "a risktaker, and commanded a vision": Peter Cowie, *Coppola: A Biography* (New York: Da Capo Press, 1994), 27–28.

29   "mental milk of magnesia": Joseph Cleary with John Sack, "Apocalypse . . . At Last!" *Penthouse*, August 1979.

29   "My reality feels like foreign movie": Eleanor Coppola, *Notes: On the Making of Apocalypse Now*, 22.

29   wonderful handheld cameraperson: Francis Ford Coppola, AI.

29   "If I knew what the basic idea was": Eleanor Coppola, *Notes: On the Making of Apocalypse Now*, 35.

29   16 mm newsreel camera: Eleanor Coppola, email to author.

29   "Francis would start talking": Schumacher, *Francis Ford Coppola*, 206.

30   "That was never my strength": Eleanor Coppola, AI.

30   they were like little Instamatic snaps: Eleanor Coppola, AI.

30   *My kids are terrific*: Eleanor Coppola, *Notes: On the Making of Apocalypse Now*, 50.

30   "exhilaration of power": Eleanor Coppola, *Notes: On the Making of Apocalypse Now*, 44.

30   suffered silently: Eleanor Coppola, email to author.

31   "It was really beautiful": Eleanor Coppola, *Notes: On the Making of Apocalypse Now*, 69.

32   "You have twenty minutes to take cover": Cindy Wood, *Apocalypse Now* interview, undated, American Zoetrope Library Archives.

32   "You couldn't see an inch": Gray Frederickson, AI.

32   "hitting you so hard": *Hearts of Darkness: A Filmmaker's Apocalypse*.

32   "115-mile-an-hour winds": Scott Glenn, *Apocalypse Now* interviews 1 & 2, undated, American Zoetrope Library Archives.

32   like a 747 flying overhead: Albert Hall, *Apocalypse Now* interview, undated, American Zoetrope Library Archives.

32   "this yellowy light": Schumacher, *Francis Ford Coppola*, 209.

32   "It's bad": Cleary with Sack, "Apocalypse . . . At Last!"

32   "seemed like days and nights": Wood, *Apocalypse Now* interview.

32   "We were all losing it": Wood, *Apocalypse Now* interview.

32 "I delivered my second daughter": Eric Althoff, "Scott Glenn Used Marine Training to Help Save 'Apocalypse Now,'" *Washington Times*, April 2015.

33 "It's not possible": Vittorio Storaro, "The American Film Institute and American Society of Cinematographers Seminar with Vittorio Storaro," Center for Advanced Film Studies, 1980.

33 "Every time we went out there": Bill Graham, *Apocalypse Now* interview, undated, American Zoetrope Library Archives.

33 "I was concerned": Graham, *Apocalypse Now* interview.

33 *Apocalypse* was a demon: Graham, *Apocalypse Now* interview.

33 "typhoon was our passage": Robert Koehler, "Kurtz's Horror Almost Coppola's Waterloo," *Daily Variety*, November 11, 1997.

33 "our hallucination": Wood, *Apocalypse Now* interview.

34 "When Marty [Sheen] came home": Jean Vallely, "Martin Sheen: Heart of Darkness Heart of Gold," *Rolling Stone*, November 1, 1979.

35 "where the dream world": Eleanor Coppola, *Notes: On the Making of Apocalypse Now*, 86.

35 "don't let me be a failure": Susan Braudy, "Francis Ford Coppola: A Profile," *Atlantic*, August 1976.

35 "guarantee of the loan": Sid Adilman, "Candid, Caustic, Cost-Groggy Coppola Spanks Yank Press," *Weekly Variety*, May 23, 1979.

35 only thing worth doing in this life: Francis Ford Coppola, AI.

36 "do good with this picture": Braudy, "Francis Ford Coppola."

36 "You're supposed to be reading": Braudy, "Francis Ford Coppola."

37 "Mona acted as a screen": Colin Michael Kitchens, AI.

37 "They sent it": Jean Autrey, AI.

37 "People would complain": Jean Autrey, AI.

37 "no money down": Jean Autrey, AI.

37 "with gusto and enthusiasm": Richard Beggs, AI.

37 "right out of *Metropolis*": Richard Beggs, AI.

38 "negative would get shipped": Mitch Dubin, AI.

38 "always running the film chain": Karen Frerichs, AI.

38 "person who is supposed": Karen Frerichs, AI.

38 "That's how things": Holland Sutton, AI.

38 "just making it up": Mitch Dubin, AI.

38 "Francis said it would": Eleanor Coppola, *Notes: On the Making of Apocalypse Now*, 98.

38 "very textured soul": Commentary, *Apocalypse Now Redux*, Paramount DVD, 2006.

39 "Stanley and Livingston": Francis Ford Coppola, *Apocalypse Now* interview, tape 9, undated, American Zoetrope Library Archives.

39 "hidden levels": Greil Marcus, "Journey Up the River: An Interview with Francis Coppola," *Rolling Stone*, November 1, 1979.

39 "Marty, it's *you*": Apocalypse Now—Conversation Martin Sheen and Francis Ford Coppola, YouTube, https://www.youtube.com/watch?v=9BkChat11cE.

39 "to fuck him up": Vittorio Storaro and Francis Ford Coppola, *Apocalypse Now* interview, Francis Talks about Kurtz, Ending, tape 14A & B, undated, American Zoetrope Library Archives.

39 "isn't an honest layer": Storaro and Coppola, *Apocalypse Now* interview.

39 "I was a raving lunatic": Martin Sheen, American Film Institute interview, December 1, 1982.

40 "Marty, go look": *Hearts of Darkness: A Filmmaker's Apocalypse*.

40 "You look like a movie star": *Hearts of Darkness: A Filmmaker's Apocalypse*.

40 "Now frighten yourself, Marty": *Hearts of Darkness: A Filmmaker's Apocalypse*.

40 Nothing is faster: Martin Sheen, American Film Institute interview, December 1, 1982.

40 he had been hiding his brokenness: Martin Sheen, *Apocalypse Now* interview, undated, American Zoetrope Library Archives.

40 "Okay, cut": *Hearts of Darkness: A Filmmaker's Apocalypse*.

41 "almost nonexistent": Sheen, American Film Institute interview, December 1, 1982.

41 "He's angry with the Church": Vallely, "Martin Sheen."

41 "You fucker": *Hearts of Darkness: A Filmmaker's Apocalypse*.

41 *I want the hatred in you to come out*: Vallely, "Martin Sheen."

41 "guilt-ridden Irish Catholic": Vallely, "Martin Sheen."

41 "Think about it": *Hearts of Darkness: A Filmmaker's Apocalypse*.

41 "My heart is broken": *Hearts of Darkness: A Filmmaker's Apocalypse*.

41 "did a dangerous and terrible": Vallely, "Martin Sheen."

41 "landmark in my life": Apocalypse Now—Conversation Martin Sheen and Francis Ford Coppola, YouTube.

41 "As you go up the river": Roy G. Levin, "Francis Coppola Discusses Apocalypse Now," *Millimeter*, October 1979.

42 "Jesus loves you, Marty": Vallely, "Martin Sheen."

42 "Martin paid a lot": Vallely, "Martin Sheen."

42 "try to have a parallel story": Dennis Schaefer and Larry Salvato, *Masters of Light: Conversations with Contemporary Cinematographers* (Berkeley: University of California Press, 2013), 220.

42 "conflict between natural energy": Schaefer and Salvato, *Masters of Light*.

43   "[Willard] is falling apart": Cowie, *Apocalypse Now Book*, 66–67.
43   "metaphor is": Gentry, "Dean Tavoularis," 93–100.
43   "For Willard": "August 13 in Pagsanjan," *Apocalypse Now* transcript, undated, American Zoetrope Library Archives.
43   "We haven't, right now": "Francis and Vittorio Talk About Problems at Dolung [*sic*] Bridge," *Apocalypse Now* transcript, undated, American Zoetrope Library Archives.
43   "I think the reason is": Vittorio Storaro and Ed Lachman Master Class, Film at Lincoln Center, YouTube, https://www.youtube.com/watch?v=8RbCBMyyKkc.
44   still was a poet-prince: Eleanor Coppola, AI.
44   "doesn't happen with Francis": Vittorio Storaro, *Apocalypse Now* interview, undated, American Zoetrope Library Archives.
44   "give that kind of idea": Storaro, *Apocalypse Now* interview.
44   "Francis is, without a doubt": Stephen Burum, "A Clash of Two Cultures," *American Cinematographer*, February 2001.
44   "Remember *Paths of Glory*": Vittorio Storaro and Ed Lachman Master Class.
44   "getting into a self-indulgent pattern": *Hearts of Darkness: A Filmmaker's Apocalypse*.
44   "What I'm coming to": "August 13 in Pagsanjan."
45   "I tend not to jump": "August 17," *Apocalypse Now* transcript, undated, American Zoetrope Library Archives.
45   "It's a crime": "August 17."
45   needed her to say: Francis Ford Coppola, AI.
45   "I don't know what I'm doing": *Hearts of Darkness: A Filmmaker's Apocalypse*.
46   far more interesting: Eleanor Coppola, AI.
46   "From the bridge on": Marcus," Journey Up the River."
46   "carnage and devastation and horror": Commentary, *Apocalypse Now Redux*.
46   "It was like Vietnam": David Breskin, "Francis Ford Coppola," *Rolling Stone*, February 7, 1991, http://david breskin.com/magazines/1-interviews/francis-ford-coppola/.
46   "people who went over the edge": Gentry, "Dean Tavoularis."
46   "Every time I look at you": Samuel Bottoms, "Samuel Bottoms 1," *Apocalypse Now* interview, undated, American Zoetrope Library Archives.
47   "I just wanted to feel like": Bottoms, "Samuel Bottoms 1."
47   "marriages broke up": Bottoms, "Samuel Bottoms 1."
47   "I don't know, Francis": Commentary, *Apocalypse Now Redux*.
47   "Freddy, that's your character": Commentary, *Apocalypse Now Redux*.
47   "like you were in a dream": Frederic Forrest, *Apocalypse Now* interview, undated, American Zoetrope Library Archives.
47   "character basically evolved": Albert Hall, *Apocalypse Now* interview, undated, American Zoetrope Library Archives.
47   "mother of the ship": Bottoms, "Samuel Bottoms 1."
47   "dove deeper and deeper": Hall, *Apocalypse Now* interview.
47   "how we got to be a family": Commentary, *Apocalypse Now Redux*.
47   Coppola was in control of all of it: Bottoms, "Samuel Bottoms 1."
48   "Everybody was opening": Bottoms, "Samuel Bottoms 1."
48   "fooling around with metaphor": Adam Nayman, "Cryptographies and Blood," *Cinema Scope* 40 (Fall 2009).
48   "fucking Charlies": Cleary with Sack, "Apocalypse . . . At Last!"
48   "got weirder and weirder": Dennis Hopper, *Apocalypse Now* interview, undated, American Zoetrope Library Archives.
49   "most amazing thing": Hopper, *Apocalypse Now* interview.
49   "So many non reasonable [*sic*] things": Eleanor Coppola, *Notes: On the Making of Apocalypse Now*, 132.
49   How basic it all was to them: Marcus, "Journey Up the River."
49   "violent, angry part": Francis Ford Coppola, "FC on Final Scenes," *Apocalypse Now* interview, undated, American Zoetrope Library Archives.
50   "We say that anger is bad": Coppola, "FC on Final Scenes."
50   "bigger than a water buffalo": Commentary, *Apocalypse Now Redux*.
50   didn't want to be seen as fat: Commentary, *Apocalypse Now Redux*.
50   "send the crew to lunch": Commentary, *Apocalypse Now Redux*.
50   "words for the process": *Hearts of Darkness: A Filmmaker's Apocalypse*.
51   "How do you judge him?": Coppola, "FC on Final Scenes."
51   "All those who want": Coppola, "FC on Final Scenes."
51   "One drive [for Kurtz] is": Coppola, "FC on Final Scenes."
51   "It's to be relaxed": Storaro and Coppola, *Apocalypse Now* interview.
51   "Everything in this production": Storaro and Coppola, *Apocalypse Now* interview.
51   "If you say I'm stressing": Coppola, "FC on Final Scenes."
55   "very magical childhood": Francis Ford Coppola interview, YouTube, https://www.youtube.com/watch?v=D9QNgHV4oQU&t=2066s.
56   "for experimental recordings": Samuel Wein, "In the Laboratory," *The Motion Picture Projectionist*, July 1929, 14.

56 "Modern methods for the production": Wein, "In the Laboratory."

56 "almost mystical place": Francis Ford Coppola: Pater Familias, Nowness, YouTube, https://www.youtube .com/watch?v=7HmiXwI2B1Y.

56 "stories of bandits": Francis Ford Coppola, Stockholm International Film Festival, 2016, YouTube, https://www.youtube.com/watch?v=ogKYljw-orU.

57 "Everything had to be remembered": Cowie, *Coppola*, 4.

57 "never forget the music": *The Family Whistle*, directed by Michele Russo, American Zoetrope, 2016.

57 "like the Italian-American Gatsby": August Coppola, *The Italian Tuning Fork: A Family Memoir*, American Zoetrope Library Archives, 20.

58 "No one knows better": Carmine Coppola to August Coppola, June 19, 1954, "Distant Vision" box, American Zoetrope Library Archives.

58 "You might counter now": Carmine Coppola to August Coppola.

59 "Dad, at their house": Francis Ford Coppola, AI.

59 "little-town mentality": Commentary, *The Godfather Part I*, Paramount DVD, 2001.

59 "what do you want to be": Sal Khan and Francis Ford Coppola fireside chat, YouTube, https://www .youtube.com/watch?v=QA81QUt5Xjs.

59 "We were very involved": Breskin, "Francis Ford Coppola."

60 "Breathe deeply, release": Francis Ford Coppola, "When Father Did Not Know Best," undated, American Zoetrope Library Archives.

60 "reality in which we live": "An Interview with Francis Ford Coppola," FFC Biographical Clippings, AMPAS Margaret Herrick Library.

60 "Hail Mary": Breskin, "Francis Ford Coppola."

61 "kid who is ugly": Maureen Orth, "Godfather of the Movies," *Newsweek*, November 25, 1974.

62 MY BEST FRIEND IS ME: Francis Ford Coppola, lyrics, undated, American Zoetrope Library Archives; Francis Ford Coppola, AI.

62 "Augie's the bright one": Breskin, "Francis Ford Coppola."

63 "He was so nice to me": David Thomson and Lucy Gray, "Idols of the King: Francis Ford Coppola Interviewed," *Film Comment* 19 (September–October 1983).

63 "a fairy tale," he said: Commentary, *The Thief of Bagdad,* Criterion DVD, 2002.

63 He did like light: Sal Khan and Francis Ford Coppola fireside chat, YouTube.

64 "only be one genius": Schumacher, *Francis Ford Coppola*, 12.

64 "If it wasn't for Augie": Michael Goodwin and Naomi Wise, *On the Edge: The Life and Times of Francis Ford Coppola* (New York: William Morrow, 1989), 17.

64 "give Daddy his break": Breskin, "Francis Ford Coppola."

64 "When's the Tucker coming?": Francis Ford Coppola, AI.

65 "It was just agonizing": Nate Penn, "Icon," *GQ*, November 2007.

65 "Dear Mr. Coppola": Stephen Garrett: "What I've Learned: Francis Ford Coppola," *Esquire*, August 1, 2009, https://classic.esquire.com/article/2009/8/1/what-ive-learned-francis-ford-coppola.

65 "It's my break!": William Murray, "Francis Ford Coppola: *Playboy* Interview," July 1975, reproduced at Scraps from the Loft, January 27, 2017, https://scrapsfromtheloft.com/movies/francis-ford-coppola -playboy-interview/.

65 "hated anybody who": Braudy, "Francis Ford Coppola."

67 "I was scared": Francis Ford Coppola, AI.

67 "my mother really": Francis Ford Coppola, AI.

67 "I used to wonder": Eve Babitz, "Francis Ford Coppola and His World," *Coast*, April 1975.

67 "'Francis' is a girl's name": Sal Khan and Francis Ford Coppola fireside chat, YouTube.

67 "regularly I was hit with the strap": Francis Ford Coppola, email correspondence, June 12, 2014, "Distant Visions" Box, American Zoetrope Library Archives.

67 "I'd get *tremendous* crushes": Breskin, "Francis Ford Coppola."

67 "I lived a tremendous fantasy life": *The Merv Griffin Show*, season 1, episode, 26, aired January 9, 1980.

68 an actual baby: Francis Ford Coppola, AI.

68 others like him: Francis Ford Coppola, AI.

68 "When a student appears": Francis Ford Coppola, AI.

68 "I've tried to believe": Francis Ford Coppola to Carmine and Italia Coppola, undated, American Zoetrope Library Archives.

69 "All I ever wanted": Francis Ford Coppola, AI.

69 TINKERBELL: Francis Ford Coppola, unmade television pilot, November 3, 1961, American Zoetrope Library Archives.

70 "It took genius": Dennis Jakob, *Apocalypse Now* interview, undated, American Zoetrope Library Archives.

71 "greatest fucking frontier": "*Elective Affinities Discussion* D, Dennis Jakob and Francis Ford Coppola in Hidden Valley, 4-6-77," audio cassette, American Zoetrope Library Archives.

71 "why have you put yourself": Dennis Jakob, *Apocalypse Now* interview, undated, American Zoetrope Library Archives.

71 "journey is not really": Jakob, *Apocalypse Now* interview.

72 his new pages: "the newspaper": Dean Tavoularis, AI.

73 "I went from being": Francis Ford Coppola, AI.

73 "I played a very political": Francis Ford Coppola, AI.

73 "first time I learned": Francis Ford Coppola, interview by Gary Leva, undated, American Zoetrope Library Archives.

73 "drama department was always": Coppola, interview by Gary Leva.

73 "The weakness of musicals": Francis Ford Coppola, AI.

73 "In the end": Francis Ford Coppola, AI.

74 "about a kid who used": Malina Saval, "Francis Ford Coppola on His Longing to Be 'Impressive,'" *Variety*, April 29, 2016, https://variety.com/2016/film/spotlight/francis-ford-coppola-hands-and-feet-the-godfather-1201762144/.

74 "he must have had eighty-seven": Goodwin and Wise, *On the Edge*, 26.

74 "eight hundred scenes": Goodwin and Wise, *On the Edge*, 28.

74 "I was astonished," Francis Ford Coppola, AI.

74 "little personal communication": "Distant Visions" Box, American Zoetrope Library Archives.

75 "I'm lazing around": Francis Ford Coppola to his parents, "Distant Visions" Box, undated, American Zoetrope Library Archives.

75 "Dear Mr. Selden": Francis Ford Coppola to Samuel Selden, April 27, 1960, American Zoetrope Library Archives.

75 "theatrical spirit": Francis Ford Coppola, Stockholm International Film Festival, 2016, YouTube, https://www.youtube.com/watch?v=ogKYljw-orU.

75 "What are you doing?": Francis Ford Coppola, AI.

77 "Do you know anything": Francis Ford Coppola, AI.

77 "Roger was such a cheapskate": Francis Ford Coppola, AI.

78 "you went to UCLA": Francis Ford Coppola Interview, YouTube, https://www.youtube.com/watch?v=D9QNgHV4oQU&t=2066s.

78 "Francis had *guts*": Bill Campbell, AI.

78 "I knew that Roger": Coppola Interview, YouTube.

78 "a *Psycho*-like scene": Francis Ford Coppola, AI .

78 "I have a small budget": Coppola to Mother, Father, Talia, July 6, 1962, "Distant Visions" Box, American Zoetrope Library Archives.

79 "I have to talk to you": Francis Ford Coppola, AI.

79 "a crazy comedy": Francis Ford Coppola, AI.

79 "we hear you have military experience": Francis Ford Coppola, AI.

80 "You should have seen it": Rex Reed, "Offering the Moon to a Guy in Jeans," *New York Times*, August 7, 1966.

80 "to shoot 75 percent": Francis Ford Coppola to William Fadiman, July 5, 1965, American Zoetrope Library Archives.

81 "two kinds of acting": Charles Champlin, "'Big Boy': Big with Man on Campus," *Los Angeles Times*, December 12, 1966.

81 "It taught me a lot": Reed, "Offering the Moon to a Guy in Jeans."

81 "things like yelling 'cut'": Reed, "Offering the Moon to a Guy in Jeans."

81 "*You're a Big Boy Now* is the most": John Mahoney, "You're a Big Boy Now," *Hollywood Reporter*, December 13, 1966.

81 "I want to make films in Denver": Champlin, "'Big Boy': Big with Man on Campus."

81 "army of vigorous youngsters": Army Archerd, "Just for Variety," *Daily Variety*, February 1, 1967.

81 "No, there shouldn't be": Francis Ford Coppola, AI.

82 "The real scandal": Axel Madison, "Coppola Breaks the Age Barrier," *Los Angeles Times*, January 2, 1966.

82 "to see Seven Arts begin": Francis Ford Coppola, "Belt Two—Seven Arts and Television" memo, undated, American Zoetrope Library Archives.

83 "utopian look at the future": Coppola, "Belt Two–Seven Arts and Television."

83 "Things to Come 1984–2000+": Coppola, "Belt Two–Seven Arts and Television."

83 Scorsese, he would think: Francis Ford Coppola, AI.

83 "want to make a film": Martin Scorsese, interview with Gary Leva, undated, American Zoetrope Library Archives.

83 *That's me*, Scorsese thought: Rodney F. Hill, "Twixt Hollywood and Art Cinema: An Interview with Francis Ford Coppola," *Cineaste* 41 (Spring 2016).

83 "He's like the older brother": "A Conversation with Martin Scorsese and Francis Ford Coppola," *USSB Hollywood Insiders*, U.S. Satellite Broadcasting, YouTube, https://www.youtube.com/watch?v=uJE3Zqb9zXY&t=2570s.

83 "his door was open to any": Steven Spielberg, interview with Gary Leva, undated, American Zoetrope Library Archives.

84 "there would be room": Spielberg, interview with Gary Leva.

84 "standing there in his black chino pants": Dale Pollock, "When George and Francis Were Friends," *Esquire*, May 1983.

84 "bored out of my mind": Thomas Maremaa, "Celluloid Dreams . . . Childhood's End," *Penthouse*, May 1974.

84 "Whatcha lookin' at?": Commentary, *Finian's Rainbow*, Warner Brothers Blu-ray, 2005.

84 "Nothin' much": Commentary, *Finian's Rainbow*.

84   "I heard a UCLA student": Francis Ford Coppola, AI.

84   *this kid has talent*: Francis Ford Coppola, AI.

85   "doing this, the camera schedule": "Coppola's Six Weeks Rehearsals Paying Off for 'Finian's' Cast," *Hollywood Reporter*, August 2, 1967.

85   "Achilles' heel": Commentary, *Finian's Rainbow*.

85   "I thought 'What would my father think?'": Commentary, *Finian's Rainbow*.

85   "He was very strict": Francis Ford Coppola, AI.

85   "George's father, Mr. Lucas": Matthew Robbins, AI.

85   "Mr. Lucas was": Matthew Robbins, AI.

85   Coppola compared him: Francis Ford Coppola, AI.

86   "never go to work every day ": Anthony Breznican, "Meet George Lucas, Office Supply Salesman, *USA Today*, May 20, 2008, http://usatoday30.usatoday.com/life/movies/news/2008-05-20-lucas-father-issues _N.htm.

86   "they thought I was dead": Aljean Harmetz, "In Lucas Valley, George Calls the Shots," *Los Angeles Herald Examiner*, July 14, 1981.

86   "living my life": Dale Pollock, *Skywalking: The Life and Films of George Lucas*, Updated Edition (New York: Harmony Books, 1983), xvi.

86   "culture relates to machinery": Lee Grant, "Lucas: Feet on the Ground, Head in the Stars," *Los Angeles Times*, December 10, 1977.

86   "We did trick animation": "Man of the Future," *Newsweek*, May 31, 1971.

86   "As families begin to break up": Joanne Williams, "Sun Interview," *Pacific Sun*, February 1980.

86   "George really started exploring": Steve Silberman, "Life After Darth," *Wired*, May 1, 2005, https://www .wired.com/2005/05/lucas-2/.

86   "Come to USC": Williams, "Sun Interview."

87   "would have upset my father": Williams, "Sun Interview."

87   "Nobody wanted to be": George Lucas, interview, American Film Institute, March 3, 2005.

87   "get out now": Walter Murch, interview with Gary Leva, undated, American Zoetrope Library Archives.

87   "fascinated with the mechanics": Michael Rubin, *Droidmaker: George Lucas and the Digital Revolution* (Gainesville, FL: Triad, 2006).

87   "I was a rising star": George Lucas, interview, American Film Institute, March 3, 2005.

87   "Neither of us talk very much": George Lucas, "Academy Tribute to Walter Murch," speech, October 6, 2000, AMPAS Margaret Herrick Library.

88   "Walk on it!": Matthew Robbins, AI.

88   "I remember him falling asleep": David Thomson, "The Secret Saver," *San Francisco*, December 1997.

88   "has a peculiar quality": Walter Murch, interview, Web of Stories, https://webofstories.com/.

88   "interested in sound": "Walter Murch interviewed by Gustavo Costantini," *The Soundtrack* 3 (July 2010).

89   "Okay, Murch": Walter Murch, AI.

89   "I never should have married you!": Aggie Murch, AI.

89   "George was the master": John Milius, interview with Gary Leva, undated, American Zoetrope Library Archives.

89   "really was, even in those days": Lucas, "Academy Tribute to Walter Murch."

89   "backed into the patio": Lucas, "Academy Tribute to Walter Murch."

90   "all sat on the grass": Milius, interview with Gary Leva.

90   "student film about": Paul Cullum and George Hickenlooper, "Wham Bam Thank You 'Nam," *Neon*, n.d.

90   "looking at each other's movies": Matthew Robbins, AI.

90   "a real obsession": Lucas, "Academy Tribute to Walter Murch."

91   "guys gonna do that film": Walter Murch, interview, Web of Stories, https://webofstories.com/.

91   "Jesus, who the hell": Pollock, *Skywalking*, 68.

91   "stopped the festival": Spielberg, interview with Gary Leva.

91   "greatest science fiction movies": "Artifact from the Future: The Making of *THX 1138*," *THX 1138: The George Lucas Director's Cut*, Warner Home Video Blu-ray, 2010.

92   "Walt Disney's version": Pollock, *Skywalking*, 68.

92   "was a disconnect": Walter Murch, interview with Gary Leva.

92   "That's George": Spielberg, interview with Gary Leva.

92   "such opulence": Pollock, *Skywalking*, 70.

92   "reason I took the scholarship": *George Lucas: Maker of Films*, PBS, 1971.

92   "That started our friendship": Milius, interview with Gary Leva.

93   "conservative Northern California family": Lee Eisenberg, "The Conversation: Francis Coppola & Gay Talese," *Esquire*, July 1, 1981.

93   "He calls me 'the kid'": Maremaa, "Celluloid Dreams . . . Childhood's End."

93   "I can sing anything!": Francis Ford Coppola, AI.

93   "Would you believe Howard Hughes?": Cutts, "The Dangerous Age."

93   "very romantic human being": Gene D. Phillips and Rodney Hill, eds., *Francis Ford Coppola: Interviews* (Jackson: University Press of Mississippi, 2004), 15

93   "I'm disgruntled": Phillips and Hill, *Francis Ford Coppola: Interviews*, 12.

93   "I could make a lot of money": Phillips and Hill, *Francis Ford Coppola: Interviews*.

94   "What I'm thinking of doing": Phillips and Hill, *Francis Ford Coppola: Interviews*, 15–16.

94   "The establishment wants": Leo Seligsohn, "Fat-Riser Finds View from Top Still Hazy," *Newsday*, November 28, 1967.

94   "a young anachronism": Steven Spielberg, interview with Gary Leva, undated, American Zoetrope Library Archives.

94   "A lot of us were involved": Carroll Ballard, AI.

95   "he was like a kid brother": Francis Ford Coppola, interview with Gary Leva, undated, American Zoetrope Library Archives.

95   "Francis's attitude was": Schumacher, *Francis Ford Coppola*, 80.

95   "we could get money": *A Legacy of Filmmakers: The Early Years of American Zoetrope*, directed by Gary Leva (2004, Leva FilmWorks).

95   "never going to be a good director": "Artifact from the Future."

95   "But this is not my thing": Lucas, interview with Gary Leva.

95   "were the Trojan horse": Michael Sragow, "Godfatherhood," *New Yorker*, March 24, 1997, https://www.newyorker.com/magazine/1997/03/24/godfatherhood.

95   "I'm starting to shoot": Phillips and Hill, *Francis Ford Coppola: Interviews*, 13.

95   "I worked on *THX*": Schumacher, *Francis Ford Coppola*, 79.

96   "I was the do-all": Mona Skager, AI.

96   "my first memories": Roman Coppola, AI.

96   "I supported that cast": Phillips and Hill, *Francis Ford Coppola: Interviews*, 15.

96   "Because we had representation": Francis Ford Coppola, AI.

96   "They were just kind of monitoring": Tony Dingman, AI.

96   "classify us as a movie": Mona Skager, AI.

96   "a snake farm": Mona Skager, AI.

96   "Literally under the cover of darkness": Coppola, interview with Gary Leva.

96   "Francis was rewriting": Mona Skager, AI.

97   "whole studio on wheels": Cutts, "The Dangerous Age."

97   "Everything I learnt": Brent Lewis, "Coppola's Coup," *Films and Filming*, November/December 1988.

97   "He didn't spell very well": Mona Skager, AI.

97   "Everybody just helped": Mona Skager, AI.

97   "send our film to New York": Schumacher, *Francis Ford Coppola*, 66–67.

97   "[Lucas and I] were sitting": Schumacher, *Francis Ford Coppola*, 67.

98   "need a special effects man": Francis Ford Coppola, "Director's Choice: *You're a Big Boy Now*," December 14, 1968, AMPAS Margaret Herrick Library.

98   "What I always learn about Francis": Eleanor Coppola, AI.

98   "The ideal way to work": Rebecca Winters Keegan, "10 Questions for Francis Ford Coppola," *Time*, August 21, 2006.

98   "The film is the force": "Close-up" on *The Conversation* Featurette, *The Conversation*, Paramount DVD, 1974.

99   "All you have is yourself": Argentina Brunetti Papers, f.37, AMPAS Margaret Herrick Library.

99   "With *The Rain People*": Philip K. Scheuer, "On the Road with *The Rain People*," *Action*, 1969.

99   "My films are unusual": Francis Ford Coppola Interview, YouTube.

99   "That's it": Ron Colby, interview with Gary Leva, undated, American Zoetrope Library Archives.

99   "They shot him!": Colby, interview with Gary Leva.

99   "big preview of *Finian's Rainbow*": Jack Warner, telegram to Francis Ford Coppola, June 24, 1968, American Zoetrope Library Archives.

100   "make a film studio anywhere": Eleanor Coppola, interview with Gary Leva, undated, American Zoetrope Library Archives.

100   "this rather thin, young guy": John Korty, interview with Gary Leva, undated, American Zoetrope Library Archives.

100   "I'm George Lucas": "Visual History with John Korty," interview by Robert Markowitz, Director's Guild of America, https://www.dga.org/Craft/VisualHistory/Interviews/John-Korty.aspx.

100   "mainly about what Francis": "Visual History with John Korty."

100   "We obviously had a lot in common": Korty, interview with Gary Leva.

100   "I mean the idea of going to Hollywood": "Visual History with John Korty."

100   "I was in this tiny apartment": "Visual History with John Korty."

100   "little soulful independent movies": George Lucas, interview with American Film Institute, March 3, 2005.

101   "We're gonna call Francis": Korty, interview with Gary Leva.

101   "I just met John Korty": "Visual History with John Korty."

101   "That's what we should do": Lucas, interview with American Film Institute.

101   "As soon as Francis is done": Korty, interview with Gary Leva.

101   "terrible on the outside": Audie Bock, "Zoetrope and Apocalypse Now," *American Film*, September 1979.

101   "This is what I want": Bock, "Zoetrope and Apocalypse Now."

101   "perfect environment": Colby, interview with Gary Leva.

101   "back Monday": Korty interview with Gary Leva.

101   "they had fishing boats": Korty interview with Gary Leva.

102   "We'll set up a studio": Korty interview with Gary Leva.

102 The difference between Francis and George: Korty interview with Gary Leva.

102 "Do you know anybody": Lucas, "Academy Tribute to Walter Murch."

102 "Come with us up the street": Walter Murch, AI.

102 "a candy store of technology": Cowie, *Coppola*, 55–56.

102 "we can have our own mix studio": Coppola, interview with Gary Leva.

103 "a Korty-like existence": Colby, interview with Gary Leva.

103 *This is heaven*: Francis Ford Coppola, AI.

103 "place out in the country": Coppola, interview with Gary Leva.

103 "we'll be independent": Coppola, interview with Gary Leva.

103 "If *The Rain People* dies": Dan Simons, "'Rain People' by the Rule Breaker," *Los Angeles Times*, September 7, 1969.

104 "George had a goofy": Matthew Robbins, AI.

104 "Come on, darling": Walter Murch, interview, Web of Stories, https://webofstories.com/.

104 "squeaky leather sounds": Walter Murch, interview, Web of Stories, https://webofstories.com/.

104 "It was like a club": Janet Robbins, AI.

104 "good in the long run": Goodwin and Wise, *On the Edge*, 91–92.

104 "I would help make sounds": Janet Robbins, AI.

105 "nervous and under great": Phillips and Hill, *Francis Ford Coppola: Interviews*, 13.

105 "It's come to the point": Phillips and Hill, *Francis Ford Coppola: Interviews*, 13.

105 "living this golden life": Phillips and Hill, *Francis Ford Coppola: Interviews*, 13.

105 "offers that I was hoping I would": Phillips and Hill, *Francis Ford Coppola: Interviews*, 15.

105 "her flight had been inspired": Francis Ford Coppola, AI.

105 "I was interested": Francis Ford Coppola, AI.

105 "sharing his life": *The Rain People* draft, American Zoetrope Library Archives.

106 "hadn't planned on it": *The Rain People* draft.

107 "pleased and proud": "Director's Choice: *You're a Big Boy Now*."

107 "film that was made by George Lucas": "Director's Choice: *You're a Big Boy Now*."

108 "a tragedy": "Director's Choice: *You're a Big Boy Now*."

108 "George died": "Director's Choice: *You're a Big Boy Now*."

108 "this pigeonholing of people": "Director's Choice: *You're a Big Boy Now*."

108 "Unions were designed": "Director's Choice: *You're a Big Boy Now*."

108 "a good symbol": Francis Ford Coppola, AI.

108 "It's the wheel of life": Francis Ford Coppola, interview with Gary Leva, undated, American Zoetrope Library Archives.

108 "The whole idea of our company": Coppola, interview with Gary Leva.

109 "Despite many clever things": Coppola, interview with Gary Leva

109 "He was so hip": Peter Biskind, *Easy Riders, Raging Bulls: How the Sex-Drugs-and-Rock 'n' Roll Generation Saved Hollywood* (New York: Simon & Schuster), 83.

109 "What [Warner chairman] Ted [Ashley and I] were trying to do": John Calley, interview with JAK Films, undated, Zoetrope Archives.

109 "studio system was ridiculous": Calley, interview with JAK Films.

109 "We'll get this thing made": George Lucas, interview, American Film Institute, March 3, 2005.

109 "We gotta wait a while": Lucas, interview, American Film Institute.

110 "How much do you need": John Milius, interview, YouTube, https://www.youtube.com/watch?v=i4nY2J1gRzg.

110 "We'll just pretend like": *A Legacy of Filmmakers*.

110 "What do you think about": Carroll Ballard, AI.

110 "Shape up or ship out": George Lucas, interview with Gary Leva, undated, American Zoetrope Library Archives.

110 "who everybody thought was extraordinary": Calley, interview with JAK Films.

110 "as the parental figure": Calley, interview with JAK Films.

110 "a way of doing films": Calley, interview with JAK Films.

111 "George, I gotta tell you": *A Legacy of Filmmakers*.

111 "Not only did I get *THX*": *A Legacy of Filmmakers*.

111 "We used to call it Wine Country": Mona Skager, AI.

111 "that's where American Zoetrope": Cowie, *Coppola*, 55–56.

111 "a weekend, a baby": *American Zoetrope 40th Anniversary Book*, American Zoetrope Library Archives, unpublished.

111 "going to change the world": Walter Murch, interview, Web of Stories, https://webofstories.com/.

111 "Literally a KEM": George Lucas, interview with Gary Leva, undated, American Zoetrope Library Archives.

112 "I spent the budget": Francis Ford Coppola, AI.

112 "I don't think we": Francis Ford Coppola, AI.

112 "work with this German equipment": Walter Murch, AI.

112 "just that youthful spirit": David Macmillan, AI.

112 "[American Zoetrope was] always": Francis Ford Coppola, "Academy Tribute to Walter Murch," October 6, 2000, AMPAS Margaret Herrick Library.

112 "what looked like simultaneous seizures": Walter Murch, interview, Web of Stories, https://webofstories.com/.

112 "It was me": Walter Murch, interview, Web of Stories, https://webofstories.com/.

113 "keep going": Milius, interview, YouTube.
113 "Boy, you're right": Lucas, interview with Gary Leva.
113 "Do you know anybody else": Lucas, "Academy Tribute to Walter Murch."
113 "That sort of mutual influence": Walter Murch, interview with Gary Leva, undated, American Zoetrope Library Archives.
113 "part of the American Zoetrope dream": Walter Murch, "Sound Minds Seminar," AMPAS Margaret Herrick Library, October 11, 2000.
113 "if you did have enough time": Murch, "Sound Minds Seminar."
113 "I somehow passed myself off": *American Zoetrope 40th Anniversary Book.*
114 "way women come out": Hal Aigner and Michael Goodwin, "The Bearded Immigrant from Tinsel Town," *City,* June 1974.
114 wanted to make a love story: Aigner and Goodwin, "The Bearded Immigrant from Tinsel Town."
114 "strictly bench players": Stephen Lighthill, AI.
115 "that Hollywood was dead": Jim Mansen, AI.
115 "I'm not sure a Hollywood crew": Jim Mansen, AI.
115 "The financing was iffy": Mona Skager, interview with Gary Leva, undated, American Zoetrope Library Archives.
115 "A lot of the time, I didn't rehearse": "*THX 1138*: Made in San Francisco," *American Cinematographer,* October 1971.
115 "It felt like working": "Artifact from the Future: The Making of *THX 1138*," *THX 1138: The George Lucas Director's Cut,* Warner Home Video Blu-ray, 2010.
115 "We were sort of getting in there": John Korty, interview with Gary Leva, undated, American Zoetrope Library Archives.
116 "Film students walk in": Louise Sweeney, "The Movie Business Is Alive and Well and Living in San Francisco," *Show,* April, 1970.
116 "The company itself": Sweeney, "The Movie Business Is Alive and Well and Living in San Francisco."
116 "about an army colonel who's": Sweeney, "The Movie Business Is Alive and Well and Living in San Francisco."
116 "could see and hear as much": Korty, interview with Gary Leva.
117 "these hippie filmmakers": Coppola, interview with Gary Leva.
117 "In the end": Coppola, interview with Gary Leva.
117 "I was a patsy": Francis Ford Coppola, AI.
117 "but we've just painted all": Coppola, interview with Gary Leva.
117 "No one knew how to work it": Coppola, interview with Gary Leva.
117 "And you saw the hand": Coppola, interview with Gary Leva.
117 "because of Marty": Coppola, interview with Gary Leva.
117 "They were threading it wrong": Mike Fleming Jr., "From 'The Godfather' Trilogy to 'American Graffiti,' 'Patton,' 'The Conversation' & 'Apocalypse Now,' Francis Ford Coppola Shares His Oscar Memories," Deadline, March 25, 2022, https://deadline.com/2022/03/francis-ford-coppola-oscars-memories-godfather-patton-apocalypse-now-1234986966/.
118 "I was so happy": Fleming, "From 'The Godfather' Trilogy."
118 "all these crazy things": Korty, interview with Gary Leva.
118 "how you guys can stand it": Korty, interview with Gary Leva.
118 "Walter and I were working": Steve Silberman, "Life After Darth," *Wired,* May 1, 2005, https://www.wired.com/2005/05/lucas-2/.
118 "a vague clinking": Murch, interview with Gary Leva.
118 "few electronic sounds": Murch, interview with Gary Leva.
119 "That's the greatest thing": Murch, interview with Gary Leva.
119 "a paradise for us": Walter Murch, Web of Stories, YouTube, https://www.youtube.com/watch?v=vIRX26iyyvc&list=PLVVor6CmEsFzCodipONmNiROhYCUWyz_U.
119 "*THX* was the best experience I had": Kenneth Von Gunden, *Postmodern Auteurs: Coppola, Lucas, De Palma, Spielberg and Scorsese* (Jefferson, NC: McFarland, 1991), 61.
119 "I owe it all to Francis": Robert Lindsey, "The New New Wave of Film Makers," *New York Times,* May 28, 1978, https://www.nytimes.com/1978/05/28/archives/the-new-new-wave-of-film-makers-a-young-group-of-writerdirectors.html.
119 "There's no question that *THX*": Dan Simons, "Cinema San Francisco Style," *Entertainment World,* March 27, 1970.
119 "The friendships of the guys": Aggie Murch, AI.
119 "If one of us got sick": Aggie Murch, AI.
120 "So it was really more of a lifestyle": Coppola, "Academy Tribute to Walter Murch."
120 "I've been waiting all my life": John L. Wasserman, "A New, Unique, Dream Studio," *San Francisco Chronicle,* December 11, 1969.
120 "ZOETROPE MEANS LIFE REVOLUTION": *Variety,* December 11, 1969.
120 "Who's the most beautiful woman": John L. Wasserman, "American Zoetrope in S.F.: A New, Unique Dream Studio," *San Francisco Chronicle,* December 11, 1969.
120 "packed, just packed": Mona Skager, AI.

120 "dyed in the wool hippies": John Milius, interview with Gary Leva, undated, American Zoetrope Library Archives.

120 a Zen anarchist: Milius, interview with Gary Leva.

120 "We were gonna change": Milius, interview with Gary Leva.

120 "impresario and public dreamer": Matthew Robbins, interview with Gary Leva, undated, American Zoetrope Library Archives.

121 "The little office on Folsom": Dean Tavoularis, AI.

121 "I read the script": Willard Huyck, interview with Gary Leva, undated, American Zoetrope Library Archives.

121 "token radical": Steve Wax, AI.

122 "And I'm talking to Orson Welles": Steve Wax, AI.

122 "resonant voice": Steve Wax, AI.

122 "[Zoetrope] was, in a sense": Declan McGrath, "Film Editing, Plumbing, and Revolution: An Interview with Walter Murch," *Cineaste* 40 (Fall 2015).

123 "And we never had the money": Steve Wax, AI.

123 "typical day at American Zoetrope": Steve Wax, AI.

123 "This is the future of filmmaking": Korty, interview with Gary Leva.

123 *What kind of quality*: Korty, interview with Gary Leva.

123 "To hell with Arriflexes": Korty, interview with Gary Leva.

123 "What I'm creating here": Steve Wax, AI.

123 "was the greatest magnet": Steve Wax, AI.

123 "You know you're like the Shadow": Steve Wax, AI.

124 "we have to go the next step": Francis Ford Coppola to Warner Bros., undated, American Zoetrope Library Archives.

124 "select and build a varying": Francis Ford Coppola to Warner Bros.

124 "scurried around arranging emergency loans": Jesse Ritter, *San Francisco Bay Guardian*, August 16, 1972.

124 "would evade charmingly": Ritter, *San Francisco Bay Guardian*.

124 "That's a good story": Lucas, interview with Gary Leva.

125 "too crazy at Zoetrope": Steve Wax, AI.

125 "You could almost time it": Robert Dalva, AI.

125 he felt it in the pit of his stomach: Murch, interview with Gary Leva.

125 "Look at this": Huyck, interview with Gary Leva.

126 "similar to *Brave New World*": Calley, interview, JAK Films.

126 "It's not the screenplay": Calley, interview, JAK Films.

126 "What happened": Huyck, interview with Gary Leva.

127 "What am I doing?": Breskin, "Francis Ford Coppola."

127 "I think that Francis was caught between": John Milius, interview with Gary Leva, undated, American Zoetrope Library Archives.

127 "There was a change in the whole industry": Gerald Nachman, "Coppola of Zoetrope—Older, Wiser and Poorer," *Los Angeles Times*, November 7, 1971.

127 "and the ground beneath Zoetrope": Nachman, "Coppola of Zoetrope."

127 "I felt Calley": Francis Ford Coppola, AI.

127 "changed our concept": "Coppola Says Para Deal 'On Leave' from Warners," *Hollywood Reporter*, October 1, 1970.

127 took your four-year-old daughter: Matthew Robbins, AI.

128 "We're here to pick up the film": Caleb Deschanel, AI.

128 "They don't like this film": "Coppola Says Para Deal 'On Leave' from Warners."

128 "Dear John": Francis Ford Coppola Letter to John Lennon, *Apocalypse Now*, American Zoetrope Library Archives.

129 "put the freaks up front": Robbins, interview with Gary Leva.

129 They'll forgive you anything: Biskind, *Easy Riders, Raging Bulls*, 99.

129 But it's not a love story: *George Lucas: Maker of Films*, PBS, 1971.

129 "Just cut five minutes from it": Lucas, interview with Gary Leva.

129 "So there was no point": Lucas, interview with Gary Leva.

129 "You don't like this?": Biskind, *Easy Riders, Raging Bulls*, 100.

130 "You didn't fight": Lucas, interview with Gary Leva.

130 "we had about a hundred people": Steve Wax, AI.

130 " all the unions were full of shit": Steve Wax, AI.

130 "We got to stop it": Steve Wax, AI.

130 "My enthusiasm and my imagination": Steven Travers, *Coppola's Monster Film: The Making of "Apocalypse Now"* (Jefferson, NC: McFarland, 2016), 66.

130 "completely communist": Lucas, interview with Gary Leva.

130 "What happened was that you had everybody": Jonathan Cott, "Francis Coppola: The Rolling Stone Interview (1982)," Scraps from the Loft, December 12, 2016, https://scrapsfromtheloft.com/2016/12/12 /francis-coppola-the-rolling-stone-interview-1982/.

131 "working minimum wage": Richard Chew, AI.

131 "[Francis] was a den mother": Carroll Ballard, interview with JAK Films, undated, American Zoetrope Library Archives.

131 "destroyed the whole idea of Zoetrope": Ballard, interview with JAK Films.

131 "I just feel about groups": Steven Spielberg, American Film Institute, September 28, 1977.

132 "Dear Francis": Kenneth I. Mancebo to Francis Ford Coppola, May 29, 1970, American Zoetrope Library Archives.

132 "No one told me": Francis Ford Coppola, AI.

132 "I have about four thousand": David Macmillan, AI.

132 "[The] American film business once again": Francis Ford Coppola, *THX 1138*, letter to Guy Flatley, American Zoetrope Library Archive.

133 "I knew nothing about this": Francis Ford Coppola, AI.

133 "was picked clean": Francis Ford Coppola, AI.

134 "Did Francis and George's dream come true?": Robert Dalva, AI.

134 "It's basically the death": Ron Colby, interview with Gary Leva, undated, American Zoetrope Library Archives.

134 "The dream": Lucas, interview with Gary Leva.

135 "some very famous woman": Eleanor Coppola, AI.

135 "I would come": Eleanor Coppola, AI.

135 "I would take these Polaroids": Eleanor Coppola, AI.

136 "Francis is actually the conceptual artist": Eleanor Coppola, *Notes: On the Making of Apocalypse Now*, 119.

136 "He has always wanted to be": Eleanor Coppola, *Notes: On the Making of Apocalypse Now*, 119.

136 "You feel him": Vittorio Storaro, Ellie & Francis, *Apocalypse Now* interview, undated, American Zoetrope Library Archives.

137 "This is difficult": Storaro et al., *Apocalypse Now* interview.

137 "Maybe in an image": Storaro et al., *Apocalypse Now* interview.

137 "It was probably the closest": Marlon Brando with Robert Lindsey, *Songs My Mother Taught Me* (New York: Random House, 1994), 430.

137 grab a buzzing fly without breaking: Martin Sheen, *Apocalypse Now* interview, undated, American Zoetrope Library Archives.

137 "Are you free": Sheen, *Apocalypse Now* interview.

137 "Hey, Dick White": Dick White, *Apocalypse Now* interview, undated, American Zoetrope Library Archives.

138 "My greatest fear": *Hearts of Darkness: A Filmmaker's Apocalypse*.

138 "have the courage to say": *Hearts of Darkness: A Filmmaker's Apocalypse*.

138 "I remember the anxiety": Eleanor Coppola, *Notes: On the Making of Apocalypse Now*, 43.

139 "put us all in a circumstance": *Hearts of Darkness: A Filmmaker's Apocalypse*.

139 dilettante: *Eleanor Coppola: Quiet Creative Force* (Sonoma, CA: Sonoma Valley Museum of Art, 2014), 31.

139 "balancing act": Eleanor Coppola letter to her mother, "Sat on Plane," undated, American Zoetrope Library Archives.

139 "This film is a twenty-million-dollar disaster!": *Hearts of Darkness: A Filmmaker's Apocalypse*.

140 "Cut, cut, cut!": Cleary with Sack, "Apocalypse . . . At Last!"

140 "I wanted to be thought of as American": Breskin, "Francis Ford Coppola."

140 "Will notify": Donna Moriarty, "Apocalypse Then," *San Francisco Bay Guardian*, August 16, 1979.

140 "turning over tables and chairs": Moriarty, "Apocalypse Then."

141 "Friendly Serving Wenches": Moriarty, "Apocalypse Then."

141 "You know, you go to Disneyland": Moriarty, "Apocalypse Then."

141 "Now, conceptual art": Dennis Hopper, *Apocalypse Now* interview, November 4, 1976, American Zoetrope Library Archives.

141 Francis, Hopper corrected himself: Hopper, *Apocalypse Now* interview.

141 a sickness: Dean Tavoularis, AI.

141 "I gasped": Jean Autrey, AI.

142 "We can give you ten dollars": Jean Autrey, AI.

142 "Francis, you're just a kid": Biskind, *Easy Riders, Raging Bulls*, 143.

142 "George, what should I do?": Maureen Orth, "Godfather of the Movies," *Newsweek*, November 25, 1974.

142 "Everybody who knew Francis": Caleb Deschanel, interview with Gary Leva, undated, American Zoetrope Library Archives.

142 "There is infinite art": *Eleanor Coppola: Quiet Creative Force*, 34.

142 "With Francis, everything": Vittorio Storaro, *Apocalypse Now Redux* interview, undated, American Zoetrope Library Archives.

143 Eleanor envied that: Eleanor Coppola, *Notes: On the Making of Apocalypse Now*, 213.

143 "So, yes of course": Bilge Ebiri, "In Conversation: Francis Ford Coppola," *New York* magazine, December 11, 2020.

143 "It's the WASP wife": *The Godfather Family: A Look Inside*, directed by Jeff Werner, written by David Gilbert, Paramount Pictures, 1990.

143 "Think of how many husbands": Murray, "Francis Ford Coppola: *Playboy* Interview."

144 "Running a set": Biskind, *Easy Riders, Raging Bulls*, 155.

144 It was *him* they hated: Commentary, *The Godfather, Part I*, Paramount, 2001, DVD.

144 "What do you think of this director": Commentary, *The Godfather Part I*.

144 "a henchman": Dean Tavoularis, AI.

144   "I was so frightened": Sragow, "Godfatherhood."

144   "My editor": "Coppola in Hollywood," *Los Angeles Times,* September 23, 1972.

145   "I don't think they're going to fire you": Fleming, "From 'The Godfather' Trilogy."

145   "a peremptory strike": Francis Ford Coppola, AI.

145   "When you play a role": Sragow, "Godfatherhood."

145   "I had my studio and my people": Bob Mottley, "Two 'Godfathers' Are Better Than One?," *New York Times,* May 3, 1974.

145   "a group of people who can": Christopher Pearce, "San Francisco's Own American Zoetrope," *American Cinematographer,* October 1971.

145   "especially if you're young": Pearce, "San Francisco's Own American Zoetrope."

146   "basically a think tank": Pearce, "San Francisco's Own American Zoetrope."

146   "I figured, 'I'll show it to them'": Sragow, "Godfatherhood."

146   "by force of his personality": Walter Murch, interview with Gary Leva, undated, American Zoetrope Library Archives.

146   "a dream girl": Francis Ford Coppola and Jack Clayton, notes in preparation of *Great Gatsby* screenplay, cassette tape, undated, American Zoetrope Library Archives.

146   "the poor boy hopelessly in love": Coppola and Clayton, notes in preparation of *Great Gatsby* screenplay.

146   "That changed my life": "Honor Role," *Hollywood Reporter,* January 18, 2008.

147   "I can fail for ten years": Paul Schrader, AI.

147   *Coppola's wrong*: Paul Schrader, AI.

147   "the most good reviews": Eleanor Coppola letter to her mother, "Sat on Plane."

148   "that it was [his] obligation": Francis Ford Coppola, interview with Gary Leva, undated, American Zoetrope Library Archives.

148   "Every incarnation of Zoetrope": Francis Ford Coppola, AI.

148   "I had money": Francis Ford Coppola, AI.

148   "I was supposed to be there for like three weeks": Peter Dornbach, AI.

148   Eleanor had it painted: Eleanor Coppola, email to author.

148   "You couldn't believe the size": Peter Dornbach, AI.

148   "the soft, cushy": Jean Autrey, AI.

149   "What's going on here?": Richard Beggs, AI.

149   "Francis always saw that the multitrack": Richard Beggs, AI.

150   "one of the most beautiful rooms": Dennis Gassner, AI.

150   "I now am as successful": "Coppola in Hollywood," *Los Angeles Times,* September 23, 1972.

150   "I'm learning. I'm trying": Ken Michaels, *Chicago Tribune,* November 5, 1972.

150   "Part of my desire": "Coppola in Hollywood," *Los Angeles Times.*

151   "This year I've overcommitted myself": "Coppola in Hollywood," *Los Angeles Times.*

151   "Don't worry, Francis": Francis Ford Coppola, AI.

151   "I cast *American Graffiti*": Fred Roos, AI.

151   "It was my first artistic experience": Michael Sragow "Inside 'Raiders of the Lost Ark,'" *Rolling Stone,* June 25, 1981, https://www.rollingstone.com/movies/movie-news/inside-raiders-of-the-lost-ark-69261/.

151   "entirely unlike a Hollywood movie": Ron Howard, AI.

152   "because he believed in George": Ron Howard, AI.

152   "We all live in two worlds": Francis Ford Coppola, *The Conversation* notes, American Zoetrope Library Archives.

152   "I never did well": *The Conversation* draft, American Zoetrope Library Archive.

153   "and before you knew it": Mona Skager, AI.

153   "I was seeing one day": Breskin, "Francis Ford Coppola."

153   "Publishing *City*": Orth, "Godfather of the Movies."

154   "and it kind of grew": Jack Fritz, AI.

154   "[Coppola] had felt that the sound": Walter Murch, "Stretching Sound to Help the Mind See," FilmSound.org, http://filmsound.org/murch/stretching.htm.

154   "As I was writing [it]": Marjorie Rosen, "Francis Ford Coppola," *Film Comment* 10 (July/August 1974).

154   "needed to give the audience": Murch, "Stretching Sound to Help the Mind See."

155   "Whenever you go outside": Walter Murch, interview, Web of Stories, https://webofstories.com/.

156   "worldizing": Richard Chew, AI.

156   "You work in sound": Walter Murch, interview, Web of Stories, https://webofstories.com/.

156   "There were many times": Michael Ondaatje, *The Conversations: Walter Murch and the Art of Editing Film* (New York: Alfred A. Knopf, 2002), 154.

156   Murch thought cutting: Walter Murch, AI.

156   "the inertia of physical reality": McGrath, "Film Editing, Plumbing, and Revolution."

157   "flinch point": Ondaatje, *The Conversations,* 269.

157   "You get to a place": Ondaatje, *The Conversations,* 9.

157   Sometimes, "the best times": Walter Murch, *In the Blink of an Eye: A Perspective on Film Editing* (Los Angeles: Silman-James Press, 1995), 50.

157   Film is like thought: Louise Sweeney, "John Huston," *Christian Science Monitor,* July 26, 1973. Collected in *John Huston Interviews,* ed. Robert Emmet Long (Jackson: University Press of Mississippi, 2001).

157 "I was just kind of watching Walter": Richard Chew, AI.

158 "It took many (many) years": Aggie Murch, AI.

158 "she never reconciled": Muriel Murch, "Eleanor Coppola on 'Notes on a Life: A Portrait of a Marriage,'" *Living with Literature* podcast, May 2, 2008.

158 "so fragile in its effect": Alfred Frankenstein, *San Francisco Chronicle*, September 14, 1972.

158 "I was not happy": Eleanor Coppola, email to author.

158 "I spent a whole day": Aigner and Goodwin, "The Bearded Immigrant from Tinsel Town."

159 "To some extent I have become Michael": Andrew Billen, "The Billen Interview: Francis Ford Coppola Explains Why He No Longer Wants to Direct Films," *The Observer*, October 30, 1994.

159 "decided to view it as the end": Roundtable Discussion with Francis Ford Coppola, *Godfather II* Press Release, Paramount Pictures, AMPAS Margaret Herrick Library.

159 "living a part of that *Godfather*": Lisa Fruchtman, AI.

159 "On *Godfather* he was": Mark Berger, AI.

159 "If you could go anywhere": Lisa Fruchtman, AI.

160 "Directors, the younger directors": Richard Albarino, "Coppola's Plans: To Lay Low in Frisco, Little Pic Project," *Weekly Variety*, March 27, 1974.

160 "Who was the star": *The Merv Griffin Show*, season 1, episode 26, January 9, 1980.

160 "The most significant fact": Albarino, "Coppola's Plans."

160 "bypass the kinds of movie deals": Richard Albarino, "Coppola: Creative Over Company Man," *Daily Variety*, August 21, 1974.

161 "creative collaboration": Albarino, "Coppola: Creative Over Company Man."

161 "macabre comedy": Albarino, "Coppola: Creative Over Company Man."

161 "Bergman is very high on you": Orth, "Godfather of the Movies."

161 "I am at the zenith": Albarino, "Coppola's Plans."

161 "I've got to start paying attention": Joseph Gelmis, "The Midwifing of 'Godfather II,'" *Los Angeles Times*, January 3, 1975.

162 "all want to buy our grapes": "Francis Ford Coppola Talks Film, Wine, and Love of Jingles," *Today*, YouTube, https://www.youtube.com/watch?v=cg5B_bfmooE.

162 "good for your picture": "A Conversation with Martin Scorsese and Francis Ford Coppola," *USSB Hollywood Insiders*, U.S. Satellite Broadcasting, YouTube, https://www.youtube.com/watch?v=uJE3Zqb9zXY&t=2570s.

163 exhibition at the Coppolas' house: Eleanor Coppola, email to author.

163 "I'm getting to be an influential person": Murray, "Francis Ford Coppola: *Playboy* Interview."

163 "I'd like to start this place": Babitz, "Francis Ford Coppola and His Word."

164 "I've already made a million": Murray, "Francis Ford Coppola: *Playboy* Interview."

165 "Everyone who has come": Eleanor Coppola, *Notes: On the Making of Apocalypse Now*, 126.

165 had reviewed the entirety of his life: Eleanor Coppola, *Notes: On the Making of Apocalypse Now*, 154.

166 "There's something really honest": Roy G. Levin, "Francis Coppola Discusses Apocalypse Now," *Millimeter*, October 1979.

166 "Sometimes a family": Éva Gárdos, interview, Apocalypse Now Revisited: Eleanor Coppola & Éva Gárdos, August 30 (year not listed), American Zoetrope Library Archives.

166 "started to get insane": Bottoms, "Samuel Bottoms 1."

166 "It felt like you were in Dante's Inferno": Frederic Forrest, *Apocalypse Now* interview, undated, American Zoetrope Library Archives.

166 "And the dreams": Forrest, *Apocalypse Now* interview.

167 It might even be a masterpiece: Eleanor Coppola, *Notes: On the Making of Apocalypse Now*, 173.

167 "What do you think you're gonna be": "'Lost and Found Sound': 5-Year-Old Sofia Coppola," *All Things Considered*, NPR, February 27, 2004, https://www.npr.org/templates/story/story.php?storyId=1721966.

167 "TOM, PLS RELAY": Coppola to Tom Sternberg, telex, *Apocalypse Now* correspondence, American Zoetrope Library Archives.

168 "PLEASE HAVE DR. REISS": Dave to Mona Skager, telex, *Apocalypse Now* correspondence, American Zoetrope Library Archives.

168 "DEAR PRESIDENT CARTER": Coppola to President Jimmy Carter, telex, *Apocalypse Now* correspondence, American Zoetrope Library Archives.

169 "MY TELEXES TO YOU": Coppola to Robin, telex, *Apocalypse Now* correspondence, American Zoetrope Library Archives.

171 "Dear John": Coppola to John Lennon, *Apocalypse Now* correspondence, American Zoetrope Library Archives.

171 "The following are the projects": Coppola to Barry Hirsch et al., telex, *Apocalypse Now* correspondence, American Zoetrope Library Archives.

173 "to live every moment": Eleanor Coppola, *Notes: On the Making of Apocalypse Now*, 176.

173 "creating the very situation": Eleanor Coppola, *Notes: On the Making of Apocalypse Now*, 177.

173 "NORMALLY, I WOULD BE FURIOUS": Coppola to Eleanor Coppola, telex, *Apocalypse Now* correspondence, American Zoetrope Library Archives.

174 "MY MOST SINCERE THANKS": Coppola, telex, *Apocalypse Now* correspondence, American Zoetrope Library Archives.

174 "IT IS IMPOSSIBLE": Coppola to Tom Sternberg, telex, *Apocalypse Now* correspondence, American Zoetrope Library Archives.

175   "this is the problem with film": Coppola to Barense, July 5, 1965, American Zoetrope Library Archives.

175   "F.F. Coppola let it be known": "Untitled Item," *Weekly Variety*, April 20, 1977.

176   "Willard's journey up the river": Cowie, *Apocalypse Now Book*, 36–37.

176   "Italians that come from": Commentary, *The Godfather Part I*, Paramount, 2001, DVD.

176   "My parents have that": Breskin, "Francis Ford Coppola."

176   "I was always in trouble": "Literary Arts: The Archive Project—Francis Ford Coppola in Conversation with Melena Ryzik," KUOW, November 15, 2017.

177   "gotten so crazy": Stephen Lighthill, AI.

177   "I didn't have any idea": Martin Sheen, *Apocalypse Now* interview, undated, American Zoetrope Library Archives.

177   "I need you to go": Barrie Osborne, American Film Institute, April 21, 2004.

177   "It's only a movie": Martin Sheen, *Apocalypse Now* interview, undated, American Zoetrope Library Archives.

177   "I completely fell apart": Schumacher, *Francis Ford Coppola*, 227.

177   "because if you stop": Tom Sternberg, *Apocalypse Now* interview, undated, American Zoetrope Library Archives.

177   "We didn't know if he": Marcus, "Journey Up the River."

177   "I was scared shitless": Francis Ford Coppola, AI.

178   "Coppola Cinema 7's": Francis Ford Coppola to Tom Sternberg, Fred Roos, and Barry Hirsch, telex, American Zoetrope Library Archives.

178   "any speculation to the contrary": Coppola to Tom Sternberg, Fred Roos, and Barry Hirsch, telex, American Zoetrope Library Archives.

178   as close to death: Eleanor Coppola, *Notes: On the Making of Apocalypse Now*, 184.

178   "He is not dead": Apocalypse Now—Conversation Martin Sheen and Francis Ford Coppola, YouTube, https://www.youtube.com/watch?v=9BkChat11cE.

178   "There are a lot of emotional memories": Schumacher, *Francis Ford Coppola*, 497.

178   "Everybody I knew who cared about us": Cowie, *Coppola*, 27–28.

178   "HAVE FULL RANGE": Coppola to Jean Autrey, telex, *Apocalypse Now* correspondence, American Zoetrope Library Archives.

179   "Where'd these come": Gray Frederickson, *Apocalypse Now* interview, undated, American Zoetrope Library Archives.

179   "like you were in a dream": Frederic Forrest, *The Merv Griffin Show*, season 1, episode, 26, January 9, 1980.

179   "He makes *Apocalypse*": Paul Cullum and George Hickenlooper, "Wham Bam Thank You 'Nam," *Neon*, n.d.

180   "was in unbelievable crisis": Walter Murch, interview, Web of Stories, https://webofstories.com/.

180   "One other thing": Walter Murch, interview, Web of Stories, https://webofstories.com/.

180   "We need six tracks now": Walter Murch, interview, Web of Stories, https://webofstories.com/.

180   *Apocalypse* would be an event: Walter Murch, interview, Web of Stories, https://webofstories.com/.

180   "Where are we going to mix?": Walter Murch, AI.

181   "When are you going": Mike Medavoy, AI.

181   "an incident occurred": Aaron H. Meister, M.D., to Dr. Klass P. Honig, November 10, 1962, American Zoetrope Library Archives.

181   "I threw myself on the floor": Coppola to Dr. D. M. Meeks, October 11, 1961, American Zoetrope Library Archives.

181   "an anxiety neurosis": Aaron H. Meister, M.D., to Dr. Klass P. Honig, November 10, 1962, American Zoetrope Library Archives

182   "GOING ON VACATION": Lucas to Coppola, telex, *Apocalypse Now* correspondence, American Zoetrope Library Archives.

182   "THANKS FOR YR TLX": Italia Coppola to Francis Ford Coppola, telex, *Apocalypse Now* correspondence, American Zoetrope Library Archives.

182   "create a big show": Stephen Burum, "A Clash of Two Cultures," *American Cinematographer*, February 2001.

182   "you couldn't buy a ticket": Eleanor Coppola, *Notes: On the Making of Apocalypse Now*, 189.

183   "IN THE EVENT": Coppola to Tom Sternberg, telex, *Apocalypse Now* correspondence, American Zoetrope Library Archives.

183   "We're getting a divorce": Eleanor Coppola, *Notes: On the Making of Apocalypse Now*, 193.

183   "impossible question of dual loyalties": Breskin, "Francis Ford Coppola."

183   but Melissa Mathison, he said: Breskin, "Francis Ford Coppola."

183   "[It's] about a husband": Cott, "Francis Coppola: The Rolling Stone Interview (1982)."

184   "cliches and predictable characters": Coppola to Carroll Ballard, telex, American Zoetrope Library Archives.

184   "I would like to clarify": "Case Histories of Business Management: A Memo from Francis Ford Coppola," *Esquire* 88, no. 5 (November 1977).

188   "trying to avoid the interior pain": Martin Sheen, *Apocalypse Now* interview, undated, American Zoetrope Library Archives.

188   "I don't know if that was Vietnam": Doug Claybourne, AI.

188   "out there for the other vets": Doug Claybourne, AI.

189   "into a giant opaque ball of gasoline": Andy Aaron, AI.

189   "Nobody move!": Andy Aaron, AI.

189   "I heard the words": Andy Aaron, AI.

189   "Is this Francis": Peter Dornbach, AI.

189   "I am emerging from": Eleanor Coppola, *Notes: On the Making of Apocalypse Now*, 230.

189   In a dream, she was a mummy: Eleanor Coppola, *Notes: On the Making of Apocalypse Now*, 214.

189   "More and more people": Cowie, *Coppola*, 116.

190   "We can do all the dreams": Biskind, *Easy Riders, Raging Bulls*, 340.

190   "These were opportunities": Francis Ford Coppola, AI.

191   "We were finished": Biskind, *Easy Riders, Raging Bulls*, 344.

191   "it's all up to you now": Biskind, *Easy Riders, Raging Bulls*, 346.

191   "If you go under, Francis": *Merv Griffin Show*, December 10, 1979. YouTube, https://www.youtube.com /watch?v=warHLZyBKAg.

191   "COPPOLA HOCKS": Jim Harwood, "Coppola Hocks Assets to UA for 'Apocalypse' End Money," *Daily Variety*, June 8, 1977.

192   "I'm willing to die": *A Million Feet of Film: The Editing of Apocalypse Now*, directed by Kim Aubry, available as a featurette on *Apocalypse Now: The Complete Dossier*, Paramount, 2006, DVD.

192   *Leave It to Beaver* story: Carroll Ballard and Scott Foundas, interview, *The Black Stallion*, Criterion, 2015, Blu-ray.

192   "You could get fifteen": Carroll Ballard, AI.

192   "I was having a terrible time": Carroll Ballard, *Daily Variety*, August 14, 1979.

193   "I want to do the scene with Mickey": Caleb Deschanel, AI.

193   "I have no illusions": Mal Karman, "The Black Stallion: Director Carroll Ballard's Struggle for Survival," *South Bay Magazine*, 1980.

193   "Good luck": "Visual History with Carroll Ballard," interview by Robert Markowitz, Directors Guild of America, https://www.dga.org/Craft/VisualHistory/Interviews/Carroll-Ballard.aspx?Filter=Full%20 Interview.

193   "regarded me as a total moron": Carroll Ballard, AI.

193   "Okay, Carroll": Caleb Deschanel, AI.

193   "I got a few pieces": Caleb Deschanel, AI.

193   as a pebble he carried: Carroll Ballard, AI.

193   a boy in the woods: Carroll Ballard, AI.

193   *We all have those friends*: Carroll Ballard, AI.

193   "If it wasn't for Francis": Caleb Deschanel, AI.

194   "previsualize": April Calou, AI.

194   "It was a one and only": April Calou, AI.

194   process of thinking: Dennis Gassner, AI.

194   "a poet with": Richard Candib, AI.

194   rumored to have been part of brothel for sailors: Dan Gleich, AI.

195   "fair amount of partying ": Dan Gleich, AI.

195   "totally massive amount of film": *A Million Feet of Film*.

195   They were all amateurs: Richard Beggs, AI.

195   "most exciting place on earth": Martha Cronin, AI.

195   "One time, I saw a piece of mail": Peter Dornbach, AI.

195   "promised land for anyone who was interested": Leana Lovejoy, AI.

196   "like going to Mecca": Dennis Gassner, AI.

196   "A Never-Neverland": Arthur Coburn, AI.

196   "Can you type?": Arden Bucklin-Sporer, AI.

196   "which only had food stuff": Holland Sutton, AI.

196   "I think she thought": Holland Sutton, AI.

196   "When postproduction": Karen Frerichs, AI.

196   "It was that casual": Karen Frerichs, AI.

196   "People just showed up": Richard Candib, AI.

196   never knew when the phone would ring: Tess Haley, AI.

196   "like somebody would walk in": Trudy Hamm, AI.

197   "Let's give everyone the day off": Tess Haley, AI.

197   "very paranoid Anna Magnani": Trudy Hamm, AI.

197   "People would walk in": Martha Cronin, AI.

197   "I didn't know how crazy": Trudy Hamm, AI.

197   "What we were doing": Trudy Hamm, AI.

198   "The mood swings": Trudy Hamm, AI.

198   "The place was crazy": Jean Autrey, AI.

198   "Everybody wound up": Karen Frerichs, AI.

198   "the cool kids": Michael Lehmann, AI.

198   "Ah, the ladies": Leana Lovejoy, AI.

198   "the law": Walter Murch, interview, Web of Stories, https://webofstories.com/.

198   "I'm the poster boy": Walter Murch, interview, Web of Stories, https://webofstories.com/.

199   "I want the film": Jean-Paul Chaillet and Elizabeth Vincent, *Francis Ford Coppola*, trans. Denise Raab Jacobs (New York: St. Martin's Pres, 1985), 79.

199 "lot of bus crash headlines": Karen Frerichs, AI.

199 "Oh my god, you went crazy": Karen Frerichs, AI.

199 "Sell the house": Sherry Rogers, AI.

199 "When you're editing": *A Million Feet of Film*.

200 "He had something in mind": Andy Aaron, AI.

200 "a leader from": Doug Claybourne, AI.

200 "I feel that it helps": *A Million Feet of Film*.

201 "Francis saw I was the guy": Jerry Greenberg, AI.

201 "What the hell are you doing?": Richard Candib, AI.

201 He had promised he wouldn't see her: Eleanor Coppola, *Notes: On the Making of Apocalypse Now*, 214.

201 Outside her body, Eleanor watched: Eleanor Coppola, *Notes: On the Making of Apocalypse Now*, 213.

201 dictionary definition of *apocalypse*: Eleanor Coppola, *Notes: On the Making of Apocalypse Now*, 213.

202 a studio within a city: Francis Ford Coppola, *Live Cinema and Its Techniques* (New York: Liveright Press, 2017), 27.

202 "Fool, fool": Dennis Jakob, *Apocalypse Now* interview, undated, American Zoetrope Library Archives.

203 "a singularly cyclic disease": Kay Redfield Jamison, *Touched with Fire: Manic-Depressive Illness and the Artistic Temperament* (New York: Free Press, 1993), 6.

204 "I come of a race": Jamison, *Touched with Fire*, 116.

204 "You know, my wife": Dennis Jakob, *Apocalypse Now* interview, undated, American Zoetrope Library Archives.

204 "fucking hit the roof": Dennis Jakob, *Apocalypse Now* interview, undated, American Zoetrope Library Archives.

204 "Word got out quickly": Tim Holland, AI.

204 "Francis, this is reel one": Dennis Jakob, *Apocalypse Now* interview, undated, American Zoetrope Library Archives.

204 "He was really affable": Tim Holland, AI.

204 "Boy, did that guy *sweat*": Dennis Jakob, *Apocalypse Now* interview, undated, American Zoetrope Library Archives.

204 "Back in the Saddle Again": Tim Holland, AI.

205 "He would occasionally scream": Tim Holland, AI.

205 "What was that noise?": Tim Holland, AI.

205 "like a knife": Francis Ford Coppola, AI.

205 "an act of God": Richard Candib, Waiting for the Apocalypse 1979, YouTube, https://www.youtube.com/watch?v=mu9kby-UaZg.

205 "What had actually happened": Francis Ford Coppola, AI.

206 "Those who didn't mind stealing": Aggie Murch, AI.

206 In May 1978: Eleanor Coppola, *Notes: On the Making of Apocalypse Now*, 266.

206 Walter Murch dreamt in silence: Walter Murch, AI.

207 young man's voice: Dan Gleich, AI.

207 "The picture, the vision": Mark Berger, AI.

207 "a quest to explore": Mark Berger, AI.

207 "Team spirit": Richard Beggs, AI.

207 "There were a lot of personal damages": Richard Beggs, AI.

208 "It was the chicken": Richard Beggs, AI.

208 "It had to be real": Richard Beggs, AI.

208 "just these headsets": Richard Beggs, AI.

208 "interior helicopter noise": Richard Beggs, AI.

208 "You be the pilot": Richard Beggs, AI.

208 "but over a relatively": Richard Beggs, AI.

208 "When Willard murders": Randy Thom, AI.

208 "was so in the zone": Andy Moore, AI.

208 "Put up reel two": Andy Moore, AI.

209 "I think if you are fully invested": Randy Thom, AI.

209 "Francis wanted even the foley": Randy Thom, AI.

209 "You'll hear five or six": Randy Thom, AI.

209 The Ghost Helicopter: Michael Sragow, "The Sound of Vietnam," *Salon*, April 27, 2000, https://www.salon.com/test/2000/04/27/murch/.

209 "Walter was using his emotion": Randy Thom, AI.

209 "was like one of those moments": Sragow, "The Sound of Vietnam."

209 he could never forget it: Vittorio Storaro, The American Film Institute and American Society of Cinematographers Seminar with Vittorio Storaro, Center for Advanced Film Studies, 1980.

209 "I, therefore had become Willard": Walter Murch, "Sound Minds Seminar," AMPAS Margaret Herrick Library, October 11, 2000, 42.

209 "*Apocalypse* was tough": Aggie Murch, AI.

209 "And Francis fucking loved that": Zoetrope typist, AI.

210 with a serial killer gleam: Zoetrope typist, AI.

210 "Everyone was exhausted": Michael Herr, *Apocalypse Now* interview, undated, American Zoetrope Library Archives.

210 "'thousand yard' stare": Herr, *Apocalypse Now* interview.

210 "What happened in Vietnam": Herr, *Apocalypse Now* interview.

210 "I would be working thirty-six": Herr, *Apocalypse Now* interview.

210 The name on the label: Zoetrope typist, AI.

211 "When am I going to read it?": Lucy Fisher, AI.

211 "No, no. This one is different": Armyan Bernstein, AI.

211 "It's one from the heart": Lucy Fisher, AI.

211 "Francis Ford Coppola": Armyan Bernstein, AI.

211 "I'm sorry to bother you": Armyan Bernstein, AI.

212 "entertaining and popular": Coppola, *Live Cinema and Its Techniques*, 70.

212 "about innocent romantic confusion": Zoetrope typist, AI.

212 "By his own admission": Zoetrope typist, AI.

213 She was the Little Mermaid: Francis Ford Coppola, *My Fairy Tale* screenplay, rough draft, June 1982, American Zoetrope Library Archives.

213 "She can't cross the street": Coppola, *My Fairy Tale* screenplay.

213 "for me a transformation": Francis Ford Coppola, AI.

213 his soul had gone up into the picture: Wendy Doniger, AI.

213 "I wasn't allowed": Francis Ford Coppola, AI.

213 "I slept in beds": Francis Ford Coppola, AI.

213 "I have done amazing things": Francis Ford Coppola, AI.

214 "and the next thing I knew": Francis Ford Coppola, AI.

214 "You have a girl in here!": Francis Ford Coppola, AI.

214 "Francis was the king": Emy Spiotta, AI.

214 "It was a real romance": Emy Spiotta, AI.

214 "about her son getting involved": Emy Spiotta, AI.

214 "Francis was so mad": Emy Spiotta, AI.

214 "just lived and breathed *Streetcar*": Emy Spiotta, AI.

214 "I'm a big consumer": Murray, "Francis Ford Coppola: *Playboy* Interview."

215 "live in the same fantasy spirit": Murray, "Francis Ford Coppola: *Playboy* Interview."

215 "Francis! No": Apocalypse Now—Conversation Martin Sheen and Francis Ford Coppola.

215 "Italians call him *regista*": 51st Annual Academy Awards, "The Deer Hunter and Michael Cimino winning Best Picture and Directing: 1979 Oscars," YouTube, https://www.youtube.com/watch?v=og8pywu8gbU.

216 "That was *old* to us": Karen Frerichs, AI.

216 "like *Midsummer Night's Dream*": Martha Cronin, AI.

216 punk rock orchestra: Dan Gleich, AI.

216 "otherwise talented": Jerry Ross, AI.

216 "Hey hey hey": Dan Gleich, AI.

216 "Happy Birthday from One Yenta": Paul Broucek, AI.

216 "All that is good in life": Gary Fettis, AI.

217 Lucasfilm, in khaki shorts: Unnamed Zoetrope typist, AI.

217 "They were all quite clean": Unnamed Zoetrope typist, AI.

217 "Bobbing for Smitchies": Paul Hirsch, "The Droid Olympics: When Editing Was a Competitive Sport," *Cinemontage*, March 1, 2005, https://cinemontage.org/the-droid-olympics/.

217 "If I ever got the bucks": Tony Chiu, "Francis Coppola's Cinematic 'Apocalypse' Is Finally at Hand," *New York Times*, August 12, 1979.

217 "really an extraordinary dream": Rubin, *Droidmaker*, 81.

218 "All the billions of dollars": Rubin, *Droidmaker*, 81.

218 "It took eight months": Rubin, *Droidmaker*, 84

218 "These kids": Lynnea Johnson, AI.

218 "We got these kids here": Lynnea Johnson, AI.

218 "Where are the kids?": Lynnea Johnson, AI.

218 "he didn't want to go back": Linda Phillips-Palo, AI.

219 "It turned out to be Gio": Karen Frerichs, AI.

219 "It was a wonderful idea": Lynnea Johnson, AI.

219 "Francis had asked me who": *The Music of Apocalypse Now*, directed by Kim Aubry, *Apocalypse Now: The Complete Dossier*, Paramount, 2006, DVD.

219 "bastardized analog-digital": Blair Jackson, "Apocalypse Now: The Music," *BAM Magazine*, October 5, 1979.

220 "like our involvement in Vietnam": Jackson, "Apocalypse Now: The Music."

220 "demands of this score": Jackson, "Apocalypse Now: The Music."

220 "laid out the instruments": Jackson, "Apocalypse Now: The Music."

220 "every primitive sound known to man": *The Music of Apocalypse Now*.

220 "I can see what": Clark Higgins, AI.

221 "We'll make media": Clark Higgins, AI.

221 "digital skyscraper": Clark Higgins, AI.

221 "in a little factory": Chiu, "Francis Coppola's Cinematic 'Apocalypse' Is Finally at Hand."

222 "It was over the top": Sherry Rogers, AI.

222 "Just let the train": Barry Hirsch, AI.

222 "saw him lose his patience": Michael Lehmann, AI.

222 "making movies will be like": Michael Lehmann, AI.

222 "Cinema's all going": Michael Lehmann, AI.

222 "spinning very fast": Francis Ford Coppola, AI.

223 L.A. screenings were just *previews*: Tess Haley, AI.

223 *"what if* we took the movie": Tom Sternberg, *Apocalypse Now* interview, undated, American Zoetrope Library Archives.

224 "Walter would come in": Karen Frerichs, AI.

224 *What if he went off a cliff*: Karen Frerichs, AI.

224 "Walter, it's time for lunch": Doug Hemphill, AI.

225 longest, most intricate sound mix: Randy Thom, AI.

225 "car has replaced": Doug Hemphill, AI.

225 "Reel two again, please": Doug Hemphill, AI.

225 the machine room: Andy Moore, AI.

225 "The machine room": Andy Moore, AI.

225 "We never left the building": Randy Thom, AI.

226 "We took off our shoes": Tess Haley, AI.

226 "I was in the navy": George Altamura, AI.

226 "most public sneak preview": Karl French, *Apocalypse Now: A Bloomsbury Movie Guide* (London: Bloomsbury, 1998), 24.

226 "Are you nervous": Tess Haley, AI.

227 "to the virtual exclusion": Andrew Sarris, "First Assault on 'Apocalypse Now,'" *Village Voice*, May 28, 1979.

227 "Find Bob Spiotta": Tess Haley, AI.

227 "Are you drunk?": Emy Spiotta, AI.

227 "all of two seconds": Emy Spiotta, AI.

227 "was a magical": Robin Supak, AI.

228 "And don't think for one second": Tess Haley, AI.

228 "What do you make now?": Tess Haley, AI.

228 "definitely a fake-it": Robin Supak, AI.

228 "on how to run movie studio": Robin Supak, AI.

228 Nor was there anything written: Tess Haley, AI.

228 "on how you handle": Tess Haley, AI.

228 "C'mon, Sofia": "apocalypse now: francis ford coppola on french press conference," Cinephile Global, n.d., YouTube, https://www.youtube.com/watch?v=-PEEGGeOSjs.

229 "I like Coca-Cola": George Altamura, AI.

II. THE APOCALYPSE

234 "It started very slowly": Barry Hirsch, AI.

235 "the most lucid account": Pauline Kael, *Notes* blurb.

235 the book brought visibility: Eleanor Coppola, email to author.

235 Eleanor withdrew from her press tour: Eleanor Coppola, AI.

235 "I was lonely": Jean-Paul Chaillet and Elizabeth Vincent, *Francis Ford Coppola*, trans. Denise Raab Jacobs (New York: St. Martin's Pres, 1985), 75.

236 "When I was first married": Cowie, *Coppola*, 7.

236 "I didn't want to lose": Breskin, "Francis Ford Coppola."

236 There was in Japan: Coppola, audio commentary, *One from the Heart*, American Zoetrope, 2004, DVD.

236 "the desire to work": Coppola, audio commentary, *One from the Heart*.

237 "my superproduction": Douglas J. Rowe, "A Special place in Coppola's 'Heart,'" *Los Angeles Times*, December 26, 2003.

237 "One [*Elective Affinities* film] will take": Jonathan Cott, "Francis Coppola: The Rolling Stone Interview (1982)," Scraps from the Loft, December 12, 2016, https://scrapsfromtheloft.com/2016/12/12/francis -coppola-the-rolling-stone-interview-1982/.

237 "It was like telling Michelangelo": Dianna Waggoner, "In Homage to the Master, George Lucas and Francis Coppola Unleash Their Clout for Kurosawa," *People*, October 27, 1080.

237 "I contacted Kurosawa": Michael Schumacher, *Francis Ford Coppola: A Filmmaker's Life* (New York: Crown, 1999), 282.

238 "We have the tremendous talent": Michael Ventura, "Coppola on Coppola."

238 "area that is perhaps so radical": Marge Costello, "Conversation with Francis Ford Coppola," *Videography*, September 1982.

239 "My idea of the perfect studio": Rowe, "A Special Place in Coppola's 'Heart.'"

240 "Army, what is love?": Armyan Bernstein, AI.

241 "little Zoetrope SWAT team": Tim Onosko, "Media Madness," *Village Voice*, April 21, 1980.

241 "Holy shit": Onosko, "Media Madness."

241 "If something goes wrong": Onosko, "Media Madness."

241 "Jerry didn't want to rehearse": Tess Haley, AI.

242 "and a little hole": April Calou, AI.

242 "worst production experience": Clark Higgins, AI.

242 "When I came back to California": Cott, "Francis Coppola: The Rolling Stone Interview (1982)."

242 "it can be Utopia": Rich Cohen, "Francis Ford Coppola's Third Act: Italy, Wine, and the Secret of Life," *Vanity Fair*, February 3, 2016, https://www.vanityfair.com/hollywood/2016/02/francis-ford-coppola-italy -wine-and-the-secret-of-life.

242 Plato's *Republic*: Patrick Goldstein, "Count Coppola," *Los Angeles Times Magazine*, August 4, 1996.

242 "school of the arts": David Rosengarten, "On Coppola's Plate, It's Food, Not Film," *New York Times*, February 16, 1994, https://www.nytimes.com/1994/02/16/style/on-coppolas-plate-its-food-not-film.html.

243 "the young people of that country": David Thomson and Lucy Gray, "Idols of the King."

243 "Dad, dad, c'mon!": "Virtual Vacation Blancaneaux Lodge - A Family Coppola Hideaway," The Family Coppola Hideaways, May 14, 2021, YouTube, https://www.youtube.com/watch?v=oJD6UisGYF8.

243 "We don't have TV sets": Goldstein, "Count Coppola."

243 "Francis was screaming": Michael Lehmann, AI.

244 "*The Empire Strikes Back* joins": Michael Coate, "The Force Defeated: Remembering 'The Empire Strikes Back' on Its 35th Anniversary," May 21, 2015, The Digital Bits, https://thedigitalbits.com/columns/history -legacy-showmanship/force-defeated-empire-strikes-back-35th.

244 "We both have the same goals": Jon Lewis, *Whom God Wishes to Destroy . . . Francis Coppola and the New Hollywood* (Durham, NC: Duke University Press, 1997), 40.

244 "trying to change a system": Lewis, *Whom God Wishes to Destroy*.

244 "Lucas has a bank called *Star Wars*": Richard Corliss, "The New Hollywood: Dead or Alive," *Time*, March 30, 1981.

244 "my hope and ambition": Electronic Imagery Conference Final Report, August 1980, American Zoetrope Library Archives.

244 "It was like a mind meld": Louise Ledeen, AI.

244 "George has many applications": Electronic Imagery Conference Final Report.

245 "psychological realities": Louise Ledeen, AI.

245 "full range of everything": Electronic Imagery Conference Final Report.

246 "a living high school": Dale Pollock, "Coppola Unveils His New Studio," *Los Angeles Times*, March 21, 1980.

247 "The optimism, the bursts": Dan Attias, AI.

247 smell of old mold and wood: Mitch Dubin, AI.

247 "be the director of design": Dean Tavoularis, AI.

248 "You shouldn't be reading that": Dana Spiotta, AI.

248 "a world that was": Armyan Bernstein, AI.

248 "Camelot of the movie business": Barry Hirsch, AI.

249 "story about a little girl": "Lucy," Sofia Coppola and Andrea, "Lucy," American Zoetrope Library Archives.

249 "We were troublemakers": Jenny Gersten, AI.

249 "Because we lived nearby": Sofia Coppola, AI.

249 "era was so glamorous": Sofia Coppola, AI.

250 "We were little rascals": Jenny Gersten, AI.

250 "I want to make *this* movie": Jenny Gersten, AI.

250 "It was so inspiring": Sofia Coppola, AI.

250 "All the people working there": Sofia Coppola, AI.

250 "It was a child's world": Jilian Gersten, AI.

250 "Francis was interested": Jill Kearney, AI.

250 "Francis was interested in everyone": Jill Kearney, AI.

251 "was like a Roman chalice overflowing": Teri Fettis, AI.

251 "I thought it was adorable": Jill Kearney, AI.

251 "Max was a real old-timer": Anne Diamond, AI.

251 "That's the kind of people": Doug Claybourne, AI.

251 *Oh my goodness*: Jill Kearney, AI.

251 "where everybody was always nervous": Ben Cowitt, AI.

252 "if you were doing a mural": Dean Tavoularis, AI.

252 "It became apparent": Thomas Brown, AI.

252 "Francis was making a think tank": Dan Attias, AI.

252 "I become my characters": April Calou, AI.

253 "brought everyone together": Dean Tavoularis, AI.

253 "knowledgeable you are": Michael Lehmann, AI.

253 "first impression" edit: "Mating Film with Video for 'One from the Heart,'" *American Cinematographer*, January 1982.

253 "creative elements of filmmaking": Clark Higgins, AI.

253 "I think where Francis was headed": Thomas Brown, AI.

253 "I want it to *be* me": Clark Higgins, AI.

254 "connected to every aspect": YouTube, https://www.youtube.com/watch?v=2pg52tzGRvs.

254 "I want images": Thomas Brown, AI.

254 "It was springtime at Zoetrope": Thomas Brown, AI.

254 *There is something crazy about all this*: Walter Murch, AI.

254 Roger Corman smiled: Roger Corman, AI.

254 "If you were in a recording studio": Jeffrey Wells, "A Film Journal Interview: Francis Ford Coppola," *Film Journal*, September 7, 1981.

254 "The Zoetrope drug policy": Dorothy Meriwether, AI.

254 "resentment and kind of nastiness": Michael Lehmann, AI.

254 "This technology shouldn't": Clark Higgins, AI.

254 "information technology, video technology": Clark Higgins, AI.

255 "advances in communication": Clark Higgins, AI.

255 *Art*, he thought, *not for the popes*: "Francis Ford Coppola: Inside the Coppola personality (1981)," Cinema Garmonboazia, April 28, 2017, YouTube, https://www.youtube.com/watch?v=2pg52tzGRvs.

255 "And he didn't even charge me rent": Lillian Michelson, AI.

255 "I never charged my home studio": Lillian Michelson, AI.

255 "within twenty minutes": Lillian Michelson, AI.

256 "I want to be a sailor": "A Pretty British Affair" (Michael Powell and Emeric Pressburger), directed by Charles Chabot and Gavin Millar, *Arena*, BBC, November 1981.

256 "I hope you will feel free": Todd McCarthy, "Michael Powell: Zoetrope's 'Sr. Director in Residence,'" *Variety*, November 14, 1980.

256 "Can Michael Powell": Dean Tavoularis, AI.

256 "It was absolutely wonderful to me": "A Pretty British Affair."

256 "I felt as if I had come home": Goldstein, "Count Coppola."

256 "He was crazy about tennis": Dean Tavoularis, AI.

257 "is something of an experiment": "Tout va bien—at Zoetrope," *Los Angeles Herald Examiner*, September 22, 1980.

257 "why Italy invented": "Tout va bien—at Zoetrope."

257 "all good American directors": "The Economics of Film Criticism: A Debate," *Camera Obscura*, 1982.

257 "a golden era of UA": Lucy Fisher, AI.

257 "not like a studio executive's life": Lucy Fisher, AI.

258 "How will I know": Lucy Fisher, AI.

258 "want me to do my job": Lucy Fisher, AI.

258 "to have meetings": Lucy Fisher, AI.

258 "What's the worst": Lucy Fisher, AI.

258 "to our collaboration": Lucy Fisher, AI.

258 "to keep [his own] nose": Bernard Gersten and John DiLeo, *My Life as It Were*, unpublished manuscript, Bernie Gerstein Papers

259 "affirmative idea develops ": "Iberia—Amsterdam to Madrid 3.X.1979," Bernard Gersten Papers.

259 "The way Gene Kelly": Tess Haley, AI.

259 "If Gene likes you": Kenny Ortega, AI.

259 "What I'm saying": Charles Schreger, "Coppola and Kelly Singin' in the Sun," *Los Angeles Times*, October 8, 1980.

260 "I hired two court stenographers": Tess Haley, AI.

260 "times when he just slept": Arne Schmidt, AI.

260 "But he's an artist": Eleanor Coppola, AI.

261 "Francis's whole thing": Eleanor Coppola, AI.

261 "shooting out our message": Clark Higgins, AI.

261 "My dad told me": Francis Ford Coppola, AI.

262 "Kenny, Kenny, Kenny!": Kenny Ortega, AI.

262 "I was becoming me": Kenny Ortega, AI.

262 was so euphoric: Kenny Ortega, AI.

262 "Janet [Hirshenson] and I have": Jane Jenkins, AI.

262 "Francis would not": Jane Jenkins, AI.

262 "It was a different mind-set": Jane Jenkins, AI.

262 job was not to say no: Susie Landau Finch, AI.

262 "It was a cattle call": Rebecca De Mornay, AI.

263 "Anybody who wanted": Aleta Chappelle, AI.

263 "Actors were calling": Jane Jenkins, AI.

263 "Nasstasja's here": Susie Landau Finch, AI.

263 "What do I": Susie Landau Finch, AI.

263 "most beautiful thing": Susie Landau Finch, AI.

263 "You were welcome": Roy Johns, AI.

264 "It was magical": Sofia Coppola, AI.

264 "Francis was constantly": Dan Attias, AI.

264 "It's the ideal situation": Tony and Ann St. John, *One from the Heart* documentary videotapes, January 7, 1980, American Zoetrope Film Archives.

264 "I wonder how Tom's doing": Arne Schmidt, AI.

264 "I usually get Francis": Tony and Ann St. John, *One from the Heart* documentary videotapes.

265 "Zeus and Hera": Tony and Ann St. John, *One from the Heart* documentary videotapes.

265 "It looked like": Arne Schmidt, AI.

265 "How's it going?": Arne Schmidt, AI.

265 "Something might have happened": Tony and Ann St. John, *One from the Heart* documentary videotapes.

265 "Kathleen had heard": Robert Hilburn, " 'Heart' LP Was Just Waits, See," *L.A. Times*, November 16, 1982.

266 "You could see it happening": Ed Rugoff, AI.

266 "sun goes down in L.A.": Robert Kensinger, AI.

266 "probably go back": Robert Kensinger, AI.

266 "He played the hell": Arne Schmidt, AI.

266 "know who Preston Sturges was": Jeff Hamlin, AI.

267 "talk to every single person": Rebecca De Mornay, AI.

267 "adoptive father": Tony and Ann St. John, "Tape 01," *One from the Heart* documentary videotapes, February 19, American Zoetrope Film Archives.

267 "brought this to show you": Tony and Ann St. John, "Tape 16," *One from the Heart* documentary videotapes, 1980, American Zoetrope Film Archives.

267 Zoetrope had prepared: *One from the Heart* documentary videotapes, 1980, American Zoetrope Film Archives.

267 "I went here when I was a kid": Tony and Ann St. John, "Tape 16," *One from the Heart* documentary videotapes.

268 "like the Pied Piper": Anne Diamond, AI.

268 "Now this is yours": Francis Ford Coppola, AI.

268 "You should have seen the look": Arne Schmidt, AI.

268 sets for *One from the Heart*: Tess Haley, AI.

268 "truly one of the objectives": Francis Ford Coppola, AI.

269 "Use 'em as bookmarks": Tony and Ann St. John, "Tape 16," *One from the Heart* documentary videotapes.

269 "lucky to have this training": Tony and Ann St. John, *One from the Heart* documentary videotapes, February 4, 1981.

269 "Joey is already": Christina Adam, "Interning with The Godfather," *Moving Image*, January/February 1982.

270 "What's he doing?": Tony and Ann St. John, "Tape 04," *One from the Heart* documentary videotapes, January 30, 1981.

270 "I think sometimes": Adam, "Interning with The Godfather."

270 "professional education": Milena Balandzich, "Zoetrope Plans High School on Lot to Encourage Students," *Hollywood Reporter*, April 9, 1980.

270 "I don't want to be minister of culture": Francis Ford Coppola, AI.

271 "Why don't *you*": Francis Ford Coppola, AI.

271 "achieved buying the television station": Tony and Ann St. John, *One from the Heart* documentary videotapes, September 27–28, 1980.

272 stretched back eons: Francis Ford Coppola, AI.

272 Technology would bring: Francis Ford Coppola, AI.

272 "My son, my son!": Gary Weimberg, AI.

272 "Pack tonight": Joanie Blum, AI.

273 "I need you guys": Joanie Blum, AI.

273 "Francis had this goal": Joanie Blum, AI.

273 "Come on, everybody": Dan Attias, AI.

273 "This is great": Dan Attias, AI.

273 "the everyday life": Lainie Kazan, AI.

273 "Wait!": Jeff Hamlin, AI.

273 "Francis lives": Joanie Blum, AI.

274 "We were in a musical": Kenny Ortega, AI.

274 "film *One from the Heart*": Ventura, "Coppola on Coppola."

274 "These guys would": Sondra Scerca, AI.

275 "People would come": Bernstein, *One from the Heart* AMPAS Screening, post-screening panel, AMPAS Margaret Herrick Library.

275 "that we not do it": Francis Ford Coppola, AI.

275 "There was not one iota": John Solomon, AI.

276 "Next please": John Solomon, AI.

276 "It wasn't a job": John Solomon, AI.

276 "Tell me about the book": Anonymous, AI.

276 "not *that* Steve Martin": Steve Martin, AI.

276 "*Ronnie Rocket* was a dream": David Lynch, Elton H. Rule Lecture in Telecommunications, *American Film Institute*, April 15, 1992.

276 "wouldn't be my film": Steve Martin, AI.

277 "Jean-Luc. Your camera's on": Susan Rogers, AI.

277 "take me to see *Raging Bull*": Ed Rugoff, AI.

277 "I kept thinking": Steve Martin, AI.

277 "Hiya, kid": Steve Martin, AI.

277 "sort of magical feeling": Steve Martin, AI.

277 "I didn't know him": Steve Martin, AI.

277 "more talent based": Lucy Fisher, AI.

277 "best four pages": Lucy Fisher, AI.

278 "brilliant, ahead of its time": Lucy Fisher, AI.

278 "find something for Mr. Vidor": Lucy Fisher, AI.

278 "This is how democratic": Lucy Fisher, AI.

278 "A general note": Tony and Ann St. John, *One from the Heart* documentary videotapes, December 30, 1980.

279 "How's your turkey?": Michael Lehmann, AI.

279 "an unqualified disaster": Vincent Canby, "'Heaven's Gate,' a Western by Cimino," *New York Times*, November 19, 1980.

280 "*Heaven's Gate*—the phenomenon": Lewis, *Whom God Wishes to Destroy*, 49.

280 "the great crafts": Lee Eisenberg, "The Conversation: Francis Coppola & Gay Talese," *Esquire*, July 1, 1981.

281 "corporate suicide": Stephen Prince, *A New Pot of Gold: Hollywood Under the Electronic Rainbow* (Berkeley: University of California Press, 2002), 39.

281 "no film business": Eisenberg, "The Conversation: Francis Coppola & Gay Talese."

281 "If that occurred in a [Twentieth] Century–Fox": Bob Spiotta, video interview with Tony and Ann St. John, American Zoetrope Film Archives.

282 "We expected our partners": Aljean Harmetz, "Coppola Is Risking It All Again," *Los Angeles Herald Examiner*, February 2, 1981.

282 "too many bed partners": Lucy Fisher, AI.

282 "Anyone in this business": Bob Spiotta, video interview with Tony and Ann St. John.

282 "through each week of shooting": Harmetz, "Coppola Is Risking It All Again."

282 "We had so much light": Gray Frederickson, AI.

283 "We've begun!": Armyan Bernstein, AI.

283 "we are changing our orientation": Gregg Kilday, "Coppola's Dream Postponed," *Los Angeles Herald Examiner*, February 3, 1981.

283 "the process of motion pictures": Kilday, "Coppola's Dream Postponed."

283 "Motion Picture technology": *One from the Heart* press conference footage, Tony and Ann St. John, American Zoetrope Film Archives.

284 film industries of Japan, Italy: Todd McCarthy, "High-Roller Coppola Gambles Studio on Future of the 'Electronic Cinema,'" *Daily Variety*, February 8, 1981.

284 "only one cinema": McCarthy, "High-Roller Coppola Gambles Studio on Future of the 'Electronic Cinema.'"

284 "hold something together": Michael Ventura, "Coppola's Woes and the Zoetrope Revolution," *LA Weekly*, February 13, 1981.

284 "The longer a film takes": Michael Goodwin and Naomi Wise, *On the Edge: The Life and Times of Francis Ford Coppola* (New York: William Morrow, 1989), 317.

284 "think Hollywood was out there rooting": Gray Frederickson, AI.

285 "How many times": Aljean Harmetz, "Coppola Risks All on $22 Million Movie," *New York Times*, February 2, 1981.

285 "After considerable thought": Francis Ford Coppola, draft of letter to Bob Spiotta and Barry Hirsch, American Zoetrope Library Archives.

286 "Francis shouldn't be shut down": Richard Corliss, "I'm Always in Money Trouble," *Time*, February 23, 1981.

286 "Francis being the emotional guy": Spiotta, video interview with Tony and Ann St. John.

286 "told them what the situation was": Spiotta, video interview with Tony and Ann St. John.

287 "Rather than lay off": Bob Spiotta Addresses Zoetrope Employees, Tony and Ann St. John, American Zoetrope Film Archives.

287 "mood here": Zoetroper.

287 "all of them had mortgages": Spiotta, video interview with Tony and Ann St. John.

287 "comprehensive package resolving this": Bob Spiotta Addresses Zoetrope Employees.

287 "responded in an incredibly supportive": Spiotta, video interview with Tony and Ann St. John.

287 "corny, non-jaded things": Spiotta, video interview with Tony and Ann St. John.

287 "Can we help": Spiotta, video interview with Tony and Ann St. John.

288 "that they would be patient": Spiotta, video interview with Tony and Ann St. John.

288 "what Zoetrope and Francis": Spiotta, video interview with Tony and Ann St. John.

288 "We're proud of it": Spiotta, video interview with Tony and Ann St. John.

288 "If a man's a friend ": Gregg Kilday, "Coppola's Troops Will Work for Free," *Los Angeles Herald Examiner*, February 7, 1981.

288 "Coppola has treated us right": Dale Pollock, "Zoetrope Workers Vote to Carry On," *Los Angeles Times*, February 7, 1981.

288 "literally in tears": Spiotta, video interview with Tony and Ann St. John.

288 "Are they ready?": Dan Attias, AI.

289 "history of Hollywood movie-making": Ann Salisbury, "Workers Give One from Heart, Pocket to Save Coppola's Film," *Los Angeles Herald-Examiner*, February 6, 1981.

289 "'I've never seen anything": Todd McCarthy, "Actor Forrest Gives Heart to Coppola Films," *Daily Variety*, February 8, 1982.

289 "scene from a Frank Capra film": Todd McCarthy, "Coppola's Employees Forgo Pay," *Daily Variety*, February 6, 1981.

289 "is virtually unprecedented": Pollock, "Zoetrope Workers Vote to Carry On."

289 "type of loyalty": Ray Loynd, "Worker-Zoetrope Honeymoon Wakes Up to Monday Reality," *Hollywood Reporter*, February 9, 1981.

289 "unable to restrain": McCarthy, "Coppola's Employees Forgo Pay."

289 "What was interesting": Bernard Gersten, memo to Ansen & Kasindorf from Bernard Gersten Vice President of Creative Affairs re: Treatment—the Zoetrope Story, undated, American Zoetrope Library Archives.

289 "Time isn't money": Francis Ford Coppola, AI.

289 "like really month to month": Kenny Ortega, AI.

289 "By risking all": *One from the Heart* documentary footage, June 24, 1981, Tony and Ann St. John, American Zoetrope Library Archives, https://vimeo.com/664542732.

289 "sharp edge of panic": *One from the Heart* documentary footage.

289 "you're feeling all": *One from the Heart* documentary footage.

289 "excitement that generates": *One from the Heart* documentary footage.

289 "All [bottom lines] tell you": *One from the Heart* documentary footage.

290 "Most everywhere you go": Ventura, "Coppola's Woes and the Zoetrope Revolution.

290 "don't sell the dream": Corliss, "I'm Always in Money Trouble.

291 "very much admire Mr. Coppola": Gregg Kilday, "$500,000 Personal Loan Helps Coppola Stay Afloat," *Los Angeles Herald Examiner*, February 21, 1981.

291 "and how Paris must survive ": *One from the Heart* documentary footage.

291 "Would you get on a plane": Rebecca De Mornay, AI.

292 "while Rome is burning": John Solomon, AI.

292 "no more incredible": Martha Cronin, AI.

292 "But that's how": Martha Cronin, AI.

292 "I sat on Rutger Hauer's lap": Holland Sutton, AI.

292 "such a nice little girl": Javier Grajeda, AI.

292 regularly ran out: Lainie Kazan, AI.

292 "bring your whole family": Lainie Kazan, AI.

292 "huge waste of money": Mitch Dubin, AI.

293 "like a cheerleading party": Sondra Scerca, AI.

293 "are you kidding": Michael Lehmann, AI.

293 "going to go down": Cynthia Kania, AI.

293 "parties were celebrations": Dennis Gassner, AI.

293 "extraordinary things happen": Coppola talk on Apocalypse Now 40 years restoration, Tribeca Film Festival, The Upcoming, YouTube, https://www.youtube.com/watch?v=YR0N9n0y1Ek.

294 "have to load in equipment": Arne Schmidt, AI.

294 "have the confidence": Arne Schmidt, AI.

294 working on a play: Cynthia Kania, AI.

294 "just to talk to us": Michael Lehmann, AI.

294 "It was like nirvana": Steve Martin, AI.

294 "small college we all wanted": Scot Haller, "Francis Coppola's Biggest Gamble," *Saturday Review*, July 1981.

294 "Tess, can you get": Tess Haley, AI.

295 "making the best movie ever": Michael Lehmann, AI.

295 Warren Beatty came: Joanie Blum, AI.

295 "hardest job I've ever done": Tony and Ann St. John, Teri Garr interview, Zoetrope Studios documentary footage, March 30, 1981. American Zoetrope Film Archives.

295 "Did they tell": Rebecca De Mornay, AI.

295 "have any life other": Tony and Ann St. John, Teri Garr interview.

295 "since the middle of December": Tony and Ann St. John, Teri Garr interview.

295 built on the psychology of color: Tony and Ann St. John, Vittorio Storato interview, Zoetrope Studios documentary footage, December 3, 1980, American Zoetrope Film Archives.

295 "follow the characters": Commentary, *One from the Heart*, American Zoetrope, 2004, DVD.

296 "infuriatingly self-confident": Garrett Brown, "The Steadicam and 'One From the Heart,'" *American Cinematographer*, January 1982.

296 "Tommy, I no-like": Cynthia Kania, AI.

296 "never light like that": Peter Semel, AI.

296 transformed bodies and minds: Peter Semel, AI.

296 "You a-see what": Armyan Bernstein, AI.

296 "Talk to Ray": Tony and Ann St. John, Zoetrope Studios documentary footage, February 23, 1981. American Zoetrope Film Archives.

296   "They're wising up": Tony and Ann St. John, Zoetrope Studios documentary footage.

297   "[would tell] me what to tell": Arne Schmidt, AI.

297   "Francis, please come in": Joanie Blum, AI.

297   "don't understand why": Joanie Blum, AI.

297   "when even staging": Dan Attias, AI.

297   "The way it was shot": McCarthy, "Actor Forrest Gives Heart to Coppola Films."

297   "I would like for you, Freddie": Jeff Hamlin, AI.

297   "This is-a your mark": Jeff Hamlin, AI.

297   "Nastassja, your expression": Aaron Latham, "Francis Ford Coppola: The Movie Man Who Plays God," *Life*, August 1981.

297   "Freddie and Nastassja": Latham, "Francis Ford Coppola: The Movie Man Who Plays God."

298   "Nastassja, be real haughty": Latham, "Francis Ford Coppola: The Movie Man Who Plays God."

298   "no way to run a railroad": Walter Murch, AI.

298   "actually became rather comical": Dan Attias, AI.

298   "feeling he was petrified": Mitch Dubin, AI.

298   "I was very actively directing": Francis Ford Coppola, AI.

298   "Francis could be told": Michael Lehmann, AI.

298   hired to say yes: Michael Lehmann, AI.

299   "Francis turned to the people": Michael Lehmann, AI.

299   "not always reasonable": Michael Lehmann, AI.

299   *This can't keep going on*: Lucy Fisher, AI.

299   "went down there one time": Jean Autrey, AI.

299   if she was sure *everything*: Jean Autrey, AI.

299   "apparently the production accountant": Jean Autrey, AI.

299   "Gio was sort of thrust": Michael Lehmann, AI.

299   "any petty cash": Tess Haley, AI.

300   "becoming more and more scary": Ceci Dempsey, AI.

300   "he wasn't singing": Franc Roddam, AI.

300   "thought I'd be doing this film": Franc Roddam, AI.

300   "If you are one": Franc Roddam, AI.

300   "give me the money now": Franc Roddam, AI.

300   "I was stuck": Lucy Fisher, AI.

301   "It was beautiful": Lucy Fisher, AI.

301   "came to get his autograph": Jack Singer, interview, Tony and Ann St. John, Zoetrope Studios documentary footage, April 3, 1981. American Zoetrope Film Archives.

301   "committed as long": Robert Lenzer, "Real Estate Mogul Jack Singer Goes Hollywood and Loves It," *Boston Globe*, March 28, 1981.

301   "Suppose I drop dead": Lenzer, "Real Estate Mogul Jack Singer Goes Hollywood and Loves It."

302   "was save the movie": Jack Singer, interview.

302   "such a cliché": Cynthia Kania, AI.

302   "fifty-five sheets": Cora Gersten, AI.

302   "Jack Singer!": Susie Landau Finch, AI.

302   "need a helicopter": Haller, "Francis Coppola's Biggest Gamble."

302   "Straighten the leg": Tony and Ann St. John, "Tape 02," *One from the Heart* documentary videotapes, March 13, American Zoetrope Film Archives.

303   "It's all right": Tony and Ann St. John, "Tape 02," *One from the Heart* documentary videotapes.

303   "dirty it up": Kenny Ortega, AI.

303   "That's it": Tony and Ann St. John, "Tape 02," *One from the Heart* documentary videotapes.

303   "have some money": Martha Cronin, AI.

304   "One Through the Heart": Martha Cronin, AI.

304   "He was bored": Martha Cronin, AI.

304   "boots-on-the-ground people": Martha Cronin, AI.

304   "put the expensive stuff": Martha Cronin, AI.

304   "Could Bob get": Jim Turner, AI.

304   "did nothing": Sonia Socher, AI.

304   "for something—he didn't": Tess Haley, AI.

304   "Bob thought": Emy Spiotta, AI.

304   "hit with a palm tree": Tess Haley, AI.

304   "glamour and the whole everything": Robin Supak, AI.

304   "Francis was not a person": Emy Spiotta, AI.

304   "couple of points where": Bob Spiotta interview, Tony and Ann St. John, Zoetrope Studios documentary footage, undated, American Zoetrope Film Archive.

305   "guys are all the same": Dan Attias, AI.

305   "deal with this crazy guy": Michael Lehmann, AI.

305   "Francis was not happy": Robin Supak, AI.

305   "Dean and Francis": Alex Tavoularis, AI.

305   "Going against Italia": Tess Haley, AI.

305 "Toward the end": Martha Cronin, AI.

305 "those times I lost my temper": Francis Ford Coppola, AI.

305 "was nothing you could do": Tess Haley, AI.

305 "He was happiest": Tess Haley, AI.

306 "that year I spent in bed": Breskin, "Francis Ford Coppola."

306 Lucy Fisher pictured him: Lucy Fisher, AI.

306 "were little puppets": Schumacher, *Francis Ford Coppola*, 297.

306 "There are Francis Ford Coppola films": Schumacher, *Francis Ford Coppola*, 309.

306 "King God," he typed: Francis Ford Coppola, "King God: A Tale for Children," 1956, American Zoetrope Library Archives.

309 "While making *One from the Heart*": Thomas Brown, AI.

309 "hiding from his debtors": Walter Murch, AI.

309 "Family and art eat": Muriel Murch, *Living with Literature* podcast, Eleanor Coppola interview.

310 "not to anticipate the kiss": Haller, "Francis Coppola's Biggest Gamble."

310 "more interested in technology": Marge Costello, "Conversation with Francis Ford Coppola," *Videography*, September 1982.

310 "pay it incrementally": Lucy Fisher, AI.

310 "Laaaaainie . . .": Lainie Kazan, AI.

310 "Wouldn't it be fun": Bob Swarthe, Bob Eberlein, Kathy Campbell, AI.

311 "Francis was completely emotional": Bob Swarthe, Bob Eberlein, Kathy Campbell, AI.

311 "Wait till Francis": Bob Swarthe, Bob Eberlein, Kathy Campbell, AI.

311 "I stayed to fire": Lucy Fisher, AI.

311 "Make it beautiful": Tony and Ann St. John, Zoetrope Studios documentary footage, December 30, 1980, American Zoetrope Film Archives.

311 Randy Roberts, cutting video, and veteran Rudi Fehr: author email with Anahid Nazarian.

311 "never gave me anything specific": Anne Goursaud, AI.

311 "passionate, unlimited hours": Chris Lebenzon, AI.

312 "will have to earn": Doug Hemphill, AI.

312 "Look what your": Doug Hemphill, AI.

312 "here's a closet": Joanie Blum, AI.

312 *This is why I fell*: Joanie Blum, AI.

312 "immediately made everyone": Gary Weimberg, AI.

313 "doesn't make sense to work": Gary Weimberg, AI.

313 "been through tremendous crises": Latham, "Francis Ford Coppola: The Movie Man Who Plays God."

313 "was always two doors away": Chris Lebenzon, AI.

313 a cloud of marijuana smoke: Gary Weimberg, AI.

313 "You won't believe it": Gary Weimberg, AI.

313 "decided the thing": Gary Weimberg, AI.

313 "you can borrow anything": Gary Weimberg, AI.

314 "other than Hollywood zillionaires": Gary Weimberg, AI.

314 "right out of the blue": Kenelm Jenour, "Coppola's Bid for Pinewood May Be Far Too Low for Rank," *Hollywood Reporter*, April 7, 1981.

314 "an idea center": Jeffrey Wells, "A Film Journal Interview: Francis Ford Coppola/Part 2," *Film Journal*, September 21, 1981.

314 "want to run Africa": Christian Spiotta, AI.

314 "three-legged coffee table": Ray Loynd, "Zoetrope Rides on Wings of 'Heart' as Par Shifts to Idle," *Hollywood Reporter*, January 13, 1982.

315 "ten worst films": "'Heart' Screening Doesn't Sit Well with S.F. Exhibs," *Daily Variety*, August 24, 1981.

315 "scenery was real pretty": Aljean Harmetz, "Embattled Coppola Plunges into TV," *New York Times*, August 26, 1981, https://www.nytimes.com/1981/08/26/movies/embattled-coppola-plunges-into-tv.html.

315 "film is unreleasable": Lewis, *Whom God Wishes to Destroy*, 63

315 "makes my relationship with the bank": Jeffrey Wells, "A Film Journal Interview: Francis Ford Coppola," *Film Journal*, September 7, 1981.

315 "like being rejected": Loynd, "Zoetrope Rides on Wings of 'Heart' as Par Shifts to Idle."

315 "there was no obligation": Lillian Ross, "Some Figures on a Fantasy," *New Yorker*, November 8, 1982.

315 "Due to Paramount's failure to comply": Coppola, American Zoetrope Library Archives.

315 "they sent out a news release": Lee Grant, "Coppola: Dreamer . . . and Doer," *Los Angeles Times*, February 9, 1982.

316 "the film event of the year": https://www.nytimes.com/1981/10/18/nyregion/coppola-s-baton-guiding-napoleon.html.

316 "I'm predicting": https://www.rogerebert.com/roger-ebert/napoleon-conquers-radio-city-music-hall.

316 "know I hide the fear": Eleanor Coppola, *Notes on a Life* (New York: Nan A. Talese, 2008), 28.

316 "going to pull this off": Janet Maslin, "Coppola Sets Up Preview, Doesn't Tell Paramount," *New York Times*, January 7, 1982, https://www.nytimes.com/1982/01/07/movies/coppola-sets-up-preview-doesn-t-tell-paramount.html.

317 "Friday, January 15": Maslin, "Coppola Sets Up Preview, Doesn't Tell Paramount."

317 Let the public decide: Maslin, "Coppola Sets Up Preview, Doesn't Tell Paramount."

317 "reaction to the system": Maslin, "Coppola Sets Up Preview, Doesn't Tell Paramount."

317 "those modern shoeboxes": Maslin, "Coppola Sets Up Preview, Doesn't Tell Paramount."

317 "Buy your plane tickets": Bob Eberlein, AI.

317 "color-corrected silent print": Chris Lebenzon, AI.

317 "We love Francis Coppola": Tony and Ann St. John, Zoetrope Studios documentary footage, January 15, 1982, American Zoetrope Film Archives.

318 "movie that cost a lot": Tony and Ann St. John, Zoetrope Studios documentary footage, January 15, 1982.

318 "people going to convene": Tony and Ann St. John, Zoetrope Studios documentary footage, January 15, 1982.

318 "For the Poowabah": Tony and Ann St. John, Zoetrope Studios documentary footage, January 15, 1982.

318 "just look at him": Teri Fettis, AI.

318 "And when the movie": Armyan Bernstein, AI.

318 "What if people": Armyan Bernstein, AI.

319 "arrangement for the distribution": Tony and Ann St. John, Zoetrope Studios documentary footage, January 15, 1982, American Zoetrope Film Archives.

321 "check had bounced": Robert Eberlein, AI.

321 "what did you think of": Francis Ford Coppola, AI.

321 "like having dessert": Tony and Ann St. John, Zoetrope Studios documentary footage, January 15, 1982.

321 "thrown out the baby": Andrew Sarris, "Riding on Coppola's Roller Coaster," *Village Voice*, January 27–February 2, 1982.

321 "work of constant astonishment": Sheila Benson, *One from the Heart* review, *Los Angeles Times*, January 22, 1982.

321 "unfunny, unjoyous": Vincent Canby, "Screen: Coppola's *One from the Heart* Opens," *New York Times*, February 11, 1982

322 "I pulled it": Francis Ford Coppola, AI.

323 "I had bought a studio": Francis Ford Coppola, AI.

323 "I like being with kids": David Thomson and Lucy Gray, "Idols of the King: Francis Ford Coppola Interviewed," *Film Comment* 19 (September–October 1983).

323 "Dear Mr. Coppola": *One from the Heart* fan mail, American Zoetrope Library Archives.

323 "Francis created this competitive": Mark Healy, "Ponyboy Stays Gold," *GQ*, March 2003.

324 "was being nurtured by Francis": Healy, "Ponyboy Stays Gold."

324 "After the experience": Francis Ford Coppola, AI.

324 "walked through fire": Healy, "Ponyboy Stays Gold."

324 "hear this all the time": *One from the Heart* fan mail, American Zoetrope Library Archives.

324 "sit on the floor together": Susan King, "'The Outsiders' Stays Gold at 35: Inside Coppola's Crafty Methods and Stars' Crazy Pranks," *Variety*, March 23, 2018.

324 "We could make a studio here": King, "'The Outsiders' Stays Gold at 35."

324 "as much production": Thomson and Gray, "Idols of the King."

325 art film for kids: Coppola interview, *Rumblefish*, Criterion DVD, 1983.

325 "now pushing forty-five": Thomson and Gray, "Idols of the King."

325 "once again paralyzed": Francis Ford Coppola to Lillian Ross, October 14, 1982, American Zoetrope Library Archives.

325 "Energy Art Death Rebirth": Francis Ford Coppola, *Megalopolis* Notes, Journal 1, December 1982, American Zoetrope Library Archives.

325 "goes to a number of friends": Francis Ford Coppola, *Megalopolis* Notes, Journal 1, February 8, 1983, American Zoetrope Library Archives.

326 "Everything in his life": Coppola, *Megalopolis* Notes, February 8, 1983.

326 *Spirit of Zoetrope*: William K. Everson, "Spirit of Zoetrope Infects Santa Fe with High Spirits and Fine Mix," *Weekly Variety*, April 20, 1983.

326 "genuine support and admiration ": Everson, "Spirit of Zoetrope Infects Santa Fe with High Spirits and Fine Mix."

327 "is very optimistic": "Zoetrope Up on the Block For 11th Time," *Daily Variety*, June 1, 1983.

327 "ultimate artistic hero": Deborah Mason, "Coppola: How to Exceed Without Really Trying," *Vogue*, September 1984.

327 "attracted me to *Mishima*": "Introduction" by George Lucas, Eiko Ishioka Papers, f. 135, AMPAS Margaret Herrick Library.

327 "have one idea": Tom Luddy interview, *Mishima: A Life in Four Chapters*, Criterion DVD, 1985.

327 "If we do this": Paul Schrader, AI.

327 "kinds of films I was doing": "Introduction" by George Lucas, Eiko Ishioka Papers, f. 135.

328 "very close to consummating a sale": Tina Daniell, "Zoetrope's Hollywood General Facing 'Involuntary' Bankruptcy," *Hollywood Reporter*, July 29, 1983.

328 "There's no deal": David Robb, "Zoetrope Moves Into Escrow and Closer to Sale," *Variety*, September 29, 1983.

328 The phone rang: Michael Lehmann, AI.

THE SHAPE OF THINGS TO COME

334 "no friends now": Francis Ford Coppola, *Megalopolis* Notes, Journal 5, December 29, 1985, American Zoetrope Library Archives.

334 "don't understand it 100 percent": Peter Keough, "Coppola Carves a Cinematic Elegy: Gardens of Stone," *Chicago Sun-Times*, May 10, 1987.

335 "The telephone rang": Eleanor Coppola, *Notes on a Life*, 16.

335 "Sofia and I flew": Eleanor Coppola, *Notes on a Life*, 16.

335 "mourning his son": Francis Ford Coppola, AI.

335 "no matter what happened": David Breskin, "Francis Ford Coppola," *Rolling Stone*, February 7, 1991, http://davidbreskin.com/magazines/1-interviews/francis-ford-coppola/.

335 wake up dreamless: Coppola, AI.

335 "serious kid of the cinema": Peter J. Boyer, "Under the Gun," *Vanity Fair*, June 1990.

335 "Would you rather": Rebecca De Mornay, AI.

336 "height of his success": Robert Lindsey, "Francis Ford Coppola: Promises to Keep," *New York Times*, July 24, 1988.

336 "is a great tree": Charles Champlin and Jack Smith, "Bad Times Behind, Coppola Dances to a Different Tune, *Los Angeles Times*, August 7, 1988, https://www.latimes.com/archives/la-xpm-1988-08-07-ca-325 -story.html.

337 "solvent company": Andrea King, "Coppola, Zoetrope Prods. File for Bankruptcy Protection," *Hollywood Reporter*, January 26, 1990.

337 "cooperate with Coppola": "Coppola to Lense High-Definition Pic," *Daily Variety*, September 16, 1988.

337 "think that dream of mine": Cowie, *Coppola*, 237.

337 "could make a dream studio": Cowie, *Coppola*, 237.

337 "That's what the human fate is": Francis Ford Coppola, *Apocalypse Now Redux* interview: Peter Cowie/ Francis Ford Coppola, American Zoetrope Library Archives.

337 "I just made *Godfather III*": Graham Fuller, "Francis Ford Coppola," *Interview*, December 1992.

337 "but as a person who had gone": Commentary, *The Godfather Part III*, Paramount Home Video, 2001, DVD.

337 "Just as Michael feels anxious": Commentary, *The Godfather Part III*.

338 "For Michael just to die": Harlan Jacobson, "Vintage Coppola," *Film Comment*, January–February 2008.

338 "You know why I did it": Richard Beggs, AI.

338 "*Godfather III* will give us": Cowie, *Coppola*, 238.

338 "Apocalypse Now, Chapter 11": Peter Hilavacek, "Apocalypse Now, Chapter 11," *Variety*, March 14, 1990.

338 "very emotional to see the movie again": Eleanor Coppola, "The Godfather Diary," *Vogue*, December, 1990.

339 incorporate the book: Francis Ford Coppola, AI.

339 "when the boundaries of my thoughts": Eleanor Coppola, *Notes: On the Making of Apocalypse Now*, "Afterword."

339 "about an old man who is dying": Fuller, "Francis Ford Coppola."

339 "I was *dying*": Fuller, "Francis Ford Coppola."

340 "raise Zoetrope from [the] dead": Ana Maria Bahiana, "Dracula and Frankenstein Raise Zoetrope from Dead," *Screen International*, November 13, 1992.

340 "buy back my studio": Army Archerd, "Just for Variety," *Variety*, September 16, 1992.

340 "I was going to 'destroy myself'": Rodney F. Hill, "Twixt Hollywood and Art Cinema: An Interview with Francis Ford Coppola," *Cineaste*, Spring 2016.

341 "fatal mistake": Francis Ford Coppola, AI.

Index

Note: The abbreviation FFC refers to Francis Ford Coppola.

About the Author

SAM WASSON is the author of seven books on film, including the *New York Times* bestsellers *Fifth Avenue, 5 A.M.: Audrey Hepburn, Breakfast at Tiffany's, and the Dawn of the Modern American Woman*; *The Big Goodbye: Chinatown and the Last Days of Hollywood*; and *Fosse*. With Jeanine Basinger, he is the coauthor of *Hollywood: The Oral History*. He lives in Los Angeles.